THE BOOK OF POSITIVE QUALITIES

To Eileen + Jake,

Thank you for your love + inspiration with your qualities. Especially P. 248 + P. 160

Jim Wo

THE BOOK OF
POSITIVE
QUALITIES

JIM DOWNS

WARNER BOOKS

A Time Warner Company

Warner Books is not responsible for the delivery or content of the information or materials provided by the author. The reader should address any questions to the author at:

The Positive Qualities Company
2888 Bluff St., #428
Boulder, CO 80301-9002
1-800-484-9668; Extension: 0984

Warner Books, Inc., 1271 Avenue of the Americas, New York, NY 10020
Visit our Web site at
http://pathfinder.com/twep

 A Time Warner Company

Printed in the United States of America
First Printing: September 1996
10 9 8 7 6 5 4 3 2 1

Library of Congress Cataloging-in-Publication Data

Downs, Jim.
    The book of positive qualities / Jim Downs.
      p. cm.
    ISBN 0-446-67140-1
    1. Character and characteristics. 2. Personality change.
   3. Change (Psychology) 4. Self-actualization (Psychology)
   I. Title.
   BF818.D68 1996
   179'.9—dc20   96-1404
                            CIP

Cover design by Cathy Saska
Book design and composition by L&G McRee

To my mother, who urged us to *be* good and is sincere in her effort to be so herself. Thanks, Mommy.

To my father, who always urged his children to "stick to the basics." Well, Daddy, here are the basics.

To all I have loved and who have loved me.

ACKNOWLEDGMENTS

Liz Wood, who did the initial typing of tapes; Judy Kain, who did the subsequent typing of tapes and definitions research, and who has shown me how unselfish love really is; Marie Fox and Colleen Ostlund, who offered critical analysis on The Positive Qualities Chart and believed in me.

Special thanks for help and encouragement: Shawn Sheehan, Jenny Tasker, Anita Downs, Jerry Downs, Judy Kain.

GUIDING PRINCIPLES

Love is all-embracing of truth, beauty and goodness.
                                                    —*The Urantia Book*

Patriotism is not enough. But neither is anything else. Science is not enough, religion is not enough, nor is love, nor is duty, nor is action however disinterested, nor, however sublime, is contemplation. Nothing short of everything will really do.
                                                    —ALDOUS HUXLEY

CONTENTS

PREFACE   XI

INTRODUCTION: MANIFESTING POSITIVE QUALITIES   1

WHY QUALITIES?   1

BALANCE IN ALL THINGS   3

CAPACITY AND GROWTH   6

"SELF" AND "OTHER"   7

CHOOSING YOUR QUALITIES   9

SELECTION   11

WHAT TO DO WITH YOUR CHOSEN QUALITIES   13

WARNING: IT WON'T BE EASY   16

START HERE   17

WHAT ABOUT CRITICISM?   18

WHAT ABOUT THE NEGATIVE?   19

THE GAP   21

WHY DO YOU EXIST?   22

INTRODUCTION TO THE QUALITIES   25

APPENDICES   543

APPENDIX 1: ALPHABETICAL LIST OF POSITIVE QUALITIES   545

APPENDIX 2: RANDOM/RANDOM PICK LIST   555

APPENDIX 3: ADDITIONAL POSITIVE QUALITIES   581

APPENDIX 4: SYMBOLS   589

APPENDIX 5: MYTHOLOGICAL, LEGENDARY, HISTORICAL, FICTIONAL, AND THEOLOGICAL CHARACTERS   597

APPENDIX 6: "BEING" AND "MEANING OF LIFE" QUOTES   601

APPENDIX 7: EXERCISES AND PROJECTS   613

APPENDIX 8: BIBLIOGRAPHY   617

APPENDIX 9: END NOTES   625

PREFACE

What is more valuable: gold or goodness, platinum or prudence, silver or self-esteem?

I have always been interested in ultimates and cosmic meanings: Why do we exist? What are the most important things to do and be in life? What are the true values? This book is my answer to these questions. I decided to gather a complete list of positive qualities. After years of searching (and I'm still looking), I have a list of more than 1800. I boiled them down to the 988 featured here.

These are not just words. They are concepts with high-minded meanings and intrinsic value. Words are powerful. They are catalysts for thoughts and feelings. Because of words, people make choices and take action. This action either helps or hinders them or others.

I intend this book to not only be information-oriented but also inspiration-oriented, meaning-oriented, and value-oriented.

I hope that the answers in this book harmonize with some of your own. I also hope that this book challenges some of your beliefs. We all need to move with wisdom through every situation that we live. There is no structured system that is just right for everyone or every circumstance.

This is a philosophy of responsibility, independence, and freedom. We all too often give ourselves over to people or ideas outside of ourselves. By "give over to" I mean that we accept without question, or a minimum investigation, tradition, the status quo, a philosophy, a political party, or the views of our parents, spouses, preachers, children, or gurus. This is a way of conveniently relieving ourselves of the burden of thinking about the most ideal action needed in each situation.

If we focus our consciousness into specific dogmas then when something doesn't fit we ignore it, fight it, or kill it.

The reasons to acquire positive qualities are many: service, religion, self-interest, tradition, humanism. We all want others to treat us with kindness, fairness, decency, and compassion, and we should direct these same qualities toward others. In the end the reason has to be a personal one. You will do so if you believe that it is the right thing to do.

The important thing is the qualities—not what I say about them but what you do about them. Make up your own theories and proceed with your own positive growth for your own personal reasons. Use this text as a guide to begin the process of becoming your highest ideas and ideals.

This book is a sampler. You get only a taste of each quality discussed. It was not feasible to fill in all that is possible. I hope that the quality you are interested in is fleshed out. If not, fill in your own notions. Contemplate and affirm your choice and act on it. Use these writings for your personal musings and for discussions with family and friends.

The source of my information was a combination of study, investigation, intuition, inspiration, logic, experience, and discussion.

THE BOOK OF
POSITIVE
QUALITIES

How to Select, Use, and Become Specific and Personal Positive Qualities

WHY QUALITIES?

There is no society in which kindness, sympathy, hospitality, or regard for others and their rights is disapproved.
—RICHARD B. BRANDT

I've noticed that people of conscience, great teachers, respected traditions, and established religions all espouse the best of their enlightenment in terms of positive qualities.

There are differences in rhetoric and different qualities are considered the foremost, but all such people and ideologies encourage those who would believe in their view to *be* loving, good, spiritual, friendly, honorable, courageous, free, compassionate, humane, wise, et cetera.

All positive-quality combinations are valid. The more there are, the greater the possibility for a harmonious balance.

We are all made up of qualities, and growth is dependent on the enhancement of these qualities. As you become your desired qualities, you recognize that you are growing—you are evolving into a better person. Using begets being. You choose to act on your information, and that choice leads to experience. That experience is then part of you. Through that experience, you actually become a different person. It is a continuous cycle. As you become your desire, you recognize a new desire. There is always another level.

My personal conviction is that the greatest of all qualities is love and that all of the positive qualities are aspects of love. As one grows in love, one realizes that there is always another and greater understanding, a deeper and more profound possibility for how one can become and manifest love.

Love is an organic reality. Although we attempt to identify it by definition and categorization, it lives freely in the personality and cannot be forced into an assigned box.

Love includes facts that are rooted in living truth. It includes meanings that are harmonized in understanding. And it includes values that are infused with goodness.

Individually and collectively, humans do endeavor to become the many qualities that are considered to be positive—often unconsciously and sometimes with selfish selectivity, but nonetheless there is always the pursuit.

Scientists are investigating the facts that make up physical reality, but once the components are known they naturally begin to coordinate the basic information. They wonder and theorize about the reasons for these facts and are curious as to the relationships that cause certain phenomena. Their quest is justified in terms of physical advantages: lowering of pain, expanding of the comfort range, and helping to clarify mysteries. Their discoveries lead to greater intellectual understanding and, in turn, to an appreciation of the meaning of things. Ultimately, if we are very clear, this understanding also leads to spiritual values: cooperation, integrity, fairness, wisdom, morality, growth, and even beauty.

The basics of the physical universe are force, matter, energy, gravity, and time, but these have no meaning or value without the qualities found on the emotional, mental, and spiritual levels. Would the universe be of any worth if there were no personalities or beings to appreciate it?

Qualities are like atoms and molecules. They are the building blocks of the nonphysical universe. When putting them together, you get the same unexpected results as in the physical world.

The next time that you use ice to soothe a burnt finger consider the components of water. Oxygen supports combustion and hydrogen is highly flammable, but when they are fused in the right proportions the magic substance of water is the result.

Our investigations and assimilations of various spiritual substances is our personal testing of what will happen when we put together the *real* substances of the universe. Qualities represent the "material" with which to build a better self and therefore a better universe.

The quality you desire has no mind, it manifests totally because of who you are and the work you do to create it. But qualities do possess their own volition. They are not personal but they do have life. Before qualities are given expression in a being with personality, they exist as active potential. Your decisions enable qualities to pierce the membrane of ego and find full expression in your personality.

The qualities you seek also seek you. As you desire an object, it finds a way to manifest for you. As you create the space in your life for its existence, it is doing everything in its power to be manifest. As you open to the dream of becoming some aspect of love, it is compelled to comply.

There are some qualities that are global, qualities that you simply must possess if any progress is to be made. These include balance, sincerity, humor, a controlled self-esteem, and, of course, love.

Some qualities are adaptable and versatile. For instance, one can be clever in a positive or a negative way. Notice the positive qualities in a negative situation. In order to be a successful thief, one has to be clever, bold, and alert; yet the thief is using this combination of positive qualities for a negative purpose. Positive aspects can be extracted from even the nastiest of acts. This helps the perpetrator come up with a plausible excuse to justify their negative behavior. Everyone always justifies their actions.

BALANCE IN ALL THINGS

There is always a need for a balance. As we become strong we must also become gentle; as we become prudent we must also be adventurous; as we seek truth we must also appreciate beauty; as we focus on goodness we must coordinate it and all of these character traits with love.

Businesspeople who have strength, determination, and drive may be successful but disliked. But if they also possess the qualities of compassion, gentleness, cooperation, and softheartedness, people will more likely be drawn to their well-rounded disposition. Powerful people need to enhance their delicate nature and pay attention to sensitivity and gentleness. They should add such pleasing qualities as humor, tact, wisdom, and flexibility. With these additions those who notice the grit will not feel its abrasiveness.

Conversely, a person who is gentle, sensitive, and thoughtful may be labeled as weak. Cherish those compassionate qualities but add or intensify strength, independence, and courage for a personality with equilibrium.

The stabilizing qualities of harmony, dignity, charisma, fairness, and insight are always needed and make the balance possible.

When you pick a quality that you want, work on bringing it into your being in your unique way. Look at your current abilities, attitudes, and skills. See how they can help you get the qualities you need.

When one pushes the boundary of a single quality the boundaries of other qualities are affected. If the intellect advances but the emotions develop at a slower rate, a person is out of balance. The emotions need to mature in order for the person to be whole.

Every quality needs its *kindred qualities* to keep it balanced: energetic/restful, decisive/obedient, analytical/poetic—these are examples of positive qualities and their strengthening kindred qualities. By nudging your known qualities and pushing the kindred qualities, your boundary is expanded.

When you focus on the quality of courage, also take into account its kindred qualities of curiosity, confidence, open-mindedness, and even-temperedness and work on them too. When you empower the kindred qualities of courage, you increase your capacity to be courageous because you have a broader base from which to go further the next time you are called on to be courageous.

The entire range of qualities is immensely greater than any single quality could possibly be. When you strengthen one quality you are strengthening the whole field.

Since all qualities are connected and each quality is a doorway into the universe, it is reasonable to surmise that when you work on those positive qualities that you already possess, you will not only enhance those qualities but you will also acquire other (even relatively remote) qualities.

We do tend to prefer our favorite qualities, but the most important qualities are those that are the most appropriate to the experience of the moment. If you respect the value of all of the qualities, it will be easier for you to flow from one to another as needed.

This connectedness can be appreciated in the association of qualities. Consider the quality of wisdom. If intuition and instinct are facets of insight, which are ways to understand intelligence, then your capacity for wisdom can be expanded when you focus on being intuitive.

You can focus on any particular quality—humor, harmony, attractiveness—wherever you better yourself, it will make you better overall, not just in that one area. If you increase your graciousness, for instance, you will feel and be more attractive. Feeling better about yourself increases your self-esteem. Or you might start with self-esteem, and as you acquire more of it you will gain more confidence and move ahead with something that you wouldn't have tried.

There is a lot of talk these days about the conflict between mind and heart. The mind primarily represents the arena for the quality of truth. The heart is the arena for the quality of goodness. There is a need for both of these qualities to be pursued, experienced, and interconnected.

It is extremely important that we live, coordinate, and integrate a wide range of qualities in order to become as universally adaptable as possible.

A person living within a limited set of qualities is moving in only one direction. That person is restricting his or her view of reality by condensing and excluding necessary options. If, on the other hand, one has a broad set of qualities, one is shining in all directions and is growing with symmetry and harmony.

It seems easier to stay in the known rather than risk the unknown. But remember that the effort is worth it.

The power of the need to fit in is very strong. Peer pressure can restrict your options. Do the beliefs of your friends, family, or society dictate what you consider to be "right" and "wrong"?

Social conventions may very well be correct for you, but it is *you* who must decide. If you are more malleable than you are self-reliant, then you may accept these external ideas as your own without question. In the hopes of modifying your judgment to be more objective, reevaluate your beliefs—especially if they come out of a book or a tradition.

There is a phenomenon that I call the "Good enough" syndrome. I've seen it in a corporate environment. It includes the "It's not my job" lament and the "I've done my share" whine.

I know a man who says that if he gets 85 percent of the job done he is successful. In fact, he usually gets 65 or 75 percent accomplished and expects someone else to take over. What's lacking is a healthy pride in doing the job correctly, accurately, and thoroughly—and a respect for the fellow workers who have to pick up the pieces.

If you are a thorough person, it may be easier to do the job yourself than to confront a coworker about doing better. If you speak out against some inequity, you may be subject to getting fired. Truly, some wisdom is called for when things get touchy.

CAPACITY AND GROWTH

Any being who has the capacity for choice has the ability to transcend their limitations.

You can go beyond your individual limitations and increase your essence of a particular quality by focusing on that quality.

Growth is part of our life. Just think of the vast difference in who you are now versus who you were when you were younger. Would you deny that you have grown and matured into a better version of yourself?

Your capacity is structured not only by genetics and environment but also by your internal landscape, your sense of self, and your desire to become better. If you work on it, you will become a new person.

When you push your subjective limits you will eventually match your objective limits. At that point you will reach an equilibrium. You are growing at exactly the rate that is possible for your state of being. This is enlightenment.

Nothing precludes the unfolding of continued growth. Even after you attain a state of enlightenment, you will still continue to progress on the never-ending journey of infinity.

If you feel a limit and say to yourself, "That's as far as I can go," then you have to look around and determine your next opportunity for growth. By continuing to work on the edges and by not believing the limits, there is continued improvement.

Maybe there is an inherent limit in certain types of qualities. For instance, there is a finite mind; however, with the theory that we use 10 percent or less of our brain, we haven't got the foggiest idea where that border is.

Even if a particular quality has a limit, there are other qualities that have no limits. They are associated with, but not restricted by, physical, emotional, or mental limits. They exist on the spiritual level—qualities like love, wisdom, and goodness.

Physical qualities have a physical limit. Physical attractiveness, for instance, is restricted by the "eye of the beholder"; but the qualities on the spiritual level grow forever.

There is probably a limit to the quality of silliness, but when you add others—whimsy, wryness, playfulness, zaniness—each of those qualities becomes greater. Play a symphony of humor in order to become a master of joy.

"SELF" AND "OTHER"

The first step to integrate any quality into your being is to recognize its value.

When you strive to gain a desired positive quality, you may think that it is totally outside of yourself, or you will probably realize that you possess some of it. But it can be observed in other people, read about, or seen on television.

As you take steps to live a quality, to bring it inside, remember that the eternal essence, the divine pattern of that quality, is fully present within your cosmic identity. Look inward for the ideal and perfect image. See yourself being a unique manifestation of this new quality.

If you have not developed a quality to the degree that you wish, you say that it is outside of you. You recognize it as "other."

First imagine that you and this "other" can be united, can coexist together, then you can make the decision to acquire it. To exemplify a quality, to demonstrate that you are in possession of it, you must do the obvious: live it. Prove to yourself and to the world that it is one of your characteristics.

As you become one with the quality, it will be difficult or impossible to see it objectively. Usually, the quality will be so much "you" that even you cannot see it subjectively.

As qualities are absorbed they are integrated and melded with the whole person. They are encapsulated and simplified as they are internalized. Consider the perfect meshing of the brain with the mind. Where does one begin and the other end?

The knowledge of who you are, your nature and personality, is a fundamental beginning. It is important to *know* yourself, but it is more important to *accept* yourself. Feel the scope and range of who you are and of what you are capable. It is important and accurate to say that you are capable of anything, but it is not practical. It is too big. You can and should start with that universal belief but then break it down to a reality that you can live today.

The only person who can truly measure your qualities is you. Candidly judge yourself. What percentages do you have of the qualities that you want or need? Look at your talents. What have you learned and experienced?

Spend time with yourself watching what it is that you do and think and say. Take that objective look at yourself. An honest, detailed look at yourself will bring you a focused perspective on the current you.

It is understood that your view of yourself is always colored by the filters of who you are. It is necessarily subjective. You are subject to and caught between your current and past experiences, your thought processes, belief systems, and myths. You can neutralize the filters somewhat by increasing your insight and intuition. Also, accepting a trusted friend's point of view will enhance your objectivity.

When you focus on something, you gain information and understanding about it. Pay attention. What do you really like? Who do you really like? For what qualities do you have an affinity? Which do you wish to emulate?

Most people naturally stay within a certain comfort range of experience, environment, thought, and emotion. This is the area of safety. The trouble is that life routinely manifests the unexpected.

It makes sense to develop the fortitude to experience a wider range of attitudes. Study and be open to all systems: religious, political, historical, scientific, philosophical, metaphysical, and self-improvement. All disciplines have a lot to offer. But all are external to the self. It is up to you to bring this information first into your body and mind, and then into your being and soul.

Stephen Hawking said, "The eventual goal of science is to provide a single theory that describes the whole universe." I believe that this is not only science's goal but also the goal of philosophy, metaphysics, and religion. This is a human goal.

We are continually expanding and modifying the theory of our personal universe in order to comprehend and encompass it. Everybody is going to have a different outlook on life, a different definition, one that changes with exploration and growth. We are bound to modify our theories of existence and our reasons for being as we acquire more information, knowledge, and experience.

Each quality can and should be experienced from both the inside out and the outside in. You experience a quality inside out by being the generator of the quality and creating it as you live your life. When you respond to a situation with the quality in your heart and mind, you are experiencing it from the outside in.

If you are in control of your life, you come from the inside and choose those things that you are going to do and be. Or you can choose who you are going to become by accepting and encompassing what comes in.

If you get blasted by a devastating experience, such as death, you have to postpone what you wanted to do and deal with this greater challenge. If you survive the crisis, your task is to continue to survive—encompass the event and expand your reality. Move the experience from an external incident to a part of your inner landscape where you eventually become comfortable with it.

I was in an electrocution and drowning accident when I was thirteen. This was a chance for me to expand my immature sense of what life was all about. The surge of electricity activated every neuron in my body, and I saw in one flash my entire life. But there was more than just the facts of those images, there was a feeling associated with them that went beyond emotion. It was value.

When I was twenty-one, my wife, Jenny, died. These events taught me that a person can continue even in the face of pain and death. Although it may take time, you can carry on.

CHOOSING YOUR QUALITIES

Choice is like oxygen—it supports all options.

When deciding on a quality, look at your underlying need. You may need the quality you have chosen but you may also need a more basic quality. The one you know you need could be the outward manifestation of a deeper need.

For example: You may feel you need the quality of decisiveness because you feel uncomfortable with a decision you know is right. You feel uncomfortable because you believe you will have a hard time defending or explaining it to others. In this case, the underlying qualities needed could be strength, courage, self-esteem, or maybe just some enhanced communication skills.

Our assimilation of qualities is often restricted by our beliefs. When you pay attention to something, you first check on your beliefs, then your ideals, ideas, and emotions. After deciding that it can fit into your personal reality, you allow yourself to begin to acquire and experience it.

The process of becoming a particular quality starts with choice, continues with preparation, and culminates in practice.

Choice is the fuel that carries you toward a quality.

Make choices. Make conscious choices. Accept unconscious choices. Accept internal reality. Accept extraneous happenings as opportunities to enhance your personal goals of becoming the qualities you are interested in.

If you continually choose to act and react to internal and external events with honesty, your choice will empower the quality to continue its existence. You, therefore, will habituate that quality, and it will become self-sustaining.

Allow the quality to unfold naturally. Qualities cannot be manufactured, they must grow. Appreciate the evolution of the quality. Enjoy it as you become it.

There are those who say "Go for it," and there are those who say "Don't force it." The important thing is that you choose. Proceed at your own pace and with your own style.

If you think of a quality, patience for instance, and say, "I sure don't have much of that one," then you've got a wonderful focus point. Since you have identified the exact issue, you can begin to work on it.

If you say, "I just can't see myself being 'dazzling,'" you are in fact *seeing* yourself being something. You see an image that is clouded by your feelings and your negative judgment. Your fantasy is one of clumsiness or crudeness. You fear failure or ridicule.

Change your attitude toward the quality (and to yourself) and you will change your vision in relation to it.

Do you not enjoy seeing young people grow? They succeed and fail, but what charms you is their willingness to proceed. The exuberance of childhood is the willingness to take the necessary steps to learn even in the face of failure.

As you become those qualities for which you have been striving, you will see that some aspects of yourself are beginning to wither. Prune these away with the courage and knowledge that the whole person will be strengthened and that the positive aspect of the pruned "branch" will be absorbed and work for the greater good.

It is said that one must die to be reborn, but there is no need for death before its time. When you plant the seed of a particular quality, let that quality grow, mature, and age properly. When a quality is old and complacent and needs rejuvenation, then it can "die" and be reborn again in a new phase and in a new state of reality. Along with its companion qualities it will mature again in the next cycle.

Nothing of value is ever lost.

SELECTION

You already possess an impressive array of positive qualities. Read the list in appendix 1 and honestly give yourself credit for who you are and who you have become. Decide in your own subjective way how much of each quality you have. Remember when you exhibited each one. Some you possess naturally and some have been hard won through adversity. Establish a position on your personal quality map of who you are now.

Selecting the qualities that you want to become is your next step in getting your "new" qualities. You could try the random-access approach— the open-to-any-page or the "I've always wanted to be" approach—to look up the quality you are interested in. But first get the big picture. Decide which quality or qualities you consider to be the ultimate. This will give you a sense of overall purpose.

Do you agree with me that *love* is the preeminent quality? Maybe you believe in a yin/yang system and postulate that there must be two qualities that share dominance. Or maybe the stability of the triangle makes you speculate that a triumvirate is appropriate. Whatever your belief, these supreme qualities will overshadow all that you do and attempt to be.

Once you have decided on your universal qualities, it is time to see how they apply to your everyday life. Note in your actions what your motives are and have been. Look beyond the actions of others and wonder what could have been the underlying qualities that made them heroes or villains. Notice how often the words that we use to describe the best of ourselves come up in conversation, advertising, news, church, the workplace. Why are you attracted to some people? What is their unique combination of positive qualities? What are yours? What qualities do you hope that your children will someday embody? How can you participate in inspiring the best in yourself and others?

Life is permeated with the opportunities to live better and become a better you. Once you are convinced of the fact that the acquisition of positive qualities is important, you will be motivated to actively move yourself to a higher plane of existence by wisely expanding your range of loving qualities.

First decide how many qualities to pick and at what intervals. You may want to select a specific quality annually or on a special occasion. Monthly would be good for choosing subcategories of your annual focus. I suggest picking two qualities per week. Daily is fun and will give you a quick look at a lot of qualities but not much time to get to know and become your choices.

Why two? Picking only one sometimes felt too restrictive for me, but try it out, it may work for you. Two qualities cover a wider range of situations, especially if they are a disparate pair. It is always fascinating to see how the two work together. More than two and it is easier to lose focus.

There are several ways to select: choose from the alphabetical or Random/Random lists in the appendix; ask a friend; listen to what your "enemies" say; ask your inner guide; make up something that works for you.

There is a certain amount of magic assumed with random picking. I would explain the "magic" this way. The mind, being as flexible as it is, gives a context to the juxtaposition of the qualities, the situation, and the personality. You make it fit.

Picking from different types helps give a balance. The following are types of qualities: hard, soft, balancing, physical, mental, spiritual, social, internal, external, progressive, safe, adventurous.

Your choice may be dictated by a negative situation. What are the positive qualities to be conscious of when you are confronted with a negative situation?

SITUATION	QUALITIES
Injustice	Fairness, Pity
Suspicion	Wisdom, Caution
Ridicule	Self-esteem, Sympathy
Bullying	Brave, Agile, Surefooted
Ignorance	Intelligence, Communication
Prejudice	Camaraderie, Honorable
Greed	Generosity, Security
Waste	Respect, Preserving
Excessive Ego	Humility, Self-control
Foolishness	Balance, Adventurous
Childishness	Innocence, Maturity
Joblessness	Talented, Steadfast

WHAT TO DO WITH YOUR CHOSEN QUALITIES

As you do *your qualities your qualities will* be *you.*

The first thing to do to acquire the qualities that you have identified is to consciously decide to *be* your qualities. Remember that you are not starting from scratch. You have previously lived these qualities. Look for the opportunity to do so again. Visualize your future self wearing your desired qualities comfortably. Surround yourself with people who have already acquired them. How do your heroes exemplify these qualities? Plug them into your current reality. Imagine yourself being the person that people talk about when they talk about someone with your chosen qualities. Continually affirm your choice. Give yourself permission. Consider each quality your "pearl of great price."

Use your creativity and imagination to acquire your desired qualities. This will help you act as if you already own them. You have to exhibit a quality in order to experience it. You are the only one who can do what must be done. Nobody is going to do it for you. But you can get help and encouragement. Share your intended qualities with a trustworthy friend. Declare your intention to acquire more of these qualities in your being.

Overlay the quality or qualities onto your personality, your actions, your thoughts, and your discussions. Put the qualities on as you would a pair of new shoes. You need to break them in.

- Study the quality. Gather information from the outside. Mull it over in your mind. Acquire the quality on an intellectual level and from there it will move down into your being level.
- When you are deciding on or are presented with long-term options, like starting or changing a career, look at your choices in relation to bunches of qualities.
- While reading about a particular quality, take time to contemplate. Start a qualities diary and write down your reflections and learning experiences. Look for a symbol for your quality. A traditional symbol is okay if you resonate with it. But an internal symbol is always better because it comes from your personal mythology. Happiness as a smiley face would be a traditional symbol; happiness as the shining smile of your daughter would be a personalized symbol.
- Consider your physical realities. Is your physical system functioning properly? Do you have any neural or chemical imbalances? Are you

in control of, or do you have a dependence upon, drugs, activity (work), thrills (adrenaline), television (entertainment), sex, sugar, food, power?

- For those who are left-brain dominated, it is good to purposefully cross over into the realm of magic—the right brain. Give yourself permission to float rather than plod and plan. Create the music and dance with freedom.

  For those who are right-brained, move over to the deliberate, logical aspects of the left brain. Move out of your feelings and structure your actions with a mathematical precision.

  Use all of your senses. Taste the qualities. Hear them in music and conversations. Feel them during your relationships with loved and not-so-loved ones. Smell them in the flowers. If you don't have any flowers, get some or give some away.

- Helping someone else foster the qualities that you are working on will give you insight into acquiring them yourself.

- It is common to forget your qualities as other things take your interest; just return to them as you remember them. If you have dedicated yourself to some ultimate quality or qualities, your actions will reflect your general focus even if you have forgotten the specific qualities of the week.

  Connect your desired qualities to past positive experiences and to qualities that you know you already possess. Connect them with something that you know you'll do in the morning: brushing your teeth, kissing your mate, enjoying your first cup of tea or coffee. Above all, practice your chosen qualities—remember and reremember them until they are habitual.

- Use the action verbs *I am, I have,* or *I will* before the quality of your choice: "I am respected"; "I have respect"; "I will be respectable." Confirm your choice: "I choose to be respectful"; "I choose to enhance my respectability." If it is necessary for your sense of fairness, then add "to some degree."

- When you deal with life's unfolding, the problems as well as the pleasures, notice your natural tendencies, the unique responses that you have developed. You may or may not like what you have developed as your responses, but for *your* reasons you have developed these actions and depend on them. By being aware of your actions as you use positive qualities, you can gradually modify your behavior to a new image of a more suitable self.

  If you are not feeling or responding or being what you believe you should be, then you must do something about it. Expose yourself to diverse ways of being: travel, read, study, expose yourself to art and entertainment, take on different jobs, meet new people. Do something nice for someone.

- Do whatever you are doing with conscious attentiveness, cheerfulness, and diligence. Keep the quality or qualities that you are striving for in mind. Write them on a piece of paper and carry them with you. Write them on the bathroom mirror with soap.

- Ask yourself the following questions: In order to be successful and happy, what qualities will I need? How will each of my known qualities enhance the qualities that I am working on? Are these the qualities that I want to work on at this stage of my life? Why is this valuable for me? How can I live it? When can I live it?

  Sometimes you will not see the answer to the question, How can I become this quality? Begin by evaluating how you already possess the quality. To what extent have you exhibited this quality? Remember that you need to look at yourself with an honest, realistic sincerity. When you are evaluating yourself there is no place for unreasonable modesty or excessive pride. It is not only a matter of recognizing that you do possess a particular quality, but also a question of degree. After you've chosen a quality, you may realize that you need to expand other qualities in order to balance a lack or an excess.

  You might be a serious person and *goofy* is one of your randomly chosen qualities; and you say, "Well, I don't have any goofiness." Remember your history. Have you ever been silly? What about playful? Do you have a sense of humor? Is there an umbrella quality under which the quality that you are seeking is located? Now you can come back to *goofy* and realize that in the categories of humor, playfulness, and friendliness, you probably have been goofy. Plug into that feeling.

- There is a natural progression from one quality to another. There are qualities that complement each other. You may have an affinity for one but shy away from another. Realize that no quality will be diminished by your acquisition of others. As a matter of fact, it will grow proportionately. Also realize that you can choose to pursue the "other" quality to the degree that you are comfortable. That's what you are going to do anyway.

- Don't worry about evaluating everything. Sometimes you won't know if you are successful without a measurable, tangible result, but sometimes you have to let go and simply move forward. You will frequently need to rely on your faith and intuition.

Do not do extensive analysis, this may lead to guilt. Look at your options objectively. There is always a transition stage that lets the old self be replaced. This is necessary for accepting and allowing the higher self to have expression and life.

- One can't *be* every quality at the same time. Most qualities are situational. As one moves through life, a combination of factors are applied to a situation to which you respond. But there is a theoretical ideal—the highest possible qualitative response. You cannot change what has happened after the fact, but you can act differently next time. You can learn and grow. One way to do this is to review what has transpired and run mental alternatives that would have been more appropriate. This lays down a neural and emotional foundation for a more appropriate, ideal, or "correct" action in the future. Then you will not just be responding to reality but also creating reality.

After an incident in your life, compare the actual scenario with the one that you would have experienced if you had let your higher self do the talking and feeling. When you refer to yourself, think of the speaker as your higher self—your superconsciousness, your God-self.

WARNING: IT WON'T BE EASY

It takes effort to improve a thing, enhance a situation, or become a better person.

Focusing on any quality is going to bring you face to face with your deficiency in that quality. If you decide to focus on giving, you may notice that you haven't given as you would have liked. You may see that you have been hesitant in this area. You will have to face what is holding you back. Do not be discouraged. Look beyond to the potential and eventual *you,* and then proceed. If you have to deal with an immaturity or an emotional block, then face it as best you can and grow. It will have to be dealt with eventually anyway.

Deciding to become a quality is not a one-time decision. There is that initial experience when you first make a wholehearted commitment, but then there is the next day and the next week and the next year. It is a continual decision to be sincere, to be faithful, to be persistent in your commitment even in the face of failure and difficulty.

You will succeed, but it is often frustrating. Continue with honest effort. You have to persevere and reinvest your energy and emotion into your decision.

The initial decision that inspires a heartfelt commitment may be profound, but even an "ultimate" experience is just one experience. You have to realize that you are still a finite, time-bound being. As you pursue living you will have other profound experiences. There will always be more significant experiences because life is an ever-expanding reality and your experience of it is also expanding.

As you act on value, *you are becoming* life.

What is your threshold of conflict? We each have our personal thresholds that we have developed over time. You've heard of the threshold of pain. Conflict and stress are associated with pain.

As you grow, your thresholds will change, and you will develop the ability and strength needed to do what is right *if* you continue to strive to grow.

START HERE

Start from anywhere—just proceed from where you are. You know that you have made mistakes. Don't think that your history is so bad that you cannot begin anew. You don't need to be a saint to begin or to continue.

Sometimes you can totally give in to a quality without regard for the consequences. You feel it when you are creating or competing in a sport or especially when you are in love.

If you find yourself being the person you'd like to be when you're with someone or in a particular situation, then recognize that as an indicator of who you can be, and focus on those qualities that you appreciate about yourself.

Make the decision to nurture that state of happiness. You'll find that you can be that person. You may seek out similar situations and similar people, but if you internalize the state of being, you will find that you can be content in dissimilar, atypical, or even negative situations.

Don't give the credit for your state of being to another person or to a situation. It is still you being you, even though the situation may be a fertile one. Giving credit to another often happens if self-esteem is low. If you can be a happy person with them, then you can also be a happy person within yourself.

When you're absorbed in an activity your mind is focused. Snatch a moment during that time and insert a conscious appreciation of what qualities you are experiencing.

When there is no activity or focus, be appreciative through relaxation, meditation, or just an open acceptance of the space. This is a special time for the quality of openness. Don't be averse to the quiet time. Don't run to the next absorbing activity. If you don't appreciate this "between time," then you can fill your life up with activity and you will be missing an important opportunity.

Ordinary tasks can be completed in an extraordinary manner. Most of your time is taken up with the consistent, mundane activities of life. Fixing dinner, washing your hair, going to work—those are the routine times when you can think about your particular qualities. Those qualities then become the focus of how you do what you are doing; therefore, you will do it exceptionally.

If you attempt to do something positive, practical, and real, you are on the right track. If you are doing something that makes you and others experience a situation with joy and goodness, then you are becoming more of the only things worth becoming: your highest ideals and your grandest and loveliest ideas.

The qualities that you emanate evoke responsive qualities from others.

WHAT ABOUT CRITICISM?

There are derogatory terms that are thrown at us from time to time, particularly when we are around immature people. But we do recognize that we sometimes deserve to be called a jerk. By adding positive elements to the experience you can turn it into something else.

If you add whimsy and sincerity, you become less of a jerk and more friendly. If you add sensitivity, you will be taking into account the feelings of the other, thus modifying your behavior and theirs. As you add positive qualities, in a proper measure, you are eliminating that which used to be recognized as negative.

When you hear a criticism, listen to the truth in it. There may be meanness or jealousy or insecurity on the part of the name-caller, but look for the reason behind the insult. Separate the truth from the negative emotional content that you feel.

If somebody calls you a wimp, they may be recognizing your gentleness and willingness to be accommodating. Accept and bless that part. But they may also be seeing a need for more strength or power in your demeanor. What they are telling you in a negative way is to strengthen those qualities in your personality that are not as robust as they need to be. You need more confidence and chutzpah in your character. People will then see that you are both sensitive and strong.

If somebody says, "Boy, you're really a slob," what is really being said is, "Please add the habits of neatness and organization to your routine."

You may not be aware of all of your actions or reactions, but others are—listen to them! It is worth valuing how people perceive you, even if that perception is foolish or even vicious. You are getting a glimpse of what is seen from the outside.

Especially listen to and take to heart the insights and observations of your friends. But you still have to decide whether or not they are correct. If not, then it is an opportunity to be gracious; take what they say with a grain of salt and dismiss it gracefully.

If you possess too much aggressiveness for instance, it will be noted as extreme and others will recognize it. If they tell you nicely, they will tell you that you are too intense, too abrupt, or too direct. You need not be less direct, simply modify your directness with more tact and add humor.

WHAT ABOUT THE NEGATIVE?

The dictionary defines negative as "lacking positive attributes." The negative has no substance or energy of its own. Shine the light of truth on it and it dissipates. The negative can also be described as possessing an imbalanced, uncoordinated, or incomplete set of positive qualities.

The negative is not a real and integral part of a person. Like the dust that collects on your body, the negative can be easily washed away with the pure water of love and the clean soap of sincerity.

It is not necessary to focus on the negative. Those with an overactive ego tend to ignore their negatives, and those with low self-esteem tend to magnify their negatives. In either case the main reason to look at the negative is to illuminate the specific positive qualities needed to fill that negative space.

Once you have decided on the positive you will notice that the negative is just a shadow. If you are exploring and going toward the positive, then the negative will be understood in the light of the positive.

"Resist not evil" is an admonition to the individual person. Wrongdoing is to be dealt with by social and divine justice not by individual revenge. Fighting evil with evil only strengthens evil, but love destroys evil altogether.

Sometimes you may find yourself honestly choosing the lesser of evils, in which case, reach for the best possible. Your choice to be positive represents progress toward the positive.

The ultimate quest has always been, and will always be, the same: to fulfill needs and wants; that is, to seek what will do you and the people that you care for the greatest good. Since this is done on an individual level, the "good" is very subjective. If you ask someone about their motives, they will justify their actions in positive terms. They will also condemn in negative terms those who do not believe as they do.

Whenever you argue for some point of view, you are defining your subjective good. By using your best logic, reason, and insight, you are explaining your motives. Since your belief system makes sense to you, it follows that others should also hold your "truths" to be self-evident. This may not be the case, of course, because another person's blend of reality leads them to different conclusions. Nonetheless, each soul needs to be loyal to their best view of reality.

Even in the most extreme examples of negative, insane logic, people are choosing what they have contrived as good for themselves. Yes, I can imagine the peculiar individual who enjoys receiving or inflicting pain, but even within this sick character the goal is still the subjective "reward."

Even hate groups define and justify their purpose in positive terms. And when people tell lies, they are using the pretense of truth. They are trying to convince you and themselves that they are being honest, but their real motivation is one of insecurity, self-interest, or apathy.

There may even be those poor souls who do not derive any joy from their deliberate and conscious choice to inflict harm and pain on themselves or others. Be that as it may, they are the exception and your quest is to the light.

Dispel the myth that one can move away from the negative. One must *move toward the positive.*

Moving away from the negative does not work except in the short run. Some real substance has to replace the negative. Negative and positive cannot inhabit the same space.

What percentage of your focus is on moving away from the negative versus moving toward the positive? Are you trying to overcome or become?

Instead of moving away from fear, move toward courage and love. Instead of moving away from frustration, move toward decisiveness and action. Instead of moving away from uncertainty, move toward knowledge and understanding. Instead of moving away from worry, move toward confidence. Instead of moving away from anxiety, move toward patience and moderation. Instead of moving away from indifference, move toward concern.

How much are you using excuses? What are the things, feelings, and circumstances that keep you from achieving your intended state of being? Regarding genuine obstacles, can you overcome them or live with them in good humor?

THE GAP

There is a gap between our current selves and our ideal selves. We are here but we want to be there. This gap will always be with us because we will never attain the ultimate goal of infinity. Since we always perceive that we are short of our goal, it sometimes feels like failure. We must resign ourselves to the fact that we will always be on the journey—always be attaining our goals and always have more to become.

Once you come to a personal understanding that you are progressing, then instead of crediting yourself with a deficiency because of this gap, you can actually appreciate it by knowing, with certainty, that you are becoming your future self.

There is a harmony in what you have been, where you are now, and who you are becoming. If you can appreciate that continuum, then you are perfect, perfecting, and perfectible.

If you are traveling to San Francisco you don't need to feel guilty about being in Salt Lake City. You are moving toward your goal and you are traveling at an appropriate speed. Since you are making progress, the gap is okay. Relax and enjoy the trip.

You do have something of what it takes to get across the chasm. The mind travels outside of time and the spirit exists independent of physical reality. You can be in time and space and independent of them too. Your ticket is the acquisition of positive qualities.

Your intentions, and the nonphysical mind, travel faster than the speed of light, therefore you should not expect to envelop a quality at the same speed. As a matter of fact, the gap between decision speed and experience speed is so great that you should expect the trip of becoming to take forever.

WHY DO YOU EXIST?

You exist to become the completeness of your highest ideas and ideals, and since your ideas and ideals will always exceed your actual being, you will be forever growing into them.

One of the basic human functions is to find meaning. Meaning is the highest attainment of the mind and can be a profound influence on the emotions, but beyond meanings are values. The quest to behold, and then to be infused with, these grand qualities is the ultimate goal of any evolving being.

The ultimate reason to focus on and bring into being the positive qualities is because those qualities are the essence of the universe—they exist! And identification with them guarantees your existence.

Qualities have spirit essence and are as consistently responsive to spiritual gravity as matter is to physical gravity. You can, by your choice, literally transform yourself from the slow physical energy of matter to the ever-living energy of spirit. You can create a spiritual mass that has the same relative force on the spirit level as a moon, planet, or sun has on the physical level.

Your physical skills will fade with age and die with your body. Your mental and emotional abilities can be buffeted about by circumstances and outside influences, but the qualities that you acquire will be with you forever. They are part of your being and part of the universe.

The solution to the ultimate anxiety—the possibility of nonexistence— is to become that which must exist. If you become the basic stuff of existence (positive qualities), you will fulfill your basic survival urge.

Incorporating positive qualities into your being, into your very self, makes your *self* endure. You are, literally, creating your own immortality. If you want to continue to exist, you must choose immortality. If you *are* existence, you cannot also be nonexistence.

Positive qualities are quite literally the keys to immortality. And as a bonus, your life will be much more rewarding while you are living it. When you choose that which you consider to be positive, you are moving toward an eventual state of alignment with what *is*.

If you experience that you exist, then you do exist—"I think, therefore I am."

The ultimate choice to exist or to cease to exist is the culmination of a long process of conscious decisions. Positive qualities cannot die. You can only lose them if you decide to forgo them.

You can make your body continue to exist by feeding and exercising it. But physical survival eventually comes to an end. You can also fulfill your emotional and mental needs during your life in the flesh. And while that is important during your physical life, in order to continue beyond the physical, you must also expand on a spiritual level.

If you want to survive death, you must exist on more than just the physical plane.

Part of the result of choice is learning, and one of the consequences of learning is growth, which is an organic process. You will find that even if you make a sincere effort to choose that which is positive and real, there is the probability that some of your decisions will be incorrect. It is to be expected that some mistakes will be made. These poor decisions can be classified as a lack of wisdom. But as you experience you can and do learn.

When fear comes at you and you choose to face it, you are bringing into your being that concept we describe as courage. You may not be the epitome of courage, but in the situation at hand, as you face the fear with your best effort, you are courageous.

The following list contains aspects that I have included with the 988 qualities in the alphabetical listings. Every quality includes at least two categories: other word forms and a definition. Use this list of options to further explore the qualities you are interested in.

I define and have further explanations following the list for the first eight items.

Definitions
Kindred qualities
Compatible qualities
Parental qualities
Familial qualities
Consequential qualities
Too far
Color
Derivative/Etymology
Synonyms
Significant date
People who exemplify/Heroes
The quality in relationships
Music/Poetry
Movement/Dance/Art/Drama/Comedy/Theater
Games/Playfulness/Humor

Fragrance
Touch
Sayings/Proverbs/Axioms/Mottoes/Quotes
Stories/Anecdotes/Parables/Analogies/Essays
Affirmations/Meditation/Prayers
Inspirations/Reflections
Considerations/Visualizations/Imagery/Fantasy
Observations/Tips/Suggestions/Advice/Admonitions
Comments/Questions
How to live this quality today
Exercises
Experiences/Practical/Realistic
Goals
Jobs requiring or that will develop this quality
Nature
Archetypes/Symbols
Historical characters/Fiction/Legends
Mythologies/Fables
Theology
Mental/Psychic
Shape/Form/Structure
Foods/Drink/Medicine
Bibliography

DEFINITIONS

I have not attempted to create a definitive dictionary. My intention is to
give the reader an idea of the quality with its positive meanings. I have
listed only those meanings that relate to the positive qualities. I examined
the definitions and all forms (adjectives, verbs, nouns, and adverbs) from
six different dictionaries. My thanks to the lexicographers.

KINDRED QUALITIES

These are balancing elements.
   All positive qualities, in order to attain their maximum value, need to
be balanced with other positive qualities. Wisdom dictates that we possess
a combination of qualities in every situation. If abandoned to isolation the
solitary quality will become inconsistent. The lack of proper and balanced
nurturing will stifle optimum growth and distort personality. If a quality is

THE BOOK OF POSITIVE QUALITIES

stripped of its necessary balancers, it eventually ends up as a negative quality.

Partner each quality with other qualities, not necessarily opposites but ones that will encourage you to maintain and retain the enthusiasm for the quality that you desire. Strength is a good thing to have, but without kindness it can turn mean. Confidence without humility turns into arrogance.

COMPATIBLE QUALITIES

These are qualities that are harmonious or work well together, such as the following:

- Glamorous and Healthy
- Devoted and Creative
- Sane, Stress Hardy, and Flexible
- Self-forgetful and Self-control

Or they are usually thought of together:

- Homey and Wholesome
- Entrepreneurial and Shrewd
- Kind and Generous

PARENTAL QUALITIES

Parental qualities are those from which the quality in question is derived. Whether a quality is parental is a subjective judgment. The chart is organized according to parental qualities. Those toward the center are the parents. Considering the linear relationships, this is not strictly true in all cases.

FAMILIAL QUALITIES

Different from synonyms in that they are in the same family, familial qualities do not necessarily have close meanings. A colorful person can also be described as having character. *Helpful* and *giving* are similar but not synonyms. Other examples: finesse and tact, graceful and free.

CONSEQUENTIAL QUALITIES

These are qualities that flow out of the acquisition of individual qualities. Certainly as you focus on one, its synonyms come to mind. But as you begin to understand and become a quality, you will also move closer to other qualities. In playfulness there is fairness, and in order to play you often need the organization of rules and roles for the players; therefore, as you are playful you are also learning about the seemingly unrelated quality of orderliness.

TOO FAR

One cannot take a quality too far if the balancing (kindred) qualities have been integrated. Consider the family of qualities of safe, cautious, practical, prudent, and consistent. The corporate and legal systems look to these as primary qualities, not so much because of their innate value but because it is easier to standardize a system and make people fit within that system. If the corporation valued the creativity, initiative, and adventuristic entrepreneurialism of the individual, the tendency toward the mediocrity of the herd and the tyranny of the policy would be counterbalanced.

One can take things too far and yet still be accepted by a society that is also taking the same things too far. Witness slavery, ethnic cleansing, and war.

POSITIVE QUALITY	TOO FAR
Adventuresome	Foolhardy
Assertive	Rude
Cautious	Fearful
Curious	Prying
Exuberant	Rambunctious
Flexible	Wishy-washy
Forward	Pushy
Individualistic	Rebellious, Overbearing
Meek	Weak
Neat	Compulsive
Relaxed	Lazy
Safe	Timid, Oppressed
Self-esteem	Arrogant, Egotistic
Sensitive	Temperamental
Spirited	Tempestuous

COLOR

If wearing or surrounding yourself with certain colors will enhance your appreciation of and the infusion of your desired quality, then you should do so. There is some science, some folklore, and some tradition to colors and quality enhancement.

THANK YOU FOR BEING POSITIVE

Pick a quality or two to emulate this week. Look them up and get some ideas on what they will mean in your life. Decide to live them. Think about them. Notice how you already possess them. See how they manifest themselves. Make them real with conscious action.

ABIDING

Word Forms: abide, abided, abode, abidance, abider, abide by, abidingly

Definitions: (1) enduring or sustaining; withstanding; **(2)** bearing patiently; tolerant; **(3)** stable; **(4)** prepared; **(5)** compliant

Synonyms: continuing, lasting, enduring, durable, steadfast, changeless, long-lived

Symbol: the *elephant* (long-lived)

ABLE

Word Forms: abler, ablest, ability, ably, ableness

Definitions: (1) having sufficient power, strength, or skill to accomplish something; **(2)** having or exhibiting superior abilities, intelligence, knowledge, talent, or competence; **(3)** having competent fortitude, vigor, or qualifications

Synonyms: capable, efficient, clever, effective, qualified, apt

Questions:
  What are your talents?
  What can you do?
  What do you appreciate?
  What do you know instinctively?
  What do you long for?
  What are your dreams?

ABOVEBOARD

Definition: straightforward; without concealment or deception; in open sight; honest

Derivation: From the difficulty of cheating at cards when the hands are above the table.

ABUNDANT

Word Forms: abundance, abundantly

Definitions: (1) marked by great plenty, ample supply; (2) fully sufficient; abounding; (3) brimming; overflowing

Synonyms: exuberant, rich, affluent, copious, wealth

Parental Quality: faith

Quote:
Consider the lilies of the field, how they grow, they toil not, neither do they spin; yet I say to you that not even Solomon in all his glory was arrayed like one of these.
—JESUS, Matthew 6:28–29

Affirmation:
All financial doors are open; all financial channels are free, and endless bounty now comes to me.
—CATHERINE PONDER, *The Dynamic Laws of Prosperity*

Advice: Forgive yourself and others and move forward with confidence. Blame and malice are burdens that hold a place in your mind and heart that could be filled with the expectant openness that is necessary for abundance.

Symbols: *vegetation; big mountain* (American Indian)

Mythologies: *Amalthea.* Zeus, grateful for Amalthea's nursing, broke off the horn of a goat and endowed it with the power to be filled with whatever the possessor desires—the horn of Plenty; Cornucopia.
The Land of Cockaigne: An imaginary country where all good things are to be had for the taking

ACCEPTING

Word Forms: accept, acceptable, acceptance, accepted, acceptability, acceptive, accepter, acceptant, acceptingly, acceptingness

Definitions: (1) receiving with pleasure; gratifying; (2) receiving with a consenting mind or willingness; (3) receiving with good grace and gracious satisfaction; (4) submitting or agreeing to; (5) understanding as true; (6) an agreeable or pleasing person; civil; (7) admittance or approval (accepted as part of the group)

Synonyms: take, admit, grateful, welcome

Familial Quality: popular

Quote:
When you really know somebody, you can't hate them. Or maybe it's just that you can't really know them until you stop hating them.
　　　　　　　　—ORSON SCOTT CARD, *Speaker for the Dead*

Reflection: They say that to receive God's grace all one has to do is to accept it. This is true, but the manner of acceptance is not passive; it is active. What you are receiving is love, and to continue the flow you must let it flow through you. You are not just a vessel but a conduit.

Tip: The giver can also think about helping the accepter accept, usually by understanding how to explain or emote acceptance.

Advice: Even though it is a sign of acceptance, silence is usually a sign of thoughtfulness or reluctance to express an opinion. Elicit a response. Verbal declaration is important.

ACCESSIBLE

Word Forms: access, accessibility, accessibly, accessibleness

Definitions: (1) approachable; (2) easy to get along with; (3) open

Synonyms: attainable, complaisant, courteous, sociable, friendly

ACCOMMODATING

Word Forms: accommodate, accommodated, accommodative, accommodatingly, accommodation, accommodator

Definitions: (1) obliging; disposed to comply and make adjustment; **(2)** makes fit, suitable, or comfortable; **(3)** furnishing with something desired, needed, or suited; **(4)** able to adapt to varying conditions; **(5)** adjusting differences; bringing into agreement or accord; reconciling; **(6)** giving consideration to; satisfying a need; **(7)** staying in line with another's expectations

Synonyms: serving, yielding, helpful

Kindred Qualities: free, independent

Too Far: conformist

Observation: The universe will accommodate your version of reality, if it can.

Suggestion: While being accommodating, be encouraging, supportive, and tolerant. If the person you are accommodating refuses to grow or is, in your opinion, growing too slowly, then you may get frustrated. But as long as the person is moving, even a little, you should be patient and helpful.

ACCOMPLISHED

Word Forms: accomplish, accomplishable, accomplisher, accomplishment, accomplishing

Definitions: (1) completed; finished; fulfilled; executed; effected; **(2)** proficient as the result of practice or training; skilled; **(3)** well endowed with good qualities and manners; complete in acquirements; educated and polished; **(4)** relates to achievement, attainment; **(5)** possessing a special skill or ability acquired by training or practice, which constitutes excellence of mind

Synonyms: perform, discharge, refined, cultured, educated, realized, brought about

Quote:

The only way round is through.

—ROBERT FROST

Parable:

They stood together resting, contemplating the future, remembering with wonder at the past. They viewed this place. None had been here before but it was familiar. They knew they were safe and they were at peace. There was an easy familiarity. They knew each other or they knew that if another was here, they were a kindred spirit. This group had reached this *now* with an eye on the individual path. But there were none who were loners. They knew that there were other groups with similar accomplishments that had made it by knowing each other's strengths and weaknesses and had committed to teamwork. By now they realized that the future goal may be interesting but that *now* was always unique. More was more but not of much value unless you had it at your personal disposal. Then you can look at yourself and recognize it as part of you and therefore part of your tools.

They moved easily here knowing that this was the time for recharge, relaxation, rest, rejuvenation, recreation, and receptivity. They also knew that they better take advantage because they would need it. The next step was study and preparation for the stage of action following that.

They knew the pattern well. They had learned that a certain pace was possible but only if one followed the flow. It was still a temptation to observe those in a different flow and go too fast or too slow. But it was getting easier to move with the confidence of knowing that they could jump into another flow if it was a continuation of the *now*.

Affirmation:

I give thanks that I am divinely equipped to accomplish great things with ease.

—CATHERINE PONDER, *The Dynamic Laws of Prosperity*

ACCOUNTABLE

Word Forms: account, accountability, accountably, accountableness

Definition: liable to be called to account; responsible; answerable

Synonym: amenable

ACCURATE

Word Forms: accuracy, accurately, accurateness

Definitions: (1) free from error, especially as the result of care; (2) not making mistakes; carefully precise; meticulous

Synonyms: exact, correct

Suggestion: Be only as accurate as necessary, but not less than needed.

Symbol: a *bull's-eye*

ACTIVE

Word Forms: act, acting, action, activate, activism, activist, activistic, activity, actor, actively, activeness, proactive

Definitions: (1) abounding in or characterized by action; busy; (2) productive of action or movement; (3) agile, quick, nimble, lively, or brisk; disposed to move; (4) marked by vigorous activity; constantly engaged in action; (5) causing or promoting movement or change; (6) requiring vigorous motion or exertion

Synonyms: alert, assiduous, spirited, sprightly, prompt, operative, industrious, diligent, energetic

Kindred Quality: relaxed

Parental Qualities: choice, decisiveness

Familial Qualities: progressive, participative

Consequential Quality: appreciation

Quotes:
When man decides, and when he consummates this decision in action, man experiences, and the meanings and the values of this experience are forever a part of his eternal character on all levels, from the finite to the final.

—The Urantia Book

Knowing is not enough; we must apply. Willing is not enough; we must do.

—GOETHE

Analogy: An automobile has to be moving in order for there to be some direction. God can't help you move in the right direction if you are parked. On the other hand, there has to be a road of some sort. God bless the road builders. You can't go driving your car into a swamp, you'd get stuck. But if you change to a hydroplane you can continue your journey.

Tip: If you're worried or unhappy, do something about it. Take a walk, put on some happy music and dance, go to sleep, watch TV—anything, just *do* something, and do it consciously.

Comment: Whether we get an idea from something we read, somebody we are inspired by, something said, from prayer, or a random thought, the action that is then taken is what gives that thought its power, its life, its value. The original thought combined with our current reality is framed and brought to life by the desire to take action and finally by taking that action. Action is the completion of decision.

Color: red

Symbols: *Mars;* the *sail;* the *spur; children* playing

ACTUALIZED

Word Forms: actual, actuality, actualize, actualizing, actualization, actually, actuate, self-actualized

Definition: to make real; realize a possibility in action

Symbol: a *golden rose*

ACUMEN

Word Form: acuminous

Definition: quickness of perception; keenness of mind or discrimination
See also: *Sagacity*

ADAPTABLE

Word Forms: adapt, adaptability, adaptation, adapter, adaptive, adaptableness

Definitions: (1) can be made suitable; can be made to fit (as for a specific or new use or situation); **(2)** adjustable to a new situation or environment (by changing one's behavior or attitudes)

Synonyms: accommodating, arranging, conforming, reconciling

Familial Qualities: flexible, obedient

Reflection: As we experience our lives, actively and passively, we also become more adaptable. Expansion comes when we look beyond the confines of the current environment: from the self, to the family, to the community, to the state, to the nation, to the planet, to the universe.

Observation: In evolution, when change occurs in the environment, the species that adapt to the change have become more flexible and more complex. When a species adapts to more than a single environment, it expands its survival boundaries.

The more successful mechanisms (or qualities) are those that have been built on a sturdy foundation and eventually become stable enough themselves to live on their own.

Just as physical evolution follows how well a species functions in increasingly complex environments, so too do we evolve on levels of the mind, soul, and spirit by what decisions we make in reaction to our internal and external environments. Because we can anticipate the future, we can also be proactive.

Color: green

ADEPT

Word Forms: adeptly, adeptness

Definitions: (1) highly skilled; thoroughly proficient; expert; **(2)** one fully skilled or well versed in any art; a master

Synonym: dexterous

Derivation: The term was originally used to describe alchemists who claimed to have found the philosopher's stone or a panacea.

ADJUSTED

Word Forms: adjust, adjustable, adjustment

Definitions: (1) accommodated to suit a particular set of circumstances or requirements; **(2)** having achieved a harmonious relationship with the environment or with other individuals

Synonyms: adaptable, conforming, fit

ADMIRABLE

Word Forms: admire, admirability, admiration, admirably, admirableness

Definition: deserving the highest esteem; inspiring approval or respect

Synonyms: wonderful, pleasing, worthy, choice, excellent

Derivation: Latin, "to wonder"

ADORABLE

Word Forms: adore, adorability, adoration, adorably, adorableness

Definitions: **(1)** worthy of or one who is receiving worship; worthy of divine honors; **(2)** worthy of the utmost love or respect; **(3)** delightful; charming

ADROIT

Word Forms: adroitly, adroitness

Definitions: **(1)** expert in using the hands or body; nimble; **(2)** cleverly skillful; resourceful or ingenious; ready in invention or execution

Synonyms: artful, dexterous, proficient

Derivation: Latin, "to set in a straight line"

ADVANCING

Word Forms: advance, advanced, advancingly, advancement

Definitions: (1) improving or making better; benefitting; promoting or furthering the good; **(2)** making progress; developing; **(3)** moving forward; proceeding

Synonyms: raising, elevating, exalting, heightening, accelerating

ADVENTURESOME

Word Forms: adventure, adventurer, adventurism, adventurous, venturesome, adventuresomeness

Definitions: (1) bold; daring; inclined to take risks; **(2)** courageous; enterprising

Synonyms: audacious, brave, daring, daredevil

Too Far: foolhardy, rash, reckless

Quotes:

The principle difference between an adventurer and a suicide is that the adventurer leaves himself a margin of escape (the narrower the margin the greater the adventure), the margin whose width and length may be determined by unknown factors but whose successful navigation is determined by the measure of the adventurer's nerve and wits. It is always exhilarating to live by one's nerves or toward the summit of one's wits.
—TOM ROBBINS, *Another Roadside Attraction*

Adventure is not in the guidebook and beauty is not on the map.
—TERRY AND RENNY RUSSELL, *On the Loose*

Symbol: a *ship*

AESTHETIC

Word Forms: aesthete, aesthetics, aesthetical, aesthetically, aesthetician, aestheticism

Definitions: (**1**) of, relating to, or dealing with the beautiful; (**2**) sensitive to art and beauty; showing good taste; artistic; (**3**) appreciative of and responsive to the beautiful; (**4**) an authority in matters of taste; (**5**) prone to cultivate and indulge in the beautiful

AFFABLE

Word Forms: affability, affably

Definitions: (**1**) easy to approach and talk to; courteous; having easy manners; (**2**) kindly countenance; benign; gracious; complaisant

Synonyms: civil, accessible, mild, urbane, polite, friendly

AFFECTIONATE

Word Forms: affect, affection, affectionately, affectionateness

Definitions: (**1**) having great love or friendliness; fondness; (**2**) proceeding from affection; indicating love; benevolent; (**3**) tender feeling; warm liking

Synonyms: attached, loving, devoted, earnest, kind, ardent

Symbols: a *kiss;* a *hug*

AFFIRMING

Word Forms: affirm, affirmed, affirmable, affirmation, affirmative, affirmer

Definitions: (**1**) characterizes one who asserts positively; states with confidence, avers, confirms; (**2**) makes a positive statement valid

Synonyms: assertive, asseverative, assuring, avouching, establishing, ratifying, declarative, pronouncing

Kindred Quality: thankful

Quotes:

An affirmation is a strong, positive statement that something is already so.

—SHAKTI GAWAIN

I will act as if I make a difference.

—WILLIAM JAMES

Affirmations:

I am a lovable person. I have the right to say "no" to people without losing their love.

—LEONARD ORR

I am (name quality) and I am growing in understanding of this quality as I continue to live it.

Observation:

You can read your environment, it is giving you some feedback. I used to think that Indians used to think <Oh, there goes a crow. That means something.> Now, I know, from my own experience, that when I see something—the crow—I'm thinking something, and then the crow shows up to affirm it while I'm thinking about it.

—JERRY DOWNS

Tips:
- Affirmations help you stay focused on the positive.
- The key to affirmations is to let your higher self, your cosmic identity, do the talking. Transfer the *self* from the ego self to the ultimate self.

Suggestions:

Applying the technique of autosuggestion to affirmations (Adapted from Catherine Ponder's *The Dynamic Laws of Prosperity*)

1. Write each affirmation ten to twenty times.
2. Work with one or more every day—at the start of the day, just before bedtime, and whenever you feel at effect.

3. Record them on tape multiple times and play back to yourself.
4. Make a list of your most meaningful affirmations.
5. Put specific names and situations into your affirmations.
6. Make your affirmation personal and invent new ones.
7. Say the affirmations in the first, second, and third persons.
8. Work with them every day until they become part of your consciousness.

Symbol: the *column;* shaking the head up and down—*yes*

AGILE

Word Forms: agilely, agility

Definitions: (1) quick and well-coordinated in movement; nimble; (2) active; lively; brisk; (3) marked by an ability to think quickly; mentally acute or aware; resourceful

Synonyms: spry, alert

Symbols: the *stag;* the *rabbit*

Fiction: *Tarzan.* In Edgar Rice Burroughs' stories of a man raised in the jungle, Tarzan became as agile as his ape family.

AGREEABLE

Word Forms: agree, agreeability, agreement, agreeably, agreeableness

Definitions: (1) pleasing; pleasant to the mind or senses; (2) willing or ready to concur or consent; (3) being in harmony; consonant

Synonyms: acceptable, grateful

Comment: You can always find something to disagree with. It is just as easy to find something to agree with. Well, I've met a few who are happiest in the midst of an argument, and it is a real challenge to douse their fires of discontent with the cool, patient waters of positive kindness. On the other hand, maybe you should just get into it with them and make their day.

ALACRITOUS

Word Form: alacrity

Definitions: (**1**) lively; gay; sprightly; (**2**) ready or prompt to act or serve; cheerful willingness

ALERT

Word Forms: alertly, alertness

Definitions: (**1**) watchful; vigilant; ready to act; (**2**) brisk; nimble; moving with promptness; active; lively; (**3**) quick to understand or respond; perceptive; (**4**) fully aware and attentive; wide awake

Symbol: an *arrowhead* (American Indian)

ALIVE

Word Forms: live, aliveness, enliven

Definitions: (**1**) in a living or functioning state; having life; (**2**) in a state of action; in force or operation; active <"Keep hope *alive*">; (**3**) cheerful; sprightly; lively; eager; animated; (**4**) having the quality of life; vivid; vibrant

Symbols: *fire* (like the living, both must consume life to stay alive); the *fountain; air*: the *breath* of Life; *bread;* the *vine*

Mythology: *Merodach.* In Babylonian mythology, Merodach is the god of life and the benefactor of humans—later in Semitic mythology, the sun god and lord of all gods.

ALLURING

Word Forms: allure, alluringly, alluringness

Definitions: (1) very attractive or tempting; enticing; seductive; **(2)** fascinating; charming

ALTRUISTIC

Word Forms: altruism, altruist, altruistically

Definition: selfless regard for or devotion to the welfare of others

People Who Exemplify This Quality: In the spring of 1991 there was a six-year-old girl who found on a New Jersey beach a bottle that contained two dollars. It also held a note that read, "Do something good with this." She decided to give it to the homeless by giving somebody a meal. With the community's help and her altruistic attitude, she was able to feed the homeless—lunch for sixty people for one day.

Quote:
> The individual can take initiatives without anyone's permission. . . .
> You do not belong to you. You belong to the universe. The significance of you will forever remain obscure to you, but you may assume that you are fulfilling your significance if you apply yourself to converting all your experience to the highest advantage of others.
> —RICHARD BUCKMINSTER FULLER

Comment: In order to acquire altruism and to experience altruistic behavior, you are going to have to submit yourself to the discomfort of recognizing needs of other people. You may have to expose yourself to injustice or prejudice. There is opportunity to turn an "unfortunate" situation into a fortunate one. The struggle blesses you with good qualities.

Color: red

AMAZING

Word Forms: amaze, amazed, amazement, amazingly

Definitions: (1) astonishing; wonderful; (2) to confound with great surprise or sudden wonder; to astound; to mystify

Synonyms: awesome, marvelous, incredible

Quote:
God sure thunk up some stuff.

—JOHN PRESTON DOWNS

AMBITIOUS

Word Forms: ambition, ambitiously, ambitiousness

Definitions: (1) an earnest desire for some type of achievement or distinction, as wealth, fame, or spiritual enlightenment, and the willingness to strive for it; aspiring; (2) requiring exceptional effort or ability; challenging; difficult <an *ambitious* project>; (3) strong yearning; eager <*ambitious* love>

Derivation: Latin "to go about"; from the practice of Roman candidates for office, who went around the city to solicit votes

Color: orange

AMELIORATIVE

Word Forms: ameliorate, amelioration, ameliorator, meliorate

Definition: tending to produce improvement

Comment: My mother said, "I had to make myself do it," when she was talking about writing an article or speaking in public. One literally does make one's *self*. The basics are all there: body, mind, choice, personality, spirit, physical environment, revelation, identity, challenge, et cetera. But you actually fashion your soul with your decisions and experiences.

AMENABLE

Word Forms: amenability, amenably, amenableness

Definitions: (1) responsible or answerable; (2) willing to follow advice; open to suggestion

Synonyms: obedient, responsive, submissive, tractable

AMIABLE

Word Forms: amiability, amiably, amiableness

Definition: possessing sweetness of temper; having a pleasant disposition; friendly; kindly; sociable; congenial

Synonyms: charming, lovable, good-natured, complaisant

Color: red

AMICABLE

Word Forms: amicability, amicably, amicableness

Definition: friendly; peaceable; characterized by good will; harmonious

Synonyms: *Amicable* always supposes two or more parties, as an amicable arrangement. A single individual would not be described as amicable, though he or she may be called friendly.

AMOROUS

Word Forms: amour, amorist, amorously, amorousness

Definitions: (1) inclined to love; loving; fond; (2) in love; enamored (of a person or thing); (3) pertaining to love; produced by love; indicating love <*amorous* delight>; (4) sexual love or lovemaking

Synonym: affectionate

AMUSING

Word Forms: amuse, amusement, amusive, amusingly, amusingness

Definitions: (1) pleasantly entertaining or diverting; (2) arousing laughter or mirth

ANGELIC

Word Forms: angel, angelically, angelicalness

Definitions: (1) of an angel or the angels; spiritual; heavenly; (2) like an angel in beauty, goodness, innocence, purity, or kindness

Quote:

Every blade of grass has its angel that bends over it and whispers, "Grow, grow."

—*The Talmud*

Exercise: The following is adapted from the *Guidelines for Use* on the Angel® Cards. Angel® Cards are small, one-by-two-inch cards with a positive quality on each. This is one way to use the Positive Qualities.

Sit quietly. Close your eyes. Breathe deeply and relax. Allow your thoughts and feelings to settle and center yourself within the light. In the stillness take some time to review your present situation. Focus on those aspects of yourself or your environment that you would like to change or improve. Set your goals simply and specifically. Move into an open, receptive space and affirm your willingness for your goals to be fulfilled. Feel a pure stream of energy entering your being. Let it move into you and fill you, lifting and expanding your awareness. Then open your eyes and select your quality or qualities.

Take time to attune to your quality. Move back into the silence and welcome it. Feel it merging with you. Open lines of communication and allow the significance of the quality to become conscious. Let it speak to you. Affirm your ability to be an open, clear expression for this energy. Visualize its essence at one with you, flowing through you and streaming into your life in harmonious and uplifting ways.

Finally, ask for a gift from the quality. Accept anything that you receive: a word, an image, or a feeling. Complete the meditation by giving thanks and writing down ways in which this quality can have greater expression in your life.

Remember your meditation in subsequent days to reaffirm your goals and reflect on how it has manifested so far.

ANIMATED

Word Forms: animate, animatedly, animation

Definitions: (1) endowed with life or the qualities of life; alive; (2) full of movement and activity; (3) lively; vigorous; full of spirit

APLOMB

Definition: imperturbable self-possession, poise, or assurance; complete and certain composure; self-confidence

APPEALING

Word Forms: appeal, appealingly, appealingness

Definition: a pleasing attraction; interesting; charming

APPEASING

Word Forms: appease, appeasable, appeasingly, appeasement

Definition: to make quiet; to calm, to still; to pacify; to soothe; to conciliate, especially by giving in to demands

APPETIZING

Word Forms: appetite, appetizer, appetizingly

Definitions: (1) stimulating or tempting to the appetite; tasty; (2) appealing or tempting

APPRECIATIVE

Word Forms: appreciate, appreciation, appreciable, appreciator, appreciatively, appreciativeness

Definitions: (1) to value or esteem; recognition of good points; conscious

of the significance, desirability, worth, or quality; **(2)** discriminating perception or enjoyment; sensitive awareness, especially recognition of aesthetic values; **(3)** expressing admiration, approval, or gratitude; thankful recognition; **(4)** to be keenly sensible of or sensitive to; **(5)** to exercise wise judgment, delicate perception, and keen insight in realizing worth;
See also: *Giving.*

Synonyms: prized, treasured, cherished, understanding

Kindred Quality: respectable

Quotes:
By appreciation, we make excellence in others our property.
—VOLTAIRE

Be prepared to appreciate what you meet.
—FRANK HERBERT, *Dune*

Tips:
- Often tell the people you love that you appreciate them.
- Recognize and appreciate the compliment your friends give you by including you in their lives.

Admonition: Appreciate the plants and animals that give up their life so that you can live. Respect the living energy that sustains you.

Comments:
- Appreciation enhances experience. One feels an experience all the deeper when one appreciates it.
- If you appreciate something, it is likely that someone else does too. Keep that in mind if you like a clean park and are wondering what to do with your trash.

Exercise: Make a list of those things that you appreciate, such as the smell of clean air, the beauty of a flower, the diversity of nature, the people in your life, or the sunrise and the sunset on the walls of the Grand Canyon.

APPROPRIATE

Word Forms: appropriately, appropriateness, apropos

Definition: especially suitable or compatible; fit or proper; relevant; to do exactly what is required under the circumstances

Synonyms: becoming, congruous, adapted, particular, apt

Comment: To do exactly what is required under the circumstances may be something very bizarre if you're a prisoner in a concentration camp, a kid in the ghetto, or even a housewife in the suburbs. But as long as you are sincere and conscious of doing the "correct" thing, then you are making a choice and you are acting in your right mind.

APPROVING

Word Forms: approve, approvable, approval, approved, approver, approvingly

Definitions: (1) to have or express a favorable attitude or opinion; (2) to like; to be pleased with; to think or declare to be good or satisfactory; to commend; (3) endorse; sanction

Synonyms: accrediting, certifying, consenting, encouraging, authorizing, supportive, promoting, praising, admiring, ratifying

Quote:
What do you call love, hate, charity, revenge, humanity, magnanimity, forgiveness?—different results of the one master impulse, the necessity of securing one's self-approval.
—MARK TWAIN

ARDENT

Word Forms: ardency, ardently, ardor

Definitions: (1) characterized by intense feeling; fervent; **(2)** intensely devoted; zealous

ARRESTING

Word Forms: arrest, arrestingly

Definition: attracting wanted attention or interest; striking; impressive

ARTICULATE

Word Forms: articulation, articulately, articulateness

Definitions: (1) clearly and effectively presented or expressed <an *articulate* argument>; lucid; **(2)** well formulated

Synonym: eloquent

Symbol: an *orator*

ARTISTIC

Word Forms: art, artful, artist, artistically, artistry

Definitions: (1) done skillfully; aesthetically satisfying; **(2)** appreciative of art and beauty; sensitive to the arts

People Who Exemplify: Michelangelo

Saying: *Ars longa, vita brevis* (Latin): "Art is long, life is short."

Quotes:
Art is the demonstration that the ordinary is extraordinary.
                                    —AMEDE OZENFANT

Be responsive to your audience. Art is making an interpretation of an experience.
                                    —JERRY DOWNS

The high mission of any art is, by its illusions, to foreshadow a higher universe reality, to crystallize the emotions of time into the thought of eternity.
                                    —*The Urantia Book*

The artist is not a different kind of person, but every person is a different kind of artist.
                                    —ERIC GILL

ASCENDING

Word Forms: ascend, ascendant, ascension, ascent

Definition: moving upward; rising or increasing to higher levels, values, or degrees

Comment: It is believed by some that after awakening on the other side of death, we automatically are given all virtue and our career of becoming Godlike is over. I believe that the struggle of progressive learning and continuing to become better is the standard throughout our universal career. The wisdom of the evolutionary program becomes more evident as we continue to live and grow.

ASPIRING

Word Forms: aspire, aspiringly, aspiration

Definitions: (1) to long, aim, or seek ambitiously, especially for something great or of high value; **(2)** ascend; soar

ASSERTIVE

Word Forms: assert, assertion, asserter, assertor, assertively, assertiveness, self-assertive

Definitions: (1) states positively; affirming; declares with assurance; **(2)** bold; confident; **(3)** demonstrates the existence of <*assert* his rights>

Synonyms: aggressive, avow, aver

Kindred Qualities: understanding, gentleness

Too Far: rude, obnoxious

Symbol: the *flag*, raised above on a pole

ASSIDUOUS

Word Forms: assiduity, assiduously, assiduousness

Definitions: (1) constant in application; unremitting; devoted; persistent; **(2)** performed with constant diligence or attention; persevering; industrious

Synonyms: attentive, sedulous, zealous

ASSURED

Word Forms: assure, assurance, assuredly, assuredness, reassure, self-assured

Definitions: (1) bold; confident; authoritative; self-satisfied; self-possessed; **(2)** convinced of the certainty or truth of a matter

ASTONISHING

Word Forms: astonish, astonishingly, astonishment

Definition: amazing; wonderful; surprising

ASTOUNDING

Word Forms: astound, astounded, astoundingly

Definition: astonishing; amazing; overwhelming with wonder

Synonym: surprising

Quote:
If we all did the things we are capable of doing, we would literally
astound ourselves.
—THOMAS EDISON

ASTUTE

Word Forms: astucious, astucity, astutely, astuteness

Definition: shrewd and penetrating; keen in discernment; exhibiting combined shrewdness and perspicacity to the point of being artful or crafty

Synonyms: sagacious, discerning, critical, subtle

Quote:
When you have an elephant by the hind legs and it is trying to run
away, it is best to let it run.
—ABRAHAM LINCOLN

ATTENTIVE

Word Forms: attend, attention, attentional, attentively, attentiveness

Definitions: (1) mindful; observant; intent; careful; (2) characterized by thoughtful regard or focus; courteous; polite; heedful of the comfort of others

Synonym: watchful

Compatible Qualities: curiosity, stick-to-itive

Parental Quality: consciousness

Familial Qualities: awake, alert, aware, concentration, focus, motivated

Consequential Quality: fair

Sayings:
Arrectis auribus (Latin): "With ears pricked up" [attentively]

Where attention goes, energy flows.
—JAMES REDFIELD

Quote:
We have two ears and one mouth so that we can listen twice as much as we speak.
—EPICTETUS

Admonition: To "pay attention" often means to listen. If we are concerned with only those things that we want to hear or the things that we want to respond to with our point of view, then we are not giving the speaker the full measure of our attention.

Comment: The key to all reality is love, so when you're driving, pay attention to where you're going.

Exercise: How good is your attention span? How long can you stare at an inanimate object? What does your mind do while you are looking at it? Do you think of its various aspects: size, shape, color, texture, taste, memory of use?

How long can you be interested in an animate scene? Witness how long you can sit in front of a TV screen. The degree to which you are absorbed in the action has a lot to do with your interest in the subject, the characters, and your curiosity of the outcome. Advertisers prepare with a great deal of effort their commercials to take advantage of the attentiveness of the paying public.

Are you motivated to keep your focus on what you need to? Is the object of your attention stimulating? Are you hungry, thirsty, or sleepy? Are you healthy? Are you in a competitive mode? All of these will affect your ability to be attentive.

ATTRACTIVE

Word Forms: attract, attraction, attractingly, attractively, attractiveness

Definition: arousing interest or pleasure; charming; alluring; inviting; engaging; winning; fascinating

Too Far: egotistical

Comment: It seems that one's physical attributes help form one's other qualities. Take, for example, an extremely attractive person. Because the outside world responds to their physical beauty, they react to that stimulus. If they get caught up in the attention paid them without balancing it with charm and humility, they may end up with an inflated sense of self-worth.

AUSPICIOUS

Word Forms: auspice, auspiciously, auspiciousness

Definitions: **(1)** successful or favorable activity; prosperous; fortunate; **(2)** propitious; opportune; kind

Synonyms: promising, encouraging, advantageous, lucky

AUTHENTIC

Word Forms: authenticity, authenticate, authentically

Definitions: (1) genuine; real; not false or copied <an *authentic* history>; **(2)** approved by authority; trustworthy; reliable

Synonyms: true, certain, faithful, credible, official, authorized

AUTHORITATIVE

Word Forms: authority, authoritatively, authoritativeness

Definitions: (1) having or proceeding from knowledge; official; **(2)** asserting control; fond of giving orders; commanding

Kindred Quality: parental

Too Far: dictatorial

Symbols: the *hand;* the *fist*

AUTONOMOUS

Word Forms: autonomy, autonomously

Definitions: (1) independent in government; self-governing; **(2)** undertaken or carried on without outside control; self-contained

Synonym: free

AVAILABLE

Word Forms: avail, availably, availability

Definitions: (1) suitable or ready for use; at hand; usable; **(2)** readily obtainable; accessible; **(3)** qualified or one who is willing to do something or to assume a responsibility <*available* candidates>

AWAKE

Word Forms: awoke, awaked, awaking, awaken, awakened, awakening

Definitions: (1) aroused or active; invigorated with new life; **(2)** to become conscious or aware of something; **(3)** to stir up; excite

Synonyms: provoked, stimulated, incited, animated

Quote:
The sleeper must awaken.
—Frank Herbert, *Dune*

Admonition: Take conscious, positive steps to be awake in each moment.

AWARE

Word Form: awareness

Definitions: (1) having knowledge or realization; conscious; cognizant; **(2)** informed; alert; knowledgeable

Synonyms: apprised, sensible, acquainted

Quote:
The Great Secret is this: one has not only the ability to perceive the world but an ability to alter the perception of it; or more simply, one can change things by the manner in which one looks at things.
—Tom Robbins, *Another Roadside Attraction*

BACKBONE

Word Form: backboned

Definitions: (1) firm and resolute character; courage; determination; firm; stability of purpose; (2) the foundation; the most substantial or sturdiest part

BALANCED

Word Forms: balance, balancing, balancer, balanceable, well-balanced

Definitions: (1) mental and emotional steadiness; (2) weighing opposing issues; deliberating or pondering ideas; (3) in a state or position of equilibrium or equal relationship; equipoise; (4) in harmony or proportion; (5) possessing bodily poise
　　See also: *Symmetrical*

Synonyms: adjusted, counterpoised, equalized

Admonition: If you are more introverted than extroverted, you may not find it easy to present yourself to the outside world. Conversely, the people who are extroverted can sometimes get lost in others and have a hard time knowing themselves. Strive for a balance: Introverted? Share your inner world. Extroverted? Meditate.

Comments:
- Balance doesn't necessarily mean attaining an opposite quality. It does mean integrated. The opposite of freedom is slavery, but the balance to freedom includes both self-respect and respect for others.
- If your life is completely peaceful, you certainly should appreciate it while you can. Yet, if life gets too sedate, you should choose to challenge yourself. Get out into the world. How can you help somebody? This will give you some tension, a little stress and strain. You need to have a little something to push against in your life.

　　Conversely, if you've got too much tension and pressure, you have to reduce it. You can be too overwhelmed to properly grow in a manner that's appropriate to your nature and character.

Exercises:

- Learn to ride a unicycle. It's good for a change in your concept of what you can do. In order to feel a positive equilibrium you must stay in motion. Also try roller-skating, ice-skating, skiing, skateboarding, and bongo-boarding. Physical manifestations of balance can translate to emotional and spiritual revelations.
- Learn T'ai Ch'uan. It is a martial art, but most people use it as a form of exercise that balances the energies.

Symbols: the *scales of justice; two;* the *wheel of fortune* (tarot); *Libra* (zodiac)

YIN	YANG
Feminine	Masculine
Passive	Active
Receptive	Giving
Dark	Light
Withdrawing	Advancing
Inhale	Exhale
Heart	Head

BEAUTY

Word Forms: beauteous, beautiful, beautify, beauties, beautied

Definitions: (1) the quality or combination of qualities in a person or thing that gives pleasure to the senses, exalts the mind, or elevates the spirit by their harmony, pattern, excellence, or truth; loveliness; (2) a particularly graceful, ornamental, or excellent quality; (3) a special grace or charm; (4) generally pleasing; very fine

Synonyms: grace, fair, seemly, picturesque, exquisite, adornment, embellishment

Saying: *Beaux yeux* (French): "beautiful eyes" [beauty of face]

Quotes:

It is not only fine feathers that make fine birds.

—AESOP

Though we travel the world over to find the beautiful, we must carry it with us or we find it not.

—RALPH WALDO EMERSON

To gild refined gold, to paint the lily,
To throw a perfume on the violet,
To smooth the ice, or add another hue
Unto the rainbow, or with taper light
To seek the beauteous eye of heaven to garnish,
Is wasteful and ridiculous excess.

—WILLIAM SHAKESPEARE, *King John*

The world in which we live needs beauty if it is not to fall into despair. Beauty, like truth . . . is a precious fruit which withstands the ravages of time, which unites generations and which prompts them to communicate.

—SECOND VATICAN COUNCIL, MESSAGE TO ARTISTS

Beauty is built into every jot and tittle of creation—into every atomic brick! Beauty soaks reality like water fills a rag.

—CHET RAYMO

Comments:

- Is it necessary to behold or to experience ugliness in order to appreciate beauty? I think not. Do you think of the beautiful when you're watching a movie about the holocaust or something horrific? Do you think about the grotesque when you're standing in awe over the Grand Canyon or looking with pleasure into the face of a beautiful person? Beauty stands in awe of itself. It is complete unto itself.

  The desire to create beauty can be inspired by the very fact of its presence, as a response to its opposite, or by its absence.
- Even if the physics of optics could explain a rainbow to the mind, the beauty of the experience must also be appreciated and is even more important to the spirit.
- Nature is the ultimate example of beauty on the material level. With nature, beauty is delicate and powerful and easy to identify. The human being is the ultimate example of beauty on the personal level.

Our first experience of another is their physical manifestation, but that skin-deep attractiveness must soon be backed up with the qualities of real beauty or the outer beauty soon becomes a sham. And if a person's outer manifestation is not so handsome or pretty, then one must be open to experiencing their inner qualities.

Experience: My experience of visiting the Grand Canyon combines varying aspects of beauty: the life-giving element of water, the juxtaposition of rock, the play of light, the human appreciation of it all, and the overcoming of the obstacles necessary to experience it. It is truly a divine gift.

Colors: yellow, or white (within which all color is contained)

Symbols: the *flower;* the *eagle*

Legend: *Helen of Troy*, the daughter of Jupiter, was a beauty who could launch a thousand ships.

Mythologies: *Frigga*, wife of Odin, is the supreme Scandinavian goddess. *Venus* is the Roman goddess of love and beauty, who was also the goddess of spring and blossom. *Blouwedd*, the Scottish goddess of youth, spring, and beauty, was a maiden who was formed of flowers and miraculously came to life.

BEHAVED

Word Forms: behave, behaving, behavior

Definitions: (1) conducts oneself well or properly; does the right things; (2) obedient; follows the rules

Comment: Respect for the rules means that you know what the rules are and that you are willing to play the game. Once you get a feel for the game, then you may decide to play by your own rules. This then adds to the scope of the game for the next generation.

BELIEVABLE

Word Forms: belief, believe, believability, believably

Definition: certainty in the existence, reliability, truth, or value of something

Suggestion: The beliefs that are particularly touchy are the ones that are considered historical or theological "facts": The earth is flat; the earth is the center of the universe; the earth was created in its full and current state five thousand years ago; Christ was born of a virgin; or the Bible (or the Koran) is the only word of God.

There is room for truth to be different from "facts." If you find that you are relying on your perception of the facts and there is a conflict, it is wise to move up a level or two into meanings and values. What is the overlaying truth?

Comment: Belief is nothing more than a theory. In science you postulate a hypothesis and then proceed to present a proof. If the proof can be carried out by another with the same results again and again, then your hypothesis is declared to be true. We cannot see what is going on outside our own life cycle except by looking at the history of our ancestors. In order to "prove" a belief we have to move out of the scientific and into the metaphysical and philosophical realms. We always use basic facts as the groundwork for proving a theory. Much of what is considered to be true is based on the agreement that one's basic assumptions are correct—then the steps taken to get to a specific conclusion are also correct, logical, or at least feel like they should be.

The most compelling validation to believe something is because you have personal experience of it.

BENEFICENT

Word Forms: benefic, beneficence, beneficently

Definitions: (1) characterizes one who does or produces good, especially performing acts of kindness and charity; (2) describes thoughts, words, or deeds resulting in good

BENEFICIAL

Word Forms: benefit, beneficially, beneficialness

Definitions: (1) advantageous; conferring positive results; useful; profitable; helpful; contributing to a valuable end; (2) receiving or entitled to receive blessings

Synonyms: beneficent, salutary, wholesome, salubrious, good, benevolent

BENEVOLENT

Word Forms: benevolence, benevolently, benevolentness

Definitions: (1) characterized by or expressing kindly feelings; (2) desiring to help others; charitable

Synonyms: benign, tender, beneficent, bounteous, generous, humanitarian, goodwilled, kindhearted, kindly, munificent, philanthropic

BENIGN

Word Forms: benignant, benignity, benignly

Definitions: (1) having a gentle or mild disposition; gracious; agreeable; (2) generous; liberal; kind; (3) favorable; beneficial

BLESSED

Word Forms: bless, blest, blessing, blesses, blesser, blessedly, blessedness

Definitions: (1) held in reverence; (2) bringing comfort, joy, pleasure, or contentment; (3) enjoying great happiness; blissful

Synonyms: felicitated, endowed, enriched, gladdened, cheerful, thankful

Kindred Qualities: humble, responsible

If you are blessed with the opportunity to serve because of your talents or the situation, seize the moment and choose to take up the responsibility. As you look back on it or forward to it, you may be humbled by the fact that you were chosen to do what was needed to be done.

Quote:
You are blessed as long as you view what happens as a blessing.
—JERRY DOWNS AND JOE BURELL

Affirmation: I am blessed on every level with happiness, success, and true achievement. I will accept what abundance comes my way with gracious thankfulness.

Mythology: In Greek mythology, *Pandora* is the first moral woman. Although traditionally Pandora's box contained all manner of ill, there is also an account that has the box holding blessings, all of which escaped, leaving only Hope.

BLISSFUL

Word Forms: bliss, blissfully, blissfulness

Definitions: (1) experiencing complete happiness, gladness, or joy; (2) cause of delight or elation

Synonyms: blessed, ecstatic, rapturous

Quote:
If one has the guts, you might say, to follow the risk, life opens, opens, opens up all around the line.

I feel if one follows his bliss, the thing which really gets you deep in the gut, and that you feel is your life, doors will open up—they *do*! If you are on your way, even if no one has done it before, it will open up.

If you follow your bliss, you will have your bliss, whether you have money or not. If you follow money, you may lose that money, and then you won't even have that. The secure way is really the insecure way.

The way in which the "richness" of the quest builds up, builds up, and continues to build up—it's terrific.

—JOSEPH CAMPBELL, *Interview with Bill Moyers*

Comment: Part of being in your bliss is being in balance. When you enhance a quality, it floods into the space where the negative qualities lurked. Bliss and fear cannot live in the same place.

BLOOMING

Word Forms: bloom, bloomed, bloomer, bloomy, bloomingly, bloomingness

Definitions: (**1**) a state or time of most beauty, freshness, or health; (**2**) rosy appearance of the cheeks; outward evidence of vitality or healthy vigor; (**3**) shining out; glowing; (**4**) growing, enriching one's life

Synonyms: flourishing, fair, flowering, blossoming, youthful, beautiful

Comment: We tend to focus in and narrow down our sense of reality, but if we see our situation as part of something larger, we can bloom out of our own mindset. Consider the tree growing on the edge of existence. I particularly love those at tree line. The fact that they are surviving in a harsh environment creates their magnificence. Your life is just like that tree. After all, you are living through difficulty and continuing to grow.

Symbol: a *flower* in bloom

BOLD

Word Forms: boldly, boldness, embolden

Definitions: (**1**) brave; intrepid; confident; (**2**) showing or requiring a fearless, daring spirit; planned with courage and zest; **(3)** unconventional; showing great liberty of style or expression; very free in behavior or manner

Synonyms: dauntless, valiant, audacious, stouthearted, high-spirited, adventurous, forward

Symbol: *youth*

BONHOMIE

Word Form: bonhomous

Definition: pleasing manner; cheerful disposition; good-natured, easy friendliness; geniality

Derivation: French, "good man"

BOUNTIFUL

Word Forms: bounty, bounteous, bounties, bountied, bountifully, bountifulness

Definitions: **(1)** abundant; plentiful; **(2)** generous in bestowing gifts or favors; munificent

BRAVE

Word Forms: braver, bravest, braved, braving, bravery, bravely, braveness, bravora

Definitions: **(1)** having or showing courage; dauntless, intrepid; **(2)** to meet or endure with courage or fortitude; **(3)** to challenge; to dare; to defy

Derivations: Latin, "barbarous"; Old Spanish, "courageous," "wild"; Danish, "brave," "worthy"

Synonyms: bold, gallant, hearty, heroic, valorous, great-hearted
    Brave, courageous, valiant, and *fearless* refer to facing danger or difficulties with moral strength and endurance. *Brave* is a general term that suggests fortitude, daring, and resolve. *Courageous* implies a higher or nobler kind of bravery, especially as resulting from an inborn quality of mind or spirit. *Valiant* implies an inner strength manifested by brave deeds. *Fearless* implies unflinching spirit and coolness in the face of danger.

Kindred Qualities: safe, practical
    Caution needs to be modified with courage and adventure, but bravery needs to be modified with the discretion of safety, practicality, and reality.

Saying: *Fortes fortuna juvat* (Latin): "Fortune favors the brave."

Quotes:
    To be brave, one must be cheerful.
                  —L. Frank Baum, *The Patchwork Girl of Oz*

    [Colonel Plum:] "There are many kinds of bravery and one cannot be expected to possess them all. I myself am brave as a lion in all ways until it comes to fighting, but then my nature revolts."
                  —L. Frank Baum, *Tik-Tok of Oz*

Fiction: Henry Fleming, the soldier in Steven Crane's *Red Badge of Courage*, is ashamed of his natural impulse to flee the horrors of war but, nonetheless, distinguishes himself as brave.

Legend: *Sir Lancelot*, the bravest of King Arthur's knights

BREATHTAKING

Word Form: breathtakingly

Definition: thrillingly or astonishingly beautiful; remarkable; exciting

BRIGHT

Word Forms: brightly, brighten, brightsome

Definitions: (1) radiant with happiness or good fortune; **(2)** cheerful and gay; lively; pleasant; **(3)** giving promise of prosperity or happiness; favorable; auspicious <a *bright* outlook>; **(4)** resplendent with charms; having a sparkling personality; animated; **(5)** an active mind; discerning; clever; intelligent; keen-witted; quick-witted; **(6)** shining in attitude, demeanor, or spirit

Derivation: Sanskrit, "to shine"

Synonyms: clear, luminous, gleaming, radiant, brilliant, witty, sunny, limpid, pellucid, resplendent, lustrous, glittering

Color: yellow

Mythology: *Aglaia* is one of the three Graces of Greek mythology, the Grace of Brilliance.
    See also: *Joyful* and *Comical*

BRILLIANT

Word Forms: brilliance, brilliantly

Definitions: (1) splendid; remarkable; illustrious; outstanding; **(2)** distinguished by unusual mental keenness or alertness; very able; talented

BROAD-MINDED

Word Forms: broad-mindedly, broad-mindedness

Definition: tolerant of various views; liberal; inclined to condone minor departures from conventional behavior

Comment: A conservative politician of this era would like to be considered broad-minded but not liberal.

BROTHERLY

Word Forms: brother, brotherhood, brethren, brotherliness

Definition: affectionate; kind; loyal; like or befitting a brother; fraternal; a good relationship with or among men

Familial Quality: sisterly

Comment: I am aware of the problem with the language, i.e., "We are all sons of God the Father." Certainly we realize that God is not a male or female entity. "The brotherhood of man" denotes all people but does not sound like it. It needs to be said that the Goddess is God and all "gods" are one.

BUBBLY

Word Forms: bubble, bubblier, bubbliest

Definition: lively; effervescent; enthusiastic; expressing joy, delight, or exultation in an irrepressible manner

BUOYANT

Word Forms: buoy, buoyance, buoyancy, buoyantly

Definitions: (1) cheerful, gay, or lighthearted; (2) encouraging or invigorating

Synonyms: sprightly, spirited, vivacious, lively, hopeful, joyous

Symbol: a *boat*

CAGEY

Word Forms: cagier, cagiest, cagily, caginess

Definition: cautious; wary; shrewd; sly; tricky; cunning

CALM

Word Forms: calmer, calmest, calmative, calmly, calmness

Definitions: (1) still; quiet; at rest; **(2)** tranquil; serene; peaceful, placid

Sayings:
  Aequam servare mentem (Latin): "Preserve a calm mind."
  Aequo animo (Latin): "with even mind" [calmly]

CANDID

Word Forms: candidly, candidness

Definitions: (1) open; frank; honest; **(2)** free from bias; disposed to think without prejudice; impartial

Derivation: from the Latin *Candidus*, meaning "white," "pure," "sincere"

CANNY

Word Forms: cannier, canniest, cannily, canniness

Definitions: (1) cautious; prudent; knowing; wary; watchful; careful; **(2)** skilled; expert; **(3)** gentle; quiet in disposition; tractable; **(4)** easy;

comfortable; **(5)** possessed of supernatural power; skilled in magic; **(6)** thrifty; **(7)** shrewd

CAPABLE

Word Forms: capability, capably, capableness

Definitions: (1) possessing physical or mental attributes required for performance or accomplishment; **(2)** possessing mental powers; intelligent; able to understand or to receive into the mind; having a capacious mind

Synonyms: adequate, competent, qualified, suitable, efficient, clever, gifted, skillful

Tip: Assess your capabilities. Start with your physical, natural endowments. Exercise and expand those to work in your favor. You have emotional, mental, and spiritual strengths as well; some are natural talents and others have been developed by the circumstances that you have lived.

CAPITAL

Word Form: capitally

Definitions: (1) the most important; chief; principal; notable; **(2)** very good; excellent; first-class

CAPTIVATING

Word Forms: captive, captivate, captivation, captivator, captivatingly

Definition: one who attracts intensely and fixedly, as by beauty or some positive quality; fascinating; enthralling; charming

Synonyms: entrancing, enchanting, bewitching

CAREFREE

Definition: free from care, worry, anxiety, or troubles
  See also: *No Worries*

Color: orange

Symbol: a *bird* (American Indian)

CAREFUL

Word Forms: care, carefuller, carefullest, carefully, carefulness

Definitions: (1) to deal with thoughtfully or with cautious concern; (2) accurately or thoroughly done or made; painstaking; (3) solicitously mindful

Synonyms: attentive, heedful, prudent, wary, watchful

CARING

Word Forms: care, cared

Definitions: (1) concerned; having thought or regard for; (2) to feel love or liking for; (3) to take charge of; to look after; to provide for

Parental Qualities: giving, kind

CASUAL

Word Forms: casually, casualness

Definitions: (1) informal, natural; (2) nonchalant

Too Far: capricious

CAUTIOUS

Word Forms: caution, cautionary, cautiously, cautiousness

Definition: using great care or prudence; wary; watchful

Synonyms: circumspect, judicious

Too Far: "Curiosity killed the cat." Curiosity not balanced by caution can be dangerous. Conversely, caution, concern for safety and security, can also be taken too far. Mediocrity and the stifling of creativity can be the sacrifice demanded in the name of security.

Visualization: Picture a wasp landing on a thistle. Talk about the epitome of caution, and yet the wasp does it with such ease.

Comments:
- Doubt is sometimes part of fear and sometimes part of caution. Take a look at the extremes and move in toward the middle from there. Regarding fear, doubt closes the mind. With caution, doubt peeks around the corner with an open mind.
- How far are you willing to go or allow other people to go into the qualities of adventuresomeness, fearlessness, or bravery? If you are responsible as a parent or as a guardian, you could be restricting growth by saying, "This is the edge that I, your guide, will not let you cross." Or you can extend your responsibility and decide to also be protective. If you are willing to push the boundaries as far as the other wants to go, then you are deciding to protect him or her from physical danger. Maybe they want to push the boundary into a possibly unsafe situation, but isn't that the nature of courage? They may or may not be able to handle what transpires when they get out there, but if they've got a friend who is willing to go with them, then the margin of error is somewhat reduced. Ultimately, the person taking the action is making the choice and taking the risk. The person supporting them and helping them is an important element in allowing them to become the person they wish to become.

  I have been alone in the Grand Canyon, miles and days from any help. When one is alone, the margin for error is reduced almost to zero. It is a palpable sensation. This can lead to fear or caution. The experience is sweeter if you are cautious in the boldest sense of the word.

CELEBRATED

Word Forms: celebrate, celebrity, celebratedness

Definition: widely known and often referred to; much publicized; renowned
See also: *Distinguished*

CELERITOUS

Word Form: celerity

Definition: rapidity of motion or action; swiftness; speed; refers to human movement or operation and emphasizes dispatch or economy in an activity or work

Synonyms: quickness, fleetness, velocity

Motto:
Certainty, Security and Celerity

—U.S. POST OFFICE

CENTERED

Word Forms: center, centering

Definitions: (1) composed and poised; in control of the mind and emotions; (2) to place or fix at or around a center; focus; (3) to gather to a center; concentrate; (4) to hold a moderate position

Symbols: the *tree* as the world axis; *one*

CEREBRAL

Word Forms: cerebrate, cerebrum, cerebrally

Definition: appealing to or conceived by the intellect rather than the emotions; intellectual

Compatible Qualities: humorous, musical, playful

In 1926 Graham Wallas, a politician and social scientist, described the four stages of creative thought: preparation, incubation, illumination, and verification. The incubation stage is often aided by walking away from the problem and doing something entirely different, particularly an activity that is a fun diversion. It is said that many mathematicians are jugglers.

CERTAIN

Word Forms: certainty, certainly

Definitions: (1) sure; true; undoubted; unquestionable; something that cannot be denied; existing in fact and truth; (2) absolutely confident; convinced; assured; (3) unfailing; reliable; dependable; (4) controlled; unerring

Synonyms: indisputable, indubitable, incontrovertible

Kindred Quality: open-minded

It is said of Hitler that he had more than one thousand books in his private library but he hadn't read even one of them because his mind was already made up. He was certain, confident, and absolutely sure that what he was doing was exactly what he was going to do. If he had possessed open-mindedness, he would have been more reasonable and unable to focus his confidence to such a destructive extent.

Comment: Heisenburg's principle of uncertainty says that no event, not even atomic events, can be described with certainty, that is, with zero tolerance. If they were exactly the same there would be no possibility for recognition. Our perception has to experience a range in order to recognize what is happening.

CHANGEABLE

Word Forms: change, changed, changing, changeability, changeful, changeably, changeableness

Definition: subject to variation or alteration in form, state, quality, or essence; passing from one state or form to another; transformative

Synonyms: modification, mutation, transmutation, transition, novelty, innovation, revolution, labile; see also: *Stress Hardy*

Kindred Qualities: playful, restful, worshipful

Sayings:

Omnia mutantur, nos et mutamur in illis (Latin): "All things are changing and we are changing with them."

Plus ça change, plus c'est le meme chose (French): "The more that changes, the more it is the same thing."

Quotes:

A tiny change today brings us a dramatically different tomorrow. There are grand rewards for those who pick the high roads.
—RICHARD BACH, *One*

The biggest reason for resisting change is the anticipation that the personal costs of the potential change will be greater than the benefits.
—J. RANDOLPH NEW AND DANIEL D. SINGER,
Industrial Engineering Magazine

When individuals resist change due to threatened self-interest, there is a tendency to camouflage the real reasons for resistance with "other reasons" the change should not be made.
—J. RANDOLPH NEW AND DANIEL D. SINGER,
Industrial Engineering Magazine

What I see without is a reflection of what I have first seen within my own mind. I always project into the world the thoughts, feelings and attitudes which preoccupy me. I can see the world differently by changing my mind about what I want to see.
—GERALD JAMPOLSKY

Change creates movement; movement creates change.
—JERRY DOWNS

He who cannot change the very fabric of his thoughts will never be able to change reality.
—ANWAR SADAT

You cannot change anyone except yourself. After you have become an example, you can inspire others to change themselves.
—PEACE PILGRIM, *Steps Toward Inner Peace*

Affirmation: I choose to change. (All of the from's and to's are inherent in the choice. You can get detailed about them after that first choice.)

Consideration: Make it harder and it will be easier to give up. Make it easier and it won't be necessary to give up. Put a lot of energy into something, and you will want to follow through.

Advice:
- It is hard to make a difficult change. It is easier if you are, or feel as if you are, forced to change by an outside agent. It is also easier if you believe that the change is a *must*. In either case the actual move takes courage and faith. There are degrees, as with all things. That is why it is a good idea to consciously decide to accept difficulty that is relatively small. Some things are physically, emotionally, mentally, and spiritually on the edge of your ability. When you have to deal with something hard, do so with a friend.
- Change is easier if you are moving toward the positive. It is more difficult when you are moving away from the negative. And, anyway, the only way to move away from the negative is to create a positive intention to do so.

Comments:
- What you think and do moment by moment are what create and change the structure of your being.
- People would be better off if they knew how to change their minds. We get stuck in the way we hold the universe. True, there needs to be an order to our existence, but there must also be the ability to let go of the established "reality" to make way for a new and better way.

Therein lies the answer. We *cannot* give up the established reality without some very good reason. Therefore, look for the good reason.

- When you decide, you are in control. When you believe or allow someone outside yourself to be in control, they are establishing the boundaries of your being.

- One important element of change is motivation. You have to be interested or threatened to act. (See *Motivated.*)

- Desire to do what you have to do. Do it well and patiently and recognize that it will get done. Don't hold any stress or antagonism in your mind as you do it. While mowing the lawn, instead of ignoring that weed, dig it out. Instead of not clipping around that tree, do so with care and enjoy it too.

- You can recreate yourself. There is a way to exchange and modify your attitude toward things that have already happened. You can do so by changing your inner self, by enhancing your knowledge, by adding to your information, by adjusting your patterns and habits, and by seeing the past in the light of your new experiences. Change the past by changing who you are. Let's say that you were in a car wreck and broke your foot—"bad" experience. You did experience pain. You may have assigned blame. You do wish that you had done something differently. But now you can change your attitude. Even though the facts of the experience stay the same, who you are in relation to that experience has changed. You now have qualities that you did not have then. The meaning of the experience becomes fuller and therefore the value of the experience is modified to become something that is other than the negative experience it once was.

  Consider this as the completion of the experience. Until you have come to peace with your past experiences and the choices that created those experiences, you will feel incomplete.

- You have choice. You are the result of your choices. The events that happen internally and the events that happen externally are responsive to your choices.

  We normally react to the world in predictable ways. This consistency is because of our unique combination of experiences and choices and because of the characteristics of our inner selves. We can free ourselves from the bounds of our patterns by expanding the repertoire of possible responses. Before you react, glance at your range of possible responses. Becoming is not only relative to who you are but also to who you have changed to. Do you have new atti-

tudes? Have you added to your qualities? You can respond differently because you are different.

Essay:

There are various factors involved in the phenomenon of change. First,
we realize a movement away from stability. We arrived at our current
fixed point of view from our finite experience and will move to a new one
from our expanded experience. The new information (catalyst for the
change) is plugged into the existing system and a new stability is eventually established.

I see a three-sphere model, each sphere within a larger one, that is
descriptive of each person's actuals and potentials.

The inner sphere represents that which a person *is* due to their experiences and decisions. This is the now. This is constantly expanding and
changing as it interacts with the second sphere. These two spheres are
where a person lives—the self.

The second sphere includes the internal and external stimuli and pressures that a person can cope with. These can, with relative ease, be
brought into the solidity of the first sphere.

In the third sphere are the hazy outreachings of the mind and unexpected and traumatic experiences. Sometimes a person feels this area to
some degree. Elements of it are continually coming into the second
sphere. This is the superconscious level of mobilization.

Something that happens in the first sphere as a result of something
coming in from the outer reaches of the third sphere could kill you or send
you to an institution. Some examples would be a traumatic physical accident, a devastating emotional experience, or a drug overdose.

The inner-most sphere is solid and is the core of who you are. The second is liquid and is your short-term potential. The third is gaseous and is
your long-term potential and expectations.

There are seven stages to change. The cycle of change begins with a catalyst—an event that touches you and has to be dealt with to maintain the
equilibrium of the system. The event can be something simple or difficult,
positive or negative. It can originate in the first, second, or third sphere.

The second step in the process is that you *feel* the event. This is a seemingly obvious thing, but nonetheless no growth will be forthcoming if it
has no internal impact. Reactions are relative to who a person is at the
time of the occurrence. The same event will have a different impact on
each individual or on the same individual at a different time.

Next, the actual work of the change is begun with a clear visualization of or feeling for what has happened. Of course, some changes are so easy for a person to deal with that the process may happen almost instantaneously. But in more difficult situations the stabilization process could take years.

The fourth step in the growth process is the breakdown into perspective. There is a gradual acceptance of the totality of the experience. One considers a series of options. What can be done about it? How do I fit these facts into my current system? Do I need a new system?

At the fifth step you should ask yourself, How do I create that new system? How do I integrate it into my old system without completely destroying the old system? Here is the rub. Some mighty strange juxtapositions find their way into our personal realities here.

The sixth is the settling of the experience—the recognition of a new individual—the balancing of a new first sphere.

The seventh phase is the mobilization of the new being. You really haven't got it unless you live it. This is also the most important place to take time out, to rest and recuperate.

This is the process of change, but change is not necessarily equal to growth. You do not want to just exchange one type of system for a different one. The alternate one could even be worse. You want to build the new person on the changeless realities of the universe. Growth is the integration of meanings and values. The greater you are able to adapt your internal environment to your external environment and experience, the greater the meaning inherent in the change.

If you refuse to accept the higher values and deeper meanings, the lower conflicts will persist.

Life is usually lived in a series of small steps and achievements. If you go outside what you can do, you will need to develop the ability and comfort to live with the new self that you are creating. Since the ideal is to always have a new self emerging from the old, it is essential to have a fluid sense of self that is above change and yet familiar with and adapting to change all the time.

Exercises:
(adapted from Denis Waitly, Nightingale-Conant Audio Tapes)

Change

1. By looking at your attitudes
2. By practicing consciously developed habits

3. By developing your personal skills
4. By clear vision
5. By strong commitment

Managing Change

1. View change as normal. Monitor your capability of adaptability.
2. Do your best to do your best. Be constructive. Rebound from disappointment and failure.
3. If the effort to change the little things far exceeds its worth, learn to live with it now and come back to it later. Keep your mind free to concentrate on bigger things.
4. Investigate ways to do things more effectively. Be inventive.

Symbols: *death; eleven;* transition from one stage to another—the *bridge;* hoping to change an expected outcome—*crossing of the fingers*

CHARACTER

Word Forms: a character, characteristic, characterize, characterful, characteristically, characterization

Definitions: (1) a distinctive trait, quality, or attribute; (2) an essential quality; nature; kind or sort; (3) an individual's pattern of behavior or personality; moral constitution; (4) moral strength; self-discipline, fortitude, or integrity; (5) a person conspicuously different from others

Synonyms: type, disposition, temperament, cast, repute

Quotes:
Character comes from following our highest sense of right, from trusting ideals without being sure they'll work.
—RICHARD BACH, *One*

Character is grace under pressure.
—ERNEST HEMINGWAY

The measure of the spiritual capacity of the evolving soul is your faith in truth and your love for others, but the measure of your human strength of character is your ability to resist the holding of grudges and your capacity to withstand brooding in the face of deep sorrow. Defeat is the true mirror in which you may honestly view your real self.

—*The Urantia Book*

CHARISMATIC

Word Form: charisma

Definitions: (1) an extraordinary power for leadership and the ability to inspire veneration; **(2)** a personal magnetism that enables an individual to attract or influence people

Quote:
If you listen you will double your charisma.

—DAVID NIVEN

CHARITABLE

Word Forms: charity, charitably, charitableness

Definitions: (1) love; benevolence; affection; good will; that disposition of heart that inclines people to think favorably of their fellows and to do them good; **(2)** liberal in judgment of others

Synonyms: generous, forgiving, benign, indulgent, lenient

Color: red

Symbol: the *girding of the loins*

CHARMING

Word Forms: charm, charmed, charmingly

Definitions: (1) extremely pleasing or delightful; entrancing; (2) to please, soothe, or delight by compelling attraction; (3) the power to gain affections; pleasingly irresistible; that which delights and attracts the heart; a fascinating or alluring quality; enchanting; (4) to subdue, especially by that which entertains and fascinates the mind; to allay or appease

Kindred Qualities: sincere, genuine, honest, integrity

Compatible Qualities: kind, helpful, complementary
One who is charming knows how to take, as well as to give, a compliment.

Familial Qualities: relaxed, poised

Consequential Qualities: attractive, friendly, intriguing

Quotes:
If you have it [charm], you don't need anything else. And if you don't have it, it doesn't matter what else you have!
—SIR JAMES BARRIE

Charm—The ability to make someone think you are *both* pretty wonderful!
—UNKNOWN

CHASTE

Word Forms: chaster, chastest, chastity, chastely, chasteness

Definitions: (1) virtuous, incorrupt; (2) free from obscenity; pure in thought and act; innocent; (3) clean; spotless, immaculate

Synonyms: modest, simple, unaffected, uncontaminated, undefiled

Symbols: the *swan;* the *unicorn*

Fiction: *Britomart*, a "Lady Knight" in Spenser's *Faërie Queen*, personified chastity and carried an irresistible magic spear. (See also: *Virginal*).

Legend: *Sir Galahad*, one of King Arthur's knights, the son of Sir Lancelot, is celebrated for his chastity. He was able to find the Holy Grail because of his great nobility and purity.

Mythology: *Bona Dea* is the Roman deity of fertility and chastity who was worshiped only by women.

CHEERFUL

Word Forms: cheer, cheery, cheerily, cheeriness, cheeringly, cheerfully, cheerfulness

Definitions: (1) animated; full of good spirits; full of life; gay; joyful; **(2)** filling with merriment; bright and attractive; **(3)** willing; hearty; **(4)** likely to dispel gloom or worry

Synonyms: lively, happy, bonny, pleasant, buoyant, sunny, sprightly, blithe, glad

Music: "Whistle While You Work"

Proverb:
A cheerful heart causes good healing.
—PROVERBS 17:22

Quotes:
The best way to cheer yourself is to try to cheer somebody else up.
—MARK TWAIN, *Mark Twain's Notebook*

Let us be of good cheer, remembering that the misfortunes hardest to bear are those which never come.
—JAMES RUSSELL LOWELL

Comment: When you are doing what you "know" you are supposed to be doing, you can be in a sublime state of cheerfulness even if the outside circumstances point to some other emotion. I believe that Christ on the cross was in a state of divine cheerfulness even in the face of apparent failure and excruciating pain because he was intensely aware that he was doing what was necessary and right.

Color: yellow

CHERISHED

Word Forms: cherish, cherisher, cherishing

Definitions: (1) treat with tenderness and affection; **(2)** take care of, foster, or nurture; **(3)** to hold dear, value highly, or appreciate; **(4)** to indulge and encourage in the mind; to harbor; to cling to <*cherish* the principles of virtue>

Familial Qualities: maternal, paternal

CHIC

Word Forms: chicly, chicness

Definition: stylish and original; effective in style; elegant; clever and fashionable

CHILDLIKE

Word Forms: child, childly, childlikeness, children, childhood

Definition: relating to or resembling a child or childhood; especially marked by innocence, trust, and ingenuousness

Saying: You are as young as you feel. [What age are you feeling?]

CHIPPER

Definitions: (1) in cheerful good humor and health; jaunty; lively; **(2)** smartly dressed

CHIVALROUS

Word Forms: chivalry, chivalric, chivalrously, chivalrousness

Definitions: (1) gracious courtesy and high-minded consideration; **(2)** possessing the qualities of chivalry, as courage, courtesy, honor, generosity, and loyalty; valiant

Comment: Even though this quality normally refers to men, that shouldn't stop women from aspiring to the noble aspects of this quality. The feminine term for chivalrous is "virago." (See *Virile.*)

Legend: *Don Quixote*, the hero of Cervantes's romance, strives to be chivalrous even though his worldview is fanciful.

CHOICE

Word Forms: choicer, choicest, choices, choose, chose, chosen, choicely, choiceness

Definitions: (1) worthy of being preferred; of special excellence; the best part of anything; **(2)** holding dear; recognizing value; **(3)** to make a choice; decide; carefully chosen; the right or privilege of choosing; option; the person or thing chosen; **(4)** to select freely after consideration; the voluntary act of selecting or separating from two or more things

Synonyms: alternative, election, exquisite, elegant, rare, dainty, delicate

Compatible Qualities: decisive, freedom

Quotes:

Life itself must be founded upon the infinite possibility for choice
and accident; and if we cannot prove that it is, we must believe that
it is. We must believe that we can change; that we can control; that
we can direct our own destinies.

—ANNE RICE, *The Witching Hour*

The only way to avoid all frightening choices is to leave society and
become a hermit, and that is a frightening choice.

—RICHARD BACH, *One*

We can have health, love, longevity, understanding, adventure,
money, happiness. We design our lives through the power of our
choices.

—RICHARD BACH, *One*

We are creators! And creators *act*.

—JACQUELYN SMALL, *Transformers*

Creators are artists. And artists create originals! I can constantly
continue to choose, moment by moment, what to put into my world.
If I opt for a negative experience, I *descend*. If I opt for a positive
experience, I *ascend* . . . and instantly, forces begin moving to manifest a positive result.

—JACQUELYN SMALL, *Transformers*

The higher choice will always be a positive one!

—JACQUELYN SMALL, *Transformers*

Pick a behavior that works.

—JERRY DOWNS

Ontogeny recapitulates phylogeny.

—LARRY NIVEN AND JERRY POURNELLE, *The Mote in God's Eye*

Note: The development of the individual repeats the stages of development of the genetic history of the organism. But because of choice it is
also possible to acquire qualities and combinations of qualities that
one's natural or environmental history have not given a person a
predilection to.

When humans "invented" the concept of the infinite, they opened the possibility of all options. They stated in one word the ultimate value of *choice*.

—JERRY DOWNS

Reflections:

- The existence of the knowns leads to the understanding of the unknowns. We know that choice, personality, experience, and all manner of positive qualities do exist. We know by personal experience that living positively is better than living negatively. Positive movement will lead to additional positive action even in the face of evil. And even though the fact of physical death is a compelling argument, it is not unreasonable to assume that we can continue our positive quest beyond the grave. If we do not continue, then there would be no reason for value to exist. A nonpersonal, mechanistic universe would have no need for love and its positive ramifications.

- Habit is analogous to motion. The first choice is like the first movements of a baby on its way to developing the walking muscles. Pulling, stretching, and crawling are the beginning of mobility. As the movement becomes habitual, as choice piles upon choice, you can move into faster modes, and then into different vehicles to be able to move at greater speeds still remaining relatively comfortable.

  Habit and inertia are related. The faster you're going with a commitment, the more momentum it has behind it because of previous decisions. If you make a bunch of decisions that move you toward honesty, and then you make a decision that moves you toward dishonesty, that one instance of dishonest behavior creates drag on the positive force, but it will probably not hold enough energy to reverse the positive momentum. The same is also true if you make many negative behavioral decisions. They build up a momentum in the direction of isolation. If you are consistently choosing the unreal, a positive decision will put the brakes on the negative behavior but won't necessarily reverse it. Albeit, the character of the decision can have a greater decelerating force. Just as a space ship going around the earth at eighteen thousand miles an hour slows down rather quickly when it enters the atmosphere, so too can a positive decision put the brakes on negative momentum if the integrity of the decision generates enough basic honest change. This may mean that in change there can be a lot of friction and pain. Consider the "good thief" on the cross. His sincerity was of such a magnitude that his continuance as a being was guaranteed. Being in heaven did not mean that he was granted a state of perfection, it means he was granted a chance to continue to choose.

- You don't have to personally experience the negative in order to know where it will go. The repercussions of such decisions are learned by observation, logic, and history. Some beings have already gone down that avenue and shown us where the path leads.

On the other hand, even the objective, observable facts of positive choices, and the certainty that they lead toward continued happiness and the joy of a worthwhile existence, may not be enough to move one in that direction. It definitely should be an influential factor, but the real motivation exists in experiencing the positive results of personal choice.

Choice is the nourishment. Choice is the fuel. You can choose to satisfy needs on the physical, emotional, or spiritual levels. A crocodile perceives, in its primitive way, its hunger and "chooses" to eat a fish. It satisfies the need—making the choice on a physical level to continue to exist. If you choose to continue on the spiritual level you must choose the fuel of positive qualities and the action of living them.

- Mistaken choices due to lack of information, lack of clarity, intelligence, social conditions, frustration, environmental conditions, and even mistaken curiosity are included in reality because choice is universal and sacred. It is one of *the* constants. Just as gravity and light are constants on the physical plane, choice is a constant on the personality plane. Even though light is a constant, there are places of darkness. So too with choice. Having the ability to choose sometimes means that an incorrect choice can be made.

Two of the major elements of choice are options and contrast. Contrast implies conflict, adversity, and difficulty. The purpose of these seemingly negative characteristics is to shine light on the positive elements of unity, clarity, harmony, and understanding. This ultimately leads to increased wisdom. Through the experience of choices, positive and negative, one can make further choices with more clarity, power, and reality.

As the individual grows in grace and wisdom through their choice and experience they help the Whole to become complete. As the Whole is evolving to its ideal, it helps the individual to become more perfect. It all works together. Thus things eventually become more ordered and less chaotic.

- Many times choice will be incorrect, but only by choosing and then consecrating that choice with action will you find that out. That is the only time you will actually feel the experience. But since you can relive it in a different way in your mind, you can learn. Then the next time you will live it differently.
- We hold on to our old selves while allowing our new selves to grow around the old. We are like coral, where the old is the structure upon which the new growth and the new life is active. The only you that is alive and vibrant is the new you. The past is the structure upon which we rely for stability. We know ourselves by who we have been, and yet we are not our structure any more than we are our body. The old self is a record of what we have chosen, and because of those choices we make new choices now. Holding on to the previous self is holding on to a dead self.

Observations:
- Choice is not only about future moments; it is about the moment you are in.
- Resistance blocks acceptance of who you are and is a friend of fear. It holds you back from choosing to be the person you dream of being and doing the things that you want to do.
- Whatever the situation—no matter how outlandish—your choices dictate *your* outcome. The situation may or may not be affected by your choice, but what happens to you is up to you.

Admonitions:
- Choice propels action; therefore, be sure that you are heading in the right direction.
- Choice is the key. Choose that which *seems* important, and as you move through life, you *will* change and alter your choosing. The more information and experience you have, the more varied will be your possible new choices.

Comments:

Positive versus Negative Choice

Consider your choice as going toward the good, not just away from the bad. It is not a matter of being good because of fear of the consequences. Preserve life because life is good and intrinsically valuable. Do not refrain from killing because it's a sin or because you will go to jail or to hell. Respect others' property because the other is worthy of respect, not because you may get caught if you take something.

If you are motivated by the negative consequences, you are at least refraining from one negative even though it is because of another negative. The consequences of an action will help clarify a choice. If the choice is to take advantage of somebody else, the possible legal consequences may curtail the behavior. Yet spiritual consequences (positive or negative) are absolutely unavoidable and inevitable.

Freedom

You are choosing to reduce your freedom if you decide to take somebody else's freedom away.

Choice Creates Reality

Since your choice is what makes your emerging reality, and since you are the one doing the choosing, you are the one choosing whether or not you are going to be a "chosen one."

Too Many Choices

Sometimes you don't think you have a choice because you have too many choices. You might be frustrated by the number of options. You feel that you don't have what it takes or that you don't have what you need. You experience this feeling because you are overwhelmed; you have not narrowed the field. The answer is to begin the narrowing process. If you take a look at your range of options and look at them objectively, you can begin to filter your options.

Accept and Reject

- When we choose to accept, we also choose to *ignore*. It would be better if in choosing to accept we were also aware of what we are choosing to reject. Consider the modern combat pilot. He is choosing the force and power and thrill of flying in an airplane that is the culmination of modern technology. He is choosing honor and duty and service to his country. But when he drops his bombs and targets his objectives, is he ignoring or choosing to reject the facts of the destruction caused? Does he realize the loss of property, life, hope, and dreams? Is it someone else's responsibility?

- Choice is inclusive and exclusive. We tend, as a species, to *ex*clude the gentle or "soft" qualities. And we tend to *in*clude the powerful or "hard" qualities. Maybe that is because a great many of the people who have been kind, peaceful, and giving have been killed. I can see that the physical and material success that these hard qualities provide is compelling and that they are necessary for their survival value. But there is a greater possibility for survival above the physical. If a person decides to include a wider range of qualities in their repertoire, they will be choosing to be successful on the emotional, mental, and spiritual levels as well.

Choice Never Stops

You are also choosing if you choose not to choose. You have to keep acknowledging that choice never stops. Choice is always in motion. Choice is absolute. Even the choice to exist or to terminate your existence.

Bad Habits

"Bad" is up to the individual to honestly assess. My wife's grandmother loved to dance but decided to agree with her religion, which taught that it was a "bad" habit, and she gave it up.

Bad habits are "breaking" mechanisms. If you decide that something is bad, you are deciding that it will slow you down. A bad habit will not move you to the light. On the other hand, a one-time bad act can be helpful in that you learn to move in the right direction by knowing, through negative experience, that the direction that the bad action just sent you was wrong. Use your bad action as a guide. Because of it you know where not to go.

Everybody has their own pace. Don't be fooled with the glamour of traveling at light speed. Most, maybe all, drugs—including power—speed you up temporarily and fool you into moving with artificial acceleration. But if you have not come by your speed naturally, there is the inevitable burnout.

Use your bad habit as a slingshot. See in it what you are striving for.

What does it give you that you need? Make that need your goal, your mission, your desire.

God's Will

Is it God's will?

People say that it is God's will if something bad happens. Most of the time they mean that God is personally creating the difficulty or disaster in order to teach a lesson. This is right only in that God set everything up. The individual still has the freedom to choose. The nature of fire is to burn, therefore, if you choose to play with fire expect to get burned. God did not manipulate your choice, He simply provided the fire for you to use. Even though a personal deity cares about you personally, He will not interfere with your choice.

As for the lessons learned, they are part of the divine setup too. As you experience something you get to know the consequences and, therefore, act and react accordingly in the future.

Jesus' Choice

It's really astounding that somebody like Jesus got crucified. This is because choice is absolute. He not only had power, but he also had complete respect for choice. It was amazing that he didn't say or do to those who intended to kill him what was needed so that they wouldn't kill him. He knew what was in their hearts and minds. Yet he also knew that the only way to make them not do what they were going to do would be to block their free will. That is exactly what he decided not to do because that would not have been divine. It would have been a manipulation of their reality and he just couldn't take their free choice away from them even though it would have meant saving his own skin.

No Choice

When do you not have choice? When you are reacting automatically. At the first moment that something happens you don't necessarily have control over your reaction—your preprogrammed responses. But remember that you created your mechanical response by your previous choices.

The choices that you make during the moment modify how you will react next time. You are creating a new default value. Fear grabs you and you face it. The next time that you are presented with fear, your response has been tempered by the fact that you chose to change your nature. You are more in control because you have decided to become the person that is in control.

Questions:
1. Am I choosing?
2. Am I choosing positive qualities for myself and others?
3. Am I choosing a balanced set of positive qualities?
4. Are my choices fair, practical, and wise?

Symbol: *crossroads*

Mythology: *Janus*, the Roman god of beginnings and endings, the guardian of portals, who had two faces, one on each side of his head

CHUMMY

Word Forms: chum, chummier, chummiest, chummily, chumminess

Definition: intimate; companionable; friendly; sociable

CHUTZPAH

Definition: supreme self-confidence; nerve; gall; audacity

Kindred Qualities: It's easy for qualities of strength and confidence to get out of hand if they are not balanced by compassion, kindness, and a willingness to see the other person's point of view.

CIVIL

Word Forms: civility, civilly

Definitions: (1) courteous and polite; mannerly; proper; **(2)** civilized

Synonyms: obliging, well-bred, affable, complaisant

Comments:
- When you choose to be civil you are creating civilization.
- Although being civil oftentimes implies an attitude that is little more than a lack of rudeness, it also implies a willingness to be tolerant. This is the beginning of the acceptance of our unavoidable differences and a practical step away from the negative and toward the positive.

CIVILIZED

Word Forms: civilize, civilizable, civilizing, civilizer, civilization

Definitions: (1) refinement of thought, manners, or taste; **(2)** educated; refined; **(3)** cultured; courteous

Quotes:
The most necessary task of civilization is to teach men how to think.
—THOMAS EDISON

To enjoy privilege without abuse, to have liberty without license, to possess power and steadfastly refuse to use it for self-aggrandizement—these are the marks of high civilization.
—*The Urantia Book*

Human dignity is the keystone of any civilization.
—CLIFFORD D. SIMAK, *City*

How to Live This Quality Today: Give people the benefit of the doubt. Examine their motives and realize that they may be doing things that you don't like, but that they have positive reasons in their minds.

Color: green

Mythology: *Isis*, the Egyptian goddess of the moon and fertility, is the one who brought civilization.

CLAIRVOYANT

Word Forms: clairvoyance, clairvoyantly

Definitions: (1) possessing the paranormal power of seeing objects or actions beyond the range of normal vision, especially the past or future or events that are happening in different locations; **(2)** having quick, intuitive knowledge of things and people; sagacity

Derivation: French, "clear," "to see"

Comment: Television has turned us all into clairvoyants.

Symbol: the *third eye*

CLASSY

Word Forms: class, classier, classiest, classiness

Definition: first-class, especially in style or manner; elegant; fine

CLEAN

Word Forms: cleaner, cleanest, cleanable, cleanse, cleanly, cleanliness, cleanness

Definitions: (1) free from flaws, imperfection, or defect; **(2)** shapely; well-proportioned; clean-limbed; lithe; **(3)** free from awkwardness; not clumsy or bungling; dexterous; adroit; clever; deft; skillful; **(4)** free from limitation or any modifying quality or circumstance; entire; complete; thorough; **(5)** free from moral corruption, guilt, or blame; innocent

Synonyms: clear, spotless, pure, purified, untarnished, sinless

Saying: Cleanliness is next to Godliness.

CLEAN-CUT

Definitions: (1) well-made; well-formed; **(2)** sharply defined; clear; **(3)** pleasing in appearance; trim; neat; wholesome

Compatible Quality: nice

CLEAR

Word Forms: clearing, clear-eyed, clearheaded, clear-minded, clear-seeing, clearly, clearness

Definitions: (1) not confused or dull; having the power of perceiving or comprehending quickly; discriminating <a *clear* intellect>; **(2)** easily seen or comprehended; free from obscurity; easily understandable; perspicuous; distinct; lucid; **(3)** evident; manifest; indisputable; undeniable; **(4)** free from perturbations; undisturbed; unruffled; serene; **(5)** free from guilt or blame; morally unblemished; innocent

Synonyms: bright, vivid, apparent, orderly, acute, obvious, plain, pure

Symbol: a clear *blue sky*

CLEMENT

Word Forms: clemently, clemency

Definition: mild in temper and disposition; forbearing; lenient; merciful; kind; tender; compassionate

CLEVER

Word Forms: cleverly, cleverness

Definitions: (1) mentally quick and resourceful; intelligent; quick-witted; astute; bright; **(2)** skillful or adroit in using the hands or body; nimble; dexterous; talented; **(3)** ingeniously or expertly made, said, or done

Parental Qualities: courage and curiosity

Symbol: the *fox*

CLIMBING

Word Forms: climb, climbable, climber

Definition: gradual or continuous progress; rise; ascend

Quote:
Climbing would be a great, truly wonderful thing if it weren't for all that damn climbing.
—JOHN OHRENSCHALL

COGENT

Word Form: cogently

Definition: compelling; convincing; having a powerful appeal to the mind; forcible; powerful; not easily resisted; pertinent; relevant

COGNIZANT

Word Forms: cognitive, cognizable, cognizance, cognize

Definitions: (1) the fact of being aware; perceptive; knowledgeable; **(2)** notice; heed; **(3)** the range of knowledge possible through observation

Familial Qualities: aware, conscious

COHERENT

Word Forms: cohere, coherence, coherency, coherently, cohesive

Definitions: (1) logically connected; clearly articulated and intelligible; **(2)** having a natural agreement; harmonious

Synonyms: united, related, consistent

COLORFUL

Word Forms: color, colorfully, colorfulness

Definitions: (1) vivid; stimulating; full of variety; picturesque; having striking or spirited elements; **(2)** a unique and charming character; pleasantly recognizable

Familial Quality: character

Symbol: a *rainbow*

COMELY

Word Forms: comelier, comeliest, comeliness

Definitions: (1) handsome; attractive; good-looking; pretty; **(2)** decent; suitable; proper; becoming

Synonyms: graceful, seemly, pleasing

COMFORTABLE

Word Forms: comfort, comforter, comfortably, comfortableness

Definitions: (1) imparting comfort and satisfaction; **(2)** content; at ease in body or mind

Synonyms: snug, pleasant, agreeable, cozy, convenient, consoled

Consequential Quality: creative

COMFORTING

Word Forms: comfort, comfortingly

Definition: encouraging; heartening; consoling; reassuring; bringing solace or cheer to someone

Synonyms: relieving, supportive

Too Far: sluggish

COMICAL

Word Forms: comedy, comic, comicality, comically, comicalness

Definition: causing amusement; humorous; funny; droll

Synonyms: absurd, laughable, ludicrous, preposterous

Compatible Quality: timing

Symbol: the *clown*

Historical Figure: *Aristophanes*, the classic Greek poet and father of comedy

Mythology: *Thalia*, one of the three Graces of Greek mythology, is the Muse of comedy and pastoral poetry. (See also: *Joyful* and *Bright*.)

COMMANDING

Word Forms: command, commandingly

Definition: controlling by influence, authority, or dignity; dominating

Synonyms: authoritative, imperious, imperative, lordly

Kindred Qualities: caring, compassionate

Symbols: *clubs* (the suit in cards); the *scepter*

COMMENDABLE

Word Forms: commend, commendation, commendably, commendableness

Definitions: (1) to express a favorable opinion; to praise; **(2)** to recommend as worthy of confidence or notice

Synonyms: approved, applauded, entrusted, recommended

Music: "You're the Tops," Cole Porter

COMMISERATIVE

Word Forms: commiserate, commiseratively

Definition: feeling or expressing sympathy, compassion, pity, empathy

Symbol: a *nurse*

COMMITTED

Word Forms: commit, committing, committable, commitment, committal

Definition: devoted unreservedly; engaged; pledged; bound

Synonyms: entrusted, consigned, confided, relegated

Quotes:
Until one is committed, there is hesitancy, the chance to draw back, always ineffectiveness, concerning all acts of initiative (and creation). There is one elementary truth, the ignorance of which kills countless ideas and splendid plans: that the moment one definitely commits oneself, then providence moves too. All sorts of things occur to help one that would never otherwise have occurred. A whole stream of events issues from the decision, raising in one's favor all manner of unforeseen incidents and meetings and material assistance which no one could have dreamed would have come their way. Whatever you can do or dream you can, begin it. Boldness has genius, power and magic in it. Begin it now.

—GOETHE

Never doubt that a small group of thoughtful, committed citizens can change the world; indeed it's the only thing that ever has.

—MARGARET MEAD

Comment: You cannot make a commitment for someone else. You might be able to provide inspiration or encouragement or help in preparation or information, but it is ultimately that person's choice, no matter how clear you are on him or her needing or being ready for the commitment.

Mythology: *Juno*, the supreme goddess of Roman mythology, wife of Jupiter, and goddess of marriage

COMMON SENSE

Definition: practical understanding or intelligence; sound judgment

Derivation: originally, the faculty that supposedly united and interpreted impressions of the five senses

Quotes:
Today's common sense is yesterday's science.

—NEILS BOHR

A walking encyclopedia will walk over a cliff, for all its knowledge of cliffs and the effects of gravity, unless it is designed in such a fashion that it can find the right bits of knowledge at the right times, so it can plan its engagements with the real world.

—DANIEL DENNETT

Common sense is instinct. Enough of it is genius.

—GEORGE BERNARD SHAW

COMMUNICATIVE

Word Forms: communicate, communicator, communication, communicable, communicativeness, communiqué

Definitions: (1) conveys knowledge of or information about; makes known; **(2)** able to transmit information, a thought, or a feeling so that it is satisfactorily received or understood
See also: *Giving*

Synonyms: revealing, disclosing, divulging, imparting, announcing, publishing, promulgating, corresponding, talkative, loquacious, articulate

Kindred Quality: order

Quotes:
As far as we can tell, human language results from a certain type of mental organization, not simply from a high level of intelligence.

—NOAM CHOMSKI

Man by means of words can communicate abstract ideas; he can benefit from experiences of others without having to be present at the time; he can make intelligent cooperative plans.

—JANE GOODALL

It is the humble man who risks his dignity to speak up for what he loves. It is the courageous man who dares contradiction and the acrimony of argument to defend his beliefs. If one loves anything—truth, beauty, women, life—one will speak out. Genuine love cannot endure silence. Genuine love breaks out into speech. And when it is great love, it breaks out into song. Talk helps to relieve us of the tiresome burden of ourselves. It helps some of us to find out what we think. It is essential for the happiest companionship. One of the minor pleasures of affection is in the voicing of it. If you love your friend, says the song, tell him so. Talk helps one to get rid of the surplus enthusiasm that often blurs our idea.

—MYLES CONNOLLY

When you live in constant communication with God, you cannot be lonely.

—PEACE PILGRIM, *Steps Toward Inner Peace*

Tip: Do it now! Talk about your conflict before it has a chance to build into something that is eating at you.

Suggestion: If you try explaining something to a friend and he or she rejects what you have to say, your explanation could be unclear or it could be that the notion just doesn't fit into your friend's framework of reality at this time. Try again later when you both have become a bit more skilled and accepting.

Comment: In trying to get a point across to another in a way that he or she will understand, you will be amazed at the insights and examples that you come up with. This happens most when you are speaking from your heart in a caring manner with the other person in mind.

Symbols: the *infinity* symbol is one of giving and receiving, the ultimate communication (see explanation under *Giving*); *water;* the *mouth* (Egyptian); *music*

COMPANIONABLE

Word Forms: companion, companionship, companionate, companionability, companionably, companionableness

Definition: good fellowship; friendly; sociable; agreeable as an associate

Synonym: comradely

Quote:
Yes, information matters; but it's really the *quality of relationships* through which information is exchanged that ultimately determines the success of an organization.
—MICHAEL SCHRAGE, "ORGANIZATIONS DON'T RUN ON INFORMATION," *Lotus*

Note: Mr. Schrage also says that the information age has failed because it has not actively and consciously included the human individual in the communication formula.

Symbol: the *round table* of King Arthur fame

COMPASSIONATE

Word Forms: compassion, compassionated, compassionating, compassionately, compassionateness

Definitions: (1) possessing sympathetic consciousness of others' distress together with a desire to alleviate it; **(2)** a disposition to pity; inclined to show mercy

Synonyms: tender, soft, indulgent, kind, clement, gracious

Quotes:
Every human being has the potential for compassion. I have chosen to pay more attention to it.
—THE DALAI LAMA, upon receiving the Nobel Peace Prize

A human being is a part of the whole called by us "Universe," a part limited in time and space. He [she] experiences the self, thoughts and feelings as something separated from the rest—a kind of optical delusion of (the personal) consciousness. This delusion is a kind of prison for us, restricting us to our personal desires and to affection for a few persons nearest to us. Our task must be to free ourselves from this prison by widening our circle of compassion to embrace all living creatures and the whole of nature in its beauty.

—ALBERT EINSTEIN

I regard it as the foremost task of education to ensure the survival of these qualities: an enterprising curiosity, an undefeatable spirit, tenacity in pursuit, readiness for sensible self-denial, and above all, compassion.

—KURT HAHN, founder of Outward Bound

I know that most . . . can seldom discern even the simplest and most obvious truth if it be such as obliges them to admit the falsity of conclusions they have formed, . . . of which they are proud, which they have taught to others, and on which they have built their lives.

—LEO TOLSTOY

Note: In your struggle to help others "see the light," understand the hold that the past has on them, that what they have experienced and fought for is often fused with their identity. Realize this about yourself, too, and be sensitive to the truth contained in different beliefs.

Mythology: *Androcles* was a Roman slave who while seeking freedom had removed a thorn from a lion's paw. When he was caught, he was doomed to fight a lion that turned out to be the befriended animal. Since the lion fawned on him, he was freed.

COMPATIBLE

Word Forms: compatibility, compatibly, compatibleness

Definitions: (1) living together harmoniously or getting along well together; (2) in agreement; congruous

Derivation: Latin, "to suffer with"

Compatible Qualities: perseverance, agreement, obliging

Comments: This is the quality of relationships.

The main type of relationship that I am referring to in the following is one of mates. There are seven primary components of a complete relationship.

1. Chemistry
2. Comfort
3. Companionability
4. Communication
5. Care
6. Creativity
7. Commitment

1. Chemistry

A. Physical

This is where it all begins. There must be an attraction. The physical senses ask to be satisfied: looks, voice, smell, touch, taste.

Compatible qualities: clean, neat

Familiarity may not be so severe as to breed contempt, but the wonder and luster does wear thin as you get to know the patterns and responses of the other person. Physical attractions lose their spark and intensity even more quickly if the extent and depth of the attraction is only hormonal.

B. Emotional

1. The emotional senses (feelings) are stimulated in symmetry with the physical.

Compatible qualities: energy, passion, sexiness

2. The emotional feeling may last a long time and even rekindle periodically, but emotions usually mellow into more tender characteristics.

Compatible qualities: gentle, snug, comfortable

3. Do not become complacent—taking the other for granted. Let him or her know your feelings.

Compatible qualities: open-hearted, open-minded

C. Spiritual

The feeling that you have found your true mate at the beginning stage is proven reliable only in time. Do not be fooled by the chem-

istry into predictions of forever. Be satisfied with the joy and energy of the moment. If there is a feeling of "all is perfect," remember that people tend to forget how to be perfect.
Compatible qualities: farsighted, playful

2. Comfort

A. Easygoing

The ease you feel with each other is a blessing when it happens in the beginning of a relationship. If it stays true over a longer time, you are truly blessed. But you have to nurture it properly for that to happen. At first the fact that you don't know all of the habits and incompleteness of each other is part of the excitement. When you are infatuated with the good feelings of passion and hope, there is an abundance of tolerance. Enjoy each other with the realization that things will change. Fortunately, people also remember how to be perfect.
Compatible qualities: consistency, sweetness, friendliness, cordiality, relaxation

B. Common ground

This is where the social, racial, age, gender, political, and religious factors come in. How will you raise the children if they are or will be present? Your family and environmental influences can be very weighty. If you realize a difference, it need not be perceived as a negative. Simply make a friendly judgment. Decide if the gap is too wide for who you are. You have an opportunity for growth in the situation. Make a judgment as to what you can expect. Every situation is different.
Compatible qualities: tolerance, nonjudgmental, judicious

C. Security

One must discover the level of security of the other. Can you support that need? Will money be an issue? How important is career? Is your mate more passionate about his or her job than you are about yours? Remember that no one can fulfill all of the needs of another.
Compatible qualities: safety, practicality, self-esteem

3. Companionability

A. The essence of relationships

Once you feel your compatibility, your true companionability is yet to be explored. This and communication are the guts of a relationship. This is your living space, your habits and hopes.

Compatible qualities: mutual interests, humor, diversity

B. Independence

Both people must feel that they have the freedom of independent thinking and action. It is essential to have a mutual respect for the existing and developing talents of the other. Each person must move independently within his or her own sphere of needs and wants even while keeping in mind those of the other. Sacrifices and compromises have to be made. Keep it balanced and fair.

Compatible qualities: sharing, helpfulness, encouragement

4. Communication

A. Conversation

Can you talk about anything? Can you share everything? Are you a good listener? Say it! Ask it! Communication need not be verbal, but your appreciation does need to be expressed.

Compatible qualities: honesty, perceptivity, sincerity, curiosity, genuineness, understanding, intuition

B. Expectations

It is important to explore expectations. Is it the white picket fence or the freedom to roam the world? What about the probability that things will change?

Compatible qualities: adaptable, broad-minded

C. Confrontation

Have you developed a constructive way of arguing, disagreeing, and making up?

Compatible qualities: diplomacy, tactfulness, discreetness, forgiveness

D. Intelligence

1. Do you have a similar intellectual range? Are your levels of schooling similar? How about the history of your experiences?

Compatible qualities: knowledgeable, insightful

2. Do you have a similar intellectual technique? If you process information mentally and the other processes it emotionally, you must realize the difference in the speed of these two methods and allow for that.

Compatible qualities: patience, logic, lucidity, mercifulness, observant

5. Care

A. You gotta have heart

Compatible qualities: heart, gentleness, sensitivity

B. Give and take

Every relationship requires a certain percentage of your energy. It is often said that a relationship is a fifty-fifty proposition. This is not true. When you are first "in love" there is no question that the mutual giving is one hundred percent. What is required in the long run is for each to continually give at the highest percent possible. You can become clear on how to give and how to receive.

Compatible qualities: considerate, courtesy, compromise, flexible, concern, contributive, polite, cooperative, respectful, forgiving, thoughtful

6. Creativity

A. Imagination

Every relationship needs an infusion of creativity.

Compatible qualities: motivation, interest, boldness, decisiveness

B. Goal setting

What are your goals? Can you share them? Do you delight in the delight of the other? Once you know what they like, give it to them.

Compatible qualities: artistry, inspiration, experience

7. Commitment

A. Practical faithfulness

Every relationship has a beginning. The time that it lasts is up to many factors. Any long-range commitment is made up of periodic decisions to continue. If you are deciding out of fear, guilt, obligation, expectation, or laziness, you are not being fair to yourself or to the other person.

Compatible qualities: wise, sensible

B. Growing

Are you giving yourself and the other the time and support to grow?

Compatible qualities: nurturing, foresight, stick-to-itive

C. Separation

When it ends as one relationship, do you have what it takes to allow it to continue as another? This includes the separation of death.

Compatible qualities: clarity, courage, curiosity, sympathy

If you don't have all seven of these elements in your relationship, then you are settling for less than you deserve or are giving more than you should.

Types of Relationships: Mother and son, mother and daughter, father and son, father and daughter, sibling to sibling, man to man, woman to woman, man and woman, employer and employed, public servant and citizen, friends, enemies, person to animal, person to project

COMPELLING

Word Form: compel

Definitions: (1) overpowering; forceful; awesome; **(2)** demanding attention; drawing notice because of interest or beauty; having a powerful and irresistible effect

COMPETENT

Word Forms: competence, competently

Definitions: (1) able or capable; duly qualified; **(2)** answering all requirements; suitable; sufficient; fit for the purpose; adequate

COMPLACENT

Word Forms: complacence, complacency, complacently

Definitions: (1) pleased, especially with oneself, one's advantages, or accomplishments; self-satisfied; unconcerned; **(2)** pleasant; kindly; complaisant

COMPLETE

Word Forms: completed, completing, completable, completer, completive, completion, completely, completeness, completedness

Definitions: (1) having all parts or elements; lacking nothing; whole; entire; full; **(2)** having all the required or customary characteristics or skills; consummate <a *complete* scholar>; **(3)** thorough; total; undivided; uncompromised

How to Live This Quality Today: You are complete right now in the sense that you are the culmination of all of your experiences so far. On the other hand, you will never be complete. Anything that you do will move you to a new state of completeness and toward your eternal goal.

COMPLIANT

Word Forms: compliance, compliantly

Definitions: (1) ready or disposed to comply to a desire, demand, or proposal; **(2)** a disposition to yield to others; flexibility

Synonyms: acquiescent, consentual, obedient, submissive

Comment: Sometimes compliance is the most appropriate quality, as the boughs of a tree in the wind.

COMPOSED

Word Forms: compose, composedly, composedness, self-composed

Definition: calm; tranquil; serene; sedate; quiet; free from agitation

COMPREHENSIVE

Word Forms: comprehend, comprehensible, comprehension, comprehensively, comprehensiveness

Definitions: (1) large in scope; covering much; inclusive; (2) having an extensive mental range or understanding; (3) able to grasp something mentally and to perceive its relationships to certain other facts or ideas

Familial Quality: open

COMPROMISING

Word Forms: compromise, compromised, compromiser, compromisingly

Definitions: (1) adjust and settle (a difference) by mutual agreement, with concessions on both sides; (2) something lying midway between, or combining the qualities of two different things

Comment: The different parties in a dispute often think that they have to give something up in order for a compromise to be effected. Although this is the case in some instances, it need not be the case altogether. *Compromising* is defined as "combining the qualities of two different things." There need not be a loss during a compromise. As a matter of fact, the new combination could bring about a novel and unexpected result. This is certainly true with the blending of positive qualities.

CONCENTRATIVE

Word Forms: concentrate, concentration, concentrator, concentrativeness

Definitions: (1) able to bring or draw to a common objective, direct toward one point, focus; (2) able to direct one's thoughts or efforts, fix one's attention on

Comment:
Shared Space Concentration

During concentration there is never one hundred percent focus except for brief periods of time, usually a few seconds. If you have great concentrative powers, that means that you not only can block out extraneous thoughts and input but also can utilize those stray inputs to enhance your directness to the task at hand. While making love, your attention is on the pleasure of yourself and your partner. That experience can be enhanced environmentally with the addition of soft covers, mood lighting, stimulating music, loving words, joking gestures, et cetera.

During problem solving and brainstorming, half of the fun is to be open to all stimuli in the framework of the solution. No matter how ridiculous the input, it may trigger some aspect of the solution that eventually is adopted.

A person with good concentration also has a very quick and discerning mind. A decision is made in a split second. Is this stray thought worth pursuing?

CONCERNED

Word Forms: concern, concerning, concernment, concernedly, unconcerned

Definitions: (1) interested or involved in some matter; **(2)** in a state of caring interest; apprehensive <a *concerned* citizen>

Too Far: reactionary, worried

CONCILIATORY

Word Forms: conciliate, conciliative, conciliatorily, conciliatoriness

Definitions: (1) overcomes distrust or hostility with friendly action, compromise, and communication; soothes anger; placates; reconciles; **(2)** makes peace between persons at variance; pacific

Synonym: engaging

CONCISE

Word Forms: concisely, conciseness

Definitions: (1) brief but exact and to the point; comprehensive; (2) giving precisely what is needed

Synonyms: succinct, condensed

Too Far: laconic

How to Live This Quality Today: Notice if the person you are talking to is very busy. If so, chatter about the kids and the weather will be a waste of time. Courtesy demands being concise.

CONFIDENT

Word Forms: confide, confidence, confidential, confidently, confidentness, self-confident

Definitions: (1) having full belief; fully assured; certain; (2) relying on oneself; bold

Synonyms: positive, sure, sanguine

Kindred Qualities: flexible, changeable

Compatible Qualities: knowledgeable, understanding

Too Far: cocky, arrogant, smart alecky

Quotes:
As is our confidence, so is our capacity.
—WILLIAM HAZLITT

Confidence ignores "No Trespassing" signs. It is as if he doesn't see them. He is an explorer, committed to following his own direction.

He studied mathematics in France and still views his life as a series of experiments. The only limits he respects are his own. He is honest and humble and very funny. After all these years, his sister doesn't understand why he still ice skates with Doubt.

—JANET RUTH GENDLER, *The Book of Qualities*

Affirmations:
By writing out words of confidence you help implant the idea more firmly in your subconscious mind, which then works harder and faster to produce happy results. Affirmations are your strongest confidence-builders.

—CATHERINE PONDER, *The Dynamic Laws of Prosperity*

Comment: In the acquisition of confidence you need at least a bit of success. You have to have some chutzpah to step out there in the first place to see if and how it works. You also need a bit of failure to overcome, to learn from, so you can go on to what does work. Success is tied to setting goals. Set up the dynamic of a positive goal. Assess the reality of your current situation, take a look at the intermediate goals in between and achieve those.

Observation: Confidence is faith in one's self.

CONFORMING

Word Forms: conform, conformed, conformity, conformable, conformation, conformingly

Definitions: (1) acting in accordance or harmony with the prevailing standards, attitudes, and practices of society or a group; to comply; **(2)** to be or become similar in form, nature, or character

Kindred Qualities: individuality, confidence

Compatible Quality: a team player

CONGENIAL

Word Forms: congeniality, congenially

Definitions: (1) agreeable, appropriate or pleasing in nature or character; pleasant; **(2)** suited or adapted in tastes or temperament; compatible; kindred; **(3)** sociable; genial; **(4)** existing or associated together harmoniously

CONGRUOUS

Word Forms: congruence, congruent, congruity, congruously, congruousness

Definitions: (1) corresponding to what is right, proper, and reasonable; fitting; suitable; appropriate; **(2)** agreeing in nature or qualities; harmonious

CONSCIENCE

Word Forms: conscienced, conscientious

Definition: the knowledge or feeling of right and wrong; the faculty, power, or principle of a person, which decides on the lawfulness or morality of actions; a compulsion to do right
See also: *Upright*

Observation: We use the measurement of personal ideals to criticize oneself and others. If you need to judge others, and if you have the knowledge of their ideals, you are better off using theirs rather than your own standards.

CONSCIENTIOUS

Word Forms: conscience, conscientiously, conscientiousness

Definitions: (1) meticulous; careful; painstaking; **(2)** influenced or governed by conscience; governed by the known, accepted rules of right and wrong; scrupulous; honest

CONSCIOUS

Word Forms: consciously, consciousness

Definitions: (1) aware of one's own existence and of external objects and conditions; **(2)** able to feel and think; awake; **(3)** aware of oneself as a thinking being; knowing what one is doing and why; **(4)** capable of or marked by thought, will, design, or perception; **(5)** deliberate; intentional

Synonyms: sensible, felt, known, cognizant, apprised

Saying: I am that I am.

Quotes:

Our great human adventure is the evolution of consciousness. We are in this life to enlarge the soul and light up the brain.
—TOM ROBBINS

People generally react to any new situation in one of four ways: Aha!, Ho-hum, Oy Vey! and Yum-Yum. These illustrate the four basic states of consciousness. . . . All else is mere elaboration.
—DAVID BRIN, *Earth*

Our ability to tell ourselves a silent narration about a future is the key to the modern conception of consciousness.
—WILLIAM H. CALVIN, NEUROPHYSIOLOGIST

Note: Calvin goes on to say that this need not be a verbal story—one needing the structure of linguistic skills—but can be a picture story—a silent movie.

If I consist of many, why do I persist in perceiving a central me at all! What is this consciousness that even now, as I think these thoughts, contemplates its own existence?
—DAVID BRIN, *Earth*

Reflections:

- I am conscious, therefore I am. If consciousness is the measure of existence, then you must experience consciousness in order to experience existence. If you do not experience consciousness, then you do not exist. I am not talking about physical existence, but ultimate existence—immortality.

  The more conscious you are, the more points time, and therefore space, you exist. In order to exist in perpetuity, those separations between consciousnesses have to be decreased to zero. This is done by choosing to be conscious, not only awake but also *alive*. Choices make you live.

  We all know that we run on automatic most of the time. It is our positive actions that increase the quantity of conscious time. The longer those conscious periods, the more "life" that is taking place. The closer together they are, the more you *exist*.

  Is it also possible that you can consciously choose nonexistence? Perhaps this means that if you choose to do negative things and do so habitually, then your sense of reality is distorted to such a point that you do not experience reality as it objectively exists. You create another reality that does not and cannot coincide with "real" reality. If everything has to have its existence inside objective reality, then a personal subjective reality that moves itself completely outside of that objective reality will eventually cease to exist. One can spend his or her time closing off all the windows and doors that are the avenues through which one moves through reality. And when the last one is completely closed there is no light of life coming into or emanating from them. In order to do that, one would have to consciously reject all truth, beauty, and goodness. That would constitute a pretty sophisticated rejection system.

- Everybody is moving in consciousness at a personal pace. Each can choose his or her own tempo of experiencing consciousness. Therefore, each can move through the universe quickly or slowly.

  If you reach a critical "spiritual speed," you will break free from inertia and become immortal. If you continually choose what you know to be wrong, the drag will slow you down and eventually you will stop. The fact that you *personally* experience your existence is the primary fact that personal consciousness does exist. If an entity never experiences its existence, then it is not a person.

- Hindu esoteric thought holds that there are seven "spirits" relative to each plane of human consciousness: Sensation, Emotion, Reflection,

Intelligence, Intuition, Spirituality, Will, and Imitation of the Divine.

Comments:
- Normally you are aware of one of three things—and only one of the three at any one time.

  1. Sensory contacts
  2. Feelings
  3. Thoughts or memories

- Oftentimes the awareness can shift so rapidly that it seems like you are experiencing more than one in the same moment. Consider a kiss: you are feeling the tactile pleasures from your lips and other skin surfaces; you are feeling the love and appreciation coming into you from the other person; you are feeling the love and affection going out from you to the other person; you are remembering and fantasizing; and you even recall that you have to put the clothes in the dryer.

  This composite is the experience of the moment. But there is also the experience of the observer self, the superconscious, the higher self. You can literally be in two places at once—experiencing the now and experiencing the experience.

  In this sense you can be on more than one level at a time. As you experience the facts of your existence, whether those are painful or pleasurable, there is also that knowing and observing level of existence. This upper level justifies the fact of existence. Your superconscious self focuses mundane reality and measures it in terms of a higher reality, and that higher reality is the purposes and values of Supreme Reality.

- It can be argued that the purpose for existence is to mesh with or be more consistent with observable reality. Science defines itself in these terms: the more accurate the theory, the more agreement with "reality" and therefore more accepted. Albeit, the accuracy is continually and almost habitually remeasured to check it against the facts of a believable reality.

  Acting positively creates a personal being that continues to exist. If your choices are positive, you are generating a subjective reality that meshes with objective reality.

  This theory will take a long time to unfold, particularly for a finite creature. Here in our earth effort, the good as well as the bad prosper or fail in what sometimes seems to be a haphazard way. Nonetheless, you know by your experience if you are growing and moving closer to that objective reality. After physical death we will get our first real proof of the results of this test. Just the fact of reawakening to our "self" will reaffirm some hope that the hypothesis is correct. If, on the other hand, some other theory of what is true proves to be correct, a different result would occur. Fact is a great changer of minds. If, say, the theory of nonconsciousness or unconscious melding with an oversoul proves to be true, then we wouldn't have much to decide because we wouldn't know ourselves as individual conscious beings capable of arguing the effects or merits of various theories.

My belief is that as an entity you will continue to experience reality in basically the same way you experience it now except you will be in different circumstances and environment. Further, I believe that you will notice a continuum of experience. In other words, you will wake up on the other side knowing your self, recognizing your existence, remembering your previous life, and continue from where you left off. Even if the external reality is significantly different, the theory should be consistent. It should still be true in the new environment that your purpose would be to make positive choices that guarantee your continued existence.

- Life is a series of minute connected and correcting steps. This moment's actions are connected to the next and the previous with the quantity and the quality of consciousness. The degree that one's actions, intentions, or experiences are conscious has an effect on your future and the larger pool of consciousness. If these experiences are positive they will shine brightly against the fabric of freedom. If negative, they will be conspicuous in their darkness.

Color: red

Symbols: an *island;* the *mirror; window(s); front; right; Saturn;* superconscious: *Jupiter*

CONSERVATIVE

Word Forms: conserve, conservancy, conservation, conservatism, conservatize, conservatively, conservativeness

Definitions: (1) inclined to preserve the existing order of things; traditional; (2) moderate; cautious; prudent; safe

Kindred Qualities: open, flexible

Too Far: conformity, closed

CONSIDERATE

Word Forms: consider, consideration, considerately, considerateness

Definitions: (1) showing kindly regard for the feelings or circumstances of others; thoughtful; **(2)** showing care; deliberate

CONSISTENT

Word Forms: consistence, consistency, consistently

Definitions: (1) harmonious regularity or steady continuity; **(2)** conducting oneself in harmony with one's belief, character, profession, or custom

Synonyms: accordant, consonant, changeless

Kindred Qualities: fairness, concern, tact, the ability to see a global view

Too Far: mediocre
　　Qualities that are often sacrificed in the corporate world in the name of consistency are flexibility and individuality. Consistency is certainly a positive quality, but kindred qualities are very much needed in order to round it out. In the attempt to be consistent, institutions will become concrete, resulting in mediocrity and apathy.

Reflection: You can remain consistent in the midst of continual and inevitable change if you are focused on positive qualities.

Admonition: Don't let your consistency get dissolved into mediocrity. If you work and hope for the good, you will have a dynamic consistency. Take a point of view that is most appropriate, reasonable, and fair in the current situation. Fear not that you will be criticized that you are promoting an "opposite" position than you previously held. That is, don't be concerned that your view in the situation at hand may appear to be different from your position on a similar but previous situation. Wisdom dictates that you pay attention to what is right at this time and proceed with poise, honesty, and tact.

Comment:

Most people know someone who they call strange or, at best, eccentric. That person may be endearing in an odd sort of way, or even repulsive; but if he or she is *consistent,* then it is easier for others to come to terms with his or her quirky nature.

CONSONANT

Word Forms: consonance, consonantly

Definition: in agreement or harmony; accordant; congruous; consistent

Synonyms: unified, suitable

Symbol: *Ouroboros,* a dragon or serpent biting its own tail

CONSTRUCTIVE

Word Forms: construct, construction, constructively, constructiveness

Definitions: (1) promoting further development or advancement; helping to improve; formative; positive; **(2)** able or helping to erect or create; **(3)** building up or somehow making better

CONTEMPLATIVE

Word Forms: contemplate, contemplated, contemplating, contemplation, contemplator, contemplatively, contemplatingly, contemplativeness

Definitions: **(1)** looking at intently; gazing; observant; **(2)** studying; thinking about with interest; meditating upon; thoughtful; having continued application of the mind to a subject; **(3)** anticipating something coming in the future; looking forward to; expectant; **(4)** a religious person devoted to contemplation of the divine and to prayer; in a state of mystical awareness of God

Synonyms: ponderous, considerate, musing

Familial Qualities: meditative, reflective

Quote:
It's so hard when contemplated in advance, and so easy when you do it.
—ROBERT M. PIRSIG, *Zen and the Art of Motorcycle Maintenance: An Inquiry into Values*

Tip: A proper environment is very conducive to a contemplative state. A natural setting seems to be ideal. Seek out a God-made or man-made garden.

Symbols: a *mandala;* a *mountaintop*

CONTEMPORARY

Word Form: contemporarily

Definition: current; modern; up-to-date; hip

Color: blue

CONTENT

Word Forms: contentment, contented, contently, contentedly, contentedness

Definitions: (1) satisfied with what one is or has; (2) ease of mind; not wanting more or different

Quotes:

Once there was a great king who gazed down from a tall tower upon a gardener who sang as he worked, and the king cried, "Ah, to have a life of no cares! If only I could be that gardener." And the voice of the August Personage of Jade reached out from Heaven and said, "IT SHALL BE SO," and lo, the king was a gardener singing in the sun. In time the sun grew hot and the gardener stopped singing, and a fine dark cloud brought coolness and then drifted away, and it was hot again and much work remained, and the gardener cried, "Ah, to carry coolness wherever I go and have no care! If only I could be that cloud." And the voice of the August Personage of Jade reached out from Heaven and said, "IT SHALL BE SO," and lo, the gardener was a cloud drifting across the sky. And the wind blew and the sky grew cold, and the cloud would have liked to go behind the shelter of a hill, but it could only go where the wind took it, and no matter how hard it tried to go this way, the wind took it that way, and above the cloud was the bright sun. "Ah, to fly through wind and be warm and have no cares! If only I could be the sun," cried the cloud. And the voice of the August Personage of Jade reached out from Heaven and said, "IT SHALL BE SO," and lo, he was the sun. It was very grand to be the sun, and he delighted in the work of sending down rays to warm some things and burn others, but it was like wearing a suit made of fire and he began to bake like bread. Above him the cool stars that were gods were sparkling in safety and serenity and the sun cried, "Ah, to be divine and free from care! If only I could be a god." And the voice of the August Personage of Jade reached out from Heaven and said, "IT SHALL BE SO," and lo, he was a god, and he was beginning his third century of combat with the Stone Monkey, which had just transformed itself into a monster a hundred thousand feet tall and was wielding a trident made from the triple peaks of Mount Hua, and when he wasn't dodging blows he could see the peaceful green earth down below him, and the god cried, "Ah, if only I could be a man who was safe and secure and had no cares!" And the voice of the August Personage of Jade reached out from Heaven and said, "IT SHALL BE SO," and lo, he was a king who was gazing down from a tall tower upon a gardener who sang as he worked.

—BARRY HUGHART, *Eight Skilled Gentlemen*

I have learned in whatsoever state I am, therewith to be content.

—ST. PAUL

Color: green

Fiction: *Roger Bontemps*, the French personification of contentment who was portrayed in a song by Béranger—Roger was always hopeful and was inclined to make the best of things.

CONTRIBUTIVE

Word Forms: contribute, contribution, contributively

Definition: giving or granting to a common fund or having a common purpose; paying a share of or making a gift toward <Through her skillful acting she was immensely *contributive* to the success of the play.>

Proverb:
Everyone must row with the oars they have.

—ENGLISH

CONTROLLED

Word Forms: control, controlling, controllability, controllable, self-controlled

Definitions: (1) having an exercise of authority over; directed; in command; (2) restrained; held back; curbed; (3) able to manage one's own temperament

Compatible Qualities: self-forgetful, self-control

Quote:

Give every man thine ear, but few thy voice;
Take each man's censure, but reserve thy judgment.

—WILLIAM SHAKESPEARE, *Hamlet*

Reflections:

- You cannot control the facts of the past. But you can control your attitude toward the facts of the past. You can control your attitude and judgment about the present and what you will do in the future. You cannot control what other people do or think or are. You can influence them but only if they are willing or susceptible to your example or power.

- There is negative control: fear, torture, sleep deprivation, threats of harm to loved ones, threats of loss of job, or loss of life. If one is to encompass the positive aspects of control one needs to persuade with logic, emotion, spiritual flavor, experience, love, cuddling, nurturing, and so on, to help others recognize their own values and move forward at their own pace. Christ said to love your enemies. If you do, you will help them just as you would your friends to get in touch with their divine selves. It is an evolutionary process and they will show themselves to be the people who they are and will progress in a more positive way rather than being forced to grow in the warped way that is inevitable if more negative pressure is put upon them. They put enough negative pressure upon themselves.

Consideration: Politicians can only tackle the hard problems with laws that cover the entire populace. People killing people with handguns is an example of a problem that is out of control. The problem began in a simpler time when guns were needed to get dinner for the family from the land. The percentage of crazies may have been just as common then, but the instant communication that we have today makes the problem seem more prevalent; also, our population is larger. Back then it was believed that the individual should be mature enough and reasonable enough to control their own actions. It was also considered obvious that those who could lose control over themselves would be able to be controlled by the majority. The problem will end when that original belief becomes a fact. The values that the individual actually possesses prevents him from shooting another person.

Laws, morals, and family rules have some influence (usually negative) in shaping the individual's choice, but in the end the individual makes the final choice.

Observation: The person asking the questions is in control of the conversation.

Comment: You need to let go of the part fear plays in your growing process. As you let go of fear, experiences will get more accessible, more exciting, but they also may get more out of your control. Ultimately they get totally out of your control. As you change from a material to a spiritual being, you are relinquishing control (of the body) in favor of cooperation (with the spirit). The soul is growing.

Recognize what you actually have control of and what you do not have control of. It is useless to try to control what is not yours to control. Life will lead you to what you need if you don't try to control it too much.

Symbol: the *chariot* (self-control)

CONVICTION

Definition: a strong persuasion or belief

Comment:

Truth and Conviction

The sincere conviction that something is true will allow the individual who holds that conviction to resonate with a power that presents an argument for truth. Yet that person could be wrong. As a matter of fact, the only thing that may be right is the sincerity of the conviction. Therefore the individual will do whatever he or she can to make the belief resonate with truth. For example, a vessel much larger than described would be needed for Noah to carry two of every species on the planet; but those who believe this "fact" sincerely, do whatever they can to make it true. They try to make it consistent with logic. If it could be proved or disproved by some objective means, then they could rejoice in their accurate belief or would have to readjust their conviction.

Actual facts or facts of belief have the resonance of truth when spoken with conviction. The individual has to decide what is truly objective or true subjectively for them.

CONVINCING

Word Forms: convince, convincer, convincingly, convincingness

Definitions: (1) satisfying or assuring by argument or proof; **(2)** persuasive of the truth, rightness, or reality of something; plausible

Comment: There is both logic and conviction in a convincing argument.

CONVIVIAL

Word Forms: conviviality, convivially

Definitions: (1) friendly; agreeable; **(2)** fond of feasting, drinking, and merry company; jovial; **(3)** befitting a feast; festive

COOL

Word Forms: cooler, coolest, cooled, cooling, coolheaded, coolness

Definitions: (1) marked by steady dispassionate calmness and self-control; **(2)** composed; restrained; **(3)** very good; pleasing; excellent; **(4)** fashionable; up-to-date; hip

Synonyms: self-possessed, fresh

Compatible Quality: stylish

Comment: What is cool may be good or bad, but if it's popular then it's acceptable. The desire to fit in and be accepted can override better judgment if the individual is immature.

Colors: blue, turquoise, rainbow

Symbols: an *ice* cube; an *icicle*

COOPERATIVE

Word Forms: cooperate, cooperator, cooperation, cooperatively, cooperativeness

Definition: a willingness and ability to work with others; teamwork

Proverb:
When spider webs unite, they can tie up a lion.
—ETHIOPIAN

Quote:
Whatever God's dream that man may be, it is certain it cannot come true unless man cooperates.
—STELLA TERRILL MANN

Reflection: Ultimately the final outcome of racial tension will be one of three separate possibilities: isolation, annihilation, or assimilation.

One of the strengths of any society is the assimilation taking place: cross-cultural relationships; cross-societal interactions; the melding of musics, ideas, and attitudes. When assimilation is done with a cooperative spirit, the new combination is a strong and unique new people.

Symbol: *fish* (teamwork)

COORDINATED

Word Forms: coordinate, coordination, coordinating

Definitions: **(1)** able to use more than one set of muscle movements to a single end; **(2)** combined in harmonious relation or action

CORDIAL

Word Forms: cordiality, cordialize, cordially, cordialness

Definitions: (1) warm; hearty; affectionate; genial; sincere; proceeding from the heart; **(2)** reviving the spirits; cheering; invigorating; giving strength; stimulating the heart

Synonym: gracious

Saying: *a bras ouverts* (French): "with open arms" [cordially]

CORRECT

Word Forms: correction, correctitude, corrective, correctly, correctness

Definitions: (1) conforming with fact or logic; true; accurate; right; free from errors; **(2)** in accordance with an acknowledged or accepted standard; proper

Synonyms: faultless, precise, exact

COURAGEOUS

Word Forms: courage, courageously, courageousness

Definitions: (1) facing and dealing with anything recognized as dangerous, difficult, or painful instead of withdrawing from it; the quality of being fearless or brave; valorous; intrepid; **(2)** that firmness of spirit that meets danger without fear

Synonyms: bold, resolute, fortitude, firm, daring, plucky, enterprising, hardy, heroic, gallant, dauntless, mettlesome
   Courage, *mettle*, *spirit*, *resolution*, and *tenacity* regard mental or moral strength in resistance to opposition, danger, or hardship. *Courage* implies

firmness of mind and will in the face of danger or extreme difficulty. *Mettle* suggests an ingrained capacity for meeting strain or difficulty with fortitude and resilience. *Spirit* also suggests a quality of temperament enabling one to hold one's own or keep one's morale when opposed or threatened. *Resolution* stresses firm determination to achieve one's ends. *Tenacity* adds to resolution implications of stubborn persistence.

Kindred Qualities: kind, curious, compassionate, confident, farsighted, open-minded

Parental Qualities: wisdom, discipline

Familial Quality: encouraging

Too Far: foolhardy

Quotes:
There are worse things than dying.

—JUDY KAIN

Courage is fear holding on a minute longer.

—GEORGE S. PATTON

One man with courage makes a majority.

—ANDREW JACKSON

With courage you will dare to take risks, have the strength to be compassionate and the wisdom to be humble. Courage is the foundation of integrity.

—KESHAVAN NAIR

Life shrinks or expands in proportion to one's courage.

—ANAÏS NIN

Courage may be the most important virtue because without it you won't have the strength to sustain any other value.

—MAYA ANGELOU (PARAPHRASE)

Note: The quality of courage is indispensable as a supporting structure for other qualities.

Inspiration: Courage is infectious. It has the ability to buoy the courage of the less courageous.

Reflection: Any method or mechanism that protects you from the fear is valuable. You can look back and say, "When I was a child, I was obedient, and therefore, I avoided fear because I was protected. When I was young, I would cower or run away, and therefore I avoided harm. When I was older, I would intellectualize and yet this was just a form of running away. But as I faced my fear, I became more courageous and balanced in the way that I handled my self and my environment." Whatever mechanism you use is valuable because it works to some degree. You cannot expect to reach the most sophisticated and appropriate method in one huge leap. Once a mechanism is recognized as less than perfect, then it is time to face the next step and develop a more polished mechanism for avoiding or facing fear.

Considerations:

- In order to experience courage, you're going to have to experience situations in which courage is a necessary element. This means difficulty. Fear allows you to experience courage.

  Courage comes into play if you need to leave something that is secure in favor of something that is adventurous, unknown, new, or exciting.

  One way of dealing with fear is giving up or releasing it. When you do that, you let it pass through you—you accept it but do not embrace it. When you feel its grip, you may process it or simply push on through it. Whatever you do, you have to control it before it can freeze your resolve.

- Courage has a lot to do with the willingness to go through fear. When you have an opportunity to go through, you face the problem with choice: to either go through or not. That's where the courage comes in.

- We each have a threshold of pain; we also have a threshold of conflict. No matter how well developed your threshold of conflict, you will create or encounter circumstances that push that limit. Measure your success against your acceptance of and management of the conflicts encountered. This includes reducing the conflict by backing off. It also includes facing it with clarity and determination, not just with willpower, but with finesse and creativity. One must have the energy and fortitude to fight, or the wisdom to hold back and do some more preparation.

Observations:
- You learn more from your failures than from your successes. Your failures give you the courage and the knowledge and the will to change things enough to create success. Think of that as an edge.
- Fear of the unknown is the greatest of fears. Your own imagination can bring you to your knees. Don't manufacture fear.
- The real problem with death is fear.

Tips:
- The antidotes to fear are gratitude, humor, appreciation, relaxation, flexibility, attentiveness, knowledge, preparedness, strength, understanding, and experience (you are not as afraid of something that you have already experienced). Courage and boldness are not really antidotes to fear, they are more reaction mechanisms.

    One of the greatest antidotes to fear is humor. When you experience fear or if your intention is to be courageous, make sure that there is a serious quantity of levity involved.
- If your focus is good enough, your attentiveness is good enough. You perceive the rattlesnake before it has a chance to bother you. Then you just take a wide path so you don't even experience the fear because your attentiveness beat you to it.

    If you are climbing a cliff you may try a handhold that you decide is a bad choice, but you have a good foothold and your other hand is in a fine position. Since you've got a good hold and are standing securely, you can see where your next handhold should be, so no fear is necessary.

Comments:
- Fear is negative power, and yet there is a way to switch fear into positive power that you control. Focus on the energy as an object. If you are inside its field, then it has control of you; but if you are outside of it, then you can take possession of it and use it for your purpose.

    When you're fearful during an experience, the thing to do is to focus on that which can be done and that which has to be done, keeping in mind what your abilities are. Test your outer limits. They can be pushed even further with the aid of adrenaline.

    Accomplishments that are achieved enkindle enthusiasm and curiosity.
- Did Rosa Parks generate the courage to sit in the front of the bus at the moment of the decision or was it a lifetime of building courage

that culminated in the defining moment of her life? I believe that it is possible for the former to be true but more often the latter is the case.

Colors: red, scarlet

Symbol: the *sword*

COURTEOUS

Word Forms: court, courtesy, courteously, courteousness

Definitions: (1) having courtlike manners; well-bred; polite and gracious; considerate of others; **(2)** actively considerate and sometimes stately politeness

Synonyms: civil, obliging, affable, conciliating, attentive, respectful

Consideration: Common courtesy is the backbone of civilization. Simple consideration of others could easily be the foundation of a new world order.

Fiction: *Sir Calidore*, a knight who typifies courtesy in Spenser's *Faërie Queen*

Legend: *Sir Gawain*, King Arthur's nephew, famous for strength and courtesy

COURTLY

Word Form: court

Definitions: (1) polite, dignified, refined, or elegant; **(2)** pertaining to, or suitable for, the court of a sovereign

Comment: Those in power in courts demand a certain conspicuous mannerliness. In the street this is known as common courtesy. Caring for the feelings and comfort of others is always appropriate.

COZY

Word Forms: cozier, coziest, cozily, coziness

Definitions: **(1)** enjoying or affording warmth and ease; snug; **(2)** marked by the intimacy of the family or a close group

CREATIVE

Word Forms: create, creation, creator, creativity, creatively, creativeness

Definitions: **(1)** to bring into being; to originate; to cause to exist; **(2)** characterized by originality and execution of thought; **(3)** productive; inventive

Synonyms: constitutive, forming, making, generative, resourceful

Kindred Qualities: harmony, practicality, talent, ability

Compatible Qualities: devoted, dreaming, playful, humorous

Familial and Consequential Qualities: There are three qualities that work well with creativity: courage, curiosity, and confidence.
   In order to be confident, you also need to be courageous. In order to be courageous, you have to have curiosity. Curiosity creates the positive impetus to venture into an unknown situation. Your fear says that there may also be difficulty in that place, but your curiosity, your inquisitiveness, your sense of wonder can be the guiding light. What does it look like? What does it feel like? What does it taste like? How will this new experience relate to something I really want? This is how curiosity leads to courage. And once you experience some courage, you become confident. Confidence allows you to commit to a course of action that surely will foster difficulty but also many experiences of joy and growth. You are then literally becoming a new person.

People Who Exemplify This Quality: There are different avenues and types of creativity. One might be creative like Einstein in math, or Mozart in music, or Lincoln in politics, or Isadora Duncan in dance, or Shakespeare with words, or I. M. Pei as an architect, or Jonathan Winters with comedy, or . . .

Quotes:
Creative thinking may simply mean the realization that there's no particular virtue in doing things the way they have always been done.

—RUDOLPH FLESCH

It is the creative potential itself in human beings that is the image of God.

—MARY DALY, THEOLOGIAN

Why should we all use our creative power? Because there is nothing that makes people so generous, joyful, lively, bold and compassionate.

—BRENDA UELAND

Creating, I have concluded, is the best window to the universe I know.

—ROBERT FRITZ, *The Path of Least Resistance*

If anything could truly change the face of our civilization, it is the creative process.

—ROBERT FRITZ, *The Path of Least Resistance*

Note: In the quotes above substitute your favorite quality. One could substitute almost any quality for *creative*.

Observations:
- In *The Path of Least Resistance*, Robert Fritz says that if you use your feelings as a standard of measurement, you will always gravitate toward what is familiar. If you are creating something new, then by its very nature it will *be* and therefore *feel* unfamiliar.

    So if you cannot depend upon feelings, then it is *wonder* that takes you forward. This means that you take the action first to find out if something works.
- One of the aspects of creativity is flexibility, meeting the conditions within which you find yourself—adaptability.

    Other creative qualities are concern for quality, responsibility, and fun.

- One of the hardest parts of being original in creativity is getting outside of the existing paradigms, especially when the established prototype is a good one. When the bird is the only model, how can humans believe that they can fly?

Tips:
- Fight destruction with creation.
- Use your natural, normal, and developed abilities in your creative endeavors.
- Conflict inhibits the creative function of the inner life. It is like a civil war in the personality. Be creative in resolving conflict.

Suggestions:
- When that inner negative voice says you don't have the talent, you don't have the will, you don't have the ability—some of which might be true—all that means is that you need to develop those qualities. If you've got a grand idea, then go get the education, or the talent, or the backing. If you don't have what it takes, persuade someone who does to help you. It takes courage to do it.
- One of the reasons that creativity comes and goes is because of the time needed to absorb the creative force. Another is the need to project it, three dimensionalize it, turn it into that which it needs to become. If one is bathed continuously in the creative juice, one doesn't have time for the practical application of the creation.

    The fact that creativity ebbs and flows is a good reason to get the gifts of the muse down on paper, onto a tape recorder, or into a sketchbook when she is whispering in your ear. Then you can return to the idea at a more normal time and in a practical manner accept the challenge and enhance the concept. You will also restir your creativity when you go back to a sketch and see the flash of brilliance there ready to be expanded from a notion into a concept and a practical reality.
- Leaving all your options open is good at the outset, but it is deadly to finalizing a creation. Commit to a particular route and reduce the possibilities and the options as you go along in order to reach a goal. The goal is a single point.

    Having contingencies, a Plan B if you fail, is reasonable, but having too many options is not workable.

Symbols: the *minstrel* (tarot); *Aries* (zodiac); *dance;* the *storm;* a *volcano;*

the *spiral;* the *spider* (web spinning); *weaving; fabric* (warp = passive; woof = active); the *mouth* (speech); the letter *R* ("The trilled *r* is onomatopoeic, alluding to thunder as the symbol of creative power; it is for this reason that most verbs in almost all languages contain the letter *r*" —J. E. Cirlot, *A Dictionary of Symbols.*)

Mythologies: *Bel* is the Father of the Babylonian gods, the creator of the world and all its people; *Osiris*, the primary Egyptian deity, is the source of fruitfulness and life, the sum of all benefits, creator and god of the Nile; *Ormazd* or *Ormuzd* ("Wise Lord") is the positive divine being of the Zoroastrians or ancient Persians, and the creator of the world.

Theology: *Brahma* is the supreme god of the Hindu trinity, and the creator; *Shiva*, the third god of the Hindu trinity—called the destroyer—represents the principles of both destruction and reproduction.

CREDIBLE

Word Forms: credibility, credibly, credibleness

Definitions: **(1)** capable of being believed; **(2)** worthy of confidence; reliable; trustworthy

Synonym: plausible

Comment: Conventional credentials—diplomas, titles, lists of accomplishments, authorship, family, children—give a person credibility.

No matter what a person says they are going to do, who they are is evident in what they have done.

Somebody might say that he or she believes in certain positive qualities, but you have to judge people on what they actually do and who they actually are, not just by what they say or what their intentions are.

CUDDLY

Word Forms: cuddle, cuddlier, cuddliest, cuddlesome

Definition: enjoys holding or laying close affectionately, hugging tenderly

Tip: Cuddling and snuggling are a nice addition to sex, both before and after. Men like to be touched, but many have the mistaken notion that it is only appropriate with sex. Men need to know that they will get fondled a lot more if they don't always take it as a sexual cue.

(I know that my generalizations about the sexes may not apply to the individual.)

Observation: Children need to be cuddled.

Symbol: a *teddy bear*

CULTURED

Word Forms: culture, cultural, culturing

Definitions: (1) artistic and intellectual regarding pursuits and products; **(2)** a quality of enlightenment or refinement arising from an acquaintance with and concern for what is regarded as excellent in the arts, letters, or manners; **(3)** exhibiting development or improvement of the mind by education and training

Synonyms: refined, accomplished, cultivated, learned, erudite, polished

CUNNING

Word Forms: cunningly, cunningness

Definitions: (1) skillful; clever; shrewd; **(2)** created with proficiency; ingenious; **(3)** pleasing; attractive; pretty in a delicate way

Synonyms: artful, crafty, sly, astute, subtle, wily

Comment: Cunning also has the negative connotation of underhanded motives, but it is easy to tell the difference when the hand is finally shown.

CURIOUS

Word Forms: curiosity, curiously, curiousness

Definition: strongly desirous to learn or know; possessing a desire to investigate

Kindred Qualities: discretion, diplomacy

Familial Qualities: adventuresome, explorative

Consequential Quality: understanding

Too Far: nosy, prying
A person's privacy should be respected. Add discretion and thoughtfulness to curiosity to temper the negative possibilities.

Quotes:
The ancient question is still awaiting an answer: What features in our brain account for our humanity, our musical creativity, infinitely varied artifacts, subtlety of humor, sophisticated projection (in chess, politics and business), our poetry, ecstasy, fervor, contorted morality, and elaborate rationalization?
—THEODORE H. BULLOCK, NEUROBIOLOGIST

Satisfaction of one's curiosity is one of the greatest sources of happiness in life.
—LINUS PAULING

Comment: When you ask a question you are exhibiting your desire for the qualities of knowledge, wisdom, and understanding. You are enhancing the qualities of curiosity and wonder. And you are exemplifying communication and possibly courage.

Fiction: *Curious George* gets in trouble because of his curiosity. He has adventures, and yet everything turns out okay.

Symbol: the *brown bear*

CUTE

Word Forms: cuter, cutest, cutie, cutie-pie, cutesy, cutely, cuteness

Definitions: (**1**) pleasingly pretty or charmingly attractive, especially in a delicate or dainty way; (**2**) clever; sharp, cunning; mentally keen; shrewd

Observation: Note that cute is not only a physical quality.

DAFFY

Word Forms: daffier, daffiest, daffily

Definition: crazy; silly; zany

Too Far: foolish

DAINTY

Word Forms: daintier, daintiest, daintify, daintily, daintiness

Definitions: (**1**) cultured and refined in taste; particular; fastidious; (**2**) elegant; tender; delicately lovely or pretty

Synonyms: choice, exquisite, fine, neat, nice, rare

Story: I was camping in the high Rocky Mountains when I first was picking qualities to emulate. The random choice of dainty was not exactly what I was looking for but I took it in stride. As I was hiking in the area, I was pleasantly surprised with the variety of dainty flowers, grasses, and soft colors. It was one of those clear, blue-sky days and even the air was dainty. I was up on a ridge at about thirteen thousand feet when I stopped to catch my breath in the thin atmosphere. Just above me a hummingbird flew over the ridge and came right for me, hesitated, and landed on my left shoulder. He must have needed a breather too. I said hello to him and he flew back a few feet, took a good look at me, and then landed again. Well, for a hummingbird a few seconds is a long time, so he was soon rested. He then took off and was out of sight in no time.

This incident taught me that odd combinations of qualities happen all the time. I knew that hummers are extremely aggressive and territorial, and while we ascribe qualities like dainty to them, they may not think so of themselves. After this I began choosing two qualities per day. I did so for about three years but found that I didn't have as much time with the qualities that I wanted, so I have since been choosing two per week.

Comment: There is room in everyone for every quality. No matter how macho you are, there is a time and place to even be dainty.

DAPPER

Word Forms: dapperly, dapperness

Definitions: (1) neat in dress or demeanor; spruce; trim; natty; **(2)** alert and lively in movement and manners

DARING

Word Forms: dare, daringly, daringness, daredevil

Definition: bold; courageous; intrepid; fearless; adventurous; brave

Quote:
It is not because things are difficult that we do not dare; it is because we do not dare that things are difficult.
—SENECA

Symbol: a *tightrope walker*

DARLING

Word Forms: darlingly, darlingness

Definitions: **(1)** beloved; very dear; cherished; dearly loved; **(2)** very pleasing; charming; cute; lovable

DASHING

Word Forms: dash, dashingly

Definitions: **(1)** spirited; engaging in vigorous action; impetuous; bold and lively; energetic; **(2)** elegant and gallant in appearance and manner

DAZZLING

Word Forms: dazzle, dazzlingly

Definitions: **(1)** surprising; overpowering with brilliant qualities; **(2)** impressing deeply; astonishing with delight

DEBONAIR

Word Forms: debonairly, debonairness

Definitions: **(1)** possessing an affable manner; genial; courteous; **(2)** suave; urbane; worldly; **(3)** gay; jaunty; nonchalant; cheerful; lively; carefree

DECENT

Word Forms: decency, decently, decentness

Definitions: (1) exhibiting proper conduct, speech or dress; respectable; **(2)** free of coarseness or indelicacy; modest; chaste; **(3)** generous; kind; fair

Synonyms: suitable, befitting, decorous, seemly, becoming

DECISIVE

Word Forms: decide, decision, decided, decisively, decisiveness

Definitions: (1) arriving at a solution that ends uncertainty or dispute; **(2)** making a choice or judgment; **(3)** showing determination or firmness; resolute

Synonyms: conclusive, unquestionable, unmistakable, positive

Kindred Qualities: vision, open-minded

Parental Qualities: faith, wisdom

Consequential Qualities: peaceful, calm

Too Far: demanding, narrow-minded

Quote:
The opposite of courage in our society is not cowardice, it is conformity.
—ROLO MAY, *Man's Search for Himself*

Note: You must be in charge of your decisions. There are elements of weakness and cowardice in conformity. Those who possess power tend to praise those qualities that will trigger an obedient response. They will say, "Be patient, be tolerant, calm down, do what I say and you'll get yours." They say that the quality of consistency equals fairness, that "we must be objective and treat everyone the same or someone will complain," as if that is a good enough reason to promote mediocrity. In the end, does the patient wait produce the promised reward? Sometimes promises cannot be fulfilled. Sometimes promises are intended to stall for time. Sometimes the promise is said realizing that memory is weak and what was promised can be forgotten or modified to suit the situation when it comes up again.

Reflection: One of the most difficult times we have is just before a decision is made. This is particularly true on important decisions: a career choice, a relationship choice, a life choice. The mind brings up lots of possibilities and what-ifs. Some of these options have fear-triggering repercussions. But once the decision is made, and you proceed with a course of action, most of that fear dissipates. There are new decisions to make. There are still doubts that come up, but if your self-reliance and self-esteem are strong, then some doubt is healthy.

Decisiveness is connected with faith. You know that your decision creates motion. You are acting, which will lead to your goal and to becoming someone different. Have the faith to go ahead and take that first step based on your powers of judgment and experience. As you begin it, and move through it, you'll find out what the next steps are to adjust to the "proper course." If it was the wrong decision, you will find that out and adjust your navigation with your new decisions.

Tips:
- Results always follow decisions; things begin to happen that fall in line with your decisions.
- Decisiveness implies follow-through with a vision and clarity of what needs to be accomplished.
- Be deliberate when you decide.

Advice: People are always looking for the general rule that will fit every specific situation. The advice I would give is to use the higher qualities to govern all that you do. Start by letting love permeate everything you do. Let personal goodness, idealized truth, and the symmetry and joy of beauty be the overriding characteristics of your choices.

When it gets down to a specific situation, let the situation dictate the specific qualities. If you are driving a car, then attentiveness is obviously important. Yet you can still use the higher quality of courtesy as well. Although paying attention will get you from point A to point B, you can always filter the specific qualities through the higher qualities.

If you're doing something highly technical, the qualities of skillful and meticulous, which are not normally considered spiritual qualities, are the most appropriate to the task at hand. But most likely you can find an altruistic reason in addition to the practical one.

It is the variableness of life's choices that keeps life interesting and makes it more complex.

Comments:

- There are degrees of decision making. There are the big decisions, the hard decisions, and the life-changing decisions that are of major import and have large effects. But the day-to-day decisions, the easy decisions, the habitual decisions, made again and again, are extremely valuable as well. They are like the sand and small stones in a dam. They are the stuff with which the big decisions are glued together.
- The military uses threat-based planning. It can be used in ordinary life as well. First identify the threats whether specific or global. Once you've established what the threat is then it's a matter of establishing a defense/offense to deal with that threat. It might be that someone is threatening your job. Well, your defense might be to do a better job, build a better rapport with the people around you or with your boss while still maintaining your integrity. It does not mean to be excessively accommodating but to do what you can to be efficient and proficient in the situation.

  Then look at your offense. Take a look at your dreams. Decide what it is that you would need to do if the threat came about. You could fight for your job if you wanted it, but on the other hand if you lost, all would not be lost because you have a plan B, you've got something to fall back on: You've always wanted to go back to school; you've wanted to write a book; you've wanted to open your own business; you've got an invention in mind—or you can go out and get another job. There are others interested in your talents. Be prepared. Then if you need to react, it is only a matter of carrying out the plan.

Kinds of Decisions

- Choice with preference: You know what you want
- The I-don't-care-just-pick-one decision
- "You decide" decision 1: I love you and want to please you
- "You decide" decision 2: I'm too lazy or uncertain to decide
- The agonizing decision: It is "too" important
- The automatic decision: the same as always
- The lesser-of-two-evils decision
- The forced-into-it-by-outside-influences decision
- The forced-into-it-by-inside-influences decision

There is a type of decision that is considered hard but really isn't if you look at it right. That decision is the "It doesn't matter to me" decision. You like both steak and pork chops, and you can't decide which you want for dinner. Since it doesn't matter you sweat and fret until you finally do pick one. Save yourself all of the agony. Just grab one. Since it doesn't matter, relieve yourself of all of your torment.

If, on the other hand, you are leaning one way or the other, use the quality of intuition to push you toward a choice.

DECOROUS

Word Forms: decorum, decorously, decorousness

Definition: displaying good manners, propriety, and good taste; proper; becoming; befitting; correct; seemly; decent

Derivation: Latin, "to be fitting"; French, "beauty," "grace"

DEDICATED

Word Forms: dedicate, dedicatedly

Definition: wholly committed to a cause, ideal, or personal goal; zealous

Affirmation: An affirmation is somewhat like an oath. You are dedicating your will to the doing of some deed or the keeping of some promise. In order to do so you need to have the firm conviction that you will be able to be true to your pledge. An affirmation is just such a confident statement.

DEEP

Word Forms: depth, deeply, deepness, deepen, deep-rooted

Definitions: (1) possessing a penetrating intellect; wise; sagacious; **(2)** engrossed; involved; **(3)** characterized by profundity of feeling; intense

Quote:
It always comes back to the same thing: go deep enough and there is a bedrock of truth.

—MAY SARTON

Symbol: the *abyss*

DEFINITE

Word Forms: define, definitely, definiteness, definitive, definitude

Definitions: (1) clearly defined or determined; precise; certain; positive; **(2)** free of uncertainty or obscurity; unquestionable; decided

DEFT

Word Forms: deftly, deftness

Definition: showing skill; expert; subtly apt; handy; dexterous

Compatible Quality: In order to be deft, you also need to be persistent and practiced.

DELECTABLE

Word Forms: delectability, delectably, delectableness

Definitions: (1) delightful; highly pleasing; giving joy or pleasure; **(2)** delicious; tasty

DELIBERATE

Word Forms: deliberation, deliberator, deliberately, deliberateness

Definitions: (1) characterized by or resulting from careful and thorough consideration; premeditated; done on purpose; **(2)** studied or intentional; aware of the consequences; **(3)** slow, unhurried, and steady; allowing time for decision for each individual action involved

Synonyms: cautious, thoughtful, voluntary

DELICATE

Word Forms: delicacy, delicately, delicateness

Definitions: (1) beautifully fine in texture, quality, or workmanship; **(2)** elegantly mild, light, or soft; **(3)** slight and subtle <a *delicate* difference>; **(4)** sensitive in feeling, understanding, or responsiveness; having a discriminating distaste for the offensive or unseemly; **(5)** finely skilled; **(6)** considerate and tactful

Kindred Quality: firm

Symbols: the *almond tree* (sweet blossoms that can be destroyed by frost); a *butterfly's wing*

DELICIOUS

Word Forms: deliciously, deliciousness

Definitions: (1) highly pleasing to the senses, chiefly to taste or smell; **(2)** very agreeable to the mind; delightful

DELIGHTFUL

Word Forms: delight, delighted, delightfully, delightfulness

Definition: giving great pleasure and satisfaction; charming

Synonyms: beautiful, gladsome, lovely, delicious, agreeable, captivating, enjoyable

DEMOCRATIC

Word Forms: democracy, democrat, democratically, democratize

Definitions: (1) existing or provided for the benefit or enjoyment of all <*democratic* art>; (2) considering and treating others as one's equals; not snobbish or prejudiced

DEMURE

Word Forms: demurer, demurest, demurity, demurely, demureness

Definitions: (1) characterized by shyness and modesty; reserved; (2) sober; sedate; (3) mature; well-mannered

DEPENDABLE

Word Forms: depend, dependability, dependably, dependableness

Definition: reliable; trustworthy; capable of being counted on

Comment: Dependable is usually the first trait that marks a true friend.

How to Live This Quality Today: Show up prepared and on time.

DESERVING

Word Forms: deserve, deserved, deserves, deservingly

Definition: worthy of merit; creditable

Consideration: The laws of the physical universe are about consumption and absorption. The laws on the emotional level are about agreement and compromise. If you apply the physical laws of consumption to the emotional level, you get rape. Physical, economic, emotional, or psychological rape is the taking of something that is not being freely given or earned.

DESIRE

Word Forms: desired, desiring, desirer, desirable, desirous, desireful, desiderate

Definitions: (1) to long for; to want; to crave; to covet; to earnestly wish to possess and enjoy; an object desired; (2) to express a wish for; to ask for; (3) sexual appetite; passion; (4) attractive; fine; an alluring person or thing; (5) worthy of desire; exciting to possess because it is pleasing, beautiful, or excellent; (6) advantageous, advisable <a *desirable* reform>

Derivation: Latin, "star" (astrology), influenced by the stars

Synonyms: pine, want, hanker, request, eager, inclination, solicit

Kindred Qualities: patient, persistent, creative, appreciative, flexible

Too Far:
  When desire is taken too far it is toxic. Consider the seven deadly sins:

  Lust: excessive desire for sexual pleasure
  Sloth (laziness): excessive desire for comfort
  Covetousness (avarice, greed): excessive desire for wealth
  Gluttony: excessive desire for sustenance
  Envy: a discontented desire for what another possesses

Pride: an extreme desire for self-aggrandizement
Anger (wrath): a drastic need to be right, safe, or strong

Quotes:

If we didn't want anything, we would never get anything, good or bad. I think our longings are natural.

—L. FRANK BAUM, *Tik-Tok of Oz*

Truly, the image makes the condition if you will make the mental image. Consciously have confidence that your desires can come true, place a picture of the desired result where you can daily view it. Your subconscious mind will make it so, and your convictions will come to pass.

—CATHERINE PONDER, *The Dynamic Laws of Prosperity*

Note: Catherine and most people attribute the power of manifestation to the subconscious mind while in reality the superconscious mind is where the real action takes place.

Affirmations:

- In order to attain your desire you must choose it; focus on it, pay attention to it; take interest in and don't be distracted from your true desire. Be specific; be definite and sincere with yourself. Write down your dominant desires.
- I give thanks for the immediate, complete, and proper fulfillment of my desires. This or something better will happen with perfect timing.

Comments:

Wanted or Unwanted Desire

Give yourself permission to look at your desire without judgment and assess your underlying need. Talk to people you trust. Then make an honest judgment.

Suppression, Repression

There is an underlying quality in suppression which connotes an exercise of willpower. If you can subdue your emotions, choose to do so when it is necessary, but *do* judge and choose. If you can hold yourself back from your desire, that is an admirable ability. Use your restraint with wisdom and an intuitive balance.

Suppressing a needed desire is just as stressful as the suppression of an inappropriate desire. Both can cause unease or even disease.

Sublimation

In chemistry sublimation is the transition of a gas to a solid or a solid to a gas without becoming a liquid. It skips a seemingly needed stage. Likewise, you can jump directly to your need. If you have made the decision that your desire is an unworthy one, you can jump over it without going through it. This is done by substitution. Focus on a higher or more noble quest. Visualize something or someone that you would like to be or have more than that has you in its grip.

Rechoose the new desire again and again. Desire is a quality of the future. If you need to control your desire do not allow yourself to be in the future. Engross yourself in the present; remove yourself from the vicinity of the temptation.

Fulfillment

If you take what you want, you will experience the consequences—good or bad.

Yearn without pain. Enjoy your desire until it is fulfilled and then enjoy what you have attained.

Clarification

Desire is often an emotional feeling. Train yourself to be more objective. Move your focus to an intellectual process and then back to the emotional. An honest appraisal of the situation is of paramount importance. Frequent reality checks help you stay on track. After all, hoping that reality is different than it is is a foolish impossibility.

It may be within your power to influence the future, especially if the change is within you. But the past is a fact. The present is the only place where action and choice and change can really occur. Albeit, you can change your attitude about the past.

Maturity

All people want things that they cannot have. But mature people find comfortable ways to live without all of their wants. They also establish mature ways to develop the skills and abundance to acquire their needs.

Questions:

What do you desire?
What is the root of what you desire?
What are your basic needs?
Is your desire a need or a want?
Is your timing right?
How do you intend to fulfill the desire?
Can the need be fulfilled another way?
Are you willing to have it if it were available right now?
What is fair?
Is it yours to take?
Is it being offered?
Do you desire pleasure, attention, recognition, power, security, happiness, attainment, love . . . ?

Symbols: *fruit;* the *apple;* the *hunter;* a *siren*

DETERMINED

Word Forms: determine, determinable, determinacy, determination, determiner, determinedly, determinedness, self-determined

Definitions: (**1**) having one's mind made up; decided; resolved; settled; (**2**) resolute; unwavering; staunch

Synonyms: firm, fixed, immovable, steady

Comment: Once you recognize that your desire is a worthy one, then pursue it with determination.

DEVELOPING

Word Forms: develop, developer, development

Definition: growing; evolving; becoming gradually fuller, larger, or better

Consideration: Potentials turn into actuals. As long as you are developing, you are becoming your ideals. It may not seem fast enough but steady progress is satisfactory. As your view of the grand reality becomes fuller and clearer, you may feel you are shrinking. It's like looking at the night sky. You may feel like an insignificant speck in a vast universe of stars and galaxies; on the other hand, you are a significant spark that can take part in the grand adventure.

Symbol: *Hair*, abundant and beautiful, represents spiritual development.

DEVOTED

Word Forms: devote, devotion, devotedly, devotedness

Definition: zealous or ardent in loyalty or affection; faithful

Too Far: fanatical

Comment: One is not devoted unless and until all one's doubts are removed. We use our powers of logic, intuition, sifting, sorting, organizing, belief, commitment, and finally faith before we allow ourselves to be enveloped in the fires of pure devotion.

Color: blue

DEVOUT

Word Forms: devouter, devoutest, devoutly, devoutness

Definitions: (**1**) expressing devotion or piety; very religious; (**2**) sincere; earnest; fervent; heartfelt

Synonyms: holy, reverent

DEXTEROUS

Word Forms: dexterity, dexterously, dexterousness

Definitions: (**1**) ready and expert in the use of the body or hands; skillful and active in manual employment; adroit; (**2**) having mental skill; expert; quick at inventing

Synonyms: artful, clever, apt

Symbol: a *juggler*

DIGNIFIED

Word Forms: dignify, dignifying, dignity, dignitary

Definitions: (**1**) worthiness; nobility; high repute; honor; esteem; (**2**) loftiness of appearance or manner; stateliness; (**3**) calm self-possession and self-respect

Color: violet

Symbol: *sun-shade* (Chinese)

Fiction: *Hermione,* in Shakespeare's *Winter's Tale*, is an example of "dignity without pride, love without passion, and tenderness without weakness."

DILIGENT

Word Forms: diligence, diligently, diligentness

Definitions: (**1**) steady in application; constant in effort or exertion to accomplish what is undertaken; assiduous; attentive; industrious; not idle or negligent; **(2)** done with care and constant effort; careful; painstaking

Synonyms: active, sedulous, laborious, persevering, indefatigable, unremitting, untiring

Quote:
Strive on with diligence.

—BUDDHA'S LAST WORDS

Symbol: *wings*

DIPLOMATIC

Word Forms: diplomat, diplomatist, diplomacy, diplomatically

Definition: tactful and clever in dealing with people; politic in conduct

Compatible Qualities: fair, open-minded

Comment: The diplomat that sticks only to small talk gets no respect and gets nothing done. The diplomat that cares only for his or her side to win will not win. The diplomat who is fair is valued.

DIRECT

Word Forms: directing, directive, directly

Definitions: **(1)** straight; not deviating; not roundabout; not interrupted; **(2)** straightforward; frank; not vague; **(3)** immediate; inevitable; consequential; **(4)** exact; complete

Proverb: You need not travel to the moon to get across the street.

DIRECTED

Word Forms: direction, director, directedness

Definitions: (1) guided, regulated, or managed; (2) knowing where you are going; having a clear purpose

DISCERNING

Word Forms: discern, discerned, discerner, discernible, discerningly, discernment

Definition: revealing insight and understanding; discriminating; capable of seeing, knowing, and judging; sharp-sighted; shrewd; astute

Quote:
The unaided human eye, under the best possible viewing conditions, comparing large areas of color, in good illumination, using both eyes, can distinguish 10,000,000 different color surfaces.
—1986 Guinness Book of World Records

Comment: It doesn't matter what some so-called expert says about it, you're going to decide for yourself anyway. You may open your ear a little bit wider if you happen to believe that the source has credentials, but even then you are going to sift it (the information) through your filters.

DISCIPLINED

Word Forms: discipline, disciplining, self-disciplined

Definitions: (1) training of the mental, moral, and physical powers by instruction, control, and exercise; (2) the result of training; self-control; orderly conduct

Synonyms: educate, drill, regulate, correct

Compatible Qualities: commitment, striving

Quotes:

Discipline is the bridge between thought and accomplishment . . . the bridge between inspiration and value achievement . . . the bridge between necessity and productivity.

—JIM ROHN

Seek freedom and become captive to your desires. Seek discipline and find your liberty.

—FRANK HERBERT, *Chapterhouse Dune*

Advice: What time of day are you the sharpest, most energetic, or most clear-headed? Are you a morning person or a late-night person? Don't fritter away this valuable time with mundane or routine tasks. Do the most difficult and important things at your optimum time.

Questions: What will it take? What must I do? Who must I become?

Symbol: the *yoke*

DISCREET

Word Forms: discretion, discreetly, discreetness

Definitions: (1) discernment or good judgment in conduct, mainly in speech; prudent; capable of preserving silence; cautious; (2) unpretentious; modest

Derivation: Old French, "prudent"; Latin, "to distinguish," "to discern"; to separate or to set apart from

Synonyms: circumspect, wary, careful

Familial Quality: perspicacity

Sayings:

Discretion is the better part of valor.

If you can't say anything nice, don't say anything at all.

Tip: Watch what you say. Project what effect it will have on the listeners and those who it may be about.

DISCRIMINATING

Word Forms: discriminate, discrimination, discriminative, discriminatory, discriminatingly

Definitions: (1) analytical; (2) discerning; perspicacious; (3) having excellent taste or judgment

Reflection: It is necessary to reevaluate periodically that which you hold to be true, particularly those things that are negative. When you come to understand that a previous belief is no longer what you now hold, let it go, but do not dismiss the whole category. I have known quite a few people who, after deciding that they did not believe in some of the precepts of the Catholic church, not only disassociated themselves with the offending concepts but with religion altogether. This is called throwing the baby out with the bathwater. One does need to discriminate, to evolve a greater understanding of reality, but this can be done surgically. Let go of the single outmoded concept and leave the remaining structure intact. Allow the space of lesser truth or error to be filled with greater truth. Keep your hope alive for a better understanding. Actively investigate superior ideas.

DISPORTING

Word Forms: disport, disported, disportment

Definition: playing; indulging in amusement; frolicsome

DISTINCTIVE

Word Forms: distinct, distinction, distinctively, distinctiveness

Definitions: (1) discriminating; differentiated; **(2)** possessing a quality, mark, or feature of difference; having that which makes or keeps something unique; **(3)** eminent; superior; famous; specially recognized or honored

Synonyms: discernment, rank, notable

DISTINGUISHED

Word Forms: distinguish, distinguishing

Definitions: (1) separated from others by superior or extraordinary qualities; eminent; noted; famous; celebrated; **(2)** having an air of distinction or dignity

Derivation: Latin, "to separate," "divide"

Synonyms: eminent, conspicuous, distinguished, celebrated, illustrious
   A person is *eminent* when they stand high as compared with those around them; *conspicuous* when they are in a position so as to be easily and generally seen and observed; *distinguished* when they have something which makes them stand apart from others in the public view; *celebrated* when they are widely spoken of with honor and respect; *illustrious* when their actions or achievements confer the highest dignity.

DIVERSE

Word Forms: diversify, diversion, diversely, diverseness

Definition: differing; different from itself; various; multiform

Derivation: Latin, "to turn in different directions"

Quote:
   Life—all life—is in the service of life. Necessary nutrients are made available to life *by* life in greater and greater richness as the diversity of life increases.
                              —FRANK HERBERT, *Dune*

Observation: Everybody needs something different.

Comment: We are all chasing it—the meaning of life, the reason for existence—down individually. In the end, we all come to the same conclusion, but it will have a million different spins on it—that's diversity; that's Divinity.

Symbol: *nature*

DIVINE

Word Forms: diviner, divinest, divinity, divines, divination, divinely, divineness

Definitions: (1) relating to or proceeding directly from God or a god; **(2)** heavenly; excellent in the highest degree; extraordinary; superb; supremely good

Prayers:
The word *divine* can be put in front of any of the qualities, depending upon which of the divine aspects you are striving for and wish to invoke.

Divine Wisdom, reveal Your Great Good.
Divine Silliness, grant me the spirit that understands things in the light of humor.
Divine Clarity, open my mind to Your pure view.

Comment: Reducing God to an *exclusive* Absolute separates the Divine Person to an infinite distance. It also makes everything less good. Elevating God as an *inclusive* Absolute allows for the most intimate and best friendship.

Symbol: The *meteorite* or any object that falls from heaven is a sacred symbol.

DOCILE

Word Forms: docility, docilely

Definitions: (1) teachable; easily instructed; (2) easily led or managed; tractable

Too Far: wimpy

Comment: When you are trying to learn something it is best if you are docile. I'm not talking about cowering in the face of a superior force. That is a different meaning. I'm talking about being attentive and easily instructed.

DOWN-TO-EARTH

Definition: practical; realistic; straightforward; earthy

Symbols: *four;* the *square;* the *cube*

DREAMING

Word Forms: dream, dreamlike, dreamed, dreamer, dreamy, dreamily, dreaminess

Definitions: (1) a state of mind marked by abstraction or release from common reality; reverie; (2) something notable for its beauty, excellence, or enjoyable quality; (3) a strongly desired goal or purpose; (4) something that fully satisfies a wish: an ideal

Quotes:
It may be those who do most, dream most.
—STEPHEN LEACOCK

Dream is the personalized myth, myth the depersonalized dream; both myth and dream are symbolic in the same general way of the dynamics of the psyche. But in the dream the forms are quirked by the peculiar troubles of the dreamer whereas in myth the problems and solutions shown are directly valid for all mankind.

—Joseph Campbell, *The Hero with a Thousand Faces*

If you can dream it, you can do it.

—Walt Disney

People who chase dreams are the most likely to catch them.

—from advertisement

If one advances confidently in the direction of his dreams, and endeavors to live the life which he had imagined, he will meet with a success unexpected in common hours.

—Henry David Thoreau, *On Walden Pond*

Parable:

Once, Chong Chou dreamt that he was a butterfly. A butterfly flittering and fluttering around, happy with himself, doing as he pleased. He did not know he was Chong Chou. But then he woke up, and there he was, solid and unmistakably Chong Chou. But he did not know if he was a butterfly dreaming that he was Chong Chou, or Chong Chou who was dreaming that he was a butterfly. Between Chong Chou and the butterfly, there must be some distinction. This is called the transformation of things.

—Lao Tzu

Reflection:

Dream versus Fact

Include in your dream the decision to do your best with what you've got. You've still got to look into your future with clarity, hope, faith, and courage but realize that these same qualities are keys for doing your best right *now*. As you are doing your best in the current situation, you are developing those qualities for the realization of your dream future. Without developing the appropriate qualities specific to your ambition, you will not be able to smoothly step into your dream.

There is a natural intuition that lets you know if you are capable of actualizing something. Unfortunately, there is a problem. This mechanism gets confused with the constricting reactions of fear. How do you separate your natural, positive knowing from the fear that keeps you from moving?

First, assess your outer world. As you do, remember and accept that you are responsible for *now* because of your decisions and choices from the past. Know what your current external realities are. Then visualize your ideal future. Then draw the curve that connects the now with the future. Compare it to the curve of where your present decisions are taking you. Then assess your inner world, especially your qualities of confidence, self-esteem, and faith. What qualities are you developing in your current reality? What qualities are needed to live your dream?

Admonition: It's important to be inspired by your heroes and yet remember that their dreams are different from yours. Being inspired by someone is different than beating yourself up for not measuring up.

Comments:
- Following your dream doesn't necessarily mean you're going to make a million dollars. It does mean that you're going to strive for what you consider to be your highest ideas and ideals. Also you may not be successful in the eyes of society if you follow your dream. If you do what you have decided and you were intended to do, you will experience happiness because you are pursuing your most enjoyable qualities.
- Don't miss out on your life. If you have a destiny, it is greater than you are, and if you do not live up to it in your own mind, then you will feel incomplete and dissatisfied.

Questions: What will you most be remembered for when you die? Will you have accomplished your fondest dreams?

Symbol: a *stormy sea*

Fiction: Sleeping Beauty in Tennyson's *The Dream*

DRIVE

Word Forms: driver, driven, driving, drivable

Definitions: (1) an inner urge that prompts activity directed toward the satisfying of a basic instinctive need; **(2)** vigorously focused toward a goal or objective; **(3)** energy and initiative; motivation; push

Tip: A lot of drive is just sticking with it.

DULCET

Word Forms: dulce, dulcetly, dulcify

Definitions: (1) sweet to the ear; melodious; harmonious; **(2)** sweet or pleasing to the mind; **(3)** pleasant or agreeable to the eye or the feelings; soothing

DURABLE

Word Forms: durability, durably, durableness

Definitions: (1) lasting in spite of hard wear or frequent use; **(2)** capable of continual use; enduring; stable

Synonym: permanent

Comment: Let difficulty roll off of your thick skin. One of the reasons that people live to a ripe old age is their ability to take things in stride. Accept the scrapes, do what you can about them, and then let them go.

DUTIFUL

Word Forms: duty, dutifully, dutifulness

Definitions: (1) performing the tasks expected or required; respectful; obedient; **(2)** proceeding from or expressive of a sense of obligation

Consequential Quality: loyalty

Quote:
> Duty does not have to be dull. Love can make it beautiful and fill it with life.
>
> —THOMAS MERTON

Symbol: the *ox*

Fiction: *Javert*, a character in Victor Hugo's *Les Misérables*, is the personification of duty and devotion.

DYNAMIC

Word Forms: dynamics, dynamism, dynamist

Definitions: (1) exhibiting energy or power in motion; involving or causing energy; **(2)** active; vigorous; forceful; **(3)** relating to or tending toward change or growth

Color: pure red

Symbol: the *ocean*

EAGER

Word Forms: eagerly, eagerness

Definition: characterized by keen or enthusiastic desire or interest; longing with anticipation; expectant

Derivation: Latin, "sharp," "keen"

Synonyms: earnest, fervent, zealous, vehement, intense, fervid

Quote:
> Expect your every need to be met, expect the answer to every problem, expect abundance on every level, expect to grow spiritually.
>
> —EILEEN CADDY

EARNEST

Word Forms: earnestly, earnestness

Definitions: (**1**) serious and intense; zealous and sincere; deeply convinced; not joking or playful; sincere; (**2**) focused; fixed; (**3**) important; not trivial

Derivation: German, "zeal," "vigor"

Synonyms: eager, urgent, fervent, warm

Kindred Qualities: humor, light

EASYGOING

Word Forms: easy, easygoingness

Definitions: (**1**) inclined to take matters in an unworried, unhurried, relaxed way; good-natured; not strenuous or agitated; (**2**) going at an effortless pace; placid

How to Live This Quality Today: You're going like a mad thing, but there are times that circumstances dictate that you cannot be hurried. At those times mellow into the easier pace. When you're waiting for the toast to pop up, when you're in an elevator, when you're on hold on the phone, you can take the time to relax or you can use it to prepare for what comes next. Either way, easy does it.

Symbol: a *hammock*

EBULLIENT

Word Forms: ebullience, ebullition, ebulliently

Definition: overflowing with enthusiasm; high-spirited; showing much exuberance or exhilaration

ECLECTIC

Word Form: eclectically

Definitions: (1) selecting or choosing from various systems or methodologies, not following any one strategy; **(2)** made up of elements selected from various sources <an *eclectic* philosophy>

Derivation: Greek, "to select," "pick out"

ECONOMICAL

Word Forms: economy, economic, economics, economist, economize, economically

Definitions: (1) careful, efficient, and prudent regarding the use of resources; thrifty; **(2)** operating with little waste or at a savings

Quote:
"All things are good in their way," said Shaggy, "but we may have too much of any good thing. And I have noticed that the value of anything depends upon how scarce it is, and how difficult it is to obtain."
—L. FRANK BAUM, *Tik-Tok of Oz*

Comment: You spend a dollar and get some bread. You eat the bread, use its energy, and then it is gone. You spend ten dollars on some gasoline, use its energy, and then it is gone. You spend ten thousand dollars on a car, use it for some years, and then it is gone. They say that the sun will finally burn out in a few billion years—then it will be gone.

On the other hand, the economy of a quality is such that as you use it, it regenerates itself and actually builds more substance. The only way to waste it is to *not* use it.

ECSTATIC

Word Forms: ecstasy, ecstatically

Definitions: (1) overjoyed; rapturous; experiencing a feeling of delight that arrests the whole mind and emotions; (2) in a state of being over-powered with joyous emotion; the condition of being beside oneself with feeling; (3) in a trance, especially one resulting from religious fervor

Derivation: from the Greek to describe a being put out of its place, "distraction," "trance"

Symbol: *jumping*

EDUCATED

Word Forms: educate, educating, education, educative, educator, educatedly, educatedness, self-educated

Definitions: (1) instructed; furnished with knowledge or principles; trained; disciplined; (2) having a cultivated mind, speech, or manner

Quotes:
What is defeat? Nothing but education, nothing but the first step toward something better.
—WENDELL PHILLIPS

The ultimate goal of the educational system is to shift to the individual the burden of pursuing their [own] education.
—JOHN W. GARDNER

What greater or better gift than to educate our youth.
—CICERO

Color: green

Symbol: the *cap and gown*

EFFECTIVE

Word Forms: effect, effectivity, effectual, efficacy, efficacious, effectively, effectiveness

Definitions: **(1)** producing a definite, decisive, or desired result; **(2)** operative; active; in effect; **(3)** making a striking impression; impressive

Synonyms: influential, forcible, potent, conclusive, convincing

Efficient versus Effective

Efficient means getting things done with the least amount of effort and time. *Effective* is used regarding the accomplishment of things, getting something done no matter if it's done efficiently or not.

Quote:
Just think of the advantage that the first warm-blooded mammal would have had at night, all the reptiles cooled down to somnolence unable to defend themselves. And all because of an abnormally inefficient animal (by cold-blooded standards!) that wasted energy by metabolizing food when it wasn't needed for movement. But this kept body temperature up and so the animal was pleasantly surprised by all the sleepy prey he encountered, which more than made up for all the wasted energy. The next time that you hear an evolutionary argument based on efficiency, remember those profligate warm-blooded animals.
—WILLIAM H. CALVIN, *The River That Flows Uphill*

EFFERVESCENT

Word Forms: effervesce, effervescence, effervescently

Definition: lively and high-spirited; vivacious; exuberant

EFFICIENT

Word Forms: efficiency, efficiencies, efficiently

Definition: directly producing the desired effect or result with a minimum of effort, expense, or waste; causative; working well; competent; able; capable
  See also: *Effective*

Quote:
  People, like everything else, work better in parallel than they do in series. . . . When things are organized socialistically in a bureaucratic series, any increase in complexity increases the probability of failure. But when they're organized in a free-enterprise parallel, an increase in complexity becomes an increase in diversity more capable of responding to *Dynamic Quality,* and thus an increase of the probability of success.
                                        —ROBERT M. PIRSIG, *Lila*

ELASTIC

Word Forms: elasticity, elastically

Definitions: (1) adjusting readily to fit the circumstances; flexible; (2) recovering quickly from emotional or physical distress; resilient; (3) receptive to new ideas; adaptable

ELATED

Word Forms: elate, elation, elatedly, elatedness

Definition: in high spirits; proud or happy; joyful; jubilant

Synonyms: exalted, delighted, overjoyed, exultant

ELECTRIFYING

Word Forms: electric, electrification, electrified, electrify, electrifiable

Definition: refers to one who causes sudden and intense excitement, arouses people to intense activity, startles or surprises, especially by doing something very inspiring or intensely interesting; thrilling

Quote:
Thunder is good. Thunder is impressive. But it is lightning that does the work.
—MARK TWAIN

Symbol: A *lightning bolt*. Lightning flashes can travel upward at 87,000 miles per second and generate 30,000°C (more than five times the temperature of the surface of the sun).

ELEGANT

Word Forms: elegance, elegantly

Definitions: (1) dignified richness and grace in manner, dress, design, or style; luxurious in a restrained, tasteful manner; (2) characterized by a sense of propriety to refinement; fastidious in manners and tastes; (3) excellent; fine; first-rate

EMERGING

Word Forms: emerge, emergence, emergent

Definitions: (1) coming forth from concealment or obscurity; appearing; coming into view; becoming visible, apparent, or known; (2) coming into being through evolution

Derivation: Latin, "to rise out," "rise up"

Symbol: a *cocoon*

EMINENT

Word Forms: eminence, eminently

Definitions: (1) standing high by comparison with others; renowned; **(2)** outstanding; remarkable; noteworthy; greatest; utmost
　See also: *Distinguished*

Synonyms: famous, illustrious, celebrated, noted, exalted

EMPATHETIC

Word Forms: empathic, empathy, empathize, empathetically

Definition: characterized by understanding, being aware of, being sensitive to, and vicariously experiencing the feelings, thoughts, and experience of another of either the past or present without having the feelings, thoughts, and experience fully communicated in an objectively explicit manner

Quote:
　Being able to feel the pain of others is a strength. It gives us incentive to avoid causing pain.
　　　　—Morgan Llywelyn, *BARD, The Odyssey of the Irish*

ENAMORING

Word Forms: amour, enamor, enamored

Definition: filling with love and desire; charming; captivating; fascinating

ENCHANTING

Word Forms: enchant, enchanted, enchantment, enchantingly

Definitions: (1) charming; irresistibly attractive; (2) bewitching; fascinating

Synonyms: entrancing, captivating, enrapturing, ravishing

Compatible Quality: trusting

ENCOURAGING

Word Forms: encourage, encouraged, encouragement, encourager, encouragingly

Definitions: (1) inspiring with courage, hope, and confidence; inspiriting; (2) hope for success; to spur on; stimulate

Synonyms: cheering, animating, emboldening

ENDEARING

Word Forms: dear, endear, endearment, endearingly

Definitions: (1) cherished or beloved; binding by ties of affection and love; (2) manifesting tender emotion; caressing

ENDEAVORING

Word Forms: endeavor, endeavored

Definition: trying hard; exerting effort; making an earnest attempt; striving

Quote:
The young fear failure. The middle-aged have come to doubt success. The elderly know both failure and success are false; it is effort alone that counts.

—DR. GEORGE SHEEHAN

Legend: the search for the *Holy Grail*

ENDURING

Word Forms: endure, enduringly, enduringness

Definitions: (1) having the capacity for remaining or continuing; durable; that which cannot be destroyed; **(2)** long-suffering; **(3)** diligent; **(4)** holding out against hardship; tolerant; unyielding

Symbols: *Saturn* (endurance); a long-distance *runner*

ENERGETIC

Word Forms: energy, energies, energize, energetically, energetical

Definition: distinguished by or exhibiting power; operating with force, vigor, and effect; spirited; efficacious

Too Far: manic, hyperactive

Quote:
I know of no other act in the local or immediate universe that requires more energy (I didn't say effort) than the act of letting go.

—JERRY DOWNS

Tip: Have projects that you like to do *and* get enough sleep.

Advice: Although it is tempting to feel anger, bitterness, or frustration when you have been wronged, you can use that energy for good. Resolve to feel pity rather than bitterness; turn the great swirl of anger into ideas of how to help and the determination to do so. If you do help the poor, sick soul who hurt you, you will become better acquainted with compassion.

If you cannot bring yourself to do anything else, at least you can pray for the person—and for yourself.

Color: orange

Symbols: the *sun, fire;* the *snake; hair*

ENGAGING

Word Forms: engage, engagingly, engagingness

Definition: winning; attractive; to draw attention or affection; pleasing

Compatible Quality: charming

ENJOYING

Word Forms: enjoy, enjoyed, enjoyable, enjoyer, enjoyment

Definition: feeling or perceiving with pleasure or satisfaction; relishing

Consideration: After the objective has been achieved, you feel good about what you have done. But before and during the process, you worry and sweat and hope. But does it feel like success while you are going through it? If you know you are going to do it, you might as well enjoy the doing of it.

ENLIGHTENED

Word Forms: enlighten, enlightening, enlightenment, enlightener

Definitions: (1) having a clearer view; illuminated; instructed; able to see or comprehend truth; free from ignorance, prejudice, or superstition; **(2)** informed; clear as to facts, meanings, values, or intentions

Tip: Whether you're enlightened or not enlightened may be relative. In either case, focusing on the positive qualities will get you there or will continue you on your way.

Colors: yellow, violet

Symbol: the *crown*

ENTERPRISING

Word Forms: enterprise, enterpriser, enterprisingly

Definition: showing an independent, energetic spirit and a readiness to commit to or experiment with; will attempt great or untried schemes; full of energy and initiative; resolute; active

How to Live This Quality Today: Write down your good ideas.

Color: red

ENTERTAINING

Word Forms: entertain, entertainment, entertainingly, entertainingness

Definition: pleasing; amusing; diverting; interesting

ENTHUSIASTIC

Word Forms: enthuse, enthusiasm, enthusiast, enthusiastically

Definitions: (1) possessing intense or eager interest, zeal, fervor; **(2)** having a strong excitement of feeling, ardor

Derivation: from the Greek, meaning "possessed by a god," "supernatural inspiration"

Consideration: Sometimes you don't get the joy of enthusiasm from doing a task, all you get is the doing of it.

Observation: When you first start something big or important you most probably have just broken through the fears of your own negative "what if's," those oppressive possibilities that, until now, have prevented you from positive action. When you overcome this swamp of negative potential pitfalls, you have risen your sight to the open blue sky, to the bright sunshine of success. Now you are given the gift of enthusiasm to start you on your way. You have taken the first decisive steps. You have faced what surely seems to be a difficult yet reasonable reality and transformed your vision to believe an optimistic possibility. You have decided to create your own future.

The problem is that the swamp really does exist. You lack the knowledge and experience. There are others willing to take advantage or who are simply looking for a free ride and fail to fulfill their promises. You may have to go north in order to eventually go south. You will most assuredly have to make compromises and unpleasant promises of your own.

The trick is to accept all of these difficulties with maturity and to reinvigorate your enthusiasm occasionally by raising your head to once again look at the good that the accomplishing and the attaining of the goal will achieve.

Comment: Enthusiasm is a hard quality to keep juiced. You eventually run out of energy. Keeping up your health helps. Connecting yourself with what is motivating, personally and altruistically, helps. You are working on something that is valuable, and that value infuses you with the enthusiasm you need to proceed.

Color: orange

ENTICING

Word Forms: entice, enticed, enticement, enticingly

Definition: alluring; lead on by exciting hope of reward or pleasure; tempting

ENTRANCING

Word Forms: entrance, entranced, entrancement

Definition: inspiring ecstasy; enrapturous; delightful; charming; enchanting

ENTREPRENEURIAL

Word Forms: entrepreneur, entrepreneurship

Definition: one who organizes, manages, and assumes the risks of a business or enterprise

Compatible Qualities: risk taker, shrewd

EQUANIMOUS

Word Form: equanimity

Definition: characterized by an evenness of mind, especially under stress; calm; composed; having a mild disposition; balanced
    See also: *Stress Hardy*

EQUITABLE

Word Forms: equal, equity, equitability, equitably, equitableness

Definition: possessing or exhibiting fairness; equal in regard to the rights of persons; distributing honest justice; giving each person their due; assigning what law or justice demands; impartial

Synonym: reasonable

Symbol: *Wyoming*, the equality state

Quotes:

[Dorothy:] "I cannot see how there can be more than one King or Queen in any one country, for were these all rulers, no one could tell who was Master."

One of the Kings who stood near and overheard this remark turned to her and said: "One who is Master of himself is always a King, if only to himself. In this favored land all Kings and Queens are equal, and it is our privilege to bow before one supreme ruler—the Private Citizen."

—L. FRANK BAUM, *Tik-Tok of Oz*

Let us be very clear on this matter: if we condemn people to inequality in our society, we also condemn them to inequality in our economy.

—LYNDON B. JOHNSON

ERUDITE

Word Forms: erudition, eruditely, eruditeness

Definition: having extensive knowledge; learned; well-read; scholarly

Color: yellow

ESSENTIAL

Word Forms: essence, essentially, essentialness, essentiality

Definitions: **(1)** the intrinsic, fundamental nature of something; basic; **(2)** absolute; complete; perfect; pure; **(3)** necessary to make a thing what it is; indispensable; requisite; vital; inherent

Affirmation: I am essential.

ESTEEMED

Word Forms: esteem, esteeming

Definition: having a high value; given a high regard or a favorable opinion; prized

Synonyms: appreciated, respected, revered

ETHICAL

Word Forms: ethics, ethicality, ethically, ethicalness

Definitions: (1) pertaining to or dealing with the principles of morality; **(2)** being in accordance with the rules or standards for right conduct or practice; faithful to the standards of a profession

ETIQUETTE

Definition: the forms, manners, and ceremonies established by convention as acceptable or required in society, in a profession, or in official life; mannerly

Comment: This is one of the qualities that involves the doing as well as the not doing. Etiquette includes not doing certain things in public as well as doing other things when appropriate.

EUPHORIC

Word Forms: euphoria, euphoriant, euphorically

Definition: experiencing a strong feeling of well-being, relaxation, happiness, and confidence

Derivation: From the Greek, meaning "the power of bearing easily"

Observation: The greatest euphoria is when you are letting pure love pass through you.

EVENHANDED

Word Forms: evenhandedly, evenhandedness

Definition: fair; treating all alike; impartial; equitable; just

EVEN-TEMPERED

Definition: placid; calm; not quickly angered, excited, or disturbed

Tip: Count to ten when you feel anger beginning to rise. It's an old trick but it works if you have a good intention.

EVOLVING

Word Forms: evolve, evolved, evolution, evolvable, evolvement

Definitions: (1) reaching a highly developed state by a process of growth and change; developing gradually; (2) unfolding; becoming disclosed; (3) exhibiting creativity along the time/space continuum; (4) freeing up, giving off, or emitting

Note: Definition 4 is "freeing up, giving off, or emitting." One way to evolve the self is by getting rid of that which is not needed. Conversely, as you radiate love and its positive manifestations, your actions result in your evolution.

Saying: The ultimate "out there" is your death. Then you are *really* out there. During this life you are still on a familiar plane, you remember where you are, you see where you are. There is a saying that we came up with on a trip in the Grand Canyon. It applies to death as well as any event that needs to be lived.

> *First you come to it.*
> *Then you go through it.*
> *Then you are on the other side.*

Even when you really are on the other side of this physical existence, you've still got the same truth. You first came to it (the fact that you were going to die), and you've gone through it (the portal of death), and you find yourself on the other side. You have to accept and encompass the fact that you have died. You must go through with doing the next thing and adapting to your new situation.

Beyond death, in the next phase of existence, you are given the next range of capacity—a new mind, a new body, a new environment, and, therefore, new attainment possibilities.

Symbols: the *fossil; steps;* a *ladder;* a *zigzag;* the *sword;* the *ziggurat* or *minaret*

EXACT

Word Forms: exacting, exactitude, exactly, exactness

Definitions: **(1)** correct; accurate; precise; adjusted; true; actual; **(2)** methodical; careful, not negligent; observing strict method, rule, or order; **(3)** meticulous; definite; precisely thought out or stated

Synonym: punctual

Familial Quality: conscientious

Saying: *ad unguem* (Latin): "to the fingernail"; "to a nicety"; "exactly" (from the use of the fingernail to test the smoothness of marble)

EXCELLENT

Word Forms: excel, excellence, excellently

Definition: being of the very best quality; exceptionally good; first-class; of great worth; superior; admirable

Synonyms: transcendent, prime, sterling, worthy, choice

EXCEPTIONAL

Word Forms: exception, exceptionality, exceptionally, exceptionalness

Definitions: (1) out of the ordinary; uncommon; rare; extraordinary; **(2)** unusually excellent; superior

EXCITING

Word Forms: excite, excited, excitement, excitingly

Definition: calling or stimulating to action; producing excitement; arousing keen interest; stirring; thrilling

Synonyms: fiery, exhilarating, invigorating

EXEMPLARY

Word Forms: exemplar, exemplarity, exemplarily, exemplariness

Definition: serving as a worthy model or example; commendable

Synonyms: laudable, praiseworthy, honorable, meritorious, excellent

EXHAUSTIVE

Word Forms: exhaust, exhaustively, exhaustiveness

Definition: testing all possibilities or considering all elements; leaving nothing out; complete; thorough

EXOTIC

Word Forms: exoticism, exotica, exotically, exoticness

Definition: having the charm or fascination of the unfamiliar; strangely beautiful; enticing

Experience: To be recognized as exotic, go someplace where you are the only one of your kind. To feel exotic, realize that you are unique.

EXPANDING

Word Forms: expand, expanded, expandable, expander

Definitions: (1) opening; spreading; unfolding; (2) enlarging in range or scope; becoming more comprehensive; developing in detail

Synonyms: diffusing, dilating, swelling, extending, amplifying

Quote:
> The great thing in this world is not so much where we stand as in what direction we are moving.
> —OLIVER WENDELL HOLMES

Visualization: There was a TV show called "Bonanza" that opened with a map being consumed by fire. It spread from the center out. I have that image as a metaphor of our expanding consciousness, of our own realization of our unfolding personality.

EXPEDITIOUS

Word Forms: expedition, expeditiously, expeditiousness

Definition: done with efficiency; speedy; prompt; quick

Derivation: Latin, "ready for action"

Kindred Quality: inventive

How to Live This Quality Today: Set yourself a job. Figure out how long it will take, and then do it in half the time.

EXPERIENCED

Word Forms: experience, experiencing, experiential, experientially

Definition: made skillful or wise through observation of or participation in an activity; practiced

Sayings:
Experto credite (Latin): "Believe one who has had experience."

There is *nothing* that will substitute for experience.

> Experience *can be attained if you . . .*
> *Care more than others think is wise;*
> *Risk more than others think is safe;*
> *Dream more than others think is practical;*
> *Expect more than others think is possible;*
> *Live on planet earth.*

Quote:
Youth is wholly experimental.

—ROBERT LOUIS STEVENSON

Affirmation: By forgiveness I have set myself free from the past. I now

face the present and the future with wisdom, security, and positive anticipation.

Inspirations:
- Ultimately, the only value of the past is what it has made you today.
  The value of your outer experiences is what they have made you
  inside.
- It is through experience that you will become someone who you
  desire to be, who you long to be, who you must be.
- God is a participant on all sides. He gets to experience what you
  choose to experience, and He gets to be the force that moves reality
  after you have chosen it. Then He gets to experience your experience
  of your actions.

Reflection: As you look back, do so with the realization that you have
accomplished things, experienced realities, and incorporated qualities into
your being. If you look into your past with worry, regret, sorrow, criticism,
hostility, or resentment, you are holding those experiences that were
unpleasant in a grip that does not free you to learn their lessons and go on.
Holding on to the negative affects your health and attitude. It is natural to
wish, sometimes very strongly if the mistake was a big one, that you had
lived those moments differently. Go with those feelings in order to forgive
yourself and possibly the others involved, and also to process the experience so that you will learn and become a new person for the future. But
do not dwell and crystallize the negative in your soul. If you just can't
seem to get a handle on what would have been the ideal action or reaction,
then just let it go, with the sure knowledge that you will be given (or give
yourself) the opportunity to experience the lesson in the future.

Considerations:
- Qualities, personality, behavior, thought, and feelings are observable
  "facts." They are observable objectively and subjectively. Therefore
  they are experiential. When something has such wide general agreement, it is considered to exist. It can be "proven" to exist with the
  most basic assumptions. "I think, therefore I am" is one famous
  statement. It might also be said as, "I am because I experience."

  The argument of physics—only that which can be measured
  exists—is only valid on the physical level. Even the scientific
  method must rely on nonphysical qualities to be considered valid.
  Would any scientist accept a theory that was not *consistent?* Or a sci-

entist that was not *honest?* Therefore, consistency and honesty and a multitude of nonphysical qualities overlay material reality.

- The only way to get through it is to go through it. If you have to get through something, and if you have to go through a contortion to do it, then it makes sense to go through that contortion. Otherwise you'll be stuck where you are until you figure out how to go through it without the contortion or acquire the necessary wherewithal to experience the contortion.
- Consider the chemistry of the body, the food you eat, your mental states and genetic patterns. All of these represent modifiers to your experience.
- One is the product of both external and internal experience. Example: You may be the beneficiary of either an affluent or impoverished upbringing. This is external. Your adult attitude—snobbish, altruistic, bitter, or nurturing—has just as much to do with your internal experience as your external.

  You could have been abused and end up abusive or end up sensitive and patient. You are prejudiced or you have a greater sense of justice—both reactions are in people who have felt prejudice against them. The external characteristics and the external situations that come to you are molding or modifying factors in your possible behavioral patterns. Sociological studies state the probabilities.

  In sociology, a particular set of circumstances occur, and the majority respond a certain way. Those may be true and good studies but the *possibility* does not necessarily make it the *probability.* The individual is just as complex as the group. The individual has control over personal choice. The individual can be overcome by the circumstances or overcome them.

Admonition: You may have a tendency to want to repeat really great experiences. Don't try to recreate the experience; you can't do it. In truth, what really created the experience in the first place was your willingness to let go of the past and hold a new experience.

Comments:
- Although the mind moves through the realms of understanding relatively quickly, it is the experience of day-to-day living that really sinks in. These experiences are how we describe our growth. The thought process may be swift but it takes time to grow.
- Experience is the most important element of growth. Choose your

experiences to open your possibilities. It is okay if they are difficult. Don't just stay with what you're used to because it's comfortable. Move out into new experiences in a prepared way, but also with curiosity and courage.

- Except for the fact that we all got here that way, nobody would believe our method of birth. My point is that we accept the most incredible things as long as we can experience them. The aspiring and acquiring of qualities is the same thing. The proof of knowing as fact, through experience, is infallible.

Exercise: Look at the choices you made that have led to the experiences that you have lived. Make a distinction between what you have chosen to experience versus what you have experienced because of some outside influence. Then look at the choices that you have made because of your experiences. You control what happens to you by your choices. You control how it happens to you by your attitudes.

EXPERT

Word Forms: expertise, expertly, expertness

Definition: very skilled; trained and knowledgeable in some field

Synonyms: adroit, clever, dexterous, proficient, adept, versed, able

Advice: Initially, modeling your actions after someone you admire gives you the courage to go out on a limb. Your imagination conjures up a successful outcome. Choices are made and actions taken. Then, once you are committed, you take over.

EXPLORATIVE

Word Forms: explore, exploration, exploratory, exploratively

Definitions: (1) in the act of exploring or looking into closely; meticulous search; strict or careful examination; **(2)** willing to travel for purposes of discovery into regions previously unknown or little known

Familial Qualities: adventuresome, curious

Consequential Qualities: experienced, knowledgeable

EXPRESSIVE

Word Forms: express, expression, expressively, expressiveness, self-expressive

Definitions: (1) possessing the ability to keenly represent one's inner thoughts or feelings in words or manners; **(2)** significant; meaningful; full of knowing <an *expressive* nod>

Familial Qualities: communicative, entertaining

EXQUISITE

Word Forms: exquisitely, exquisiteness

Definitions: (1) very lovely; extraordinarily fine; delicately beautiful; appealingly distinctive; dainty; **(2)** carefully done or elaborately made; unique excellence of execution; **(3)** highest quality; admirable; accomplished; perfected; **(4)** highly sensitive; keenly discriminating; fastidious

Synonyms: choice, consummate, refined, matchless

EXTEMPORANEOUS

Word Forms: extemporary, extempore, extemporization, extemporize, extemporaneously, extemporaneousness

Definitions: (1) composed, performed, or uttered offhand, without previous study or preparation; unpremeditated; impromptu; **(2)** adept at speaking without preparation; **(3)** made for the occasion; improvised

Derivation: Latin, "out of the time," "at the moment"

Admonition: When speaking extemporaneously, speak from the heart and project the consequences of your words.

EXTRAORDINARY

Word Forms: extraordinarily, extraordinariness

Definition: going beyond what is usual, regular, or customary

Derivation: It is interesting that this word is made by combining two words that by themselves would not be considered anything special: *extra* and *ordinary*. Put them together, add a personality, and you do get someone truly special.

EXTROVERTED

Word Forms: extrovert, extravert, extraverted, extroversion, extraversion, extroversive, extrovertive, extrovertively

Definitions: (1) the act or habit of being predominantly concerned with and obtaining gratification from what is outside the self; **(2)** friendly; uninhibited; gregarious; exuberant

Kindred Qualities: courteous, sensitive

EXUBERANT

Word Forms: exuberance, exuberantly, exuberate

Definitions: (1) overflowing; superabundant; lavish; effusive; **(2)** abounding in high spirits and vitality; full of joy and vigor

Synonyms: copious, plenty, plentitude

Too Far: rambunctious

FABULOUS

Word Forms: fabulously, fabulousness

Definitions: (1) almost impossible to believe; incredible; astonishing; **(2)** exceptionally good or unusual; marvelous; superb; exceedingly great; wonderful

Derivation: Latin, "celebrated in fable," "legendary"

Symbol: the *dragon*

FAIR

Word Forms: fairness, fairly, fairer, fairest, faired, fairing, fair-haired, fair and square, fair-minded, fair play

Definitions: (1) pleasing to the eye or mind, especially because of fresh, charming, or flawless qualities; lovely; beautiful; **(2)** clean; pure; free from anything that might impair the appearance, quality, or character; attractive; **(3)** open; frank; honest; just; equitable; impartial; **(4)** civil; pleasant and courteous

Synonyms: reasonable, clear, candid, unprejudiced

Comment: Every circumstance cannot be fair, but if all parties enter a situation with a fairness of mind, then they will have a better chance of ending up with a satisfactory outcome for all. Take into consideration not only your concern for your interest but also a healthy concern for the other person's interest.

FAITH

Word Forms: faiths, faithful

Definitions: (1) possessing complete trust, confidence, or reliance on a person, statement, thing, or deity as trustworthy; (2) faithfulness; fidelity; loyalty; allegiance

Synonyms: belief, credence, conviction

Compatible Quality: trust

Familial Qualities: innocent, open

Consequential Quality: loyalty

Too Far: If you take faith too far from the practical qualities, you will believe that all problems have solutions and that nothing is beyond your reach. If you take practical too far you will be blind to the richness of creative possibilities.

Sayings:
Gardez la foi (French): "Keep the faith."

God helps those who help themselves.

Quotes:
Faith is something that anybody in their right mind would not believe in.
—ARCHIE BUNKER

Faith is nothing more than the conscious choice of the God within.
—GANDHI

DORIS: It's not a question of faith it's just common sense.

FRED: Faith is believing in things when common sense tells you not to. Don't you see it's not just Kris [Kringle] that's on trial, it's everything he stands for. It's kindness and joy and love and all the other intangibles.

DORIS: Oh, Fred, you're talking like a child. You're living in a realistic world and those *lovely intangibles* of yours are attractive but not worth very much. You don't get ahead that way.

FRED: That all depends on what you call "getting ahead." Evidently you and I have different definitions.

DORIS: Oh, these last few days we've talked about some wonderful plans. Then you go on an idealistic binge. You give up your job. You throw away your security and you expect me to be happy about it.

FRED: Yes, I guess I expected too much. Look, Doris, someday you're going to find that your way of facing this realistic world just doesn't work and when you do, don't overlook those *lovely intangibles*. You'll discover they are the only things that are worthwhile.

—*Miracle on 34th Street* (1947)

Parable: There is the old story (Persian) of a thief who was to be executed. As he was being taken away, he proposed a bargain with the king: In one year he would teach the king's favorite horse to sing hymns. The king agreed!

Later, the other prisoners watched the thief singing to the horse and mocked him. "You will not succeed," they told him. "No one could." But the thief was not worried. He told them, "I have a year, and who knows what might happen in that time? The king might die. The horse might die. I might die. And perhaps the horse will learn to sing."

Prayer:

My Lord God, I have no idea where I am going. I do not see the road ahead of me. I cannot know for certain where it will end. Nor do I really know myself, and the fact that I think I am following Your will does not mean that I am actually doing so. But I believe that the desire to please You does in fact please You. And I hope I have that desire in all that I am doing. I hope that I will never do anything apart from that desire. And I know that if I do this You will lead me by the right road, though I may know nothing about it. Therefore I will trust You always, though I may seem to be lost and in the shadow of death. I will not fear, for You are ever with me and You will never leave me to face my perils alone.

—THOMAS MERTON

Reflection: Faith is the answer to doubt. When you are mistaken, criticized, abused physically or emotionally, it is natural to second-guess yourself, but go back to what you *know*. You may not understand intellectually all of the details, but you do know in your gut some very clear and unarguable facts. Make sure that those facts are flexible enough to fit any situation, and are fair enough to fit any person. Look at the qualities involved. Are you taking into consideration compassion and communication along with power and courage?

If you look back later, with a more mature overview, and understand that you were wrong, can you at least be able to say that you were sincere? And since you see things differently, you can do better next time. You can also make a point of letting other people know what you learned in the hope that they will learn the lesson without so much pain. But mostly, you can achieve by *being,* by exemplifying the new you that knows by fact, experience, and faith more than you knew before, because you *are* more than you were before.

Consideration: Consider the awesomeness of Christ on the cross. Experiencing incredible physical pain and outrageous moral and political injustice, in the face of what anyone would call obvious failure, his character was still gentle and merciful. His faith was so clear; he knew how things really could be, should be, and would be. Even in this incredible situation, he just continued to be himself. He made sure his mother would be taken care of by John. He made sure to forgive his killers. He comforted the thief on the cross next to him. He also decided not to use his superhuman powers. He had lived as a man and would die as a man. When love is your nature, you have to be loving.

Advice: People will sometimes try to discourage you. This is the time to hold on to what you sincerely believe is right. This difficulty is the fire that helps you to know the essential substance of your faith.

Admonitions:
- Have the faith to do the next necessary thing.
- Don't let the facts get in the way of your faith. The situation may not be the best, but that is no reason to believe that it will always remain

so. Have faith and know in your heart that resolution, harmony, and growth are inherent.

If the situation is terrific, that is no reason to forget that you deserve it. Appreciate the experience as it is happening.

Comments:
- Faith in the survival of supreme values is the core of personal survival. If you have faith in and therefore bring supreme values into your being, you and them will thrive. Faith tells you that supreme values will survive and if you cannot be separated from them, then you will survive with them.

  Before you become a quality you don't know its significance, but you believe that being that quality will be worth it. You are staking your existence on an assumed fact. That is faith.
- Emotional feeling helps one believe in something. But faith goes deeper—down to the center of knowing. You may believe in a political leader today, but next month your belief has shifted because of subsequent events. Emotion can be washed away with the next flood of experience. But faith is the rock solid foundation. Faith is the riverbed, belief is the water, emotion is the motion of the water.
- Faith is the natural state of acceptance of a child's mind. From this point of openness the child continually encounters those experiences of conflict that are the initial and cumulative alterations in this faith characteristic. Taking the continuity of these childhood experiences and reactions as a unit, we see the growth of self-identity and how the person subsequently relates to and copes with his or her particular problems.
- It is "unreasonable" during the hard times to have faith, but if you have faith then, you are acquiring a deeper level of faith than when things are going well.

Experience: The experience of being reborn happens to those who make the supreme decision to align with a higher reality.

Colors: blue, red, white

Symbols: the *feather;* the *shield*

FAITHFUL

Word Forms: faithfully, faithfulness

Definition: firmly adhering to duty; exhibiting true fidelity; loyal; true to allegiance; constant in the performance of duties or services; honest; conscientious

Synonyms: consistent, staunch, incorruptible

Motto:
Semper Fidelis (Latin): "Always faithful"

—U.S. Marine Corps

Symbol: the *dog*

Fiction: *Abdiel*, an angel in Milton's *Paradise Lost,* was faithful during the Satanic default—"faithful found among the faithless."

FAMILIAL

Word Forms: family, familiar

Definition: pertaining to or characteristic of a family

Consideration: The family is the basic unit of society, then comes the clan, tribe, state, and nation. Once we all see that we are all of the same family, we will have a chance for world peace.

Symbols: the *chain;* the *Ruby Slippers* (which were silver in the original written version) that Dorothy of Kansas wore in *The Wizard of Oz* when she declared, "There's no place like home."

FAMOUS

Word Forms: fame, famously, famousness

Definitions: (1) widely known; celebrated; renowned; distinguished; **(2)** honored for achievement; eminent

Synonyms: illustrious, conspicuous, noted, prominent

Kindred Quality: Humility. You need to keep your ego in check and accept your fame with an appropriate measure of humility.

Compatible Qualities: self-acceptance, success

Reflection: A person who is not famous will not be given as much credit for brilliance or erudition as one studied in and labeled as an expert in his or her field, even though the unknown person may say or do the same thing with just as much refinement. The exception is children, who we consider brilliant because of their innocence. If we do not accept brilliance where we find it, we are narrowing our field and accepting wisdom and knowledge from an unrealistically small population. This is why authors have a common habit of quoting those who are trusted and traditional soothsayers to give foundation and substance to their words.

Comment: Normally famousness is something that is attributed to you by others. But it is important to look at yourself in an objective light too. What is it that you have accomplished or achieved? Give yourself the credit you deserve and you will be enhancing your honesty, your self-acceptance, and your self-esteem.

FANCY

Word Forms: fancier, fanciest, fancies, fancied, fanciful, fancying, fancily

Definitions: (1) light; whimsical; possessing a playful imagination; **(2)** ornamental; decorated; elaborate; **(3)** able to perform intricate and difficult tricks; exhibiting superior skill; **(4)** to like; to be pleased with; have amorous fondness for

FANTASTIC

Word Forms: fantasy, fanciful, fantastical, fantasticality, fantastically, fantasticalness

Definitions: (1) produced or existing only in imagination; not real; **(2)** whimsical; capricious; chimerical; **(3)** extraordinarily great, to the point of defying belief; **(4)** eccentric

FARSIGHTED

Word Forms: farseeing, farsightedly, farsightedness

Definition: having foresight and good judgment

Quote:
  The long run is possible only if we consistently take care of the short run.
          —WILLIAM H. CALVIN, *The River That Flows Uphill*

Comment: Sometimes you can see farther into the future than others. The farther you see, the greater the difficulty in bridging the gap with your contemporaries. The problem then is that you have no company in your vision. Or worse yet, you are sanctioned because you are politically incorrect. Don't let the skepticism of your peers get to you. You may not be able to convince them of your superior view, but you must remain true to your reality. Yet you must also be wise and recognize the myopic views of those in positions of power. Consider Galileo, who dared to agree with Copernicus that the sun, and not the earth, was the center of the solar system. He lived in the times of the inquisition and the likes of Pope Urban VIII, who was deaf to any new ideas. (Urban even had the birds in the Vatican gardens killed because they disturbed him.) Galileo faced the torture of the rack and decided to disavow his "blasphemous" claim. He lived out the rest of his life under house arrest.
  New ideas can be dangerous to established creeds.

Symbol: a *telescope*

FASCINATING

Word Forms: fascinate, fascination, fascinator, fascinatingly

Definition: charming; captivating; to attract by delightful qualities; extremely interesting; compelling

Derivation: Latin, "to bewitch," "to enchant," "to put under a spell"

Synonyms: entrancing, alluring, enrapturing, enamoring

Comment: If you possess a balanced and broad range of positive qualities, you will be naturally fascinating.

FASHIONABLE

Word Forms: fashion, fashionability, fashionably, fashionableness

Definitions: (1) observant of or conforming to the fashion of the day, particularly in dress but also in thought and deed; **(2)** current; popular; stylish; modern

FAVORED

Word Forms: favor, favorable, favorite, favoritely, well-favored

Definitions: (1) treated with or looked upon with friendliness or approval; **(2)** endowed with especially good qualities; **(3)** enjoying special advantages; privileged

Familial Quality: fascinating

FEARLESS

Word Forms: fearlessly, fearlessness

Definition: free from fear; bold; courageous; intrepid; undaunted; brave

Quote:
Fear is just a negative guess about an uncertain future.
—JOE BURULL

Observation: If you gamble and win you've got guts. If you gamble and lose you've got a learning experience. There's a fine line between foolish and fearless.

Comment: The fear is what makes me scared.

FEISTY

Word Forms: feistier, feistiest, feistily, feistiness

Definitions: (1) full of animation, energy, or courage; spirited; exuberant; (2) having or showing a lively aggressiveness; spunky; plucky

Symbol: the *badger*

FELICITOUS

Word Forms: felicitate, felicity, felicitously, felicitousness

Definitions: (1) suitable to the occasion; well-chosen; apt and to the point; (2) apropos and pleasing in expression or style; (3) happy; pleasant; delightful; enjoyable
See also: *Appropriate*

Derivation: Latin, "to make happy"

Synonyms: timely, successful, opportune, joyous

FERTILE

Word Forms: fertility, fertilization, fertilely, fertileness

Definitions: (1) fruitful; rich; producing in abundance; prolific; **(2)** productive in mental achievements; inventive; ingenious; having abundant resources

Synonyms: fecund, luxuriant; *fertile* denotes the power of producing, *fruitful* the act.

How to Live This Quality Today: Write down your ideas.

Symbols: *seeds; frogs; grapes;* the *cat*

Mythology: *Baal*, an ancient Semitic god of fertility

FERVENT

Word Forms: fervor, fervid, fervency, fervently, ferventness

Definition: having or showing very warm or intense spirit, feeling, or enthusiasm; ardent; passionate; zealous; earnest

Too Far: extremist

FESTIVE

Word Forms: festival, festivity, festively, festiveness

Definition: for or suitable to a feast or festival; joyous; gay; mirthful

Observation: You can come to a joyous gathering with a festive spirit, but even if you don't the prevalent emotion is contagious.

Symbol: *streamers*

FETCHING

Word Forms: fetch, fetchingly

Definition: attractive; pretty, charming; pleasing; captivating

FIDELITY

Word Form: fidelities

Definitions: (**1**) faithfulness; careful and exact observance of duty, or performance of obligations or vows; good faith; (**2**) firm adherence to a person or party with which one is united or bound; loyalty; (**3**) accuracy; exactness

Derivation: Latin, "faith," "trust"

Synonyms: conscientious, trustworthy, trusting, fealty, allegiance, constancy, integrity

Symbol: *turtledoves*

FINE

Word Forms: finer, finest, finely, fineness

Definitions: (1) the superior or best quality; of high or highest grade; excellent; **(2)** delicate in texture or workmanship; **(3)** highly skilled; accomplished; **(4)** performed with extreme care and accuracy; **(5)** showing subtle ability or nicety; discriminating; **(6)** physically trained or hardened close to the limit of efficiency; **(7)** characterized by refinement or elegance; polished; **(8)** healthy; well; **(9)** sophisticated in appearance; smart; **(10)** good-looking; handsome

Synonyms: beautiful, attractive, showy, dainty, choice, rare

FINESSE

Word Forms: finessed, finessing

Definitions: (1) extreme delicacy or subtlety in performance, skill, or discrimination; **(2)** smooth and tactful, as in handling a delicate situation; **(3)** artful strategy, cunning

Synonyms: crafty, adroit

Compatible Quality: sensitive

FIRM

Word Forms: firmer, firmest, firmly, firmness

Definitions: (1) fixed; steady; stable; unshaken; not easily moved; **(2)** unchanging; resolute; constant <a *firm* faith>; **(3)** showing determination; positive; **(4)** full of or indicating strength; vigorous

Synonyms: robust, close-knit, staunch, steadfast, unyielding, tenacious, unfaltering, rugged, sturdy

Kindred Quality: soft

Symbol: the *leg;* the *column*

FIT

Word Forms: fitter, fittest

Definitions: **(1)** adapted for a certain end or purpose; **(2)** proper; right; appropriate; **(3)** ready; prepared; trained; qualified; **(4)** in good physical condition or excellent trim; healthy

FITTING

Word Forms: fittingly, fittingness, befitting

Definition: suitable or appropriate; proper or becoming

Synonyms: expedient, congruous, apposite, apt, competent, adequate, seemly, conformable

FLAIR

Definitions: **(1)** a natural talent, aptitude, or ability; bent; knack; **(2)** a uniquely attractive quality (as elegance, smartness, or sophistication); style; **(3)** instinctive perceptiveness; discernment

How to Live This Quality Today: Notice what qualities your friends have a flair for. Weave that recognition into the conversation. By doing so you will be building a flair as an artful complimenter.

FLAMBOYANT

Word Forms: flame, flamboyance, flamboyantly

Definitions: (1) strikingly bold or brilliant; showy; **(2)** extravagantly dashing and colorful

How to Live This Quality Today: Wear bright colors.

FLEXIBLE

Word Forms: flex, flexile, flexibility, flexibly, flexibleness

Definitions: (1) yielding to influence; tractable; **(2)** capable of responding or conforming to changing or new situations; **(3)** adaptable physically, emotionally, or mentally

Synonyms: pliable, pliant, supple

Too Far: wishy-washy

Quote:
Most moral codes say "either-or" . . . while the universe itself seems to be filled instead with a whole lot of "maybes."
—DAVID BRIN, *Earth*

Reflection: Flexibility can be experienced on many levels. On the physical, a flexible set of muscles helps in your supple and graceful movement. On the emotional, flexibility is essential for dealing with the variability of life's situations.

As one acquires a broad and balanced set of positive qualities, flexibility is an inevitable result.

Comments:
- Prisoners of war who survived, first decided to survive and then were flexible enough to do and be whatever it took to survive.
- I've noticed that people have an incredible capacity to juxtapose seemingly impossible concepts in their psyche, such as killing for peace or cheating for success. Be aware of these incongruities in yourself. If you find that you are justifying a point of view, you could take that as a clue to something that you may be forcing to fit.

FLOURISHING

Word Forms: flourish, flourisher, flourishingly

Definitions: (1) increasing in wealth or honor; prosperous; **(2)** at the peak of development, activity, or influence; to be in one's prime
    See also: *Growing*

Derivation: Latin, "to blossom," "flowering"

Synonyms: thrive, triumph

FLOWING

Word Forms: flow, flows, flowed, flowingly

Definitions: (1) moves steadily in an agreeably effortless or rhythmic way; **(2)** to have a smooth, satisfying, harmonious continuity

Comments and Questions: What happens when the point between giving and receiving gets choked off? The internal energy doesn't flow. There are always physical ramifications to the balance between giving and receiving. It is true that physical illnesses are the result of both external and internal causes. If you are not doing what you know you need to be doing or are doing what you know you should not be doing, the internal energy turns in on itself and gets wacky. It can turn into cancers or nervous disorders or headaches or ulcers or even a suppression of the immune system.

    The difficulty comes in measuring that balance. You have to make subjective judgments. Are you taking care of the duties of daily living with honest effort? Are you doing interesting things with interesting people? Are you enjoying what you are doing? Are you proceeding smoothly from one thing to the next? Are you facing your difficulties instead of creating them? And if you have created a problem, are you doing your best to return things to balance?

Symbol: *river water*

Mythology: *Alpheus*, a Greek river god

FOCUSED

Word Forms: focal, focus, focusing, foci, focusable, focuser

Definitions: (1) brought into a center of activity or attention; (2) fixed on one object or purpose; concentrated

Compatible Qualities: determined, motivated

Parental Qualities: disciplined, joyful

Familial Qualities: attentive, thorough

FOLKSY

Word Forms: folk, folksier, folksiest, folksily, folksiness

Definitions: (1) friendly or neighborly; sociable; (2) very informal; familiar; unceremonious; casual; unpretentious

Derivation: Middle English, "people"

Familial Qualities: down-to-earth, homey

FORBEARING

Word Forms: forbear, forbore, forbearer, forbearance, forbearingly

Definition: patient; long-suffering; self-controlled when subject to annoyance or provocation

Familial Qualities: stick-to-itive, determined

Symbol: the *ox*

FORCEFUL

Word Forms: force, forcefully, forcefulness

Definitions: (1) acting with power or full of energy; vigorous; (2) effective; cogent; telling

Kindred Qualities: This is a quality that is positive in combination. It needs always to be balanced with a range of other qualities depending on the circumstances. As a parental disciplinarian you need to be *forceful* yet *tender*. A person in a potentially threatening situation needs to be *forceful* and *prudent*. In a rough and tumble game the combination would be *forceful* and *playful*.

Too Far: insensitive, bully

FORESIGHTED

Word Forms: foresee, foresight, foresightful, foresightedly, foresightedness

Definitions: (1) possessing the power of seeing beforehand; prescience; (2) having thoughtful regard or provision for the future; prudent forethought; (3) exhibiting the ability to project to oneself or others the consequences of actions taken

Quotes:
Lacking foresight, evolution is simply opportunistic, retaining those features that were available when opportunity knocked.

It [evolution] even created the capacity for music and poetry and humor—somehow.
—WILLIAM H. CALVIN, *The River That Flows Uphill*

Comment: All of the confusion, frustration, and sorrow that are caused by war, greed, corruption, and ignorance have hope of being turned to solutions if large numbers of people, individually, decide to focus on the good. People may be turned to the positive because they have a faith or a belief that compels them to seek the light. It may be because it is economically advantageous. Or they may do so because of the misery they have wrought upon themselves or that is wrought upon them. Where there is misery there often is collective complicity.

The most permanent of these disasters is the ongoing destruction of plants, animals, and habitats that will take another hundred generations to rebuild if they come back at all.

We need to extend our vision into the future. But more importantly we need to extend our love and concern to those people who will be facing these sad consequences. After all, they are our children.

FORETHOUGHTFUL

Word Forms: forethought, forethoughtfully, forethoughtfulness

Definitions: (1) characterizes one who thinks or plans out in advance; one who premeditates; (2) having prudent thought for the future; foresightful

Mythology: The name *Prometheus* means "forethought." Prometheus was a Titan of Greek mythology who stole fire from the gods and gave it to humanity. He was tortured severely by Zeus for his insolence. Evidently, the myth writers wanted us to realize that, with forethought, we can weigh the potential good of our actions against the potential personal grief. Forethought does not always protect you from difficulty.

FORGIVING

Word Forms: forgive, forgave, forgivable, forgiver, forgivingly, forgivingness

Definitions: (1) characterizes one who gives up resentment against, stops being angry with, or pardons; (2) giving up all claim to punish or exact penalty for; overlooking; abandoning vengeful feelings
   See also: *Ventilious*

Synonyms: absolving, releasing, excusing, exonerating, exculpating

Kindred Qualities: imagination, communication

Familial Qualities: tolerance, acceptance

Significant Date: International Forgiveness Week, the first week of February

Saying: *Ira furor brevis est* (Latin): "Anger is a brief madness."

Proverb:
Anger is as a stone cast into a wasp's nest.

—MALABAR

Quotes:
If you're harboring the slightest bitterness toward anyone, or any unkind thoughts of any sort whatsoever, you must get rid of them quickly. They aren't hurting anyone but you. It is said that hate injures the hater not the hated.

—PEACE PILGRIM, *Steps Toward Inner Peace*

Nature does abhor a vacuum, and when you begin moving out of your life what you do not want, you automatically are making way for what you do want. By letting go of the lesser, you automatically make room for your greater good to come in.

—CATHERINE PONDER, *The Dynamic Laws of Prosperity*

Forgiveness is the fragrance of the violet that clings fast to the heel that crushed it.

—GEORGE ROEMISCH

Affirmation:
I fully and freely forgive you. So far as I am concerned, that incident between us is finished forever. I wish you no harm. I am free and you are free and all is again well between us.

—CATHERINE PONDER, *The Dynamic Laws of Prosperity*

Meditation: Start with several deep breaths, all the way down into your solar plexus, all the way down into your being. Calm yourself. Open yourself. Visualize the divine essence of forgiveness at your crown chakra at the top of your head. Ask for this forgiveness to be a part of you. You have experienced it before and you want to experience it more fully. See it in all its colors. Let it settle into your mind. "I will forgive every thought I've had that needs forgiving. I will allow my mind to forgive all who need forgiving. I will forgive myself for all that needs forgiving."

Breathe forgiveness into each part of your body. Linger on each area as long as the forgiveness is doing its job. Move to your eyes and forgive all the anger that you have emitted from them. Forgive all of the pain that you have seen. Relax them, replace the pain with forgiveness. Replace the forgiveness with harmony, symmetry, and beauty. Move the divine energy of forgiveness to your ears, say, "I forgive everything that I have heard that needs forgiving." Move to your nose, forgive all evil smells. Move to the mouth and throat. Forgive yourself for all that you've said in a hurtful tone—purifying your communication.

Accept divine forgiveness. Move to your arms and hands. Forgive them for any actions that they have done. If your forgiveness is pure, the negative no longer exists, they are taken care of. Especially linger in your heart where you have hurt people in your relationships, or they have hurt you. All is forgiven, all is evaporated. Make sure you forgive for all ills, real or imagined, that have come to you or that you may have introduced into someone else's mind.

Breathe into your gut and especially release all the anger and frustration that you have been holding. All hurt and anguish are gone. The power of divine forgiveness is absolute. You are clean. Space is now open for new hope, for new life.

Move now to your hips and your genitals. Forgive yourself for all sexual misconduct. Forgive yourself for all of your guilt.

Go to the base of your spine and realize that a lot of what you felt you had to do, you did because of survival. Forgive yourself and allow yourself to be whole.

Move into your thighs and your knees. Forgive your legs for all of the fear, for every time you've run away, for every time you've physically or wishingly kicked someone. Relax your feet, now you have happy toes. Let all of these ills sink into the earth and into the ether, they don't exist anymore. They are all gone. They are replaced with divine harmony.

Move back up through you feet, your calves, your knees, your thighs, with a ball of harmonious and merciful energy. It is a cleansing glow of light, all of the molecules of your being are being replaced. Move back up through your spine. The ball of light at the base of your spine now has replaced all failure. Everything is calm. You are a new person. Move into your heart, breathe freely, it's all okay now, it's all gone. Your arms are free, your shoulders are relaxed, you've got new vitality. You can begin again—a clean slate.

You will now communicate your new hope, all that has transpired before is gone and forgiven. You will see the world with new eyes; you will smell the freshness. When you hear ill and when you see ill you will automatically transmute it and do something positive about it. Your mind is a new mind, fresh, decent, willing, and open. Give thanks to the divine power of forgiveness and the divine substance of mercy for renewing you.

Move back up to your crown chakra and let the divine essences float there and live there, renewing your body and soul. Keep filling your blood stream, your neurons, and your cells with the divine energy. There is a pulsating, glowing light filling your whole being.

When you are ready, come out of your meditation gently and continue your life in grace.

Going through the forgiveness meditation, don't push away any specific instances that come up, but don't linger on them either. Don't try to bring them up; there is no need for specific detail. Be generous with all of the forgiveness.

Note: Adapt this meditation to fit any quality that you desire.

Prayer:
God grant me the serenity to accept the things I cannot change, courage to change the things I can, and the wisdom to know the difference.

Observation: Anger is part of d*anger.*

Causes of Anger

1. Frustration, irritation, or a threat to safety
2. Unfair treatment—real or imagined
3. Offended or endangered beliefs
4. Dissatisfaction with oneself—a need for self-esteem
5. Exhaustion or chronic fatigue
6. Physical illness—unable to do what you could normally do
7. Some kinds of mental illness

Destructive Anger

1. Acting out your anger by striking out verbally or physically at others or yourself
2. Denial and repression
3. Anger turned inward results in depression.
4. Self-administered drugs and alcohol lead to problems and don't help you deal with the root causes of the anger.
5. Driving while angry is a bad idea. You surely would not have driving safely on your mind.

Constructive Anger

1. If you feel tired or frustrated and find yourself lashing out at a friend for what may at the time seem like a good enough reason but probably isn't, stop, explain that you are feeling stressed out and irritable, and then do yourself a favor and take your needed rest.
2. Use words rather than physical violence. When someone is reasonable, even though that person is stressed, he or she is recognized as someone with poise.
3. Talk to a friend or give yourself a good talking to.
4. If the problem involves a relationship, first talk with the person, but if it is serious enough ask a mutual friend to arbitrate.
5. Seek psychiatric or other forms of therapy. You may have a chemical imbalance that needs to be corrected with a change of diet or even prescription drugs.
6. Be objective rather than subjective. Focus on the problem and not on the person. Focus on what is important to you.
7. Use the anger energy to do something constructive.
8. Get a massage.
9. Give it time.
10. Put a wash cloth on your face and the back of your neck.
11. Learn forgiveness. First you must forgive yourself.
12. Say a prayer, meditate.
13. Take a shower, take a walk, read a book, play catch, run around the block, scream, cry, dance.

Tip: Forgive yourself and anyone in your past, present, or future. Ask in your heart that they forgive you. Freedom is about clean lines of energy. Blame and grudges block freedom's flow. Continue positively from where you are.

Suggestion: Bless those who have harmed you or whom you have harmed—real or imagined. Some damage is deep and painful, so begin with people who are easier to forgive. Practice forgiving and it will get easier. It may or may not be your responsibility to seek an active resolution to your problem in the form of counseling, meetings, letters, et cetera, but at least, in your own mind and heart, forgive and set free both the other person and yourself.

Communicate whenever possible. But you have to know (or believe) that the other wants to communicate with you.

Comment: To err is human but to forgive is divine. The best part of an argument is when you make up.

The Stages of Forgiveness

1. Decide to forgive
2. Forgive yourself
3. Forgive the other
4. Believe or imagine how the other can forgive you
5. Assume the other has forgiven you
6. Assume the other is forgiving him- or herself
7. Forget it

FORMAL

Word Forms: form, formality, formalize, formally, formalness

Definitions: (1) being in accordance with the usual requirements, customs, or conventions; observant of conventional requirements of behavior or procedure; punctilious; **(2)** done or made in orderly, regular fashion; methodical; **(3)** having a regular arrangement or pattern; symmetrical

Synonyms: precise, ceremonious, exact

FORTHRIGHT

Word Forms: forthrightly, forthrightness

Definitions: (1) free from ambiguity or evasiveness; straight to the point; direct; outspoken; candid; frank; **(2)** immediate

Kindred Qualities: delicate, sensitive

FORTIFIED

Word Forms: fortify, fortification, fortifier, fortifiable

Definitions: (1) possessing physical strength, courage, or endurance; invigorated; **(2)** one with added mental or moral strength; encouraged

Familial Quality: mettlesome

Tip: When you don't feel loved or loving, or even if you do, take stock of your positive qualities; you'll feel stronger and better able to continue on.

FORTITUDE

Word Form: fortitudinous

Definition: strength of mind in the face of pain, adversity, or peril; patient courage
  See also: *Courageous*

Derivation: Latin, "strong," "powerful"

Comment: It is by facing stress, conflict, difficulty, and problems that you acquire the qualities of strength, fortitude, and bravery.

FORTUNATE

Word Forms: fortune, fortunately, fortunateness

Definition: having, bringing, or coming by good luck; favorable; auspicious

Synonyms: fortuitous, prosperous, successful

Tip: If you are fortunate, appreciate it.

Question: Can you generate this quality? You will notice that the people with a certain set of qualities are fortunate. Either they have a talent and fortune comes as a result, or they are nice to be around, so they are sought-after companions. Either way, you can develop your natural abilities or your positive personality traits in order to create your personally fortunate situation.

Mythology: *Fortuna*, the Roman goddess of fortune

FORWARD

Word Forms: forwarder, forwarding, forwardly, forwardness

Definitions: (1) mentally advanced; precocious; (2) progressing onward; (3) prompt; ready; eager; (4) bold; pert

Too Far: pushy

FOURSQUARE

Word Forms: foursquarely, foursquareness

Definitions: (1) firm; solid; unyielding; unhesitating; (2) having bold conviction; frank; forthright; direct

Kindred Quality: lighthearted

FOXY

Word Forms: fox, foxier, foxiest, foxily, foxiness

Definitions: (1) slyly clever; cunning; crafty; sharp; **(2)** physically attractive, especially in a sexually alluring way (slang)

FRAGRANT

Word Forms: fragrance, fragrantly, fragrantness

Definition: having a pleasing scent; sweet-smelling

Synonyms: perfumed, balmy, aromatic, odoriferous, spicy

Quote:
> The scent of jasmine travels only with the wind, but the fragrance of holiness travels even against the wind.
>
> *—The Dhammapada*

Comment: All of the senses have intrinsic value.

Symbol: *flowers; perfume*

FRANK

Word Forms: franker, frankest, frankly, frankness

Definition: open; ingenuous; candid; free in expressing what one thinks or feels; free from reserve, disguise, or guile; clearly evident; plain

Derivation: Middle Latin, "free," "at liberty"

Synonyms: honest, sincere, undisguised

Kindred Qualities: articulate, compassionate

Too Far: brusque, piercing

FRATERNAL

Word Forms: fraternity, fraternize, fraternalism, fraternally

Definitions: (**1**) relating to or involving brothers; friendly; brotherly; (**2**) in a generic sense, refers to the familial connection between all people, male and female; (**3**) characterizes one who gives special attention or favor to individuals because they are family or are as close as family.

Symbol: fellowship: the *garland*

FREE

Word Forms: freer, freest, freed, freeing, free and easy, freedom, freehanded, freehearted, freethinker, freewill, freely, freeness, guilt-free

Definitions: (**1**) able to move in any direction; loose; (**2**) unhindered; unhampered; (**3**) able to choose for oneself; not restricted by anything except one's own limitations or nature; (**4**) spontaneous; (**5**) not constrained or stilted; smooth, easy, and graceful; (**6**) generous; liberal; lavish; profuse; abundant; copious; (**7**) frank; straightforward; (**8**) open to all

Kindred Quality: Respect. When people feel freedom without any constraints, they *know* that they can do anything. This includes taking what they want even if it belongs to someone else. Add the quality of respect for person and property, and freedom is truly free.

Compatible Qualities: artistic, expressive

Saying: Freedom is the power to choose your chains.

Comments:
- An individual or a society experiencing fear is usually willing to give up freedom in favor of security and protection, which oftentimes means the reduction of personal freedoms.

    Freedom is a given, like gravity, but our choices (which is also a universal principle) restrict our freedom. In our restrictions of freedom we say, "I cannot do this" or "I must do that." We say that we are free, but there are a lot of restrictions on our freedom.

We restrict ourselves by agreeing to the rules of society (driving on the right side of the road) or religion (eating fish on Friday). Or we are subjected to control by others, which is usually carried out by fear or violence. Consider the workplace: you conform not only to keep your job but because you may be branded as someone who is not a team player or is a trouble maker.

• If you are possessed by your possessions, you are not free.

THE FIRST AMENDMENT TO THE CONSTITUTION OF THE UNITED STATES

Congress shall make no law respecting an establishment of religion, or prohibiting the free exercise thereof; or abridging the freedom of speech or of the press; or the right of the people peaceably to assemble and to petition the Government for a redress of grievance.

FREETHINKING

Word Forms: free, freethinker, free thought

Definitions: (1) characterizes a person who forms opinions on the basis of personal reason, independent of authority, tradition, or established belief; (2) one who accepts the possible validity of all modes of thought or action; open-minded

Kindred Quality: cooperative

Familial Qualities: independent, individualistic

FRESH

Word Forms: fresher, freshest, freshen, freshly, freshness

Definitions: (1) having the color and appearance of youth; (2) not impaired by time; not forgotten or used; **(3)** original, spontaneous, and stimulating; **(4)** vigorous; lively; having new energy; not tired

Synonyms: brisk, strong, unfaded, florid, ruddy, novel, recent

Tip: Keep your thoughts fresh. Always be on vacation.

Comment: With the eyes of love, even the distasteful seems fresh.

FRIENDLY

Word Forms: friend, friendlier, friendliest, friendship, friended, friending, friendliness

Definitions: **(1)** showing kindly interest and good will; amicable; **(2)** cheerful; comforting; supportive; helpful; **(3)** disposed to peace; **(4)** attached to another by affection or esteem; a favored companion

Synonyms: propitious, helpful, sympathetic, conciliatory

Consequential Quality: love

Proverbs:
A man who would have friends must show himself friendly.
—JEWISH

True friendship is like sound health, the value of which is seldom known until it is lost.
—CHINESE

Quotes:
Become interested in your fellows; learn how to love them and watch for the opportunity to do something for them which you are sure they want done.
—JESUS, *The Urantia Book*

To find a friend one must close one eye—to keep a friend, two.
—NORMAN DOUGLAS

No man is a failure who has friends.
    —CLARENCE, GEORGE BAILEY'S ANGEL IN *It's a Wonderful Life*

So long as we love, we serve. So long as we are loved by others, I would almost say, we are indispensable; and no man is useless while he has a friend.
                                        —ROBERT LOUIS STEVENSON

Comment: True friendship is a gift of sublime self-forgetfulness. Being overly focused on oneself will drain your energy. But if you focus on your task or your loved one, you will have more energy and motivation to persist.

Symbols: *shaking hands; crossed arrows* (American Indian)

Legends: Syracusans *Damon and Pythias*. Pythias was condemned to death but was allowed to return home to finalize his affairs. Damon took his place on the chopping block, but Pythias returned in the nick of time to save him from execution. In reward for this show of friendship, they were both set free.
    Nisus and Euryalus. In Virgil's *Aeneid*, Nisus died valiantly attempting to save his best friend Euryalus.

FRISKY

Word Forms: frisk, friskier, friskiest, friskily, friskiness

Definition: lively; frolicsome; playful; gaily active

FROLICSOME

Word Forms: frolic, frolicsomely, frolicsomeness

Definition: merrily playful; full of gaiety and mirth; sportive; lighthearted

FRUGAL

Word Forms: frugality, frugally, frugalness

Definitions: (1) economical; not spending freely or unnecessarily; saving; sparing; not profuse, prodigal, or lavish; (2) entailing little expense; requiring few resources

Too Far: stingy

FRUITFUL

Word Forms: fruitfully, fruitfulness

Definitions: (1) very productive; prolific; plentiful; fertile; (2) producing results; profitable; rich, abundant

Compatible Quality: generous

Color: red

Mythology: *Vertumnus*, a Roman god of gardens, crops, orchards, and spring

FULFILLED

Word Forms: fulfill, fulfilling, fulfiller, fulfillment

Definitions: (1) characterizes one whose expectations have been met; satisfied; (2) completed; brought to an end; accomplished; realized; performed

Comment: When one accomplishes one's desires (a form of self-love) then one feels fulfilled, especially if it is done unselfishly.

Symbol: a *single rose*

FUN

Word Forms: funner, funnest, funned, funning

Definitions: (1) lively, gay play or playfulness; merriment; amusement; sport; recreation; joking; **(2)** a source or cause of enjoyable distraction, as an amusing person or thing

FUNNY

Word Forms: funnier, funniest, funnily, funniness, funny bone

Definition: comical; droll, causing laughter; amusing

Synonym: humorous

Quote:
  To find something funny one only has to look at themselves.
          —JAY WARD, THE CREATOR OF "ROCKY AND HIS FRIENDS"

Symbol: *laughing*

GALLANT

Word Forms: gallanted, gallanting, gallantry, gallantly, gallantness

Definitions: (1) brave; high-spirited; courageous; heroic; noble-minded; **(2)** showing polite attention; courteous; chivalrous; courtly; **(3)** having to do with love; amorous; **(4)** gay; splendid; magnificent; **(5)** exhibiting dashing behavior and ornate expression; **(6)** stately; imposing; grand

Synonyms: intrepid, fearless, valiant, bold

GAMESOME

Word Forms: game, gamesomely, gamesomeness

Definition: sportive; playful; frolicsome; merry; gay

GAY

Word Forms: gayer, gayest, gaiety, gaily, gayness

Definitions: (1) joyous and lively; merry; happy; lighthearted; exuberant; high-spirited; (2) given to social life and pleasures

Synonyms: blithe, sprightly, sportive, hilarious

GENEROUS

Word Forms: generosity, generously, generousness

Definitions: (1) liberal in giving or sharing; unselfish; bountiful; (2) free from meanness or pettiness; magnanimous; noble-minded; gracious

Kindred Quality: practical

Too Far: poverty

Quote:
If you get great pleasure and joy out of giving of yourself, then your "selfishness" manifests itself as generosity.
—JUDY KAIN

Parable: The Bible story of the employer who paid those who worked all day the same as those who worked just at the end of the day, shows that generosity is a greater quality than consistency.

Comment: Generosity does not mean only the giving of money. It also includes the sharing of ideas, establishing positive systems and infrastructure, caring for emotional needs, even helping control those who cannot control themselves.

Symbol: a *mountain* (Chinese)

GENIAL

Word Forms: congenial, geniality, genially, genialness

Definitions: (1) warmly and pleasantly cheerful; cordial; kindly; friendly; amiable; sympathetic; **(2)** imparting warmth, comfort, or life

Synonyms: merry, hearty, revivifying, restorative, inspiriting

GENIUS

Word Forms: geniuses, genii

Definitions: (1) extraordinary intelligence surpassing that of most intellectually superior individuals; a person who possesses such intelligence; **(2)** an outstanding gift for some specialized activity

Synonyms: talent, wisdom, faculty, aptitude, ability, ingenuity, capacity, cleverness

Kindred Qualities:
A man with genius is unendurable if he does not also possess at least two other things: gratitude and cleanliness.
—FRIEDRICH WILHELM NIETZSCHE

Quotes:
Everyone knows about Newton's apple. Charles Darwin said his *Origin of the Species* [*sic*] flashed complete in one second, and he spent the rest of his life backing it up; and the theory of relativity

occurred to Einstein in the time it takes to clap your hands. This is the greatest mystery of the human mind—the inductive leap. Everything falls into place, irrelevancies relate, dissonance becomes harmony, and nonsense wears a crown of meaning.

—JOHN STEINBECK

Mediocrity is self-inflicted and genius is self-bestowed.

—WALTER RUSSELL

Comment: Genius is not just relegated to math (Einstein) or music (Mozart) or writing (Shakespeare). You can be a genius of any quality or talent. The Scottish write of a genius for friendship.

Genius is not only bestowed, it can also be developed.

Symbol: a single *pearl*, usually hidden (Chinese)

Legend: Ancient Roman belief held that each person is assigned a guardian spirit at birth. This spirit is referred to as a *Genius* and is the person's natural ability. It carries the person's destiny and inspires the person to become the genius they are.

GENTEEL

Word Forms: genteelly, genteelness

Definitions: (1) well-bred or refined; polite; elegant; (2) stylish or fashionable

Derivation: Latin, "of noble birth"

Familial Qualities: ladylike, gentlemanly

GENTLE

Word Forms: gentler, gentlest, gentled, gentling, gently, gentleness, gentlefolk, gentleperson, gentlewoman, gentleman, gentle-hearted, genteel

Definitions: (1) refined or polite; **(2)** generous; kind; **(3)** serene; patient; **(4)** mild; moderate

Synonyms: placid, pacific, quiet, soft, peaceful, mild, meek

Kindred Qualities: determined, strong

Saying: *Suaviter in modo, fortiter in re* (Latin): "Gently in manner, strongly in deed"

Comment: We associate gentleness with the sense of touch; but even though we cannot physically touch most people, we can touch their hearts with the kindness of a smile, touch their minds with an encouraging word, or touch their funny bones with a sense of humor.

Symbol: the *unicorn*, symbolizing gentleness and longevity (Chinese)

GENTLEMANLY

Word Forms: gentleman, gentlemanliness

Definition: pertaining to or becoming a man of good breeding; polite; complaisant

Note: If you pick this quality and you are female, then use those qualities that are described and look up *Ladylike.*

GENUINE

Word Forms: genuinely, genuineness

Definitions: (1) real; true; authentic; not artificial; not counterfeit <a *genuine* manuscript>; **(2)** sincere and frank; honest and forthright

Synonyms: natural, unadulterated, unaffected, veritable

Comment: When, on the one hand, one seems genuine and honest and on the other hand has selfish motives, then the person's true purpose isn't really known until time clarifies it. But you may be able to see through the facade from the outset. If not, then wait patiently because eventually the individual will show his or her true self. Remember the old saying: "Actions speak louder than words."

Oftentimes people say that they are motivated by a positive quality and yet are taking steps and actions that go against the very qualities that they profess to hold in such high regard.

GIFTED

Word Forms: gift, giftedly, giftedness

Definitions: (1) endowed by nature with a great talent, ability, or faculty; **(2)** exceptionally intelligent
See also: *Genius*

GIVING

Word Forms: give, gave, given, giver

Definitions: (1) to transfer one's own possession freely to another without asking anything in return; **(2)** devoted to a cause, occupation, pursuit, or goal

Kindred Quality: appreciation

Too Far: co-dependent, insecure, victim
You can sacrifice yourself under necessary situations, but sacrifice can be negative. If you give beyond the need, you could be depriving the other of a valuable learning experience and allowing yourself to be a victim. Or if more is taken than is needed, the receiving gets turned into greed.

Quote:
What fulfills you is not what you keep but what you give away.
—Madelyn Manning Mims, 800-meter gold medal Olympian

Analogy: Giving and receiving can be seen in the infinity symbol (∞). Divide the symbol in half horizontally. The bottom half of the symbol is the giving side; the top half is the receiving side. Divide it left and right. The left is the self; the right is the other. Whatever you've got to give crosses over through the central point. It goes into the other person's receiving chamber, the top portion of the other side. The quantity, quality, and value of the giving is dependent on the capability, maturity, and capacity of the person giving, but also on his or her attitude toward the receiver.

The quantity and quality being given is modified by the receiver's capacity and ability in receiving. A flood of good could be given (information, goods, services, love) but the receiver can only receive what he or she allows. God gives us unlimited love, but we can receive only according to our willingness, maturity, and experience.

If this closed loop is flowing perfectly, if there are no choke points, the flow of energy increases. The size and volume of the opening has to increase as well.

Greed creates a choke point. It is the desire to receive and hold with no reciprocal giving. The reason for this greed is usually insecurity, but the result is an ingesting of a greater quantity of material than is needed. This causes mistrust, alienation, and bloating.

The saying goes, "The more you give, the more you receive." The true compensation for giving is on a spiritual level with satisfaction, learning, and the experience of giving. These are much more valuable than the temporary rewards of money, privilege, or prestige, albeit, these physical rewards can be deserved also.

Tips:
- There is not only pleasure in receiving but also in giving.
- If you continually give, you will continually have.
- The more people receive, the more they "have" to give.

Comment: There is a natural flow to the energy of giving and receiving. Give with all the generosity in your heart. Receive with all the genuine, gracious appreciation you possess.

Giving is considered a positive quality, and taking normally is considered a negative quality. On the other hand, taking can also be positive. Certainly we take every day from the plant and animal kingdoms for our sustenance. And what do we give back? There has to be, as in everything, a balance.

One of the most generous gifts is to graciously accept the love that is given to you. Those who are giving to you are doing so out of the goodness of their hearts. It is only right for you to appreciate their gifts.

Consider the kiss. If you're kissing someone you love, it is your wish that the kiss is received with as much appreciation as you are delivering it. But if the other person is concentrating too much on giving you a kiss, then they may not be receiving yours. It is important to know how to receive.

Experience: I once stood in an unnamed side canyon in the Grand Canyon and was overwhelmed by the absolute beauty surrounding me— flowers, colors, rocks, water. Even the air was pristine, pure and sapid. I was strong, healthy, and happy and I realized through the intensity of that beauty that this point in time and this place in space were a gift created by a Divine Being specifically for me. It didn't matter how many millions of years it took to create the universe and the planet. No matter the evolution and weathering of the rocks. That was just the price that was freely and lovingly paid to give me that moment in time. All that was left for me to do was to experience the appreciation and to appreciate the experience. And so it is for each "now."

Symbol: *infinity* (∞)

Legends: *Santa Claus*, based on the person of Saint Nicholas (Dutch: Sant Nikolaas), the bishop of Myra, the patron saint of children
Kris Kringle: "Kris" is derived from *Christ* and "Kringle" from *kind.*

GLAD

Word Forms: gladder, gladdest, gladden, gladly, gladness, gladsome

Definitions: (1) pleased; affected with pleasure or joy; happy; cheerful; (2) wearing a gay appearance; showy; bright; (3) pleasing; exhilarating

Synonyms: delighted, gratified

Fiction: *Pollyanna,* also known as the Glad Girl, who finds good in everything and is brightly optimistic, created by Eleanor H. Porter

GLAMOROUS

Word Forms: glamour, glamorize, glamorously

Definition: fascinating personal attraction; alluring charm

Compatible Quality: healthy

GLEEFUL

Word Forms: glee, gleefully, gleefulness

Definition: merry; gay; joyous; full of delight

GLOWING

Word Forms: glow, glowingly

Definitions: (1) radiating health and high spirits; (2) warmly favorable or complimentary <a *glowing* account of her work>; (3) ardent zeal; animated excitement or passion; elated; (4) exhibiting rich and warm color or feeling

Derivation: Old English, "bright," "to glitter"

GOAL ORIENTED

Definition: focused on the end or final purpose; characterizes one who intends to accomplish everything he or she sets out to do

Music: "Walking in a Winter Wonderland"

Quotes:
Take care to get what you like or you will be forced to like what you get.
—GEORGE BERNARD SHAW

One has half the deed done who has made a beginning.

—HORACE

The limitations define how you are to proceed.

—JERRY DOWNS

I had 5,000 ways of proving that I was getting closer to where I wanted to go.

—THOMAS EDISON after 5,000 "failed" experiments
on the light bulb

The last step depends on the first. The first step depends on the last.

—RENE DAUMALL

Having a goal sometimes limits your flexibility.

—JUDY KAIN

Note: Don't get so narrow in your goal that you forget about your higher purpose.

Purpose is a general direction toward which you wish your life to move. Resolutions, on the other hand, are goals that help contribute to your purpose. Once you have stated your purpose, set up a plan to achieve it. Look at the resources that are available, and think about which ones are needed.

It's important to have a taste of success. Also, make sure you reward yourself when you meet your short-term goals.

—GEORGE SHEEHAN, M.D., "Peak Performance! Coaching
your Internal Team," *Taking Care Magazine*

Inspiration: You alone do not need to arrive at all of the determination you need to experience your goals. You need not be the sole cause and effect of your results. As a matter of fact, if you depend only upon yourself, your results will be limited to your personal sphere of reality. If you expand to include other people, you have opened yourself up to a much broader range of possibilities.

Did you ever wonder what magnificent music Mozart or any of the great composers would have been able to produce with today's technology; what about the great inventors, artists, and engineers? We can and should build on the accomplishments that have been made before us.

But if you expand beyond the personal and the collective to include cosmic principles, then you will be connecting yourself to universe reality—unlimited creativity. The more you choose the source, the closer you will emulate the source. As you become it, the more you will be an instrument of it, and it will flow through you.

I believe that this source is personal—a wise and loving God. But even if you have come to the conclusion that the universe is nothing but a grand mechanism, doesn't it still behoove you to allow your goals to be aligned with the workings of that system? Wouldn't your greatest successes be when you work with what works?

One of the greatest gifts of life is choice. Your range of choice is as broad as your consciousness. Goal setting focuses your mind and action on attainment and results. Align your mind with the Higher mind; target your goal on your highest ideas and ideals and you will truly be on the road to success.

Consideration: Contemplate the difference between that which *is* value and that which *has* value.

Observation: One cannot underestimate the need for *discipline* in goal setting. The thing to remember is who is in control. Is your discipline being imposed from without—from parents, bosses, society, religion, or friends—or is it being generated from within? You are fulfilling your needs because of your inner desire.

It is good to have a combination of both the outer and the inner. But when an external force becomes too controlling, meet it with the wisdom of an appropriate inner force. You could choose to fight fire with fire, in which case dominance will be achieved by the one with the superior strength. Or you could choose to avoid the fight by using communication, reason, law, justice, inventiveness, resolve, and understanding.

In order for internal discipline to take precedence, one must be highly *motivated*. External motivation is often a forced motivation. Internal motivation may have fear or pity as elements but can be made more powerful with hope, responsibility, curiosity, and love.

Tips:
- You are an end in yourself—work for *you* as a goal.
- Have a project that you are excited about, that you are looking forward to, that will draw you out of bed in the morning.
- Do not listen to those who say it cannot be done. It is your goal. You *know* that you can do it. It is your vision and you will do it at your pace.

- Beware of being a slave to your goals. Be happy about your goal each day that you are accomplishing it.

Advice: I know it is dangerous to focus on negative motivation to get somewhere. But if you notice that you are motivated because of the "going away from" method of action, then understand that in yourself and consciously decide to "move away" while changing your strategy to a more positive method.

When you find yourself in the midst of a thought beginning with "I cannot do this because . . ." grab hold of the thought and take control. First, turn it off and then turn it around to a positive. As usual, this is much easier to say than to do.

Focus on the thought consciously. Put it through a test—the inner test of doubt. After all, if your idea/ideal is strong enough to overcome the negative, then it certainly has the thrust, once it gets off of the ground, to sail for a while. Then all you need to do is to continue the propulsion and keep adjusting and balancing the thrusters to maintain course and speed.

So, go ahead, put your best idea through your hardest tests—only make sure *you* are in charge, not that negative attitude.

Does not the understanding of the risk, the willingness to face the challenge, and the courage to look your fear in the face necessitate that you be conscious of the negative side? The key is that you be in control of your choices.

Admonition: Keep on plugging, keep choosing, keep doing what you need to be doing. Take action, have courage, and you will grow and move forward, no matter where your starting place is.

Comments:
- Inspiration, intuition, instinct, and luck are alternatives or additions to goal setting. Goal setting is a left-brain technique and it certainly does work. But there are also other possibilities of attaining one's goals.

    You could win the lottery. Hey, it happens! Put out a buck for a ticket and hope for the best. That'll solve your financial goals, if you use the money wisely. But it won't help you lose that weight you want to lose, or calm that temper that you've got, or enhance your determination.

    Then, again, there's rich old Uncle Henry, who's got billions and billions, and he could leave you his estate. That would take care of a few of your financial worries.

On your physical goal of losing that weight, you could get stranded on a desert island and have nothing to do but climb trees to get coconuts and get plenty of exercise by walking around the island looking for food. You'll end up with a pretty nice physique after a while.

Or you could begin the goal setting techniques that will get you there. The goal may be physical, mental, emotional, or spiritual, but you cannot get to it without focusing on and acquiring those qualities that are needed for you to experience what you choose.

• The question "Where will I get the time?" is valid. If you are dedicated to your family and holding a job that nurtures that family, then feel good that you are succeeding in that. You must begin from where you are. And add to what you are already doing. All the more reason that you choose a goal (and qualities that are necessary to *be* that goal) that is highly motivating. You will have to really want it to squeeze out some more energy and enthusiasm in your "free" time if you are already putting in a full effort.

Questions:

1. What is my life's purpose?
2. What do I admire?
3. Who do I admire?
4. Why have I chosen this goal?
5. What price will I pay to achieve my goal?
6. How will my goal contribute to my life?
7. What is my contribution to all life?
8. How will things change when I succeed?
9. Who will give me feedback as I progress?
10. Who will support and contribute to my success?
11. What will be the rewards of success?
12. How close to my self-image is my goal?

Goal Setting:

Life Purpose

1. List two or more of your unique positive qualities.
2. List ways that you like to express these qualities.

3. What does your success look like?
4. Combine into a single statement. Example: "I am communicating with clarity and kindness my understanding and appreciation of reality in a practical and creative way."

Qualities Needed to Accomplish Your Goals

1. Desire
2. Motivation
3. Determination
4. Skill, talent
5. Stick-to-itiveness

How to Do It

1. Know your life purpose.
2. Decide
   - on your *strategy* as well as your goals,
   - on your *tactics* as well as your goals,
   - on your *target* as well as your goals.
3. Visualize your goals.
4. Write them down.
5. Make a plan.
6. Believe in your goals and yourself.
7. Look at the obstacles to overcome as opportunities.
8. Start.
9. Act: Delegate or do it yourself.
10. Continue—be persistent.
11. Look forward to accomplishments.
12. Don't listen to people who say it won't work.
13. Don't be dejected by your failures.
14. Understand the rewards you are going to get.
15. Complete it.
16. Get acknowledgment from others and from yourself.

Goal Setting (Earl Nightingale, *A Course in Winning* audio tapes)

1. Select a motivating and compelling goal.
2. Define it in your own words—be specific and concise.
   - Begin with six-month to one-year goals.
   - State it as if it has already been reached.

- Use action modifiers.
- Use emotion words (enthusiastic, happy).
- State it in the present tense and be *positive*.
- Use personal pronouns ("I weigh a trim, athletic 165 pounds and enjoy exercising every day").

3. Always direct your self-talk stimulation toward what you desire— *positively*.
4. Read your goal two to five times a day, or use a tape.
5. Break down bigger goals into smaller tasks.

Goal Setting (Zig Ziglar, *A Course in Winning* audio tapes)

1. Identify the goal.
2. Set a deadline for achievement.
3. List the obstacles to overcome.
4. Identify the people and groups to work with.
5. List the skills and knowledge required to reach your goal.
6. Develop a plan of action.
7. List the benefits.

Measurable Goal Setting

Once you focus on the quality or qualities that you desire, you must also make sure that you've got a measurable proposition.

Go ahead and establish a goal: "I want to be happy." Then ask yourself what it is that has made you happy. After remembering your historical happiness you will be able to better project what would likely give you happiness in the future. These occurrences need not be measurable, but often they will be. Measurable: this week's paycheck, my first car, my first house. Unmeasurable: Daddy's hugs, Mommy's rock-a-bye-baby, my first kiss, the sun on my face, looking into a lovely face that is looking back at me with love.

Seven Types of Goals

1. Physical: appearance, medical, exercise, weight, nutrition
2. Family: loving, listening, supporting, forgiving, respecting, time together
3. Financial: earning, saving, investing, budgeting, insurance, credit

4. Social: humor, listening, self-confidence, manners, caring, friendship
5. Mental: imagination, attitude, education, reading, curiosity
6. Career: job satisfaction, effectiveness, training, understanding, purpose, competence
7. Spiritual: inner peace, meaning, gratitude, religious study, God-consciousness

Color: red

GODLY

Word Forms: god, goddess, godlike, godlier, god-fearing, godliness

Definition: filled with love for God; pious; devout; religious; aspiring to conform to God's design

Quotes:
God is Love, and whenever you reach out in loving kindness, you are expressing God. God is Truth, and whenever you seek truth, you are seeking God. God is Beauty, and whenever you touch the beauty of a flower or sunset, you are touching God.
—PEACE PILGRIM, *Steps Toward Inner Peace*

Why indeed must "God" be a noun? Why not a verb . . . The most active and dynamic of all?
—MARY DALY, THEOLOGIAN

God can only do *for* you what God can do *through* you by means of your thoughts and ideas.
—CATHERINE PONDER, *The Dynamic Laws of Prosperity*

Note: And your persistent decision to yield to your higher ideals

Reflection: The easiest definition of God is that God is Love. A personal, positive, creative being. The most objective definition I've seen is from *The Urantia Book*: "Man has always thought of God in the terms of the best he knew, his deepest ideas and highest ideals. Even historic religion has always created its God conceptions out of its highest recognized values. Every intelligent creature gives the name of God to the best and highest thing he knows."

Tip: When you meet god, treat god like God. Since everyone is god, treat everyone like God.

Comment: There is always someone who is stronger or smarter or wiser than you are. Many times it is only your perception of them in relation to your perception of yourself.

If they truly are godly, they will not flaunt their superiority. A superiority that is most probably specific to one area or is a superficial difference. They may be older, or more experienced, or female while you are male, or Polynesian while you are Inuit. But even though you may admire, or even envy, those strengths and differences, you need not push yourself down while elevating them.

Remember that you are also growing and are "better" in some respects than some others. There are also people who are "better" than those you admire.

Why is it that sometimes differences are cause to deify and other times are a cause for a negative prejudice?

Color: blue

GOOD SELF-IMAGE

Definition: a positive concept of oneself or one's capacity

Observation: It is ironic how often those with a poor self-image usually have a sensitive perception of the values of others: "I'm no good but look at how wonderful so-and-so is."

Subjective reality is folded in such a way that the person with a poor self-image cannot see or accept his or her own positive qualities. Consider Marilyn Monroe; her beauty was certainly obvious to an adoring and desiring public and she surely must have been aware of it, but it was not enough. Those who study theatrical art say that she was a talented actor but her lack of self-esteem helped to destroy her.

Structure: The following is from the article "Anxiety—Recognition and Intervention," which appeared in *The American Journal of Nursing.*

Components of a Good Self-Image

- Satisfaction of personal wants
- Satisfaction of personal goals
- Satisfaction of personal expectations
- Reasonable control of self
- Reasonable control of environment
- A sense of usefulness
- A sense of productivity
- A sense of belonging
- An ability to understand and be understood—communication

Threats to a Good Self-Image

- A sense of helplessness
- A sense of isolation, alienation, or loneliness
- A sense of insecurity (a threat to identity)
- Fear

GOOD WILL

Word Form: good willed

Definitions: (1) benevolence; friendly disposition; **(2)** willingness; cheerful consent

Saying:
Good will to all

                                             —CHRISTMAS WISH

GOODHEARTED

Word Forms: goodheartedly, goodheartedness

Definitions: kind and generous; benevolent; charitable; well-meaning

GOODNESS

Word Forms: good, goodly, good-tempered

Definitions: (1) excellence of character, morale, or virtue; **(2)** generous and kindly feelings; benevolence; **(3)** the best part

Sayings:
The golden rule: Do unto others as you would have them do unto you.

If darkness is, then darkness is good.
—MBUTI

Quotes:
The good I meet with goodness; the bad I also meet with goodness.
—LAO-TSE

It is amazing how complete is the delusion that beauty is goodness.
—LEO TOLSTOY

It is noble to be good and it's nobler to teach others to be good, and less trouble.
—MARK TWAIN at the opening of the Mark Twain Library

Consideration: The results of being good are usually evident.

Advice: When in doubt, focus on the good, focus on what you know to be correct and true. Ask your heart whether or not you are doing the right thing. Ask your friends, but your friends may be more cautious, more conservative than your ideals, so even though they are well-meaning you are going to have to take their response with a grain of salt. It may mean that they are not willing to take the steps that you are willing to take. Use your intuition.

Comment:

Leaky Goodness

If you are good to one, they get the direct benefit of that act of kindness. But what good does it do others? Since you are practicing goodness to one you and they will be more likely to give it to others as well, so your personal benevolent acts leak over to the outside world. No matter how private your goodness, you are adding to the greater good.

GOOD-HUMORED

Word Forms: good humor, good-humoredly, good-humoredness

Definition: possessing a cheerful temperament; good-natured

GOOD-NATURED

Word Forms: good nature, good-naturedly, good-naturedness

Definition: naturally mild in temper; not easily provoked; amiable

Synonyms: *Good-natured* denotes a disposition to please and be pleased. *Good-tempered* denotes a spirit that is not easily ruffled by provocation or other disturbing influences. *Kind* denotes a disposition to make others happy by supplying their wants and granting their requests. *Obliging* stresses a friendly readiness to be helpful.

GOOFY

Word Forms: goof, goofier, goofiest, goofily, goofiness

Definition: silly; good-hearted

Kindred Quality: thoughtful

Compatible Quality: good timing

Too Far: absurd

Exercise: Watch Goofy cartoons.

GORGEOUS

Word Forms: gorgeously, gorgeousness

Definitions: (1) showy; fine; splendid; glittering with gay colors; brilliant; **(2)** magnificent; beautiful; superb

GRACED

Word Form: grace

Definition: adorned; embellished; exalted; dignified; honored

Music:

> *Amazing Grace! (how sweet the sound)*
> *That sav'd a wretch like me!*
> *I once was lost, but now am found*
> *Was blind, but now I see.*

Saying: There, but for the grace of God, go I.

GRACEFUL

Word Forms: gracefully, gracefulness

Definitions: (1) possessing beauty or charm of form, composition, movement, or expression; elegance with appropriate dignity; **(2)** exhibiting an attractive quality, feature, or manner; **(3)** having a sense of what is right and proper; decent; **(4)** merciful; clement

Familial Quality: free

Exercise: Dance!

Symbols: the *swan;* a ballet *dancer;* the *hummingbird*

GRACIOUS

Word Forms: graciously, graciousness

Definitions: (1) having or showing kindness, courtesy, charm, good taste, or generosity of spirit; **(2)** tactful and delicate; urbane; refined; **(3)** merciful; compassionate; **(4)** possessing divine grace; virtuous; good

Synonyms: benignant, mild, tender, cordial, affable, genial, sociable

Comment: It is because of God's graciousness that we were given the gift of choice; besides, He had to give us choice so that we would be able to grow and discover our own divinity, thus freeing Him from His infinity.

GRAND

Word Forms: grandeur, grandly, grandness

Definitions: (1) great; illustrious; powerful; (2) splendid; magnificent; (3) noble; sublime; lofty; (4) conceived or expressed with great dignity; (5) important; distinguished

Synonyms: elevated, exalted, majestic, superb

Color: green

GRATEFUL

Word Forms: gratify, gratitude, gratefully, gratefulness

Definitions: (1) causing, feeling, or expressing thanks; appreciative; (2) agreeable; pleasing; acceptable; affording pleasure

Synonym: refreshing

Comment: Gratitude is a key to abundance, fulfillment, and a happy life. It's difficult to have a painful or melancholy attitude when you are grateful. Gratitude is a general antidote to any downward spiral of stress, depression, or conflict. You will still have to deal with the difficulties at hand, but you will be able to do so with a more chipper attitude. Cultivate the attitude of gratitude.

GREAT

Word Forms: greater, greatest, greatly, greatness, greathearted

Definitions: (1) having distinctive importance; momentous; renowned; (2) marked by nobility of thought or action; (3) unusual in ability of achievement; highly gifted; illustrious; superior; eminent; (4) impressive; remarkable; (5) absorbed or enthusiastic; proficient; skillful; (6) excellent; splendid; fine

Synonyms: majestic, grand, powerful

Quotes:
God is great, God is good, like a God ought'a should.
—JERRY DOWNS

Since the quality of greatness is wholly determined by the content of goodness, it follows that, if you can through grace become good, you are thereby becoming great.
—*The Urantia Book*

Greatness is a transitory experience. It is never consistent. It depends in part upon the myth-making imagination of humankind. The person who experiences greatness must have a feeling for the myth he is in. He must reflect what is projected upon him. And he must have a strong sense of the sardonic. This is what uncouples him from belief in his own pretensions. The sardonic is all that permits him to move within himself. Without this quality, even occasional greatness will destroy a man.
—FRANK HERBERT, *Dune*

Note: The word *sardonic* is said to derive from a plant that grows in Sardinia, which when eaten produces convulsive laughter that ends in death.

GREGARIOUS

Word Forms: gregariously, gregariousness

Definition: fond of the company of others; social

Color: red

GROUNDED

Word Forms: ground, groundedly, groundedness, well-grounded

Definitions: (1) fixed or set, as on a foundation, cause, reason, or principle; settled, as in concrete; **(2)** stable and sturdy

Comment: What's good about hitting rock bottom is that you now have a firm and grounded place from which to continue.

GROWING

Word Forms: grow, grew, grown, grower, growth, growingly

Definitions: (1) advancing; improving; making progress; **(2)** developing to full stature or maturity; becoming adult

Sayings:
You have to crawl before you can walk.

A child cannot do the things of an adult.

You can progress beyond who you are, but you have to be who you are now.

Growth is the turning of potentials into actuals.

No one grows in a vacuum.

Quotes:
Growth is awareness plus risk-taking.

—JACK CANFIELD

Sometimes a *Dynamic* increment goes forward but can find no latching mechanism and so fails and slips back to a previously latched position. Whole species and cultures get lost this way. Sometimes a static pattern becomes so powerful it prohibits any *Dynamic* moves forward. In both cases the evolutionary process is halted for a while. But when it's not halted, the result has been an increase in power to control hostile forces or an increase in versatility, or both. The increase in versatility is directed toward *Dynamic Quality*. The increase in power to control hostile forces is directed toward static quality. Without *Dynamic Quality* the organism cannot grow. Without static quality the organism cannot last. Both are needed.

—ROBERT PIRSIG, *Lila*

The worst potential competition for any organism can come from its own kind. The species consumes necessities. Growth is limited by that necessity which is present in the least amount. The least favorable condition controls the rate of growth. (Law of the Minimum)

—FRANK HERBERT, *Heretics of Dune*

Reflections:
- People advanced enough to be living ideas beyond their generation are often judged to be both saints and freaks, and in either case are considered a threat to the status quo. The value of the status quo is that it seems to be a protection from the pain of change. There is almost always pain in growth. The trick is to grow at a natural rate. When you force growth, that growth is painful. Growth along with playfulness is less painful.
- If one is more prepared by one's attitude, upbringing, and perhaps even genetics to accept certain types of change, then when those changes occur, one will have something of a blueprint, a map, or a path to get from his or her current state of existence to the new state of existence. In that new state of existence, the difficulty has been incorporated and understood, and it is not difficult anymore.

Observations:
- You can stifle or enhance the growth of a plant by observing those elements that make it grow at its minimum or optimum potential. Consider the beauty of the bonsai.
- Growth is greatest where external pressures are least. The greatest growth occurs in the presence of the greatest freedom.

- The fact of an expanding universe should have been realized earlier. If a static universe existed, then gravity would cause the universe to contract and eventually collapse back in on itself. An expanding universe is a dynamic universe. You also have to be an expanding "universe" otherwise you collapse in on yourself. That is the quality of *growth*. If you are continually growing, you are a dynamic entity. If you are a static entity you eventually become a stagnant entity. Where there is no growth there is no life. So life by its very definition has to have motion, and in a spiritual sense that motion is the acquisition and attainment of positive qualities.

Tips:
- Stable growth means having a ratchet mechanism. A ratchet holds something in a stationary position while energy is placed on the system to move the system. As you grow you need to retain the appropriate stability on the "lesser" level as you expand into the greater.
- You have to have some kind of a guiding system if you're going to be going somewhere. And growth is going to a different state of mind or a state of some higher "beingness." This guiding system is experience. If it is "right," stay on course; if "wrong," adjust course.
- Everyone has heard of the threshold of pain, but there are lots of different thresholds: conflict, failure, success, stress, confusion, security, boredom, filth . . .

  Some people might fail once or twice and decide that's enough; other people can get kicked around all their lives—two different thresholds. It is partly the threshold of pain, because it is painful to fail, but if you are doing what you love, then you are not really failing.

  Notice what your thresholds are. In order to grow, you will need to push your boundaries, and your thresholds are a very good measure of those boundaries.

Admonition: The most potent poisons that kill or retard growth are prejudice and ignorance. That is why an examination of one's beliefs and belief systems is important. Is there a conflict with your highest ideals and your structured beliefs? If so, develop the courage to choose the best you know. If your belief system says to love your enemy but you don't even know your neighbor or you are afraid of someone because of his or her skin color, then there is a lack of harmony between what you believe and what you want to believe.

Comments:
- The following are conditions under which growth will be stifled:

  1. The difficulties are too extreme for the individual
  2. You are too busy to grow
  3. You are too stressed to grow
  4. Your life is too easy
  5. You are prejudiced

- All types of growth don't necessitate adversity, but all types of growth necessitate a change from one state of stability through a state of flux to another state of stability. The level of difficulty is personal. One person's difficult way is another person's smooth highway.

  The ideal is to grow both externally and internally within the range that you choose and at just the appropriate level of difficulty. The pace should take a wavelike pattern with valleys of less difficulty allowing for rest and assimilation and peaks of greater difficulty to stretch your ability.

  There is often conflict in growth. There are two keys to solving this problem:

  1. Understand that conflict is part of growth and be resigned to it as a fact.
  2. Learn to anticipate or even like the conflict. It is possible to recognize conflict as opportunity. Use the qualities of the past as stable groundwork from which to move.

- There must be something to grow into and grow against. In order to be courageous, one must have a situation where nerve is necessary. In order to be altruistic, one must have a situation where giving is necessary. In order to have poise, one must experience or witness rudeness and decide to be respectful.

  Some qualities are supportive qualities. One is patience. For instance, both patience and energy are necessary elements of courage. Is discretion the better part of valor? If so, then patience is part of courage. Knowing when and if to fight and when to hold back are both needed.

  Some supportive qualities are more neutral in nature. For example, information or knowledge of a situation are important to courage. You wouldn't know when to hold back or to move forward unless you had the understanding upon which to base your decision.

• The following are the primary components of successful growth:

1. Choice
2. Loyalty to your choice
3. Enjoyment of your choice
4. Sharing your qualities

Essay:
What is the ultimate reason for learning? To grow, to become, to unfold. But to what end and for what purpose? It is your choice. Your choices are most efficient if they are directed toward your personal concepts of what you consider to be the highest, noblest, or most "real" ideas and ideals. Focus on any of the levels: physical, emotional, intellectual, or spiritual.

All information is filtered first through your thoughts and feelings then through your belief system. The final step before something is included into your being is on the experiential level.

Learning is associated with information and knowledge. Growth is associated with movement from one state of being to another. One can learn without growing but one cannot grow without learning, because growth must be accompanied by the infusion of something of value—a higher quality. A machine can learn but it cannot feel or acquire a higher value.

Sooner or later, all those who ask the ultimate questions will realize that at least part of the answer has to do with continuous growth.

All along the way, the held system of belief will be focusing the mind. *It does not matter what the belief system is.* You could be an agnostic or a religionist. You could believe that you will die and disappear or continue to live and grow forever. We will find out soon enough. But what does matter is that you continue to grow. Only with growth will you expand to encompass your ever greater potential.

Question: Why do people sabotage their own growth? Is it because of a lack of self-esteem, a lack of direction, or a lack of commitment?

Colors: green, red-orange

Symbols: the *tree;* a *field of grain;* any growing *vegetation;* the *stag*

GUIDING

Word Forms: guide, guidingly

Definition: leading; conducting; directing; superintending

Compatible Quality: charismatic

Familial Qualities: leadership, confidence

Legend: *Nestor*, a wise king in Greece, the chief advisor during the siege of Troy

Mythology: *Mentor* was a friend and tutor of Odysseus. Athena sometimes took his form as an advisor; a *mentor*, thus, is a wise and trusted counsellor.

GUMPTION

Word Form: gumptious

Definitions: (1) initiative; resourcefulness; **(2)** courage; spunk; guts; **(3)** common sense; shrewdness

Derivation: Middle English, "to understand," "heed"

GUSTO

Definitions: (1) enthusiastic and vigorous enjoyment or appreciation; **(2)** vitality marked by an abundance of energy and enthusiasm

GUTSY

Word Forms: guts, gutsier, gutsiest, gutsiness

Definitions: (1) daring or courageous; nervy; plucky; forceful; **(2)** robust, vigorous, or earthy; lusty

HANDSOME

Word Forms: handsomer, handsomest, handsomely, handsomeness

Definitions: (1) good-looking; attractive; well-proportioned in appearance; **(2)** graceful in manner; possessing propriety and ease; adroit; **(3)** neat; correct; moderately elegant; **(4)** liberal; generous; gracious

HANDY

Word Forms: hand, handier, handiest, handily, handiness, neat-handed

Definitions: (1) dexterous; ready; adroit; skilled use of the hands; **(2)** ingenious; performing with skill and readiness

Synonyms: useful, helpful

HAPPY

Word Forms: happier, happiest, happily, happiness, happy-go-lucky

Definitions: (1) lucky; fortunate; favored by circumstances; **(2)** having or causing a feeling of great pleasure, joy, or contentment; glad; pleased; satisfied; delighted; **(3)** exactly appropriate to the occasion; suitable and clever; felicitous; apt

Synonyms: successful, merry, blithesome, blissful, prosperous

Quotes:
The rules of a happy life:

1. Don't sweat the small stuff
2. It's all small stuff

—GEORGE ELLIOT

I hope you find, as I did, that happiness comes from noticing and enjoying the little things in life.

—BARBARA ANN KIPFER, *14,000 Things to Be Happy About*

No man is more unhappy than the one who is never in adversity; the greatest affliction of life is never to have been afflicted.

—TRYON EDWARDS

Effort does not always produce joy, but there is no happiness without intelligent effort.

—*The Urantia Book*

Suggestion: Decide to be happy—sincerely and completely no matter what. I mean happy in the manner of the third definition above, "exactly appropriate to the occasion." When you are happy in this way you are truly on your way to being content.

We all want to be happy, but sometimes we are not happy. But you can transcend happy and be Happy anyway. Even when you find yourself in an unhappy state of mind, you have to move forward in time anyway, so move forward with a positive, hopeful attitude. This will displace your actual attitude. Then you would be living on two levels: the level of practical, realistic, daily life and the level of higher, farseeing life. As you experience your actions, words, deeds, and people, project your sensibility and understanding toward how you want to feel and think.

The difference between Happy and Joyful is situational. It is hard to be happy while you are in pain, but the higher quality of joy can be experienced even in the face of difficulty.

Symbols: the *bat* (Chinese); a *leaf* (Chinese); *water maidens;* the *thunderbird* (American Indian); the *sun* (American Indian)

HAPPY-GO-LUCKY

Definition: trusting cheerfully to luck; carefree; happily unworried or unconcerned; easygoing; lighthearted

Comment: When you trust it all to God, you can afford to be happy-go-lucky.

HARDY

Word Forms: hardier, hardiest, hardily, hardiness

Definitions: (1) bold; brave; daring; resolute; intrepid; courageous; (2) strong; firm; compact; stout; (3) confident; full of assurance; (4) indefatigable; rendered firm by exercise; vigorous

Synonyms: inured, robust, stouthearted, resistant, enduring

HARMONIOUS

Word Forms: harmony, harmonies, harmoniously, harmoniousness

Definitions: (1) adapted to each other; having the parts combined in a proportionate, orderly, or pleasing arrangement; congruous; (2) having similar or conforming feelings, ideas, or interests; in accord or agreement

Saying: Sing in harmony—live in harmony.

Quotes:

We need to re-discover the vast, harmonious pattern of the natural world we are a part of, the infinite complexity and variety of its myriad components, the miraculous simplicity of the whole. We need to learn again those essential qualities in our bodies, the alertness of our minds; curiosity and the desire to satisfy it, fear and the will to conquer it.

—JAMES RAMSEY ULLMAN, *Age of Mountaineering*

As long as you are working for your selfish little self, you're just one cell against all those other cells, and you're way out of harmony. But as soon as you begin working for the good of the whole, you find yourself in harmony with all of your fellow human beings.

—PEACE PILGRIM, *Steps Toward Inner Peace*

No life can be in harmony unless belief and practice are in harmony.

— PEACE PILGRIM, *Steps Toward Inner Peace*

Reflection: Relationships in harmony make music.

Comment: An individual needs to have a sense of self that is in harmony with a healthy worldview. When one changes, the other must also change. If they are out of sync, one will experience anxiety during the process of reestablishing the balance.

The key is to include in your worldview the realization and acceptance of the fact of changes, and to include in your inner being an expanding ability to deal with change. The qualities to focus on are flexibility, growth, wisdom, tolerance, courage, understanding, and acceptance.

There is no getting away from conflict, but one must always seek to harmonize the difficulty.

Colors: blue, green

Symbols: the *lyre; three; justice* (tarot); the *whale*

HEALING

Word Forms: heal, healer, health, healingly

Definitions: (1) restore to health; to make sound, well, or healthy again; **(2)** reconcile; to make up

Comment: Healing is what the individual who is ill brings to the curing process.

Colors: magenta, pink, orange, green

Symbols: The *Staff* of the Roman and Greek god of medicine, *Aesculapius*, is the medical symbol and is a staff entwined with one serpent that represents peace, wisdom, and healing. The *Caduceus* with two serpents is also associated with healing because it is the symbol for the Roman god Mercury, who was the god of medicine. The Romans used the caduceus as a symbol of moral equilibrium and good conduct. The wand represents power, the snakes wisdom, the wings diligence, and the helmet symbolizes lofty thoughts.

The month of *June* is the month of healing.

Historical Figure: *Hippocrates*, the Father of Medicine, a Greek physician who lived 460(?) to 377 B.C.

HEALTHY

Word Forms: health, healthier, healthiest, healthful, healthily, healthiness

Definitions: (1) well-being and vigor of body, mind, or spirit; salutary; **(2)** being in a sound state; enjoying fitness; hale; robust; **(3)** conducive to life; wholesome; salubrious; **(4)** prosperous; flourishing

Sayings:
A votre sante (French): "To your health" [used as a toast].

The body is a temple.

Affirmation:
I give thanks for ever-increasing health, vitality, and beauty on all levels of my being.
　　　　—CATHERINE PONDER, *The Dynamic Laws of Prosperity*
　　　　(paraphrase)

Reflections:
• There is an understandable tendency to make attempts to limit the amount of pain that one experiences. On the surface, this seems reasonable. But consider all of the reasons that you need or would prefer to choose pain.

1. If by experiencing a smaller amount of pain you hope to avoid a greater amount
2. If you believe that your sacrifice will protect someone you love or something you believe—like an ideal

3. If by suffering you will give life to another—birth
4. You may wish to continue to allow your current, and therefore known, pain rather than choose a change that may or may not produce a new pain.
5. If by feeling pain you know that you will be getting a reward— like good physical conditioning
6. If the pain is part of the game and the fun of the game outweighs the pain involved
7. If by experiencing the discomfort you will receive the wage you need to sustain your livelihood
8. If pain is a part of the adventure
9. If you cannot reach your goal without it

- If you know your pain and confront it with courage, you won't have to resort to avoiding it. The fearful use different ways to restrict their pain. One way is to be anesthetized with drugs or alcohol, or by making choices that reduce the need to confront the difficulty, that is, find a comfortable niche and allow a minimal amount of change to occur. The logic is that change equals pain. Although there is also pain involved in just keeping your mouth shut and trying to limit your boundaries.

    Another way that the psychologically imbalanced and the emotionally immature manifest their need to reduce their own pain is by creating it in others. There's an extreme example in criminals, of course, but even a "normal" individual will lash out at a stranger, a friend, or family when he or she is in pain or is frustrated or fearful. It is difficult to experience gentleness and patience when you're also experiencing pain or anger, but it is possible.

Colors: pink, green, red

Symbol: *five*

HEART

Word Forms: hearten, heartfelt, hearty, dearheart, big-hearted, great-hearted, heartsease, heartsome, pure-hearted, single-hearted

Definitions: (1) the seat of emotion; **(2)** tenderness; affection; loving character; **(3)** the capacity for kindness; benevolence; **(4)** courage; hardihood; **(5)** inmost thoughts or feelings; consciousness or conscience; **(6)** enthusiasm; energy; spirit; resolution; **(7)** the vital or essential part; the real meaning; the core

Compatible Qualities: relaxed, joyful, soft, peaceful, playful

Music:
You've gotta have heart, miles and miles and miles of heart.
                    —"MILES AND MILES AND MILES OF HEART"

Saying:
Le coeur a ses raisons que la raison ne connait point (French): "The heart has its reasons that reason knows nothing of."

Quotes:
In spite of everything, I still believe that people are really good at heart.
                    —ANNE FRANK (1929–1944), *The Diary of Anne Frank*

Every heart that has beat strong and cheerfully has left a hopeful impulse behind it in the world.
                    —ROBERT LOUIS STEVENSON

Symbols: the center of the body, therefore, the center of eternity—the *heart;* the heart of the universe—the *sun;* the heart of the earth—*gold;* the *lotus flower*

HEARTY

Word Forms: heartier, heartiest, heartily, heartiness, hardihood

Definitions: (1) sincere; warm; cordial; proceeding from the heart; **(2)** full of health; sound; strong; **(3)** unrestrained expression; vigorous; exuberant

HELPFUL

Word Forms: help, helpfully, helpfulness

Definition: rendering aid or assistance; useful; giving service

Compatible Quality: friendly

Saying:
If someone comes to you asking for help, do not say in refusal, "Trust in God. God will help you." Rather, act as if there is no God, and no one to help except you.

—HASIDIC

Quotes:
Like the blind man standing on the corner waiting for somebody to lead him across; all of us, at some point in our lives, need some help.

—JOE FRAZIER

One has a right to criticize, who has a heart to help.

—ABRAHAM LINCOLN

Parable: There was a preacher who believed in God's help. Now his church was in danger from the rising waters of a flood. When it was time for evacuation, he got all of his parishioners out safely and then went back to the church. The police came in a squad car and said it is time to go, but he refused, saying, "I will put my faith in God. He will save me." Later he was on the second story of the church with the water rising fast and the rescue squad came by in a boat to pick him up, but he refused them, saying, "Thank you kindly, but I am not leaving. God will save me." Finally he had to get onto the roof and hold onto the steeple with the raging waters all around him. A National Guard helicopter arrived to save him, but again he refused them, saying, "God will help me." Well, the preacher was drowned. When he got to heaven he asked God why He didn't help him in his time of need. God said, "What do you mean? I sent you a car, a boat, and a helicopter!"

Tip: Simply be willing to be helpful and you will have the opportunity.

Constrain your willingness so that you are not pushy about helping where it is unwanted.

HEROIC

Word Forms: hero, heroical, heroine, heroism, heroize

Definitions: (1) brave; bold; intrepid; noble; renowned; (2) characterizes men of godlike strength or courage; (3) exalted; eloquent; high-flown <as *heroic* words>; (4) daring and risky, but used as a last resort <as *heroic* measures>

Synonyms: fearless, valiant, gallant

Quote:
> The hero is the man of self-achieved submission.
> —Joseph Campbell, *The Hero with a Thousand Faces*

Symbols: heroic striving—*Hercules;* the *sun*

HIGH-MINDED

Word Forms: high-mindedly, high-mindedness

Definition: having or showing high ideals, principles, and feelings

Color: yellow

HIGH-SPIRITED

Word Forms: high-spiritedly, high-spiritedness

Definition: full of spirit or natural fire; vivacious; boldly courageous; noble; mettlesome

HOLY

Word Forms: holier, holiest

Definitions: (1) possessing spiritual and moral worth or aims; **(2)** evoking or meriting reverence or awe

Too Far: sanctimonious

Color: red

Symbol: the *halo*

HOMEY

Word Forms: home, homier, homiest, homeyness

Definition: having qualities associated with home; comfortably familiar; cozy; informal

Compatible Quality: wholesome

HONEST

Word Forms: honesty, honestly, honestness

Definitions: (1) honorable; held in reverence; respectable; **(2)** creditable; praiseworthy <an *honest* day's work>; **(3)** commendable; seemly; **(4)** truthful; trustworthy; possessing integrity; **(5)** showing fairness and sincerity; frank; **(6)** innocent
  See also: *Upright*

Kindred Quality: decisiveness

Too Far: insensitive, naive

Quotes:

> *The devil can cite Scripture for his purpose.*
> *An evil soul, producing holy witness,*
> *Is like a villain with a smiling cheek,*
> *A goodly apple rotten at the heart:*
> *O what a goodly outside falsehood hath!*
> —WILLIAM SHAKESPEARE, *Merchant of Venice*

"Honesty"—(absolutely indispensable in science)— . . . is probably the least likely marvel ever to have emerged out of self-centered human minds.

> —DAVID BRIN, *Otherness*

Consideration: If you are dishonest and you feel guilty about it, that's good! It's good because it shows you that there is a discrepancy between what you do and what you idealize as proper behavior. Guilt is an intermediate step to honesty. It is a level of awareness that is essential for further progress. But eventually you must move away from both the guilt and the dishonesty.

Observation: A person finding themselves in a compromising situation will have their honesty tested.

Comments:
- Honesty is gentle, kind, and clear. When honesty has clarity, it also has purity.
- Honesty must be guided by wisdom. You need to know when to speak and when to hold your tongue. Honesty is like sunshine and shade. Sometimes you want one, and sometimes you want the other.
- No matter what the external moral or immoral pressures, integrity and honesty begin with you. You still have the choice. The soldier taking orders still has the personal decision whether or not to pull the trigger.
- When prejudice has been institutionalized upon a culture, race, or religion, the oppressors have a vested interested in maintaining the self-serving, "justified" dishonesty. They have lots of company in upholding the lie that they live, and look for any reason to prop up the injustice. When the oppressed is courageous enough to speak the truth, there is a genuine perceived threat to the oppressor. The threat is described in loss of jobs and safety, and many other reasonable excuses, but at the base of it still lies the oppression.

HONORABLE

Word Forms: honor, honorability, honorably, honorableness

Definitions: (1) worthy of great respect; highly regarded; estimable; (2) actuated by principles of honor; a scrupulous regard to probity, rectitude, or reputation

Synonyms: nobility, dignity, spirit, renown, upright

Quote:
What is honored in a country is cultivated there.
—PLATO

Note: What is honored in the self is also cultivated there.

Symbol: the *turtle*

HOPEFUL

Word Forms: hope, hopefully, hopefulness

Definitions: (1) desire for good accompanied with a belief that it is obtainable; expecting to get what one wants and needs; (2) having the vision, energy, and ability to turn dreams into reality

Synonyms: expectation, confidence

Compatible Qualities: optimism, determination

Consequential Quality: long-suffering

Music: "Over the Rainbow," E. Y. Harburg

Quotes:
Hope is an orientation of the spirit, an orientation of the heart. It is . . . the certainty that something makes sense, regardless of how it turns out.
—VACLAV HAVEL

Hope springs eternal in the human breast.

> —ALEXANDER POPE

Hope is a good thing, maybe the best thing and no good thing ever dies.

> —*The Shawshank Redemption*

If the universe seems to be trying to destroy you, the best way to fight back is with hope.

> —DAVID BRIN, *Brightness Reef*

Cartoon:

Snoopy cartoon

1st frame: Snoopy complains of a feeling of meaninglessness and emptiness.
2nd frame: Charlie Brown enters with a bowl full of dog food.
3rd frame: Snoopy exclaims, "Ah, meaning!"

Observation:

The Basics in Life:

1. Values
2. Meanings
3. Hopes—goals and desires
4. Needs
5. Experiences

Tip: As you make up a new life, that's the only life that is.

Comment: You can get there from here. You can always get to nirvana or normalcy or wherever you want to get, even if you are at rock bottom. Be grounded where you are and continue your journey.

Colors: orange, blue, green, rainbow

Symbols: the *anchor; seed;* the *helmet*

HOSPITABLE

Word Forms: hospitality, hospitably, hospitableness

Definitions: (1) receiving and entertaining strangers and guests with generous kindness and in a friendly manner; **(2)** offering a pleasant or sustaining environment; **(3)** liberal and generous in disposition and mind; receptive or open to new ideas

Admonition: If you cannot be hospitable at least be civil.

Mythology: *Baucis and Philemon* were an affectionate couple who hospitably entertained Jupiter and Mercury. In gratitude their little house was turned into a palace. In response to their wish to be together always, they were turned into twin trees when they died.

HUGGABLE

Word Forms: hug, hugged, hugging, hugger, huggle

Definition: inviting a close embrace; cuddly

How to Live This Quality Today: Hug someone.

HUMANE

Word Forms: humanely, humaneness

Definition: having what are considered the best qualities of humankind; kind; tender; merciful; considerate; sympathetic; compassionate; benevolent, et cetera

Quote:
Eliminate irrelevant and inaccurate communications about what it means to be male or female, black or white, young or old, rich or poor, disabled or temporarily able-bodied, or to hold a particular belief system.
—ROSALIE MAGGIO, *The Non-Sexist Word Finder*

HUMANITARIAN

Word Forms: human, humanity, humanitarianism, humanistic

Definition: a person promoting human welfare and social reform, especially through the elimination of pain and suffering; a philanthropist

HUMBLE

Word Forms: humbler, humblest, humility, humbly, humbleness

Definitions: (1) free from pride or vanity; modest; meek; (2) respectful

Synonyms: unassuming, unobtrusive, unpretentious

Prayer:
    Number seven of the Alcoholics Anonymous twelve-step program:

    We humbly ask God (as we understand the concept) to remove our shortcomings.

Symbol: *shoes*

HUMOROUS

Word Forms: humor, humorously, humorousness

Definitions: (1) funny; comical; jocular; amusing; droll; risible; (2) having the power to speak or write in the style of humor; fanciful; playful; exciting laughter

Quote:
    Imagination was given to man to compensate him for what he is not; a sense of humor to console him for what he is.

                               —FRANCIS BACON

Observation: A sense of humor is just as important as the physical senses.

HUSTLE

Word Forms: hustled, hustling

Definitions: (1) proceed or work rapidly or energetically; **(2)** aggressive, especially in business; **(3)** to urge, prod, or speed up

HYGIENIC

Word Forms: hygiene, hygienical, hygienics, hygienically

Definition: promoting good health; healthful; sanitary; clean

HYPNOTIC

Word Forms: hypnosis, hypnotically, hypnotize, hypnotism

Definition: fascinating; spellbinding; entrancing

IDEALISTIC

Word Forms: idea, ideal, idealist, idealistically, idealization

Definitions: (1) behavior or thought based on a conception of things as they should be or as one would wish them to be; **(2)** striving to achieve one's ideals

Quote:
> *Ideas* may take origin in the stimuli of the outer world, but *ideals* are born only in the creative realm of the inner world.
> —*The Urantia Book*

Color: yellow

ILLUSTRATIVE

Word Forms: illustrate, illustratively

Definition: the quality of elucidating and making clear what is obscure

Derivation: Latin, "clear," "bright," "lustrous"

Compatible Quality: artistic

ILLUSTRIOUS

Word Forms: illustriously, illustriousness

Definitions: (1) conspicuous; a reputation of greatness or renown; **(2)** conferring luster or honor; brilliant
    See also: *Distinguished*

Derivation: Latin, "clear," "conspicuous," "distinguished"

Synonyms: glorious, noble, eminent, celebrated, famous

IMAGINATIVE

Word Forms: imagine, imagination, imaginatively, imaginativeness

Definitions: (1) using or showing vision, creativity, or productive talent; **(2)** able to conceptualize or feel a situation other than that within one's personal experience

Synonyms: conceptive, ideal, poetical, romantic, inventive, original

Too Far: Imagination taken to an animated level becomes fantasy.

Fantasy taken too far makes for an unreal inner world. Balance your fantasy with hands-on experience and follow-through.

Quotes:
> What is now proved was once imagined.
>
> —WILLIAM BLAKE

> Don't rely on words or equations until you can picture the idea they represent.
>
> —LEWIS EPSTEIN AND PAUL HEWITT

> You can find in a text whatever you bring, if you will stand between it and the mirror of your imagination. You may not see your ears but they are there.
>
> —MARK TWAIN

> Imagination is more important than knowledge.
>
> —ALBERT EINSTEIN

> Most people look at what is and never see what can be.
>
> —ALBERT EINSTEIN

> Look about you this moment: Everything you see and touch was once [an] invisible idea until someone chose to bring it into being. Any powerful idea is absolutely fascinating and absolutely useless until we choose to use it.
>
> —RICHARD BACH, *One*

Comments:
- No matter how qualified or deserving you are, you will never reach a better life until you imagine it for yourself and allow yourself to have it.
- You can use your imagination against yourself too. People use their imaginations all the time. They're very creative about how they should feel—good or bad. Most of the negative self-talk is pure imagination.

Color: yellow

Symbols: *flight; wings;* the *moon; Gemini* (zodiac)

IMITABLE

Word Forms: imitate, imitability, imitableness

Definition: worthy of being copied or imitated

Question: Would you want someone to follow your example and carry on your work?

IMMACULATE

Word Forms: immaculacy, immaculately, immaculateness

Definitions: (1) pure; innocent; perfectly correct; (2) spotless; unstained; without flaw, blemish, fault, or error

IMMUNE

Word Forms: immunity, immunize

Definition: being safe; exempt from or protected against something disagreeable or harmful

Admonition: Immunize yourself from fear with love, from sorrow with laughter, from loneliness with friendship.

IMPARTIAL

Word Forms: impartiality, impartially, impartialness

Definition: (1) equitable; just; fair; (2) objective; not biased in favor of one party more than another; unprejudiced
    See also: *Nonjudgmental*

Familial Quality: open

Comment: Being impartial does not mean that you are indifferent, disinterested, or that you do not care, just that you are willing to take the facts as you see them without putting any undue judgment on them. You do eventually have to judge some things, but if you are open, you will be treating the people and the situation more fairly.

IMPECCABLE

Word Forms: impeccability, impeccably

Definition: immaculate; exemplary; without defect or error; faultless; flawless

People Who Exemplify This Quality:
Impeccable is a snappy dresser. He likes clean lines and he always smells good. Some people think of him as rigid, but when they get to know him they see how graceful he really is. Especially if they witness him performing the tango with his favorite dance partner, *Pizazz*.

Impeccable plays Chopin with his little brother, *Punctilious*, whom he affectionately calls "Punky" in private.
                    —AFTER THE STYLE OF JANET RUTH GENDLER IN
                    The Book of Qualities

IMPERIAL

Word Forms: imperially, imperialness

Definitions: (1) pertaining to an empire or to an emperor; (2) commanding; maintaining supremacy; sovereign; (3) majestic; august; magnificent; regal; imperious

Question: What would it be like if every man acted like a king and every woman a queen?

IMPORTANT

Word Forms: import, importance, importantly

Definitions: (1) having much significance, value, or influence; outstanding; great; of exceptional consequence; (2) deserving special notice or attention; noteworthy

Synonyms: relevant, dignified, momentous, essential

Affirmation:
I am inherently important and uniquely designed to do my own thing so perfectly that no one else in the world can do it like me.
—JACQUELYN SMALL, *Transformers*

IMPRESSIVE

Word Forms: impress, impression, impressively, impressiveness

Definitions: (1) makes an imprint on the mind, feelings, or senses; has the power to affect or excite attention and feeling; (2) arouses admiration or respect

Synonyms: imposing, important

Observation: If you do something well, it will impress someone. There is an exception to this. In an organization where the job is to create a smooth flow, the smoother things go the less the people who create that smoothness leave an impression. This is because the organization is primarily dealing with that which does not go well and those who don't know how or care to do an excellent job. It takes a wise and observant manager to occasionally set aside the handling of difficulties and praise those who make his or her life easier because they can be relied on to make things work so well that they are invisible.

IMPROVING

Word Forms: improve, improvable, improvement, improvingly

Definition: raising to a higher or more desirable state or value; making better

Synonyms: advancing, enhancing, progressing, proficient

Comment: Although there are those times when we experience a burst of flourishing growth, most of the time "becoming" is like watching paint dry—sure and steady. It takes time but it looks good, even as it is drying. Unlike paint, acquiring qualities continues to grow in beauty beyond the drying time.

IMPROVISATIONAL

Word Forms: improvise, improvisation, improvisationally

Definition: makes do with the tools and materials at hand, usually filling an unforeseen and immediate need; spontaneously creative

INCISIVE

Word Forms: incise, incision, incisively, incisiveness

Definition: penetrating, piercing, or keen intellect; clear and direct thought; sharp; acute intuition

Derivation: Latin, "to cut into"

Compatible Quality: concentration

INDEFATIGABLE

Word Forms: indefatigability, indefatigably, indefatigableness

Definition: persistent; persevering; unwearied; untiring; not exhausted by labor; not yielding to fatigue

Synonyms: assiduous, sedulous, unremitting, unwearied

Comment: The positive qualities are like a whole field of pearls of great price. Each is worth an inexhaustible effort.

INDEPENDENT

Word Forms: independence, independently

Definitions: (**1**) self-determining; not subject to the control or influence of others; free from the rule of another; self-governing; (**2**) self-directing; not subject to bias, persuasion, or influence; not obsequious; (**3**) self-commanding; free; easy; bold; unconstrained

Synonyms: separate, unrestricted

Saying: If it is to be, it is up to me.

Quotes:
No one is entitled to be given answers to the problems that beset them. If you wish to know the truth of things, you must find it out for yourself.
—TERRY BROOKS, *The Black Unicorn*

Steps to Financial Independence

(Adapted from Catherine Ponder, *The Dynamic Laws of Prosperity*)

1. Be quiet, meditate, and ask.
2. Decide to achieve financial independence and get a sense of peace about the rightness of it for you.

3. Make a detailed mental picture of what you really want.
4. Proceed as you feel led. Do not try to force or hurry your way to fulfillment.
5. Quietly continue to persevere in whatever ways are revealed to you. Stick to it and you will succeed!
6. Realize that your dreams of financial independence have already come true on the mental plane and that every good thing already exists.
7. Remind yourself often of what you have already accomplished.

Comments: People who have had too much to drink may want to be independent and believe that they are capable enough to drive, but a sober person should judge if the threshold has been crossed and take control.

INDIVIDUALISTIC

Word Forms: individual, individualist, individualistically

Definition: characterizes one who pursues an independent course in thought or action

Too Far: rebellious

Quote:
[The Cowardly Lion:] "To be individual, my friends, to be different from others, is the only way to become distinguished from the common herd. Let us be glad, therefore, that we differ from one another in form and disposition. Variety is the spice of life and we are various enough to enjoy one another's society; so let us be content."
                                              —L. FRANK BAUM, *The Lost Princess of Oz*

Comment: If you are not working with an organization, and especially if you are not very gregarious, then one of the things that has to be strong is your confidence and faith that what you are doing is what you are supposed to be doing, that it is good and valuable. If you are writing a book, are a lone artist or an independent adventurer, then you have an opportunity to develop the characteristics of individuality.

Structure: In *Discover* magazine (May 1992), Jerold M. Lowenstein explains in his article on the Human Genome Project that all human beings are 99.9 percent genetically identical. But since the number of human DNA base pairs equals approximately 3 billion, the 0.1 percent difference amounts to 3 million bases. It is this 3 million that insures our individuality. Even in identical twins individuality is unmistakable. And that is only on the physical level. Then take into consideration environment, experience, and attitude.

Symbol: *Leo* (zodiac)

INDOMITABLE

Word Forms: indomitability, indomitably, indomitableness

Definition: firm; not easily discouraged, defeated, or subdued; unyielding; unconquerable

Too Far: overbearing

INDUSTRIOUS

Word Forms: industry, industriously, industriousness

Definition: diligent; hard-working; constantly, regularly, or habitually occupied; assiduous

Synonyms: busy, active, laborious, sedulous

Saying: *Hoc age* (Latin): "Do this!" [Apply yourself to your thing.]

Quotes:
[Johnny Dooit:] "The only way to do a thing is do it when you can, and do it cheerfully, and sing and work and think and plan. The only real unhappy one is he who dares to shirk; the only real happy one is he who cares to work."
            —L. Frank Baum, *The Road to Oz*

The harder you work, the luckier you get.

—GARY PLAYER

Symbol: *bees*

INFLUENTIAL

Word Forms: influence, influencially

Definition: having the capacity or power to produce great effects on others by intangible or indirect means; effective

Synonyms: potent, forcible, persuasive, controlling, guiding, authoritative, leading

INFORMATIVE

Word Forms: inform, information, informatively, informativeness

Definition: imparting knowledge through language, facts, lore, data, music, or entertainment; instructive; answering questions

Familial Quality: service minded

Symbol: The *raven*. Odin, the supreme Scandinavian deity, had two ravens who told him of everything that went on in the world.

INGENIOUS

Word Forms: ingenuity, ingeniously, ingeniousness

Definitions: (1) having an ability to originate new combinations of ideas; inventive; (2) skilled at making things work; resourceful; (3) witty; well formed; well adapted

Derivation: Latin, "having unusual capacity," "gifted with genius"

Synonyms: talented, clever

Compatible Quality: genius

INGENUOUS

Word Forms: ingenue, ingenuously, ingenuousness

Definitions: (1) fair; candid; free from reserve, disguise, or equivocation; **(2)** innocent; naive

Synonyms: open, frank, ingenuous
People who are *open* speak out at once about what is uppermost in the mind; people who are *frank* do so from a natural boldness; people who are *ingenuous* are actuated by candor and love of truth, which makes them willing to speak their minds without reserve.

INITIATIVE

Word Forms: initial, initiate, initiatively

Definitions: (1) taking the first step or move; responsible for beginning or originating action; **(2)** the attribute of originating new ideas or methods; to think and act without being urged; enterprising

Kindred Qualities: insight, courage, experience

Quote:
The biggest things are always the easiest to do because there is no competition.
                                        —WILLIAM VAN HORNE

Comment: Initiative sometimes "fails" because an educated guess has to be made on things with which you don't have experience or information.

Your guesses become a new set of circumstances upon which to base the next experience in your quest for qualities. If you get negative feedback, you have an opportunity to work on communication and understanding. Since you decided to take the initiative, the gamble was worth it.

INNER-DIRECTED

Word Form: directed

Definition: directed in thought and action by one's own scale of values as opposed to external norms

Parental Quality: faith

Comment: When focusing on the inner realm, you will discover subconscious, conscious, and superconscious. You will know the superconscious by its feel. This is the area from which your higher impulses and a sense of right action emanate. This is what to heed.

INNOCENT

Word Forms: innocence, innocently

Definitions: (1) free from guilt or sin, especially through lack of knowledge of evil; blameless; guiltless; faultless; (2) without guile or cunning; lacking sophistication; ingenuous

Synonyms: pure, undefiled, virtuous, immaculate, spotless, simple

Comment: The quality of innocence is normally attributed to the purity and beauty of a new baby. It is such a compelling quality that we are instantly drawn to that bright bundle of pure potential. As time goes on, add to that personality the qualities of sincerity, grace, charm, and wonder and the innocence blossoms dynamically into a splendid, mature soul.

Color: white

Symbols: *sheep;* a sleeping *baby*

INNOVATIVE

Word Forms: innovate, innovation, innovatively, innovativeness

Definition: able to change or alter by introducing something new

Compatible Quality: cooperative

INQUISITIVE

Word Forms: inquire, inquiring, inquisitor, inquisitively, inquisitiveness

Definition: inclined to seek knowledge by discussion, investigation, or observation; given to research; eager for knowledge; curious

Compatible Quality: informative

Symbol: the *question mark* (*?*)

INSIGHTFUL

Word Forms: sight, insight, insightfully, insightfulness

Definitions: (1) power to see into a situation; penetrating; perceptive; **(2)** the act or result of apprehending the inner nature of things or of seeing intuitively

Synonyms: discerning, introspective, acumen, shrewd, keen, clever, perspicacious

Kindred Quality: prayerful

INSPIRING

Word Forms: inspire, inspiration, inspirable, inspiringly

Definitions: (1) having an animating effect upon; influencing, stimulating, or impelling; inducing to some creative or effective effort; **(2)** capable of moving a person to a particular feeling or idea; **(3)** to be filled with the spirit

Quote:
Inspiration may be a form of superconsciousness, or perhaps of subconsciousness—I wouldn't know. But I am sure that it is the antithesis of self-consciousness.

—AARON COPLAND

Comment: If you focus on the positive, even in your criticisms of a person or a situation, you are helping to transform both the situation and the person.

It is easy to feel badly when treated poorly. There are so many ways to be treated poorly. But if you lash out in anger and frustration, you will only be successful in creating more anger and resistance. In hoping to control an ugly situation, you may be able to box it up. But the person or people who have created the negative have not been changed.

Containment may be necessary as a first resort. Society and the individual do have the right to protect themselves. But force from the outside is not the final solution. The final solution is for people to possess the qualities within themselves that will make it impossible to do the negative things that they have done before. When you inspire people with the positive, they tend to act in accordance with their higher qualities.

Color: blue

Symbol: the *torch*

INSTINCTIVE

Word Forms: instinct, instinctively

Definition: inspired by a natural tendency or propensity; arising spontaneously; being independent of judgment or will

Synonyms: intuitive, inborn, automatic

Quote:
For all the talk you hear about knowledge being such a wonderful thing, instinct is worth 40 of it for real unerringness.
—MARK TWAIN

Observation: Something experienced becomes instinct. This may be how abilities and qualities are passed on genetically.

Symbols: the *house;* the *steed*

INSTRUCTIVE

Word Forms: instruct, instruction, instructively, instructiveness

Definition: conveying knowledge; serving to educate or inform

Comment: Teachers are some of our most valuable citizens.

INSTRUMENTAL

Word Forms: instrument, instrumentally, instrumentality

Definition: conducive, as an instrument or means to some end; contributing aid; useful; helpful

Prayer: Lord, make me an instrument of your peace.

INTEGRATED

Word Forms: integrate, integrating, integration

Definition: formed, coordinated, or blended into a functioning or unified whole; united

Quote:
When we try to pick out anything by itself, we find it is tied to everything else in the universe.

—JOHN MUIR

Symbols: a *necklace;* a *sheaf* or *bundle; interlocking fingers*

INTEGRITY

Definition: the quality of being of sound moral principle; uprightness of character; honest and sincere; incorruptible

Compatible Qualities: complete, firm

Suggestion: Trust the higher self to do what is right instead of manipulating the ego self to live up to your expectation.

Symbols: a *rock* or *stone;* the *lover* (tarot)

INTELLIGENT

Word Forms: intellect, intelligence, intelligently

Definitions: (1) knowing; understanding; well informed; sensible; skilled; having wisdom; having an active, discerning mind; acute; (2) guided or directed by mind; rational; quick to learn

Synonyms: *Intelligent, clever, alert*, and *quick-witted* mean mentally keen or quick. *Intelligent* stresses success in coping with new situations and solving problems. *Clever* implies native ability or aptness. *Alert* stresses quickness in perceiving and understanding. *Quick-witted* implies promptness in finding answers in debate or humor and in devising expedients in moments of danger or challenge.

Admonition: There are seven types of intelligence as proposed by Howard Gardner in *Frames of Mind*: linguistic, logical/mathematical, musical, spatial, kinesthetic, knowing oneself, and knowing others.

Recognize that you have all types of intelligence to some degree. What is important is to keep expanding all areas of yourself. It is easier to do so in the area(s) that is (are) comfortable, but it is possible to develop the other areas too. Do this by putting yourself into the path of learning and by dealing with confrontations as you move through life.

Comment: If you believe that you are not intelligent, you are probably underestimating yourself. Test your limits. You will tend to hold yourself within what you think to be true. You can always underestimate and be more confident of success, but if you overestimate, with a dash of prudence, you will attain greater results.

Color: yellow

Symbols: the seat of intelligence—the *heart;* the *sun; wings;* a *lamp; Virgo* (zodiac)

INTERESTING

Word Forms: interest, interested, interestingly

Definition: exciting attention or curiosity; attractive

Quote:
Happiness goes like the wind, but what is interesting stays.
—GEORGIA O'KEEFFE

Suggestion: Being genuinely interested in what is wonderful in others will excite them to exhibit the best of themselves. And you will be inspired to find ways to help them feel free to show their endearing qualities.

INTIMATE

Word Forms: intimacy, intimately, intimateness

Definitions: (1) closeness with warm friendship developed through long association; very familiar; **(2)** indicative of one's deepest nature; intrinsic; essential

Quotes:

People didn't understand that true intimacy did not consist of sexual intercourse, which could be done with strangers and in a state of total alienation; intimacy consisted of talking for hours about what was most important in one's life.

—KIM STANLEY ROBINSON, *Red Mars*

Color: orange-brown

INTREPID

Word Forms: intrepidity, intrepidly, intrepidness

Definition: resolutely fearless; bold; brave; undaunted; possessing enduring fortitude

Derivation: Latin, "not trembling or shaking with fear"

Symbol: the *boar*

INTRIGUING

Word Forms: intrigue, intriguingly

Definition: arousing intense interest or curiosity by the display of fascinating qualities

INTROSPECTIVE

Word Forms: introspect, introspectively, introspectiveness

Definition: looking into one's own mind, feelings, reactions, or motives; observation and analysis of oneself

Derivation: Latin, "to look within"

INTUITIVE

Word Forms: intuit, intuition

Definition: characterizes one who immediately knows or learns of something without the conscious use of reasoning; possessing instantaneous apprehension, the sixth sense, inner sight or insight; instinctual

Kindred Qualities: faith, self-confidence, freedom

Quotes:
> You can count how many seeds are in the apple, but not how many apples are in the seed.
>
> —KEN KESEY

> To the rationally minded the mental processes of the intuitive appears to work backwards.
>
> —FRANCES WICKES

Reflection: Intuition is the mind's gift to experience. It is in between knowledge and experience. With intuition you can know something that you haven't actually experienced.

Some things you can only get through experience, but intuition can help you get it. And some things you only need to get through intuition. Intuition makes learning more efficient.

Comments:
- Intuition is more conducive to success in a calm, relaxing environment, free from distraction. This peaceful situation can be external but must be internal. In a busy environment where your mind is filled with thoughts, if you have a quiet space inside, the intuitive answers can still flow.

- Intuition is a short cut to solution. There are the plodding, analytical steps of getting from A to Z, but intuition travels faster than the speed of logical thought.
- Intuitive clarity is not only the sharp vision of mental clarity but also the knowing feeling of an emotional rush.
- Intuition can be a flash of genius or a gentle nudge. While pondering a problem, your intuition says, "This is the way," but it also says, "That's not exactly it." Heed also that "negative" intuition that pushes you away from some course of action.

How to Live This Quality Today: Follow your hunches faithfully and you will develop a faith and clarity that will lead you to your "right way." Another course of action may be a better one for the majority, but if you are acting on your inner guidance, you will feel more in control, more confident, and comfortable. If you are wrong, you will know that it was your choice. Plus you are learning what is a productive hunch and what is not.

Colors: indigo, yellow

Symbols: the sound of the *flute;* the *sun;* the planet *Mercury; window(s); water*

INVENTIVE

Word Forms: invent, inventively, inventiveness

Definition: adept at producing something new; creative; ingenious

Saying: Necessity is the mother of invention.

Quote:
There are three stages in the life cycle of any scientific idea. First, it's treated as a joke. Next, it's taken seriously but considered to be impossible. Finally, people admit that it's possible, but they insist that it's trivial.
—MICHAEL ROSE, Mathematical Geneticist, *Discover*, June 1992

Observation: If you lose something you once had, you have a great opportunity to be inventive. I know a man who was left-handed and lost his left arm in a motorcycle accident; it is amazing how inventive he has gotten with his right hand.

Suggestion: Give workers their fair share of the profit for their inventiveness within the workplace. Call it the Inventive Incentive. If the organization takes the profit and the credit for the employees' inventiveness, there is less incentive for the individual to be open to creativity.

Symbol: a *light bulb*

INVESTIGATIVE

Word Forms: investigate, investigation, investigatory

Definition: Curious and deliberate in research; the action or process of searching minutely for truth, facts or principles; a careful inquiry to find out what is unknown in the physical or moral world either by observation and experiment or by argument and discussion

IRRESISTIBLE

Word Forms: irresistibility, irresistibly, irresistibleness

Definitions: (1) that which cannot be successfully resisted or opposed; superior to opposition; **(2)** tempting to possess; enticing; alluring

JAUNTY

Word Forms: jauntier, jauntiest, jauntily, jauntiness

Definitions: (1) gay and easy in manner or bearing; airy, sprightly; perky; **(2)** stylish; chic

JOCULAR

Word Forms: jocularity, jocularly

Definitions: (1) merry; given to jesting; habitually jolly; (2) containing jokes; sportive; not serious; playful; witty

Observation: A joke that makes fun of or belittles someone is no joke.

Comment: It takes some discretion and tact to know when to interject some jocularity into a serious situation. It could be the best thing to break the tension and get people seeing things in perspective again or it could be the most tasteless thing to do. It's all in the timing and reading the situation accurately.

JOIE DE VIVRE

Definition: a delight in being alive; carefree, buoyant enjoyment

Derivation: French, "joy of living"

Symbol: a full head of *hair*

JOLLY

Word Forms: jollier, jolliest, jollied, jollity, jollying, jollies, jollily, jolliness

Definitions: (1) merry; gay; lively; full of life and mirth; jovial; (2) expressing, inspiring, or exciting frivolity and gaiety; (3) cheerfully festive; (4) delightful; charming

Derivation: Probably Icelandic, refers to the feast of Christmas

Synonyms: sportive, sprightly, joyous

Legend: *King Cole*, a legendary British King, was noted for his joviality ("Ol' King Cole was a merry old soul").

JOVIAL

Word Forms: joviality, jovialize, jovially, jovialness, jovian

Definition: good-humored; good-natured; convivial; jolly; merry; joyous

Derivation: under the influence of Jove or Jupiter, the chief Roman god

Color: orange

JOYFUL

Word Forms: joy, joyfully, joyfulness

Definition: feeling, expressing, or causing a very glad feeling; happiness; great pleasure; delight
   See also: *Comical, Bright*

Synonyms: rapture, ecstasy, exultation

Quote:
   Grief can take care of itself, but to get the full value of joy you must have someone to divide it with.
                              —MARK TWAIN, *Puddin'head Wilson*

Symbols: the *butterfly* (Chinese); a *ship* plowing through the sea

Mythology: *Euphrosyne*, one of the three Graces of Greek Mythology— these three sisters had control over pleasure, charm, elegance, and beauty in human life and in nature.

JUBILANT

Word Forms: jubilate, jubilee, jubilance, jubilation, jubilantly

Definitions: (1) characterizes a time of happy celebration and rejoicing; **(2)** spontaneously expresses joy; triumphant; exultant

JUDICIOUS

Word Forms: judicial, judiciously, judiciousness

Definition: possessing sound judgment; discreet; prudent; wise

Synonyms: sagacious, expedient, sensible, well-judged, well-advised, politic, discerning, thoughtful

Sayings:
Judgment comes from experience. Experience comes from poor judgment.

Ex pede Herculem (Latin): "from the foot of Hercules" [From a part we may judge the whole.]

Reflection: On judgment day, God is not going to ask you what you have done but who you are becoming.

Observation: The problem with a jury of one's peers is the redneck jury who sentenced a fourteen-year-old black boy to death because he spoke flippantly to an older white woman. Then when the jury who tried him were put on trial, their peers declared their actions just.

Symbol: *Jupiter*

JUST

Word Forms: justice, justify, justly, justness

Definitions: (1) upright; proper; having principles of rectitude, honesty, and righteousness; **(2)** equitable; impartial; fair

Saying: *Fiat justitia, ruat caelum* (Latin): "Let justice be done though the heavens fall."

Motto:
Justitia omnibus (Latin): "Justice for all."
                                                    —DISTRICT OF COLUMBIA

Quotes:
Appropriate anger can be a force for good. Anger has provoked good and courageous people to come forward and defend the rights of those who are powerless to defend themselves.
                    —ABIGAIL VAN BUREN, *The Anger in All of Us and How to Deal with It*

It is wise to disregard laws when they conflict with justice.
                                    —L. FRANK BAUM, *Tik-Tok of Oz*

Injustice anywhere is a threat to justice everywhere. We are caught in an inescapable network of mutuality, tied in a single garment of destiny. Whatever affects one directly affects all indirectly.
                    —DR. MARTIN LUTHER KING JR., Letter from Birmingham City Jail

[Justice] is the first virtue of social institutions, as truth is of systems of thought.
                                                    —JOHN RAWLS

Comment: Justice has a lot to do with seeing reality from the "other's" point of view.

Symbols: blindfolded woman with scales—*Lady Justice;* justice—the *crane;* the *sword; fourteen*

Mythology: *Astraea*, in Greek and Roman mythology, the goddess of justice who became the constellation Virgo

KEEN

Word Forms: keener, keenest, keenly, keenness, keen-witted

Definitions: (1) acutely or finely perceptive; extremely sensitive, responsive, or alert; **(2)** having great acumen; shrewdly intelligent; astute; **(3)** animated by strong feeling or desire; **(4)** eager; interested; enthusiastic; **(5)** great; wonderful; marvelous

KIND

Word Forms: kindhearted, kindly, kindliness, kindness

Definitions: (1) gentle and considerate; disposed to be helpful and solicitous; good and tenderhearted; friendly; generous; **(2)** affectionate; loving; agreeable; **(3)** inclined to give pleasure or relief; sympathetic

Synonyms: well-disposed, courteous

Quotes:
[Tollydiggle:] "It is kindness that makes one strong and brave."
—L. FRANK BAUM, *The Patchwork Girl of Oz*

Perfect kindness acts without thinking of kindness.
—LAO-TSE

Symbol: the *dolphin;* the *elephant*—kindness, compassionate, and loving (Hindu)

KNIGHTLY

Word Forms: knight, knightliness

Definition: exhibiting those characteristics associated with knights, specifically chivalry, dignity, bravery, honesty, and goodness

Comment: If you are female and pick this quality at random, look at the characteristics involved; they are not the sole purview of the male world to contemplate and to live.

Symbol: the *sword*

Legend: *King Arthur*, the legendary British king who may have lived in the sixth century A.D., who fostered the idea of right versus might

KNOWLEDGEABLE

Word Forms: know, known, knowing, knowingly, knowingness, know-how, knowable, knower, knowledge, knowledgeability, knowledgeably, knowledgeableness

Definitions: (1) well-informed; intelligent; keen; to perceive or understand as fact or truth; **(2)** possessing insight or understanding; to apprehend with clarity and certainty; **(3)** to have a memory of; to be familiar with; recognize; **(4)** to be aware of; have information about; **(5)** have experience with; practiced

Synonyms: learned, skillful, erudite, comprehension

Kindred Quality: interested

Familial Qualities: *Incisive*—penetrating knowledge; *insightful*—knowledge about the inner nature of things; *instinctive*—knowledge from a previous generation; *intuitive*—knowledge without the conscious use of reasoning; *perspicuous*—an ability to communicate with the inner other

Sayings:
Nosce te ipsum (Latin); *Gnothi seauton* (Greek): "Know thyself."
—SOCRATES

Action begets knowledge. Information begets understanding.

Knowledge is power.

Quotes:
I was gratified to be able to answer promptly. I said, "I do not know."
—MARK TWAIN

"Knowledge for its own sake"—this is the last snare set by morality: one therewith gets completely entangled with it once more.
—FRIEDRICH WILHELM NIETZSCHE

[Merlin:] "It is never wise to turn aside from knowing, however the knowing comes"
—MARY STEWART, *The Hollow Hills*

We only get in trouble when we think about it. When we don't think about it, we know who we are.
—JOE BURULL

When and if we have found and understood the complete irreducible laws of physics, we certainly shall *not* thereby know the Mind of God. We will not even get much help in understanding the minds of slugs. . . . Instead our position will be like the chess player who has learned the rules of chess, or a would-be pianist who can now read all the notes. This skeletal knowledge is certainly not enough for skillful play. As we approach such understanding, it is the end of the beginning, not the beginning of the end.
—FRANK WILCZEK, Professor of Physics, *Discover*

Things are known in the knower after the manner of the knower, not after their own manner of existence.
—THOMAS AQUINAS

Consideration: What do you consider to be the essentials? What do you consider to be the most important, basic realities? That's what you will act on. When you are considering an automobile, there are certain things that the vehicle must have or you will not buy it. When you are picking friends, a job, a spouse, or a religion you have a certain criteria in mind. There are certain things that are essential.

At one time we understood what those essential things were because we decided that they were to be essential. But once we established their basic value we bundled them up into a tidy package and put them into our mind and soul and forgot their importance. They are our personal, basic, fundamental realities. Put your mind to reconsidering what they are. That understanding will help you know what you consider to be your "self."

Admonition: See yourself through other people's eyes. Recognize what it is that turns them on. If you know what it is that other people appreciate about you, whether it is your natural or acquired qualities, then you can enhance those qualities.

Comments:
- Information is located in books, but Knowledge is acquired through an interactive and personal involvement with the information. A thing must be experienced, oftentimes repeatedly, before it becomes part of your inner knowing. Even then some things cannot be retained without continued practice.
- It is ironic that *agnostic* has the root meaning "to know." Isn't it just as reasonable to know that God does exist when using the senses?

Question: How do you know that you know?

Colors: violet, yellow

Symbols: the *Tree* of Knowledge; a rolled papyrus *scroll*

Structure:

Types of Knowing

Memories: fragmentary, faded by time, clouded by emotion; replaced by other memories; adjusted by desire; focused by repetition; induced by smells, tastes, sound, sight, or touch; *Experiential*: past, present, or future; *Dreams*: movies, plays, TV, day-dreams, imagination, guessing; *Convictions*: the visualization of a goal completed; *Reminders*: images that look like or remind you of other images, i.e., Rorschach ink blots, clouds

LADYLIKE

Word Forms: lady, ladylikeness

Definition: like a lady in manners; genteel; well-bred; refined; polite; well-spoken
See also: *Gentlemanly*

Note: If you pick this quality and you are male, then use those qualities that are described and look up *Gentlemanly*.

LAID-BACK

Definition: relaxed; easygoing; carefree

How to Live This Quality Today: Lie back in a hammock and watch the clouds go by and count your blessings.

LAUDABLE

Word Forms: laud, laudability, laudably, laudableness

Definition: praiseworthy; commendable

How to Live This Quality Today: Do what you are supposed to do.

LAW-ABIDING

Word Forms: law, law-abidingness

Definition: abiding by or keeping to the law; obeying the law

Quotes:
Only outer peace can be had through law. The way to inner peace is through love.
—PEACE PILGRIM, *Steps Toward Inner Peace*

Mere obedience to the law does not measure the greatness of a nation. . . . The true test is the extent to which the individuals composing the nation can be trusted to obey self-imposed law.
—LORD JOHN FLETCHER MOULTON

Comment: Laws, rules, and regulations have been made to state the obvious, like the protection of the innocent, but also because some will take unfair advantage when the opportunity is available. When that happens, society makes a law.

On the other hand, you can be so willing to do the right thing that straying from the law is merely a mistake or may even be necessity because of circumstances as with civil disobedience.

Questions: What should be allowed? What level of freedom should be given? The level that the individual can cope with or what the society can deal with?

How can you be sure that something like nuclear material or the idea of freedom can be handled safely and responsibly?—only time, trust, and common sense as safeguards. Learn from history and hope for positive possibilities.

Symbol: the *Archpriestess* (tarot)

LEADERSHIP

Word Forms: lead, leader

Definitions: (1) ability to influence, exert authority; **(2)** characterizes one who advances an idea or enhances the progress of a project, usually with the cooperation of others

Kindred Quality: the ability to listen

Compatible Qualities: humility, mercy

Familial Quality: experienced

Too Far: bossy, domineering

Way Too Far: tyrannical

Quotes:
If you think about it, people love others not for who they are, but for how they make us feel. We willingly follow others for much the same reason. In order to *willingly* accept the direction of another individual, it *must* feel good to do so.
—IRWIN FEDERMAN, PRESIDENT AND CEO, MONOLITHIC MEMORIES

If I had to choose one quality to distinguish the best new leaders, it is "openness to criticism," the passion for continual self-development, which teaches the leader to value the development of others.

—MICHAEL MACCOBY, *The Leader*

Tip: Once a decision is made do four things: (1) Commit to it even if you don't agree with it entirely; (2) be sure that all of the members of the team are likewise committed; (3) make a plan on how to achieve the goal; and (4) decide whom the decision will affect and let them know before they get broadsided.

Advice: Lead by questioning, by asking for suggestions and by consensus. Make it obvious that each member of the team is valuable, that they have something to offer. Encourage participation and risk taking.

Admonition: If you ask for input, respond to it.

Comments:
- The lubricant between a leader and a team is dialogue, communication. A leader has to be sensitive to and find out what the expectations of the others are. An individual or a group can give up their individual judgment to the leader, but only if it is specifically needed and agreed to be the right thing to do.

   If a person gives up control to another, that person should be willing to give the leader support with his or her opinions, ideas, and forgiveness. The person being led can look at the situation as a learning experience and not get into blame if the experience is not what he or she wanted or expected.

   You should not give up the responsibility for your own decisions easily.
- If a person takes the responsibility for others, he or she has to expect that others will want to assess rewards or blame for success or failure. But the leader needs to understand that that is the choice of the individual others.
- There are different types of leader-follower relationships: sergeant-private, teacher-student, manager-employee, parent-child—and they all have different degrees of learning, risk, control, intention, and care involved. The situation and the individuals dictate what pressure needs to be exerted.

- Consider time in your leadership duties. Have you got deadlines? Can you afford to teach someone to do a task or must you get someone who has the skill already?

There has to be the willingness to let people push whatever edges they can. There are times when it is better to have a group get in sync on the project. The time to get everyone up to speed is longer, but in the end the reward is increased cohesiveness, consistency, safety, and efficiency. Then the team for the next project is already moving forward as a unit.

LEARNED

Word Forms: learn, learning, learnedly, learnedness

Definition: having or showing profound or extensive education; well-informed; erudite

Sayings:
Ab uno disce omnes (Latin): "From one, learn to know all."

Docendo discimus (Latin): "We learn by teaching."

Fas est et ab hoste doceri (Latin): "It is right to learn, even from an enemy." [If you can't say, "I don't know," you don't learn.]

Quotes:
As soon as you say you know the answer there is no where else for you to go. You can stay where you are or repeat where you have been.

—JERRY DOWNS

[Merlin:] "The best thing for being sad is to learn something. That is the only thing that never fails. You may grow old and trembling in your anatomies, you may lie awake at night listening to the disorder in your veins, you may miss your only love, you may see the world about you devastated by evil lunatics or know your honor trampled in the sewers of baser minds. There is only one thing for it then—to learn. Learn why the world wags and what wags it. That is the only thing which the mind can never exhaust, never alienate, never be tortured by, never fear or distrust and never dream of regretting. Learning is the thing for you. Look at what a lot of things there are to learn—pure science, the only purity there is. You can learn astronomy in a lifetime, natural history in three, literature in six. And then, after you have exhausted a milliard lifetimes in biology and medicine and theocriticism and geography and history and economics—why, you can start to make a cartwheel out of the appropriate wood, or spend fifty years learning to begin to learn to beat your adversary at fencing. After that you can start again on mathematics, until it is time to learn to plough."

—T. H. WHITE, *The Once and Future King*

Ninety-two percent of what you learn is linked with something that you learned before you were 10 years old!

—GLORIA FRENDER

Note: Connect what you want to learn to something already known but also link the new material with something that is strongly desired.

Reflections:
- You can acquire the quality of being a learned person by studying, by experiencing, by gathering knowledge and information, by finding out better ways to assimilate that information, and by being able to store and retrieve that information. If you express it in such a way as to impart it to someone else so that that person can pick up on it more efficiently, then you are learned.
- The difference between what you've learned and what you've become is the difference between a memory imprint and a soul imprint.

Consideration: People arrive at certain plateaus in their philosophies. They arrive there through logic, experience, a flash of brilliance, or simply acquiesce to a belief system. At this plateau there may be a feeling of finality. There are many who stop there, assuming that that is the end. Since they've got *the* answer, they don't have to be open or expand their consciousness. What people do is recycle back through the same concepts over and over again because of the fear of the next step.

Observations:
- Learning is not just the ability to answer questions. Learning is most complete when the learner designs the questions.
- The elements of learning that are essential are that it is instructive, contagious, experiential, fun, and valuable.

Comment: People spend a tremendous amount of time learning the body of knowledge of a particular field in order to build on it without reinventing the wheel. But as the amount of information in the category grows it eventually has to split into subcategories.

Another technique is to build faster tools with which to manipulate the information, i.e., computers. It is the wise person who learns how to find the information rather than trying to memorize all of it.

With the acquisition of qualities, we cannot ignore 90 percent of the quality's attributes just because all that has been said about it cannot be absorbed into the brain. Luckily it works on a different level. As you become the essence of a quality, you increase your capacity to assimilate its totality and complexity. Qualities are amorphous and flexible enough to be lived in a wide range of situations. Plus, there is plenty of time.

LEGITIMATE

Word Forms: legitimacy, legitimize, legitimation, legitimately, legitimateness

Definitions: (1) lawful; in accordance with established rules, principles, or standards; (2) logical; in accordance with the laws of reasoning; valid; (3) genuine; real; not false or spurious; justified <a *legitimate* complaint>

LEISURELY

Word Forms: leisure, leisureness, leisureliness

Definition: deliberate; slow; unhurried; without haste; laid-back

LENIENT

Word Forms: lenience, leniency, leniently, lenity, lenitive

Definitions: (1) indulgent; agreeably tolerant; merciful; not strict or severe; mild; having an easygoing forbearance; **(2)** having a soothing influence; relieving pain, stress, or harshness

Derivation: Latin, "soft," "mild"

LEVELHEADED

Word Forms: level, levelheadedly, levelheadedness

Definition: having common sense and sound judgment; sensible; possessing an even temper

LEVITY

Word Form: levities

Definition: lightness of mind, character, or behavior; frivolity; lack of seriousness

Derivation: Latin, "lightness," "gaiety"

LIBERAL

Word Forms: liberality, liberalize, liberally, liberalness

Definitions: (1) favorable to progress or reform, as in political or religious affairs; **(2)** free from prejudice or bigotry; tolerant; **(3)** free of or not bound by traditional or conventional ideas, values, or judgments; open-minded; **(4)** generous and willing to give; **(5)** given freely or abundantly; bountiful

Kindred Quality: conservative

LIBERTY

Word Forms: liberties, at liberty

Definition: freedom from restraint, the body is at liberty when not confined, the will or mind is at liberty when not checked or controlled; people enjoy liberty when no physical force operates to restrain their actions or volitions

Derivation: Latin, "free"

Symbol: *footwear*, since slaves walked barefoot

LIGHT

Word Forms: lighted, lighten, lighthearted, lightly, lightness, enlighten

Definitions: **(1)** knowledge; enlightenment; mental illumination; **(2)** free from care; cheerful; gay; **(3)** animate; bright

Synonyms: buoyant, easy, unencumbered, gentle, delicate, lively

Saying: A candle's light is best seen in the dark.

Quotes:
Only those who live up to the highest light they have find their lives in harmony. Those who act on their highest motivations become a power for good.
—PEACE PILGRIM, *Steps Toward Inner Peace*

Concentrate on living according to the light you have, so that you may open yourself to more light.
—PEACE PILGRIM, *Steps Toward Inner Peace*

Let there be light: and there was light. And God saw the light, and that it was good.

—GENESIS 1:3,4

Symbols: *dew;* the *diamond; gold;* the *lamp*

Mythology: *Balder,* the Scandinavian deity of light and peace, who was wise and beautiful

LIGHTHEARTED

Word Forms: lightheartedly, lightheartedness

Definitions: (1) free from care or anxiety; gay; **(2)** cheerfully optimistic and hopeful; easygoing

Comment: Even if things are difficult on the material level, with a focus on the positive, your personal spiritual connection can be lighthearted. It may not change your funky mood, but you can be heartened by your faith.

LIKABLE

Word Forms: like, likability, likableness

Definition: having qualities that compel approval; pleasant; agreeable; attractive; genial

Advice: You should try to love everybody but you don't have to like everybody. Albeit, if you look for their motives, you will probably see reasons to like them.

LIMBER

Word Forms: limbered, limbering, limberly, limberness

Definitions: (1) capable of being shaped; flexible; **(2)** having a supple and resilient mind or body; agile; nimble

Synonyms: pliant, pliable, lithe

Comment: There are two obvious ways to get physically limber: one is stretching and one is yoga. To get mentally limber, read new ideas and communicate. Keep that brain muscle flexible.

Food: The herb Gotu Kola, or Indian pennywort, is said to assist in the transference of the synaptic connections. When that word is just on the tip of your tongue or your thoughts are just not flowing smoothly, Gotu Kola might help.

LIONHEARTED

Word Forms: lionheart, lionheartedness

Definition: exceptionally courageous or brave; magnanimous

LITHESOME

Word Forms: lithe, lithesomely, lithesomeness, lissome

Definition: pliant; limber; nimble; supple; flexible

LITURGICAL

Word Forms: liturgy, liturgies, liturgist, liturgics, liturgically

Definition: pertaining to the established formulas for public worship or the entire ritual for formal group worship

Observation: There is a combining power when a group of sincere people get together for the uplifting of their hearts in worship.

LIVELY

Word Forms: live, livelier, liveliest, liveliness

Definitions: (1) brisk; vigorous; active; (2) cheerful; airy; (3) spirited; exciting; stimulating; (4) strong; energetic; intense; stirring; (5) brilliant; fresh; (6) quick to rebound, to spring back; resilient

Synonyms: *Lively, animated, vivacious, sprightly*, and *gay* mean keenly alive and spirited. *Lively* suggests briskness, alertness, or energy. *Animated* applies to what is spirited, active, and sparkling. *Vivacious* suggests an activeness of gesture and wit, often playful or alluring. *Sprightly* suggests lightness and spirited vigor of manner or of wit. *Gay* stresses complete freedom from care and overflowing spirits.

LOFTY

Word Forms: loft, loftier, loftiest, loftily, loftiness

Definitions: (1) elevated in character, quality, or condition; sublime; exalted; eminent; dignified; (2) noble in sentiment or diction

Derivation: Old Norse, "air," "heaven"

Synonyms: high, stately, proud

Kindred Quality: humble

Too Far: stuck-up

Symbol: *winged sandals*

LOGICAL

Word Forms: logic, logicality, logically, logicalness

Definitions: (1) the art of thinking and reasoning justly; **(2)** using correct rationality; **(3)** necessary; to be expected because of what has gone before; that which follows as reasonable or sensible

LONG-SUFFERING

Word Form: long-sufferingly

Definition: bearing injuries or provocation for a long time; patient; not easily provoked

Kindred Quality: hope

Consideration: If you know that you can and will do your best "under the circumstances" then you are a practitioner of long-suffering. The "circumstances" may be a singular incident and something that is negative (an accident, victimization, being in the wrong place at the wrong time) or the "circumstances" can be plural (all of the events of our lives). We are all putting up with difficulty. The consequences may be a change or an adjustment for the foreseeable future.

Even if everything is going well, you have to deal with the repercussions of internal growth and external change.

Symbol: the *ox*

LOOSE

Word Forms: looser, loosest, loosen, loosen up, loosed, loosing, loosely, looseness

Definitions: (1) having a flexible or relaxed character; **(2)** not confining or bound; free

Too Far: sloppy, uncaring

LOVABLE

Word Forms: love, lovability, lovably, lovableness

Definition: worthy of love; endearing; possessing qualities that attract love or admiration; amiable

LOVE

Word Forms: loving, lover, lovingest, lovable, loved, lovely, loverly, beloved, lovesome, lovebird

Combining Phrases: in love, loving-kindness, love affair, love beads, love boat, lovebug, love child, loved one, love feast, love handles, love-in, love knot, love life, love match, love potion, lovey-dovey, love seat, loving cup, love interest, well-beloved

Definitions: (1) a deep devotion or affection for another person(s) or sometimes a thing, idea, or ideal; to hold dear; cherish; **(2)** to feel a lover's passion, devotion, or tenderness; **(3)** one who is beloved

Compatible Qualities: friendship, trust, caring, respect, honesty

Consequential Quality: self-forgetfulness
    Love is blind. When you are doing something you love or are with someone you love, you are in a state of enjoyment or bliss that is oblivious to all ills. When you are in love you think not of yourself but your joy lies in thinking of ways to delight, comfort, and interest your loved one.
    At play one is enveloped in the excitement, interest, and concentration on the goal.

Too Far: smothering love

Music: "All You Need Is Love"—The Beatles

Sayings:
    Aloha oe (Hawaiian): "Love to you"; "Greetings"; "Farewell"

    Amor vincit omnia (Latin): "Love conquers all things."

Quotes:

Love is better than chocolate, but sometimes chocolate is easier to find.

—JUDY KAIN

If you love, you are welcome in the universe; if you are loved, you are at home here.

—FRANK PITTMAN, M.D.

That which is done out of love always takes place beyond good and evil.

—FRIEDRICH WILHELM NIETZSCHE

If I have prophesy and know all mysteries and all knowledge, and I have all faith as to move mountains, yet do not have love, I am nothing. Love is patient and kind and rejoices with the truth. Love bears all things, believes all things, hopes all things, endures all things. Love never fails.

There abide faith, hope and love but the greatest of these is love. Pursue love, yet keep zealously seeking all of the spiritual gifts.

—1 CORINTHIANS 13:2–13; 14:1

You live that you may learn to love. You love that you may learn to live. No other lesson is required.

—MIRDAD

> *Good shepherd, tell this youth what 'tis to love.*
> *It is to be all made of sighs and tears:—*
> *It is to be all made of faith and service:—*
> *It is to be all made of fantasy,*
> *All made of passion, and all made of wishes;*
> *All adoration, duty, and observance;*
> *All humbleness, all patience, and impatience;*
> *All purity, all trial, all obeisance.*
> —WILLIAM SHAKESPEARE, *As You Like It*

A single human unloved can set the universe afire.

—FRANK HERBERT, *EYE, Death to a City*

Affirmation: I am deliberately and joyously radiating divine love to myself, my friends, and all the world.

Inspiration: God provided the universe with the original patterns of truth, beauty, and goodness out of the unified reality of love. It is like the splitting of white light into a rainbow. Truth, beauty, and goodness are equivalent to the primary colors of red, yellow, and blue. Further diffusion and mixing of the basics creates all of the possibilities of colors and qualities.

Reflections:

- The question "What is the purpose of life?" is one that we seek until we realize that the answer is "To love." But then, that's the enlightenment-type of answer. Although it is the ultimate answer, it is the simple and basic answer. It doesn't tell you what it means. So then the next questions: "What is love?" and "How do I love?" open a Pandora's box. The diversity is expressed in the concepts of all of the underlying positive qualities that make up the nature and value of love. Each positive quality can be traced to the source of love. Each positive quality emanates and is connected to its kindred and familial qualities.

  Love's components can be felt and observed. You can experience goodness, truth, and beauty. If you focus on the truth aspects, you recognize justice, faith, wisdom, and courage. If you focus on the beautiful aspects, you will appreciate symmetry, humor, and relaxation. If you focus on goodness, you will feel generosity, kindness, and nobility.

  Each quality begets other qualities and needs other qualities to fulfill itself.

- One of the characteristics of love is that it can be experienced and viewed on so many different levels. The highest level, the most spiritual level, is the intense desire to do good to and for other people. But not just people. All life is included. The universe is included. Even the creature giving love to the Creator.

- In this day and age when people say "I love you," what some mean is "I appreciate what you do for me" or "I really like the pleasure you give me." Although those are facets of love, this is one reason why romantic love fails: the desire to be loved without the balancing need to love another selflessly in return.

Observations:

- Love is contagious.
- Love does not ignore or even transform the negative—it utterly destroys, evaporates, and obliterates it.

Suggestions:

- Do everything with love.

- Love should not be reserved only for those who love you. Those with a love deficit need love the most.

Comments:

- The key to love is not receiving love but is in giving love. The more you give love, the more you understand it, the more you appreciate it, the more you have of it.
- The love that a person feels deeply for another motivates him or her to be the person that the other will love.

    When two people love each other they each strive to be the person that the other is in love with. There is a strong desire to live up to the loving image that is held up to you by your lover. As you appreciate and love yourself as being as wonderful as the one who loves you, you not only become that ideal being but even better. Love lifts both the loved and the lover beyond themselves.
- When you love someone, even the simplest and most innocent mannerisms and traits are appreciated with fondness.
- Love is infinite. As you approach what seems like the culmination of love, you are experiencing a relative state of perfection. You can plateau to a new level, but there will always be greater heights and more valuable connections of understanding, being, and growing.

How to Live This Quality Today:

- In order to experience love, you must love someone, including yourself. Go out of your way to do something that would be pleasing to yourself or to someone else, physically, emotionally, mentally, or spiritually.
- Acts that you can do to or for someone you love:
Take a walk together.
Talk to each other, revealing yourself.
Be interested in the affairs of the other.
Give the other support and encouragement.
Find agreement on important topics.
Be warm and tender.
Have a romantic dinner by candlelight.
Sit close together and touch.
Give the other flowers.
Give the other hugs and cuddles, kisses and snuggles.
Say "I love you."
Write a love letter.
Appreciate the other.
Let the other know that you are thinking about him or her.

Color: red

Symbols: The *heart;* the *hearth; Venus; five;* a *pyramid* could be a symbol of love with each of the other qualities as one of the blocks—love is the foundation, the culmination, and an integrated whole: one love.

Fiction: *Beauty and the Beast,* the fairy tale illustrating the triumph of love over externals

Mythologies: *Ishtar*, the Babylonian goddess of the evening star, fruitful goodness, and the patroness of love; *Kama*, the Hindu god of love; *Anteros*, in Greek mythology, the god of mutual love; *Aphrodite*, the Greek goddess of love and beauty; *Astarte*, the Greek goddess of love and fertility; *Eros*, the Greek god of love; *Ashtoreth*, the Phoenician goddess of love and fertility; *Cupid*, the Roman god of love; *Freya*, the Scandinavian goddess of love and beauty

LOVELY

Word Forms: love, lovelier, loveliest, lovelies, loveliness

Definitions: (1) having a beauty that appeals to the heart or mind as well as to the eye; charmingly or gracefully beautiful; **(2)** highly pleasing; delightful; **(3)** having a great moral or spiritual beauty

LOYAL

Word Forms: loyalty, loyally, loyalness

Definitions: (1) unswerving in allegiance; constant and faithful in any relation or obligation implying trust, confidence, or care; **(2)** the willing bond of the self to a cause, leader, or friend

Parental Qualities: faith and duty
   One cannot help but be loyal to what is held in faith.

Familial Quality: growth

Quotes:
The back of the arrow follows the front as if from love and loyalty.
—MARK HELPRIN, *Refiner's Fire*

Live loyally today—grow—and tomorrow will attend to itself.
—*The Urantia Book*

Comments:
- The ideal of loyalty is eventually spoiled if what you are loyal to is focused on selfishness.
- Love may not be the primary motive of a relationship. It may be duty or tradition or obedience, but if the people involved persist with loyal action, they will end up loving.

Symbol: the *dog*

LUCID

Word Forms: lucidity, lucidly, lucidness, pellucid

Definitions: (1) distinct; presenting a clear view; easily understood; intelligible; transparent; **(2)** sane; mentally sound; rational; **(3)** shining; bright; resplendent

LUCKY

Word Forms: luck, luckier, luckiest, luckily, luckiness

Definition: accompanied by or having good fortune

Synonyms: *Lucky, fortunate, happy,* and *providential* mean meeting with unforeseen success. *Lucky* stresses the agency of chance in bringing about a favorable result. *Fortunate* suggests being rewarded beyond one's deserts. *Happy* combines the implications of lucky and fortunate with stress on being blessed. *Providential* implies the help or intervention of a higher power.

Saying: Luck is where opportunity and preparedness meet.

Parable:

I understand the following to be an old Zen story. I read it in *Sadhana—A Way to God*, by Father Anthony de Mello, S.J.

There is a Chinese story of an old farmer who had an old horse for tilling his fields. One day the horse escaped into the hills and when all the farmer's neighbors sympathized with the old man over his bad luck, the farmer replied, "Bad luck? Good luck? Who knows?" A week later the horse returned with a herd of wild horses from the hills, and this time the neighbors congratulated the farmer on his good luck. His reply was, "Good luck? Bad luck? Who knows?" Then, when the farmer's son was attempting to tame one of the wild horses, he fell off and broke his leg. Everyone thought this very bad luck. Not the farmer, whose only reaction was, "Bad luck? Good luck? Who knows?" Some weeks later the army marched into the village and conscripted every able-bodied youth they found there. When they saw the farmer's son with his broken leg they let him alone. Now was that good luck or bad luck? Who knows?

Everything that seems on the surface to be an evil may be a good in disguise. And everything that seems good on the surface may really be an evil, depending on your attitude.

Symbols: supreme intelligence, which triumphs over life and death—a lidded *urn; horseshoes;* a *shell* (Chinese); *gold* (According to east Indian tradition, gold brings both prosperity and luck, and is considered sacred to the gods.)

Types of Luck: tough luck; fool's luck; dumb luck; bad luck; good luck; blind luck; lady luck; beginner's luck

LUMINOUS

Word Forms: lumen, luminosity, luminously, luminousness

Definitions: (1) radiating or reflecting light; shining; bright; **(2)** intellectually brilliant; readily intelligible; **(3)** clear; enlightened or enlightening

Symbol: illumination—*Aquarius* (zodiac)

LUSCIOUS

Word Forms: lusciously, lusciousness

Definitions: (1) richly satisfying to the senses or the mind; **(2)** sexually attractive; seductive; voluptuous

LUSTROUS

Word Forms: luster, lustrously, lustrousness

Definitions: (1) bright; luminous; brilliant; splendid; illustrious; **(2)** having qualities that shine pleasingly to the observer

LUXURIOUS

Word Forms: luxury, luxuriate, luxuriously, luxuriousness

Definitions: (1) the best and most costly things that offer the most physical comfort and satisfaction; fond of or indulging in the use and enjoyment of such things; **(2)** splendid; rich; comfortable

Derivation: Latin, "extravagance"

LYRICAL

Word Forms: lyre, lyric, lyrist, lyricism, lyrically, lyricalness

Definition: (1) poetic, musical, songlike; **(2)** expressive of feeling and emotion, especially spontaneous enthusiasm; exuberant, rhapsodic; **(3)** characteristic of high, light, and flexible qualities

MAGICAL

Word Forms: magic, magically

Definitions: (1) describes any unusual, seemingly inexplicable or extraordinary power or influence; **(2)** mysteriously impressive; beautiful

Quotes:

What they say in Alcoholics Anonymous is that you cannot stop drinking. Everybody who ends up in AA has tried every way they know to stop drinking. The only way you can stop drinking is by turning things over to a power greater than yourself. You have to determine what that power greater than yourself is. Some people say it's a redwood tree they found in the forest when they were out walking and looking for inspiration. Some people say it's God. Some people say it's the stars. Every type of person who has had most of their brain cells burned out still gets sober through some magical thing. So, for me, I would say, it was magic.

—JOE BURULL

Logic gives you what you need; magic gives you what you want.
—TOM ROBBINS, *Even Cowgirls Get the Blues*

Comment: At least some kinds of magic are connected with generosity. Consider the incident with the loaves and fishes. Christ was compelled by compassion and generosity to feed the assembled people. The multitudes didn't exactly take things in the spirit given. They said, "Great, something for nothing, a free lunch."

From the outside, magic looks like something is happening that cannot happen. Magicians are revered because they seem to have more power and therefore more freedom and control.

You may not have the resources to create loaves and fishes but you do have the resources to do something. You do have the power and freedom to be sympathetic or empathetic. You can be giving and sharing. Abundance is available to everyone.

Goal: The goals of magic in the prescientific age were the same as those of science: to predict the future and to influence the environment.

Symbols: the *wand;* a *net;* the *whistle; abnormal objects or persons;* the *right hand*

Legend: *Merlin,* the enchanter in the legends of King Arthur

MAGNANIMOUS

Word Forms: magnanimity, magnanimously, magnanimousness

Definitions: (1) noble in mind; elevated in soul or in sentiment; rising above pettiness or meanness; generous in overlooking injury or insult; showing or suggesting a lofty and courageous spirit; **(2)** exhibiting nobleness of soul; liberal and honorable

Derivation: Latin, "great mind" or "great soul"

Synonyms: high-minded, high-souled, great-souled, exalted, unselfish

Familial Quality: forgiving

Color: yellow

MAGNETIC

Word Forms: magnet, magnetically

Definition: possessing an extraordinary power or ability to attract <*magnetic* personality>; charismatic

MAGNIFICENT

Word Forms: magnificence, magnificently

Definitions: (1) splendid; imposingly beautiful; grand; rich or sumptuous;

(2) exalted; noble; sublime; very fine; superb

Synonyms: glorious, gorgeous, stately

People Who Exemplify This Quality: Michelangelo Buonarroti. I have to assume that he was magnificent because his sculptures of David and the Pietà, his painting of the Sistine chapel, and his architecture of St. Peter's Basilica are such fine examples of magnificence.

MAJESTIC

Word Forms: majesty, majestically

Definitions: (1) august; having dignity of person or appearance; noble; **(2)** splendid; elevated; lofty; grand; stately

Derivation: Old French, "greatness," "grandeur"

MALLEABLE

Word Forms: malleability, malleably, malleableness

Definitions: (1) capable of being altered or controlled by outside forces or influences; yielding; **(2)** a capacity for adaptive change; amenable

Kindred Quality: sturdy

Familial Quality: flexible

MANEUVERABLE

Word Forms: maneuver, maneuverability

Definition: able to move skillfully toward an objective or away from an obstacle; shrewd; able to devise a stratagem or scheme

MANNERLY

Word Forms: manners, mannerliness, well-mannered

Definition: showing good conduct; polite; courteous; well-behaved

MARVELOUS

Word Forms: marvel, marvelously, marvelousness

Definitions: (1) the highest kind or quality; notably superior; **(2)** causing wonder, astonishment, or surprise; wonderful; **(3)** miraculous; supernatural; extraordinary

Comment: With a healthy and humble sense of self, a self-assessment of being marvelous would not be egotistical. Give yourself credit for your magnificence.

MASTERFUL

Word Forms: master, masterfully, masterfulness

Definitions: (1) authoritative; having the ability or power to control; **(2)** showing skill or knowledge that makes one master of a subject; expert

MATERNAL

Word Forms: mother, mom, mommy, maternally, maternity, maternalize

Definition: motherly; characteristic of a mother or motherhood—loyal, supportive, protective, loving, giving
    See also: *Paternal*

Quote:
Teach your children what we have taught our children, that the earth is our mother. Whatever befalls the earth befalls the children of the earth.
—CHIEF SEATTLE

Symbols: *water;* the *gorge;* the *forest;* the *ocean;* the *oven;* the *goose*

MATTER-OF-FACT

Word Forms: matter-of-factly, matter-of-factness

Definition: true to the unembellished facts; literal; straightforward

Kindred Qualities: tactful, honest

MATURING

Word Forms: mature, maturity, maturation

Definitions: (1) being brought to full growth or development; **(2)** perfecting; developing or working out fully; completing

Quote:
Maturity: to have regained the seriousness that was had as a child at play.
—FRIEDRICH WILHELM NIETZSCHE

Reflections:
- Maturity is the move from an egocentric universe to an other-centered universe.
- We traverse through survival, security, duty, subjective self-interest, giving in order to receive, pitiful altruism, helpfulness, generosity—and a person can get stuck in any one of these levels.
- Giving selflessly, in order to be truly mature, must include self-esteem, power, and the ability to clearly and compassionately communicate, especially in a confrontation.

Comment: Children try to establish their identity. One of the immature ways that they do so is by exaggerating the differences that they see. Somebody who has glasses is called four-eyes, somebody who is large is fat. There is a lack of subtlety in their differentiation between themselves and others. A person can go through life with these immature prejudices.

Some adults of any race hold that someone who has a different skin color or a different genetic structure is superior or inferior. The prejudice gives the immature person a comparison to judge themselves by. As long as they do not have the traits that they describe to themselves as negative, then it follows that they must be superior.

The mature person goes beyond the facade of the physical or historical and if there is a need to judge will do so based on the character of the individual.

Physical, emotional, psychological, intellectual, social, and historical differences are facts. Generalizations, especially negative generalizations, are very dangerous and cannot fit all of any class.

Exercise: It is very instructive to listen to yourself on tape. Put what you're thinking on the tape and then listen to it some time later. You get a sense of who you were and how your mind worked. You will hear what you considered to be of value and who you used to be. Compare your current thoughts about the same subject to what is on the tape. The taped thoughts may sound somewhat immature. So you will get a sense of how your thoughts have progressed as you have grown.

Experience:
The Five Stages of Grief

1. Denial and isolation
2. Anger
3. Bargaining
4. Depression
5. Acceptance

You may not be able to bypass the stages of grief but you can move through them efficiently. Don't allow yourself to wallow in your defeat or sorrow.

MEDITATIVE

Word Forms: meditate, meditation, meditatively, meditativeness

Definitions: (1) contemplation or reflection; muse; **(2)** to think about doing; to plan; **(3)** to hold a superior attitude in mind

Synonyms: study, ponder, consider, ruminate, cogitate

Compatible Qualities: peaceful, comfortable, reflective, calm, confident, restful

Tip: Relaxation is an integral part of meditation. The meditative state establishes a link between the mind and the spirit. Relaxation leaves you open to receive.

Advice: In meditation be sure that your focus is concentrating on the superconscious rather than the subconscious mind. Do this with worship and with a prayerfully appreciative attitude.

Meditations:
- To develop a particular quality that you want, meditate on that quality. Sit quietly, breath deeply, be calm. Chant "Om." Then visualize at the top of your head, at the crown chakra, the divine essence of that quality. Invoke it to fill your aura with itself. Next move it into your mind, contemplating the aspects of the quality that have to do with your thinking process. Open yourself to it. Ask the quality to fill you totally with itself. Give it permission to be what it needs to be in your life.

  Move it down into the throat chakra, again asking and giving permission that your communication skills be indicative of that quality. Linger on each area. As you move to the heart chakra, feel the joy of the quality, feel the substance of it enriching your life. Continue this process through all of the chakras but also throughout your body, down to the bottoms of your feet. Immerse yourself in the quality, knowing that it is now part of you. Allow it to infuse you. Return the energy up through your body to its source and then all the way back down again. Wash this energy like waves throughout your physical, mental, and spiritual systems several times. Let is settle comfortably.

Visualize the quality sinking into the earth and stabilizing there, rooting as you take the steps in your new life with this quality in your being. You are grounded in your new quality.

At the end of the meditation, thank the divine quality and thank yourself for being open and allowing yourself to become this quality.

This is a good meditation to do in the beginning of the week when you pick a quality or two. If you pick two qualities, first do this meditation on one quality at a time. Then combine the two qualities in a separate meditation later in the week.

Do this exercise in a group if you can; and if you do, include a prayer that the others will be successful and that the energy will fill not only the individual but all of the group. (See meditation for *Forgiving*.)

Mirror Meditation

- The idea here is to visualize or imagine yourself looking into a mirror in your mind. This could also be done looking into a real mirror. "See" yourself in your various states, dwelling on each state for a period of time.
  1. Look at yourself as you see yourself.
  2. Concentrate on the image of your objective self.
  3. See yourself as a friend would see you.
  4. Look at your ideal self. Project the image of a perfected self. What does that person look like, act like, feel like? Remember the most positive of your experiences.

Color: black

MEEK

Word Forms: meeker, meekest, meekly, meekness

Definition: not inclined to resentment; serene; not violent; a gentle disposition

Derivation: Middle English, "soft," "pliant," "gentle"

Synonym: *Mild* implies a temper that is, by nature, not easily provoked. *Meek* implies a spirit that has been schooled to mildness by discipline or suffering.

Familial Qualities: patience, forbearance

Too Far: weak

Poetry:

> *Meekness*
> *Holds no fear*
> *Is full of faith*

Symbol: the *lamb*

MELLOW

Word Forms: mellowly, mellowness

Definitions: **(1)** pleasant; agreeable; free from tension or discord; **(2)** made gentle, soft, and sympathetic by age or experience

MELODIOUS

Word Forms: melody, melodic, melodiously, melodiousness

Definition: musical; agreeable to the ear by a sweet succession of sounds; harmonious

Reflection: The melody of one's life is something that you feel. Listen for it. It may be sweet or raucous, but if it is yours, you can play it.

Symbol: the *flute*

MEMORABLE

Word Forms: memory, memoir, memorability, memorably, memorable-ness, memorandum, memorial, memorabilia

Definitions: **(1)** worthy of being remembered; easily remembered; famous; **(2)** illustrious; celebrated; distinguished; notable; striking

Synonyms: great, conspicuous, prominent, extraordinary, remarkable

MERCIFUL

Word Forms: mercy, mercifully, mercifulness

Definition: compassionate; tender; having disposition to forgive, be kind, or helpful

Synonyms: *Mercy, charity, clemency, grace,* and *lenity* mean a disposition to show kindness or compassion. *Mercy* implies compassion that forbears immediate punishment. *Charity* stresses benevolence and good will shown in tolerance and broad understanding of others. *Clemency* implies a mild or merciful disposition in one having the power or duty of punishing. *Grace* implies a benign attitude and a willingness to grant favors or make concessions. *Lenity* implies lack of severity in punishing.

Quote:
    Mercy is based on the foundations of justice, fairness, patience and
    kindness—in that order.
                            —*The Urantia Book* (paraphrase)

Reflection: A person who has done a disservice, dishonor, or wrong does have to make up for this fact. One of the first steps is to apologize. But apology may not be enough. It may be necessary to perform some kind of compensation either to the individual or to the community.

    When is the compensation complete? Has the person become one who would not do again what was done? Has the individual changed to the extent that he or she has become trustworthy?

The person wronged needs to accept the apology and give forgiveness in its due time.

Color: blue

MERITORIOUS

Word Forms: merit, meritoriously, meritoriousness

Definition: worthy of reward or notice; deserving fame or happiness; praiseworthy

Derivation: Latin, "to earn," "to gain," or "to deserve"

Advice: Do the next thing. Do it well and your reward has been given.

MERRY

Word Forms: merrier, merriest, merriment, merrily, merriness, merry-making

Definitions: (1) full of fun and laughter; lively and cheerful; gay; mirthful; joyous; jolly; **(2)** marked by cheerfulness or festivity

Synonyms: Sportive, sprightly, vivacious, blithe, jocund, jovial, merry-andrew—one whose business it is to make fun of others. (This last term is said to have originated with one Andrew Borde, a physician in the time of Henry VIII, who attracted attention and gained patients by making facetious speeches.)

Saying: *Gaudeamus igitur* (Latin): "Let us then be merry."

Proverb:
A merry heart makes a cheerful countenance.

—PROVERBS 15:13

Mythology: *Momus*, the Greek god of laughter

MESMERIZING

Word Forms: mesmerize, mesmerized, mesmeric, mesmerism, mesmerizer

Definition: compellingly fascinating; spellbinding

METAMORPHIC

Word Forms: metamorphose, metamorphosis, metamorphically

Definition: possessing the ability to change; exhibiting striking alteration in character, appearance, or condition

Derivation: Greek, "transformation"

Comment: We currently live in our body and have our identity in our temporal ego. We function in our mind and act from our personality. If one identifies with positive qualities, then a transition begins to take place—a shift from the material to the spiritual. The mind and personality move to the soul, which becomes the seat of the cosmic identity. This is effected with a persistent choosing of that which we know to be right. It takes a steadfast heart and above all true sincerity.

Symbols: the *butterfly;* the *frog*

METAPHYSICAL

Word Forms: metaphysics, metaphysically

Definitions: (1) pertaining to the nature of being; essential reality;

(2) based on abstract and subtle reasoning; (3) relating to the transcendent or to a reality beyond what is perceptible to the senses; supernatural

Comment: Metaphysics is one bridge between the material and the spiritual. Other bridges are humor and music.

METHODICAL

Word Forms: method, methodically, methodicalness

Definition: acting in a systematic way; painstaking; meticulously careful; deliberate

Compatible Quality: patience

Comment: Time and a methodical steadfastness are creative. The subcontinent of India used to be in the southern hemisphere. As it moved north it ran into the northern landmass and has pushed up the Himalayas. There used to be a great mountain range in the area of the Grand Canyon. It was washed away millions of years before the Colorado River ever began its work. We also have millions of years to become our most magnificent selves.

METICULOUS

Word Forms: meticulously, meticulousness

Definition: taking extreme care with minute details; precise; thorough; methodical

People Who Exemplify This Quality: Pan Xixing of Wuxi, China, wrote, "True friendship is like sound health, the value of which is seldom known until it be lost," twice on a human hair in March 1990.
—The 1992 Guinness Book of World Records

METTLESOME

Word Forms: mettle, mettlesomely, mettlesomeness

Definition: (1) full of spirit; courageous; brisk; fiery; (2) possessing constitutional ardor

Derivation: a variant spelling of metal, used in a figurative sense

Comment: *mettlesome* is not to be confused with *meddlesome*, which means to interfere in the affairs of another without their permission.

MIGHTY

Word Forms: might, mightier, mightiest, mightily

Definitions: (1) having great bodily strength or physical power; very robust or vigorous; commanding; (2) important; momentous; (3) great; wonderful; colossal

MILD

Word Forms: mildly, mildness

Definitions: (1) soft; gently and pleasantly affecting the senses; sweet; (2) tender and gentle in temper or disposition; kind; compassionate; merciful; clement; indulgent; easy; (3) calm; tranquil; mellow; meek

MINDFUL

Word Forms: mind, mindfully, mindfulness

Definition: regarding with care; bearing in mind; heedful; observant; watchful; attentive; aware

Quote:
The mind is the connecting link between the formed and the unformed world.
    —CATHERINE PONDER, *The Dynamic Laws of Prosperity*

Comment: One of the mind's purposes is to be a vector, to point a direction by posing questions and by comparing what you say you want to do to what you actually do.

MINISTERIAL

Word Forms: minister, ministerially

Definitions: (1) serving as an instrument or means; helpful; **(2)** to be service oriented; to give care or aid; **(3)** to provide information, often of a religious nature

MIRTHFUL

Word Forms: mirth, mirthfully, mirthfulness

Definition: merry; jovial; festive; full of merriment

Synonyms: *Mirth, glee, jollity,* and *hilarity* mean a feeling of high spirits that is expressed in laughter, play, or merrymaking. *Mirth* implies generally lightness of heart and love of gaiety. *Glee* stresses exultation shown in laughter, cries of joy; delight. *Jollity* suggests exuberance or lack of restraint in mirth or glee. *Hilarity* suggests loud or irrepressible laughter or high-spirited boisterousness.

MODERATE

Word Forms: moderated, moderating, moderation, moderately, moderateness

Definitions: (1) avoiding excesses and extremes; keeping within reasonable bounds; temperate; sober; steady; **(2)** mild; calm; gentle; not violent; nonviolent

Saying: *Meden agan* (Greek); *Ne quid nimis* (Latin): "Nothing in excess"

MODERN

Word Forms: modernity, modernistic, modernly, modernness

Definition: up-to-date; contemporary; not old-fashioned or obsolete; recent; fresh; new; novel

MODEST

Word Forms: modesty, modestly

Definitions: (1) having or showing a moderate or humble opinion of one's own value, abilities, or achievements; unassuming; **(2)** shy or reserved; not forward; **(3)** behaving according to a standard of what is proper or decorous; decent; pure; **(4)** showing moderation; not extreme or excessive; **(5)** quiet and humble in appearance or style

Synonyms: unobtrusive, coy, becoming, chaste, virtuous

MORAL

Word Forms: morality, moralize, moralist, morally

Definitions: (1) dealing with or capable of making the distinction between right and wrong in conduct or character; good; **(2)** designating support that involves approval and sympathy but without action <*moral support*>

Synonyms: *Moral, ethical, virtuous, righteous,* and *noble* mean conforming to a standard of what is right and good. *Moral* implies conformity to established sanctioned codes or accepted notions of right and wrong. *Ethical* suggests the involvement of more difficult or subtle questions of rightness, fairness, or equity. *Virtuous* implies the possession or manifestation of moral excellence in character. *Righteous* stresses guiltlessness or blamelessness. *Noble* implies moral eminence and freedom from anything petty, mean, or dubious in conduct and character.

Quotes:

Morality is not a simple set of rules. It's a very complex struggle of conflicting patterns of values.

The most moral activity of all is the creation of space for life to move onward.

—ROBERT PIRSIG, *Lila*

Above all, we must realize that no arsenal or no weapon in the arsenals of the world is so formidable as the will and moral courage of free men and women.

—RONALD REAGAN, FORTIETH U.S. PRESIDENT

If your morality gets in the way of your humanity it's time for another look.

—JERRY DOWNS

A crime in one society can be a moral requirement in another.

—FRANK HERBERT, *Chapterhouse Dune*

Inspiration: Number four of the Alcoholics Anonymous twelve-step program: We have made a searching and fearless moral inventory of ourselves.

Symbol: moral equilibrium—the *caduceus* (a wand entwined with two serpents and wings)

MOTIVATED

Word Forms: motive, motivative, motivate, motivating, motivator, motivation

Definitions: (1) furnished with an incentive or a goal; **(2)** causing or having the power to cause motion; incite, impel

Synonyms: *Motive, impulse, incentive, inducement,* and *spur* mean a stimulus to action. *Motive* implies an emotion or desire operating on the will and causing it to act. *Impulse* suggests a driving power arising from personal temperament or constitution. *Incentive* applies to an external influence (as an expected reward) that will incite to action. *Inducement* suggests a motive prompted by the deliberate enticements or allurements of another. *Spur* applies to a motive that stimulates the faculties or increases energy or ardor.

Kindred Quality: service minded

Quotes:
By their fruits you shall know them.
　　　　　　　　　　　　　　　—Jesus, Matthew 7:20

In gaining entrance into the kingdom of heaven, it is the motive that counts. God looks into your heart and judges your inner longings and sincere intentions.
　　　　　　　　　　　　　　—Jesus, *The Urantia Book*

Affirmation:
I feel healthy. I feel happy. I feel terrific. I am riding a consistent, persistent wave of good fortune.
　　　　　　　　　　　　　　　—W. Clement Stone

Observations:
Motivation will take the form of desire or concern.

The Seven Motivating Conditions

1. Love—altruism, encouragement
2. Hope—reward, desire
3. Curiosity—interest
4. Obligation—duty
5. Necessity—protection, survival
6. Fear—guilt, embarrassment, doubt, concern
7. Hate—revenge

The Ladder of Motivation

1. Love
2. Delight
3. Wisdom
4. Need
5. Want
6. Comfort
7. Pleasure
8. Discomfort
9. Restriction of freedom
10. Fear
11. Pain
12. Death

Tips:

- *Momentum and inertia*: Once you get moving, you have a better chance to continue.
- How to get up in the morning: Be motivated by something you want to do (internal) or have to do (external).
- Variety is the spice of life. Change what you are doing often enough to keep it interesting.
- The more efficient you are at a task the more that task can be fit into a shorter attention/time span. But the more interesting it is the longer you will be able to continue it.
- Keep your motives high, pointed toward your finest ideas and ideals.
- Repeat and repeat your decision to impress the subconscious mind with the sincerity of your decision.

Comments:

- Motivation is sometimes affected by promises. But then you have to decide that the one doing the promising can or will come through on the promise.
- When your motivation is survival and you have to do it, you simply do do it. If you can synthesize or juxtapose that level of need with a goal that you have, then you will proceed as ardently as if it were an absolute necessity.
- Sometimes you are convinced by a clever argument or the logical alignment of facts. You compare this information with your inner knowledge and are motivated to act. But if your knowing is con-

firmed by your inner wisdom, you (almost) cannot help but to act on it since it *is* the source that moves you.

- The "Just do it" or "Do it now" philosophy implies that you have focused your desires down to one option.

Questions:

How long is your attention span?
How are you motivated?
How do you provide motivation?

Exercises:

The following is adapted from *A Course in Winning*, audio tapes, "On Motivation and Procrastination," by Jimmy Calano and Jeff Salzman, founders of CareerTrak seminars.

1. Get started.
2. Plot it out.
3. Break it up.
4. Do the first step immediately to build momentum.
5. Make sure you can do it.
6. Get what you need.
   - Tools
   - Expertise
   - Time
   - Intestinal fortitude
7. Remind yourself how good you are—accomplishments.
8. Begin each day with the most important and difficult task.
9. Visualize completion.
   - Relax
   - Enjoy achievements
   - Go over details
10. Do it for ten minutes.
11. Commit publicly—invite others to monitor your progress.
12. Reward yourself for accomplishment of a specific goal.
13. Become an automaton.
    - Just do it
    - Put one foot in front of the other

The following is a Denis Waitly contribution to *A Course in Winning*, audio tapes.

Actions Toward Positive Self-Motivation

1. Replace the words "can't" and "try" with "can" and "will."
2. Focus all of your attention and energy on the achievement of the objective that you are involved in right now.
3. Failure is only a temporary change in direction to set you straight for your next success.
4. Make a list of five of your most important wants or desires, write next to each what the benefit or payoff is when you achieve it. Look at the list the last thing at night and the first thing upon rising.
5. Be solution-oriented when presented with a problem.
6. Seek and talk to someone this week who is doing what you want to do—and doing it well, and get the facts from them. Learn about other winners in the field. Go to conferences, courses, and seminars. Read books.
7. See yourself enjoying the rewards of your success.
8. Repeat again and again about your goals. "I want to—I can. I want to—I can."

MOXIE

Definitions: (1) vigor; energy; pep; verve; (2) courage; boldness; nerve; determination; perseverance; (3) know-how; expertise

MULTIDIMENSIONAL

Word Forms: dimensional, multidimensionality, multidimensionally

Definitions: (1) refers collectively to the elements and aspects that make up a complete personality; (2) the integration and harmony of the body, mind, and spirit; (3) having the ability to adapt and be comfortable in a variety of social and physical settings; (4) having the ability to function adequately on the physical, emotional, mental, and spiritual levels of being

Kindred Quality: multidisciplined

MULTIDISCIPLINED

Word Forms: disciplined, multidiscipline

Definitions: (1) proficient or skillful in a variety of fields of study; **(2)** engaged in multiple training that corrects, molds, or perfects the mental faculties or moral character

MULTIFACETED

Word Form: facet

Definition: having many interesting sides or aspects to one's personality; complex; intricate

MUNIFICENT

Word Forms: munificence, munificently

Definition: liberal in giving or bestowing; generous; lavish

Synonyms: bountiful, helpful, open-handed

MUSICAL

Word Forms: music, musician, musicality, musically, musicalness, philo-musical

Definitions: (1) capable of creating music; **(2)** having the pleasing harmonious qualities of music; melodious

Synonyms: dulcet, concordant, rhythmical, mellifluous

Saying: Nobody can conceive of music in hell and no one can imagine a heaven without it.

Quotes:
Music is the effort we make to explain to ourselves how our brains work. We listen to Bach transfixed because this is listening to a human mind.
— LEWIS THOMAS

If music be the food of love, play on.
— WILLIAM SHAKESPEARE, *Twelfth Night*

Mythologies: *Apollo*, the Greek and Roman god of music, poetry, prophecy, archery, and medicine; *Euterpe*, the Greek Muse of music and lyric poetry; *Orpheus*, a Greek musician who could charm beasts and make trees and even rocks move to the melody of his lyre

Historical Figure: *St. Cecilia*, the patron saint of music

NATURAL

Word Forms: nature, naturalize, naturally, naturalness

Definitions: (1) in accordance with what is found or expected in nature; **(2)** real; not artificial; **(3)** innate or inherent qualities or ability <*natural* talent>; **(4)** possessing the higher qualities of human nature; **(5)** an inherent sense of right and wrong <*natural* rights>; **(6)** marked by easy simplicity; at ease; free from affectation

Synonyms: ingenuous, spontaneous, intrinsic, normal, true, original

Quotes:
I reckon there's as much human nature in some folks as there is in others, if not more.
— EDWARD NOYES WESTCOTT

Nature reaches out to us with welcoming arms, and bids us enjoy her beauty.
— KAHLIL GIBRAN

The best remedy for those who are afraid, lonely or unhappy is to go outside, somewhere where they can be quite alone with the heavens, nature and God. Because only then does one feel that all is as it should be and that God wishes to see people happy, amidst the simple beauty of nature.

—ANNE FRANK, *The Diary of Anne Frank*

Observation: I've noticed that people expect others to possess the natural talents that they possess. If it is easy for them, it's obvious that it should be easy to others. It is surprising and sometimes frustrating when they realize that others do not have that ability. It is even more astonishing that they may not even want to enjoy it.

Recognize and be thankful for your inherent gifts, but also have compassion for others who do not have the positive qualities that you have naturally.

NEAT

Word Forms: neater, neatest, neaten, neatly, neatness, neat-handed

Definitions: **(1)** trim; tidy; clean; orderly; **(2)** precise; systematic; **(3)** marked by skill or ingenuity; adroit; **(4)** fine; admirable; **(5)** shapely; well-proportioned; a simple, pleasing appearance; **(6)** cleverly or smartly phrased or done

Too Far: compulsive

NECESSARY

Word Forms: necessaries, necessity, necessarily, necessariness

Definitions: **(1)** essential, indispensable, or requisite; **(2)** unavoidable; inevitable

Affirmation: I am necessary.

NEIGHBORLY

Word Forms: neighbor, neighborhood, neighborliness

Definition: friendly; showing kindness or helpfulness; sociable

Synonym: amicable

People Who Exemplify This Quality: Mr. Fred Rogers

Quote:
God did not come to me through a mystical experience, but through a human being, a neighbor, an agent of his love.
—ELIZABETH KILBOURN

NERVY

Word Forms: nerve, nervier, nerviest, nervily, nerviness

Definition: showing calm courage; unexpectedly bold

NEW

Word Forms: newer, newest, newly, newness, renewed

Definitions: (1) having never existed or occurred before; **(2)** pure; unspoiled; **(3)** rejuvenated; refreshed in spirits; healthy; **(4)** contemporary; recent; fashionable; **(5)** beginning again; making another start

Synonyms: *New, novel, modern, original,* and *fresh* mean having recently come into existence or use. *New* applies to what is freshly made and unused or has not been known or experienced before. *Novel* applies to what is not only new but strange or unprecedented. *Modern* applies to what belongs to or is characteristic of the present time or the present era.

Original applies to what is the first of its kind to exist. *Fresh* applies to what has not lost its qualities of newness such as liveliness, energy, brightness.

Saying: Obsolete the old with the new.

Quote:
Scientists treat a new idea the same way that the body treats a foreign substance: it is rejected.
— WILLIAM H. CALVIN, *The River That Flows Uphill*

Advice: When you come up with something new, innovative, or different, do not be dismayed at the criticism that you will experience. Expect it, anticipate it, even welcome it, for these are the fires within which your idea is purified.

Symbol: *thirteen*

NICE

Word Forms: nicer, nicest, nicety, nicely, niceness

Definitions: (1) pleasing; agreeable; delightful; **(2)** amiably pleasant; kind; thoughtful; considerate; **(3)** requiring great accuracy, precision, skill, or delicacy <*nice* workmanship>; **(4)** refined as to manners, language, or character; **(5)** virtuous; respectable; decorous; **(6)** good; excellent; a generalized term of approval; having very wide appeal

Synonyms: dainty, exquisite, fine, exact, correct

Too Far: naive

Saying:
If you don't have anything nice to say, don't say anything at all.
— MATERNAL WISDOM

Quote:

It's nice to be nice to the nice.

—FRANK BURNS, "M*A*S*H"

Comments:

- Since everyone wants others to be nice to them, it makes sense to make the effort to accommodate that desire. The likelihood of their being nice back increases dramatically—even though that may not or should not be your motive.
- If someone is not nice, make up a reason why that person is not, or better yet, ask him or her. Knowing why gives you a better appreciation of, and tolerance for, the individual's poor behavior.

NIMBLE

Word Forms: nimbler, nimblest, nimbly, nimbleness

Definitions: (1) light and quick in motion; moving with ease and celerity; lively; swift; **(2)** quick and clever conception, comprehension, or resourcefulness; **(3)** sensitive; responsive

NO WORRIES

Definition: carefree; untroubled; nonchalant

Sayings:

Sans souci (French): "without worries"

Australian: "No worries, mate."

Quote:

What, me worry?

—ALFRED E. NEUMAN, *Mad* magazine

NOBLE

Word Forms: nobler, noblest, nobility, noble-minded, nobly, nobleness, noble-souled

Definitions: (1) famous, illustrious, or renowned; having eminence, dignity, excellence, or fame; worthy; (2) having or showing superior moral qualities or ideals; (3) grand; stately; splendid; magnificent; magnanimous

Derivation: Latin, "to come to know"

Synonyms: exalted, majestic, high, imperial, august, generous, lofty

Quote:
Noble aim, faithfully kept, is as a noble deed.
—WILLIAM WORDSWORTH

NONCHALANT

Word Forms: nonchalance, nonchalantly

Definition: coolly unconcerned; unexcited; centered

Familial Quality: cool

NONJUDGMENTAL

Definition: avoiding judgments based on one's personal or especially moral standards

Quotes:
> We judge ourselves by what we feel capable of doing, while others judge us by what we have done.
> —HENRY WADSWORTH LONGFELLOW

> In judging others, folks will work overtime for no pay.
> —CHARLES EDWIN CARRUTHERS

Reflection: Judgment is essential to survival. But there are variations of judgment. A person who demands an empirical proof for *all* reality is closing down reason. Did ultraviolet and infrared exist before the instruments were available to detect them? If you *must* have proof you are doomed to wait until someone with the faith focuses the lens so that you can see.

A person who moves judgment to the negative realm of prejudice is closing down freedom. A person who judges that their version of reality is the only one, and demands that others step into that mold, is closing themselves to the possibilities and truths that other realities offer.

Add a full measure of humanness to your judgment and you won't have to worry about the beast of imbalance.

Advice:
- Use your judgment to protect yourself from dangers.
- Open your heart to judge yourself with a penetrating honesty and a lighthearted mercy. It is a nervy act.

Comments:
- Another person or society can only be judged justly using *their* own set of rules and moral standards. If you judge them with yours, you see them incorrectly and probably unfairly.

    Conversely, if you judge yourself by their standards, you reduce the value of your experience.
- Judgment from others is almost always resented unless you completely trust them and give them permission to judge you.

Symbols: the *void*—not the absence of life but the absence of conflict; *nothingness*

NORMAL

Word Forms: norm, normality, normalcy, normalize, normally

Definitions: (1) conforming to or consisting of a pattern, process, or standard regarded as usual or typical; natural; regular; **(2)** well-adjusted; without marked or persistent mental aberrations

NOTEWORTHY

Word Forms: noteworthily, noteworthiness

Definition: worthy of observation or notice especially because of some special excellence; outstanding; remarkable; notable

NOURISHING

Word Forms: nourish, nourishment, nourishingly

Definition: promoting or sustaining life, growth, or strength

NURTURING

Word Forms: nurture, nurtured

Definitions: (1) characterizes one who promotes development by providing nourishment, support, and encouragement during the stages of growth; **(2)** raising; training; educating; **(3)** to further the development of; foster

Synonyms: *Nurture* is to train with a fostering care. *Nourish* denotes to supply with food or cause to grow. *Cherish* is to hold and treat dearly.

Color: green

Symbols: *Mother Earth; mommy*

OBEDIENT

Word Forms: obey, obedience, obediently

Definition: complying with authority; yielding willingly to commands, orders, or injunctions; performing what is required or abstaining from that which is forbidden

Synonyms: dutiful, docile, tractable, amenable

Quotes:
> Yet the concept of civil disobedience, as practiced by such nonviolent practitioners as Martin Luther King, carries with it a further stipulation: that those who for moral reasons disobey the law must do so consciously and with full willingness to suffer whatever penalties their disobedience brings.
> —RUSHWORTH M. KIDDER

Comment: Active participation in obedience includes your positive choice in the action. Begrudging obedience is less than ideal.

Fiction: *Griselda*, a heroine of Chaucer's *Canterbury Tales* who is subjected to cruel trials to test her patience and obedience, is ever meek and long-suffering and never complains.

OBJECTIVE

Word Forms: objectivity, objectify, objectivize, objectively, objectiveness

Definitions: (1) free from prejudicial personal feelings or opinions; unbiased; (2) real; actual phenomena; external to the mind as distinct from inner or imaginary feelings and thoughts; **(3)** something that one's efforts are intended to attain or accomplish; purpose; goal; target

See also: *Realistic*

Quotes:

Objectivity does not mean detachment, it means respect; that is, the ability not to distort and to falsify things, persons and oneself.

—ERICH FROMM

The scientist's job is to explore everything. No matter the difficulties! To stay open, to accept ambiguity. To attempt to fuse with the object of knowledge. To admit that there are values shot through the whole enterprise. To love it. To work toward discovering the values by which we live. To work to enact those values in the world. To explore—and more than that—to create!

—KIM STANLEY ROBINSON, *Red Mars*

Reflection: It is a most difficult thing to be truly objective. We look at the world through our subjective experiential view. To those who do not experience the wisdom of a larger view, statements like "Love your enemy" are truly baffling. The only reason to even consider that statement as reasonable is if you believe that Christ was genuinely objective.

Observations:

- An astute observer must have a keen sense of insight into motivation if he or she is to explain the actions of others.
- Objectivity works best on the factual level. The physical sciences thrive on objectivity in experimentation. Observation can be reproduced. If another person performs the same experiment with the same results, we call it true. But as soon as an opinion arises from the facts, the possibility of conflict arises.
- What would the scientific approach be if it did not include the more etheric qualities? A scientist must have *integrity* and be *honest, curious, exact, efficient,* and *proficient.* These qualities allow the experiment to be conducted in the first place. These qualities are the back-

drop of the experiment—the human/spiritual part of the experiment that allows the observer to believe that the results are valid.

- Curiosity and wonder make us take the time and effort to seek the truth. Therefore, the positive qualities are the real purpose and meaning of experience.

Tips:
- Solicit multiple subjective views.
- Give yourself permission to hold your current point of view. Remember that you are a sincere and reasonable person. And, if need be, give yourself permission to change to another position as your open-mindedness and open-heartedness allow you to find a new ground upon which you can then comfortably stand.

Comments:
- Objective reality can be described in two ways. One is the "true" objective reality, that is, reality that is indisputably from *the* objective point of view. This would include all reality from the finite to the absolute.

  The second type of objective reality is collective, subjective reality. The agreement of a group of people becomes objective reality. This is the collective consciousness or social reality. Subjective reality can align with either reality.

  The qualities which we experience are existential and experience is the key. We subjectively correlate our experience of the world to what we call objective reality. We communicate to other beings who verify our point of view with their subjective reality and their personal experience. When there is an agreement, we call that objective.

- On the absolute level there are some absolute truths. These are unknowable by objective means and yet we have conceptualized them. Where else would the concepts of absolute, universal, and infinite come from?

OBLIGING

Word Forms: oblige, obliger, obligee, obligingly, obligingness

Definitions: (1) helpful; ready to be of service; courteous; civil; **(2)** under a debt of gratitude; appreciative

Synonyms: obliging, accommodating, kind, and complaisant

Both *obliging* and *accommodating* imply making a gracious and welcome gesture. *Oblige* emphasizes the idea of doing a favor and often with some effort. *Accommodate* emphasizes providing a service or convenience. One is *kind* who desires to see others happy. One is *complaisant* who endeavors to please. One who is *obliging* performs some actual service, or has the disposition to do so.

Compatible Qualities: amiable, pleasing

OBSERVANT

Word Forms: observe, observable, observance, observation, observantly

Definitions: (1) one who pays strict attention to; keenly watchful; **(2)** quick to notice or perceive; alert; **(3)** conforming to law, custom, religion, or ritual

How to Live This Quality Today: Use your peripheral vision.

Comment: The only way we can know what's going on inside other people is to see what they say and do outside themselves, the decisions they make, and the actions they take.

Fiction: *Sherlock Holmes,* famous detective of Sir Arthur Conan Doyle, who had incredible powers of observation and deductive reasoning

OKAY

Word Forms: okays, okayed, okaying

Definitions: (1) all right; satisfactory; adequate; sufficient; **(2)** correct, permissible, or acceptable; **(3)** feeling well; **(4)** safe; sound; **(5)** estimable, likable, or dependable

OPEN

Word Forms: opened, opening, opener, openest, openly, openness, open-eyed, open-faced

Definitions: (1) affording approach, view, passage, or access; available; **(2)** not secret or hidden; **(3)** expanded; unfolded; **(4)** receptive; not closed to new ideas; **(5)** generous; liberal; **(6)** frank; candid; direct; honest; **(7)** ready to do, hear, see or receive anything; fully prepared; attentive

Too Far: gullible

Reflection: There are those who say that you are already all that you need to be or will ever be; that all you need to do is allow it; just be open and don't get in your own way.

Advice: Give other people's belief systems a healthy respect. Be open to their sense of reality and order. They have experience and sincerely understand the place that they are in. You may judge that place to be a small box, but after all, you are in a box of your own. Realize that you, and hopefully they, are evolving and expanding. Tomorrow you may stand with them on more compatible ground because of the compassion you showed toward them today.

Comment: People are fond of saying, "I went into this philosophy or idea with a healthy skepticism—I even wanted to prove it wrong—but I was convinced that it was correct." But it is unwise to approach an idea with an overabundance of skepticism. That is sure to prevent you from reaping the benefits that are available. A healthy, honest skepticism prevents you from being naive, but a healthy openness helps you grow.

Honest openness might occasion that you are taken in by an idea that seems plausible. Until you learn, you may even be gullible. You may look the fool because you were willing to be open, but you also are respected for your honor and you gained the experience unlike the skeptic who because of fear kept closed.

OPENHANDED

Word Forms: open, openhandedly, openhandedness

Definition: generous; liberal; munificent

Symbol: the removal of the right glove

OPEN-HEARTED

Word Forms: open, open-heartedly, open-heartedness

Definitions: (1) candid; frank; (2) generous; kind; benevolent

Too Far: bleeding heart

OPEN-MINDED

Word Forms: open-mindedly, open-mindedness

Definitions: (1) receptive to new ideas; free from bigotry or prejudice; (2) willing to communicate or debate a point; impartial

Compatible Qualities: decisive, focused

Too Far: filterless

The ultimate brainwashing would be a totally open mind. If people accept without question, or concern for contradiction, anything and everything presented to them, they would be perfect tools for manipulation.

Saying: Minds are like parachutes; they only function when open.

OPPORTUNISTIC

Word Forms: opportune, opportunity, opportunist, opportunistically

Definition: takes advantage of conditions that are favorable to the attainment of a goal; open to success

Sayings:
Today's stumbling blocks are tomorrow's stepping stones.

If your "master" is a strong one, then your success as a "slave" is your opportunistic attitude.

Regrets are temptations fulfilled or opportunities unfulfilled. Learn from your regrets.

Quote:
When one door closes another door opens; but we so often look so long and so regretfully upon the closed door, that we do not see the ones which open for us.

—ALEXANDER GRAHAM BELL

Observation: Problem solvers and risk takers are opportunistic.

Suggestion: If your life becomes too placid, you will be happier if you choose to extend yourself a challenge. If your life is too hectic, take the opportunity to relax.
Difficulties can be seen as blessings and hardships as opportunities to acquire some positive personal qualities. If you are not experiencing any difficulties, then appreciate this peaceful time with thankfulness that equals the intensity of your difficult times.

Admonition: You never regret the positive things you try. You only regret the things you wish you had done. Would you rather do it and regret it than not do it and regret that you hadn't tried it?

If you regret what you have done, then at least you've done it and not been scared away from a difficult but desirable situation. If you regret what you have done, the regret can be transformed into a learning experience. Forgive yourself and go on. Forgiveness and reflective thought are the transforming mechanisms of changing the regret into a positive learning process (even if all that you've learned is that you don't want to do it again).

OPTIMISTIC

Word Forms: optimal, optimism, optimist, optimum, optimize, optimistically

Definitions: (1) takes the most hopeful view of matters; expects the best outcome in any circumstance; looks on the bright side of things; **(2)** believes that good will ultimately triumph over evil and that virtue will be rewarded

Kindred Qualities: realistic, practical

Quote:
Optimist: "Daydreamer" more elegantly spelled.
— SAMUEL CLEMENS, *Mark Twain's Notebook*

Comment: While listening to a political convention, I realized that politicians are caught in a trap of projecting an overly optimistic point of view because everybody who they are trying to appeal to is demanding that they solve the problems that exist. In order to receive the confidence of the electorate, they have to make optimistic promises. Politicians trying to get votes will project an optimistic image no matter what.

Even an honest politician is hampered by the fact of having to meet the requirements of optimism. If the politician does, in all sincerity, believe that he or she can accomplish what is promised, then he or she might be naive. Social problems are so large, diverse, and involved that such grand promises are blind to the facts of reality. On the other hand, if he or she realizes that all that can be done, and all that should be promised, is to take actions that will move toward the solutions, then he or she is being more honest.

ORDERLY

Word Forms: order, ordered, orderliness, well-ordered

Definitions: (1) methodical; neat; tidy; well-arranged; (2) well-behaved; law-abiding; peaceable; harmonious

Synonyms: systematic, regular

Saying: A place for everything and everything in its place.

Quote:
Robert's Rules of Order

> No minority has a right to block a majority from conducting the legal business of the organization. No majority has a right to prevent a minority from peacefully attempting to become a majority.

Comment: We experience such delight when something falls into place. Just as nature abhors a vacuum, nature loves order.

Symbols: spiritual order—*three;* moral or perfect order—*seven;* universal order—*ten;* cosmic order—*twelve*

ORGANIZED

Word Forms: organize, organizing, organization, organizer

Definitions: (1) brought together; cooperative for a common objective; (2) arranged, established, or instituted; brought into being

Tip: The key to order is putting like objects together.

Suggestion: A simple and effective way of getting organized is by beginning your day making a list and ending it making notes.

ORIENTED

Word Forms: orient, orientation

Definitions: (1) intellectually or emotionally directed; **(2)** having a good sense of direction; **(3)** knowing where one stands in relation to various moral, political, or religious opinions

Quote:
Living is not necessary, but navigation is.
—POMPEY

Symbols: the *east, sunrise;* the *North Star;* a *pyramid*—the four cardinal directions and a central apex

ORIGINAL

Word Forms: origin, originality, originally

Definitions: (1) first in order; preceding all others; the beginning; **(2)** arising or proceeding independently; inventive; novel; **(3)** thinking or acting in an independent, creative, or individual manner

Quote:
A mind that's afraid to toy with the ridiculous will never come up with the brilliantly original . . .
—DAVID BRIN, *Brightness Reef*

OUTGOING

Word Form: outgoingness

Definition: interested in and responsive to others; friendly; sociable; gregarious

OUTSTANDING

Word Form: outstandingly

Definitions: (1) prominent; conspicuous; striking <*outstanding* courage>; **(2)** superior or distinct; excellent; wonderful

PACIFISTIC

Word Forms: pacific, pacifist, pacifism, pacify, pacifistically

Definitions: (1) characterizes one who opposes war and the military solution; one who proposes that all disputes be settled by arbitration; **(2)** nonviolent; peaceable

Kindred Qualities: humor, luck, strength

Compatible Qualities: moral conviction, patience, courage, objective, compromising

Familial Quality: *Satyagraha* (Sanskrit): literally "Insistence on Truth"; pressure for social and political reform through friendly passive resistance

Inspiration: Leo Tolstoy at the age of fifty experienced a religious conversion to the Gospel of Peace and lived his last thirty years preaching the ethic of nonviolence.

Advice: Remember that there is personal pacifism and political pacifism. Do not castigate yourself if you are not Gandhi with his combination of personal and political pacifism. Your personal belief, that *might* does not make *right,* is laudable. You do what you can in your daily life to live peaceably.

Comment: To make political pacifism work there must be unity, loyalty, courage, and mutual respect.

Bibliography: *Lest Innocent Blood Be Shed: The Story of The Village of Le Chambon and How Goodness Happened There*, Philip P. Hallie

This is the true story of effective nonviolent resistance to Nazism. The townspeople sheltered and saved the lives of many hundreds of Jews even though the penalty was deportation or death.

Read from and about Gandhi.

Read from and about the Quakers.

PAINSTAKING

Word Forms: painstakingly, painstakingness

Definition: showing diligent caution and effort; careful

PANACHE

Definition: dashing elegance of manner; spirited self-confidence; flamboyance; verve, carefree

Historical Figure: *Savinien Cyrano de Bergerac*, French dramatist, novelist, and duelist, 1619–1655

PARAGON

Definition: a model or pattern of excellence or perfection

People Who Exemplify This Quality: *You* are a paragon because you live a standard that you have decided is right for you. You can be an example of goodness simply by being good.

PARENTAL

Word Forms: parent, parentally

Definition: fatherly or motherly; tender; affectionate

Tips:
- Know how to let your child learn. Give him or her the tools, instruction, encouragement, and then the freedom.
- Notice what talents your child has naturally. Expose him or her to lots of options. Give your child the benefit of your observations about his or her talents and interests.

PARTICIPATIVE

Word Forms: participate, participatory, participation

Definition: being or willing to be a part; sharing; partaking

PARTICULAR

Word Forms: particularity, particularize, particularly, particularization

Definitions: **(1)** unusual; special; worthy of attention and regard; not ordinary; noteworthy; **(2)** detailed; meticulous; **(3)** singularly nice in taste; precise; fastidious

Synonyms: appropriate, distinct, exact, exclusive

PASSIONATE

Word Forms: passion, impassioned, passionately, passionateness

Definitions: **(1)** compelled or ruled by intense emotion or strong opinion; fervid; zealous; expressing or showing profound feeling; emotional; enthusiastic; vehement; **(2)** easily aroused to or influenced by sexual desire; ardently sensual; amorous

Derivation: Latin, "to endure," "to suffer"

Quote:
Indeed, what could *Reason* ever accomplish for mankind by itself, without *Passion* to drive it on?
—DAVID BRIN, *Earth*

Color: bright red

Symbols: *blood;* a *storm*

PASTORAL

Word Forms: pastorally, pastoralness

Definition: characteristic of pleasant rural life; peaceful, simple, and natural; innocent; idyllic

Proverb:
A butterfly never hurries—even when pursued.
—CHINESE

Symbols: the *shepherd;* the *farmer*

Fiction: *Beulah*, in Bunyan's *Pilgrim's Progress*, the idyllic land of sunshine and delight

Mythologies: *Ceres*, the Roman god of agriculture and fruits of the harvest; *Cybele*, the Phrygian goddess of nature; *Demeter*, the Greek god of agriculture and fruitfulness

PATERNAL

Word Forms: paternity, paternally

Definition: fatherly; characteristic of a father or fatherhood—loyal, supportive, protective, loving, giving
See also: *Maternal*

Symbols: the *sun;* the *umbrella*

PATIENT

Word Forms: patience, patiently, compatient, omnipatient

Definitions: (1) the will or ability to wait calmly or endure pain or trouble without complaining, losing control, or making a disturbance; quietly tolerating delay, confusion, or inefficiency; **(2)** refusing to be provoked or angered by an insult; **(3)** forbearing; tolerant; **(4)** steadiness, endurance, or perseverance in performing a task; diligent; **(5)** quiet action

Derivation: Latin, "to suffer"

Synonyms: constant, composed, equanimity, fortitude, stoic, poise, imperturbable, long-suffering, persistent, self-possessed
   Patience refers to the quietness or self-possession of one's own spirit. *Resignation* refers to the submission of your will to the will of another.

Kindred Qualities: adaptable, foresight, humor, initiative, prepared

Compatible Qualities: accommodating, assertive, open, perspicacious, persistent

Note: Having the focus to pay attention to something and being *persistent* enough to continue to pay attention to it, will develop *patience* while you are getting it done.

Parental Qualities: faith, hope

Familial Qualities: kindness, tolerance, serenity

Consequential Qualities: confidence, creativity, decisive, freedom, insight, peace, progress, self-discipline, self-esteem, stress hardy, wisdom

Quotes:
   Nothing so needs reforming as other people's habits.
   —MARK TWAIN

The greatest gift of stone is patience.

—BARRY HUGHART, *The Story of the Stone*

Patience ceases to be a virtue when it permits others to waste our time.

—PAULINE M. SCHMIDT

Patience is easier if you have respect for the person or thing with which you are trying to be patient.

—JUDY KAIN

Adopt the pace of nature; her secret is patience.

—RALPH WALDO EMERSON

Story: You're all strung out, a hard day at work, you want to take a bath, relax in hot water. Just thinking about that bath, oh, it's going to be great. But the damn bathtub takes forever to fill up! You're impatient. It is not the bathtub's fault, it's filling up as fast as it can. You start to think about that. That's the key to patience!—it is happening. The impatience is within you. You are the source of the stress because it's not happening fast enough for your personal satisfaction. If you're satisfied with the pace at which something is going, then you won't be impatient. And sometimes you can take action to make it go faster. If you do that, you are also enhancing your patience because you are an active participant in moving it along.

Part of the impatience is that you are already strung out; you've already got that impatience built up. Anything that doesn't happen to your instant gratification is going to build on that impatience. The trick is to not let the steam get compressed in the first place. Study the suggestions under *Stress Hardy*.

Affirmation: I choose to be patient. The more patient that I am, the sooner that I will know what my next course of action will be.

Consideration: Don't expect your inner self to change instantly. There are instances of that, usually in extreme crisis, but you can't go around having a life of total crisis all the time. Expect that you will succeed. Work with patience and continual focus. Give yourself the same time it takes for a human baby to be born.

Visualization: Sit quietly. Put on some soft, instrumental music. Relax. Open your heart. Close your eyes.

You are walking in the woods. To get to the clean running stream, you need to go through the brier patch. You move into its jumbled branches but it doesn't take long to get entangled. You know that you cannot stay where you are. You know that clear ground is ahead. At first you move too quickly and are pricked and torn by the merciless thorns. The pain quickly teaches you to move with caution. Yet you realize that you also need resolve and deliberation. You settle into the pace that is necessary. You pick the ripe berries and enjoy their sweet reward. You are thankful. You stop to remove a thorn that is stuck in your leg. You notice that you are not annoyed by the inconvenience. You bend down to smell the rose that gave you its thorn. As you go on you move with more confidence and realize that you are being pricked less and less. You understand that your movements are graceful. You catch the flight of the butterfly just as you are feeling the joy of the dance. You make your last move into the clearing. You feel relieved and yet, now that you've got the hang of it, you're almost looking forward to the next encounter. Take off your shoes and cool your feet in the water.

Enjoy the rest of your journey.

Observation: It is easier to be patient with those that we judge to be ignorant than those who we think should know better.

Tips:
- To acquire patience teach someone something.
- One of the aspects of patience is realizing how long it takes something to manifest. Allow that time to be.
- A key to patience is to be diligently present.

Admonition: Use the memory of your experiences of the past as fuel to illuminate the present. Project your mind and heart into some possible futures and your choices will be clearer. Hold with a sensitive, confident faith that the meaning and value of the present will be revealed.

Comments:
- Patience is often misunderstood as a quality of inaction. Think instead of the "nonactive" time as active anticipation. The hungry hunter who is quiet and attentive knows that the moment to move will soon be at hand and that he must be ready.

- There is a time tension that the patient person sets up, which creates a sense of an appropriate, proper, and favorable outcome. That is, a realization that all will truly be well, which brightens the present with its hope and begins the journey into the future. If you cannot see or sense that lighter day, look farther into the future or into a different one.
- Those in power, whether political, parental, industrial, or educational, tend to say, "Be patient." Not for any altruistic desire that those who they give this advice to become more spiritually rounded, but because they want a quiet, docile, nonactive populace. They want it to be tolerant and dutiful. What is really being demanded is not patience but obedience.

The true nature of the quality of patience has more to do with movement. Patience will deliver the intended goal. If one also has a steadfast intention and hard-working development, there will be consistent progress toward a goal.

Sometimes your patience is not more than a passive, hopeful wish that what you want will come your way. But if that is the only level of activity possible, then you are being actively patient; your desire to participate in the advancement toward your goal is being met.

How to Live This Quality Today: You might be standing in line to talk to the teller at the bank. While you're there, you can be organizing your banking needs. If this is done, occupy your mind with something else that you enjoy doing. No time to waist on boredom. Read a book. Talk to the people in line with you. Think about what you need to do when you leave the bank. Plan your vacation.

Symbol: the *tortoise*

Legend: *Enid*, in Arthurian legend, a lady who was a model of constancy, loyalty, and patience

Bibliography: Read about the patience of Job. Although Job has been much credited with patience, I think that his story is primarily one of faith. But patience is one of the roots of faith.

PEACEFUL

Word Forms: peace, peaceable, peacefully, peacefulness, peacemaker, peacekeeper, pax

Definitions: (1) in a state of mental or physical tranquility or quiet, security, or order; quietly behaved; composed; **(2)** describes the state of harmony in personal relations, concord between governments or organizations; **(3)** one who reconciles between unfriendly parties

Synonyms: calm, pacific, repose, order, gentle, mild, serene, friendly

Compatible Qualities: *satyagraha,* compassion

Saying: *Pax vobiscum* (Latin): "Peace be with you."

Quotes:

Peace is empowerment, justice and the struggle for justice. Peace is personal, relational, local, national, international, global. Peace is not found, it is created by continual attention and effort. [There is no way to peace, peace is the way.]
—JOEL EDELSTEIN (LAST SENTENCE IS QUAKER)

Non-violence is more powerful than all the armaments in the world. It is mightier than the mightiest weapon of destruction devised by the ingenuity of man.
—MOHANDAS KARAMCHAND GANDHI

Here certainly is the golden maxim: Do not do to others that which we do not want them to do to us.
—CONFUCIUS

What is hateful to you, do not to your fellow men. That is the entire law, all the rest is commentary.
—THE TALMUD

Hurt not others with that which pains yourself.
—UDANA-VARGA

This is the sum of duty: do naught to others which if done to thee would cause thee pain.

—THE MAHABHARATA

All things whatsoever ye would that men should do to you, do ye even so to them.

—THE BIBLE

No leader is going to give us peace, no government, no army, no country. What will bring peace is inward transformation which will lead to outward action. Inward transformation is not isolation, not a withdrawal from outward action. On the contrary, there can be right action only when there is right thinking, and there is no right thinking when there is no self-knowledge. Without knowing yourself, there is no peace.

—KRISHNAMURTI

If we cannot adjust our differences peacefully we are less than human.

—FRANK HERBERT, *Heretics of Dune*

[Merlin:] "To plant a garden is the chief of the arts of peace."

—MARY STEWART, *The Last Enchantment*

Insofar as you have peace in your life, you reflect it into your surroundings and into your world.

—PEACE PILGRIM, *Steps Toward Inner Peace*

There is no greater block to world peace or inner peace than fear.

—PEACE PILGRIM, *Steps Toward Inner Peace*

Note: She goes on to say that what we fear we learn to hate, then we have both fear and hate. Love dissolves fear and hate.

Prayer:
Lord, make me an instrument of your peace.
Where there is hatred, let me sow love,
Where there is injury, pardon,
Where there is doubt, faith,
Where there is despair, hope,

Where there is darkness, light
and where there is sadness, joy.
Divine Master, grant that I may not so much seek to be consoled as
*   to console;*
To be understood as to understand;
To be loved as to love;
For it is in giving that we receive,
It is in pardoning that we are pardoned;
And it is in dying that we are born to eternal life.
   —GIOVANNI FRANCESCO BERNARDONE, SAINT FRANCIS OF ASSISI

Consideration: Are you going to be a warrior or a peacemaker? Now, warriors often make war in the name of peace, but there is a huge distinction. And the difference is the consciousness. If you have the qualities of compassion, gentleness, and concern in your character, they will balance out the qualities of strength, power, and force. In war one is compelled to use the means of war. You must consider your enemy as unworthy of life, victimized innocent bystanders as necessities of the struggle; your own comrades are expendable. The use of the most intense power is justified to "win." But to be a peacemaker there is a need to get inside the mind and heart of your opponent. You need to have the compassion to understand and to help them. Your fight is for fairness. It is possible to be a warrior and a peacemaker.

Observation: There will be no lasting peace until people see more security and profit in peace than in offensive or defensive aggression.

Advice: One of the greatest threats to peace is *facts*. Most of what an argument is about is the different understandings, views, and beliefs about what the facts are.

Establish what each party holds to be the facts, but then move on. If there is an argument on these "facts," it can then go round and round, each side trying to prove that its facts are the good facts and the other guy's facts are bad facts, each trying to make the other side give up its position and accept the opposite view. If the view of the future is a vision of peace, the view of the past can be held as objective history.

Peace Pilgrim's Steps Toward Inner Peace (in no set order)

- Be willing to face life squarely.

- Realize that every problem impacts growth to the degree that it is attempted to be solved.
- Live what you believe with the highest light you have.
- Give priority to the good you are motivated toward and start to act on that good.
- Simplify your life. Balance needs with wants and harmonize inner and outer well-being.

Admonition: Overcome
Evil with Good
Falsehood with Truth
Hatred with Love
Ugliness with Beauty
Selfishness with Thoughtfulness
Need with Service

Symbols: the *dove;* the *olive tree;* the *crane* (Japanese)

Color: blue

PENITENT

Word Forms: penance, penitence, penitently

Definition: having regret of sin or offense and willingness to atone; repentant; contrite

Comment: If you do something that you know to be wrong, you will eventually have to reverse the injury. To feel a need to take positive action is a first step. You may not be able to remove the harm done to the specific person. What you can do is change who you are. Then you will act differently to all.

PEPPY

Word Forms: pep, peppier, peppiest, peppily, peppiness

Definition: energetic; vigorous; lively; spirited; brisk

PERCEPTIVE

Word Forms: perceive, percept, perceptible, perception, perceptivity, perceptual, perceptively, perceptiveness

Definitions: **(1)** showing keenness of insight, sympathetic understanding, or intuition; discerning; **(2)** observant; a quick capacity for comprehending

Too Far: nosey

Quotes:

Eskimos see sixteen different forms of ice which are as different to them as trees and shrubs are different to us. Hindus, on the other hand, use the same term for both ice and snow. Creek and Natchez Indians do not distinguish yellow from green. Similarly, Choctaw, Tunica, the Keresian Pueblo Indians and many other people make no terminological distinction between blue and green. The Hopis have no word for time.

—ROBERT PIRSIG, *Lila*

If the doors of perception were cleansed, everything would appear as it is: infinite.

—WILLIAM BLAKE

Observation: In our attempt to simplify complex activities or processes, we tend to isolate individual aspects of the system. This is like turning off a movie projector and studying the film one frame at a time. One will get a detailed look at the individual frames but will never be able to perceive the dynamic spirit or emotional content of the performance.

PERFECT

Word Forms: perfected, perfecting, perfecter, perfection, perfectionist, perfective, perfectly, perfectness

Definitions: (1) complete in all respects; without defect or omission; sound; flawless; **(2)** in a condition of complete excellence in skill or quality; faultless; most admirable; **(3)** completely correct or accurate; exact; precise; **(4)** without reserve or qualification; pure; complete; total; **(5)** expert; proficient; completely effective; thorough

Kindred Qualities: common sense, down-to-earth

Compatible Qualities: realistic, compromising

Quotes:

Be perfect, therefore, as your heavenly Father is perfect.

—Matthew 5:48

The most important question to ask at any one moment is, "How is this perfect?"

—Joe Burull

When we realize a total of something as we are experiencing it, we are for that moment, perfect.

—Jacquelyn Small, *Transformers*

Consideration: The following excerpt and the Three Stages of Perfection are from Scofield, a biblical scholar.

The word "perfect" as the Bible uses it of men, does *not* refer to sinless perfection. Old Testament characters described as "blameless" or "wholly devoted" were obviously not sinless. Although a number of Hebrew and Greek words are translated "perfect," the thought is usually either "completeness in all details" (Hebrew: *tamam*; and Greek: *katartizo*) or "to reach a goal or achieve a purpose" (Greek: *teleioo*).

Scripture recognizes that Christians do not attain sinless perfection in this life.

Three Stages of Perfection

1. *Positional perfection*, already possessed by every believer of Christ (Hebrews: 10:14)
2. *Relative perfection*, i.e., spiritual maturity, especially in the will of God, love, holiness, patience, and "everything good." Maturity is achieved progressively, "perfecting holiness" and "Are you now being made perfect?" Perfection is accomplished through the gifts of ministry bestowed to "prepare God's people."
3. *Ultimate perfection*, perfection in soul, spirit, and body

Tip: Perfect is doing the next thing that is possible for you to do and doing it with a positive intention.

Comment: One does not become instantly perfect, but one is as perfect in the moment as one allows oneself to be. There are both absolute and relative perfection. Since we are finite beings we have to accept the fact that we are in the realm of relative perfection. If you compare absolute perfection to finite perfection there is a dramatic gap. But there need not be any negative connotation applied to relative perfection simply because the gap exists. Perfection is still perfection even in its most immature or child-like manifestation.

Question: Can you be perfect if you can't deal with your perfection?

Symbols: the *circle; ten*

PERFECTIBLE

Word Form: perfectibility

Definition: capable of improvement or progressive refinement

Comments:
- You can damn the failure that you have had, but know that damning the failure doesn't really do any good. As a matter of fact, it does more harm. The only thing to really do is to, as quickly as possible, focus on improvement. The lesson has been learned. Since we are

living inside time, there is the possibility of repeating or not repeating the past.

- You have to take into consideration your ability, the social situation, and the circumstance to determine how "perfect" you can be in the situation. The perfect act takes all variables into consideration and melds them with mindful wisdom. Relative perfection is subjective. Keep your eye on the ideal. Maintain your honorable intention. Strive for perfection. As you learn and grow you refine the subjectivity and it gets better as you go.
- Don't be *too* perfect. If you are too perfect, you may be too cautious, too locked into your idea of what is perfect and unwilling to leap beyond your known understanding and into the greater realm beyond where chance and possibilities and mistakes and growth and greater freedom abound.

The perfect is the *now* and the perfecting is the *becoming*.

PERKY

Word Forms: perk, perkier, perkiest, perkily, perkiness

Definitions: (1) spirited; aggressive; briskly self-assured; **(2)** jaunty; cheerful; pert; gay; saucy

PERMISSIVE

Word Forms: permissible, permission, permissively, permissiveness

Definitions: (1) allowing freedom; tolerant of behavior or practices disapproved of by others; indulgent; lenient; **(2)** granting or expressing consent

PERSEVERING

Word Forms: persevere, persevered, perseverance, perseveringly

Definition: persists in pursuing something in spite of obstacles, opposition, or discouragement; steadfast in purpose

Synonyms: constant, indefatigable, resolute, tenacious

Quote:
Great works are performed not by strength, but by perseverance.
—SAMUEL JOHNSON

PERSISTENT

Word Forms: persist, persistence, persisting, persistently

Definitions: (1) refusing to relent; continuing, especially in the face of opposition or difficulty; persevering; **(2)** continuing to exist or endure; lasting

Kindred Qualities: daring, fearless, diversity

Quotes:
Keep on plugging.
—JOHN PRESTON DOWNS

Nothing in the world can take the place of persistence. Talent will not; nothing is more common than unsuccessful men with great talent. Genius will not; unrewarded genius is almost a proverb. Education will not; the world is full of educated derelicts. Persistence, determination alone are omnipotent.
—RAY KROC, FOUNDER OF MCDONALD'S

It just goes to show, if you are persistent, something gets done.
—ANY PARENT TO A CHILD WHO HAS JUST ACCOMPLISHED A PROJECT

A great deal depends upon the thought patterns we choose and on the persistence with which we affirm them.
—PIERO FERRUCCI

Affirmation:
I refuse to give up. I shall continue, firmly, steadily and insistently until the good appears.
—CATHERINE PONDER, *The Dynamic Laws of Prosperity*

Comment: The person who asks for something 30 or 40 or even 150 times, and finally gets it, has figured out how to ask for something.

PERSONABLE

Word Forms: person, personably, personableness

Definitions: (1) having an agreeable or pleasing personality; **(2)** having a well-formed body; graceful; attractive

Familial Qualities: friendly, well-groomed

PERSPICACIOUS

Word Forms: perspicacity, perspicaciously, perspicaciousness

Definition: having keen mental perception and understanding; discerning

Derivation: Latin, "to look through"

PERSPICUOUS

Word Forms: perspicuity, perspicuously, perspicuousness

Definition: clear and explicit in statement or expression; easily understood; lucid; not obscure or ambiguous; plain; distinct

Comment: Perspicuity is the mirror image of perceptive. It takes perceptivity to the inside of the other people's understanding. It is a clarity about how they perceive the world, so that the argument is presented with the language that they are familiar with. There is no need to use force or trickery. Perspicuous people help others assimilate softly, recognizing what the others can digest. Maybe what is needed is mother's milk or maybe some roughage is okay. Sincerity and kindness gently move the information into their systems so that it is assimilated easily.

The reason most people have trouble doing this is because they can't get out of themselves long enough to get into someone else.

PERSUASIVE

Word Forms: persuade, persuasion, persuasively, persuasiveness

Definitions: (1) causing someone to do something, especially by reasoning, urging, or influence; to prevail upon; **(2)** inducing someone to believe something; convincing

Synonyms: win over, entice, exhort

Comment: If you think you possess someone, you will try to run that person's life and in doing so you will be running your own life poorly.

Symbol: the *Empress* (tarot)

PERT

Word Forms: pertly, pertness

Definitions: (1) lively; brisk; sprightly; in good spirits; **(2)** forward; saucy; bold; **(3)** jaunty and stylish; chic

PHILANTHROPIC

Word Forms: philanthropy, philanthropist, philanthropical, philanthropically

Definition: possessing benevolence toward the whole human family; demonstrating universal good will, especially as manifested by donations of money, property, or work to needy persons or to institutions advancing human welfare

Derivation: Greek, "love of humanity"

PHILOSOPHICAL

Word Forms: philosopher, philosophy, philosophic, philosophize, philosophically, philosopheme

Definitions: (1) devoted to a study of the processes governing thought and conduct; theory or investigation of the principles and laws that regulate the universe and underlie all knowledge and reality; (2) rational; sensibly composed; calm in a difficult situation

Derivation: Greek, "love of wisdom"

Symbol: the *Archpriest* (tarot)

PHOTOGENIC

Word Forms: photo, photogenically

Definitions: (1) artistically suitable for being photographed; (2) possessing the ability to project an inner beauty

People Who Exemplify This Quality: Eleanor Roosevelt, Albert Einstein

PHYSICAL

Word Forms: physicality, physician, physicist, physique, physics, physically, physicalness

Definitions: (1) perceptible through the corporeal senses; subject to the laws of nature; natural; **(2)** having material existence; of or relating to the body

Affirmation: My body is a safe and pleasurable place for me to be. My body is a temple.

PIONEERING

Word Forms: pioneer, pioneered

Definition: going before into that which is unknown or untried, sometimes to prepare the way for others

Compatible Quality: courageous

Parental Qualities: faith and freedom

Familial Quality: adventurous

Symbol: the *covered wagon;* a *space capsule*

PIOUS

Word Forms: piety, piously, piousness

Definitions: (1) having or showing religious devotion; godly; **(2)** sacred, distinguished from secular; reverent; righteous

Color: blue

Symbol: filial piety—the *stork*

PIQUANT

Word Forms: piquancy, piquantly, piquantness

Definitions: (1) agreeably pungent or stimulating to the taste; pleasantly sharp or biting; **(2)** exciting interest or curiosity; stimulating; provocative

Synonyms: spirited, lively, smart, clever, charming

PITY

Word Forms: pities, pitied, pitiful, pitying, pityingly

Definition: sympathizing with the grief or misery of another; compassion or fellow-suffering; empathy

PIZAZZ

Definitions: (1) energetic; vigorous; vital; spirited; **(2)** attractive style; dash; flair; sparkle

Compatible Quality: entertaining

PLACID

Word Forms: placidity, placidly, placidness

Definitions: (1) gentle; quiet; undisturbed; equable; **(2)** serene; mild; unruffled; calm; tranquil; peace of mind

Derivation: Latin, "to please"

PLAYFUL

Word Forms: play, played, playing, playfully, playfulness

Definitions: (1) fond of fun; frisky; indulging a sportive fancy; frolicsome; **(2)** humorous; joking; merry

Synonyms: lively, jocund, gay, vivacious, sprightly

Kindred Qualities: balance, fairness

Consequential Qualities: orderliness, sharing
    When a child, or anyone, plays they learn that it is fun to be associated with other individuals.

Saying: All work and no play makes Jack a dull boy.

Quotes:
    If all the year were playing holidays, to sport would be as tedious as work.
                                        —WILLIAM SHAKESPEARE, *Hamlet*

    In a sense, all science, all human thought, is a form of play. Abstract thought [is the way we are able] to continue to carry out activities which have no immediate goal (just as other animals play while young) in order to prepare . . . for long-term strategies and plans.
                                        —JACOB BRONOWSKI, MATHEMATICIAN

    The creation of something new is not accomplished by the intellect but by the play instinct acting from inner necessity. The creative mind plays with the objects it loves.
                                        —CARL G. JUNG

Symbols: *swings;* the *seal*

PLEASANT

Word Forms: please, pleasantry, pleasure, pleasantly, pleasantness

Definitions: (**1**) agreeable to the mind or to the senses; (**2**) having an agreeable manner or appearance; attractive; amiably cheerful; enlivening; (**3**) gay; lively; merry; jesting; jocular; playful; sportive

Synonyms: gratifying, good-humored, humorous, jocose, amusing, witty

Too Far: hedonistic

Admonition:
- Beware the enslaving power of pleasure.
- It takes courage to choose to live a life that includes, but also transcends, pleasure.

Comment: If your goal is strictly pleasure, comfort, and the accoutrements of an easy life, then you will work to acquire those things. But admit what you are passing up to satisfy the pleasure goal. Pleasure has its value, but so do any and all of the other individual qualities. Life is sweetest when you are in the process of acquiring a wide range of qualities. Pleasure for oneself without care for others will only lead to selfishness.

PLIABLE

Word Forms: ply, pliability, pliancy, pliant, pliably, pliableness

Definitions: (**1**) easily bent; yielding to pressure without breaking; supple; lithe; (**2**) flexible disposition; docile; readily yielding to moral influence, arguments, persuasion, or discipline; tractable; (**3**) adjusting readily to varying conditions; adaptable

PLUCKY

Word Forms: pluck, pluckier, pluckiest, pluckily, pluckiness

Definition: marked by courage; spirited; brave; resolute

POETIC

Word Forms: poet, poetical, poetics, poeticize, poetry, poetically

Definitions: (1) written or spoken word that formulates a concentrated imaginative awareness of experience; language chosen and arranged to create a specific emotional response through meaning, sound, and rhythm; **(2)** possessing the peculiar beauties of poetry; sublime; **(3)** imaginative

Comment: Rap is poetry as an acceptable, popular, and communicative medium. Whatever is wonderful and good can be fused with culture.

Symbol: *words*

Historical Figures: *Chaucer*, the Father of English poetry; *Homer*, the Father of epic poetry

Mythologies: *Bragi*, the Scandinavian god of eloquence and poetry; *Erato*, the Muse who presided over lyric poetry; *Calliope*, Greek and Roman Muse of eloquence and heroic poetry

POISED

Word Forms: poise, poising

Definitions: (1) composed, dignified, and self-assured; **(2)** being in balance or equilibrium

Quote:
It is to the mind of perfect poise, housed in a body of clean habits, stabilized neural energies, and balanced chemical function—when the physical, mental and spiritual powers are in triune harmony of development—that a maximum of light and truth can be imparted with a minimum of temporal danger or risk to the real welfare of such a being. By such balanced growth does man ascend.
                                                              —*The Urantia Book*

POLISHED

Word Forms: polish, polishing

Definitions: **(1)** smooth; soft; **(2)** refined; elegant; polite; **(3)** flawless; expert; without error

POLITE

Word Forms: politer, politest, politely, politeness

Definitions: **(1)** polished or elegant in manners; refined in behavior; **(2)** courteous; considerate; tactful; complaisant; civil; **(3)** exhibiting warm cordiality; genteel

Compatible Quality: friendly

POPULAR

Word Forms: popularity, popularize, popularly

Definitions: **(1)** commonly liked, approved of, or admired; **(2)** having many friends; well-known; **(3)** suited to or pleasing to the intelligence or taste of the target audience

Synonyms: beloved, favorite, fashionable, savoir-faire

Kindred Qualities: self-esteem, modest, discreet, gentle, gracious, decent

Compatible Qualities: quick-witted, mannerly, tactful, humorous

Parental Qualities: friendly, personable, confident

Familial Qualities: agreeable, kind, cool, charming, interesting

Consequential Qualities: leadership, charisma, communicative, confident

Comments:
- You know what you are attracted to. Let those aspects of yourself shine through. If you are attracted to the qualities in another that are not as strong in yourself, that does not mean that you need to focus on becoming those qualities first. Focus first on the qualities that you already have naturally through living your life. And then expand your repertoire of qualities.
- Decide who it is important to be popular with. To be accepted by some people is not worth your effort. If they will not accept you unless you take actions that are negative, then don't bother with them. Don't forget about common sense. Get yourself out of a bad situation before you get into it.

    You have to decide what you want to be, not what they want you to be. Associate with people with whom you can feel comfortable. You must like yourself, but you cannot have a mutual admiration society of one.

Questions:
- Are you nice to be around?
- Do you have the tendency to hide or shade your best qualities because you believe it would not be popular to show them?

    Go ahead and exhibit yourself. As you do, you will acquire the finesse to be yourself with the attitude that is acceptable.

POSITIVE

Word Forms: positivity, positively, positiveness

Definitions: (1) good; ideal; favorable; the best of a kind; **(2)** independent of changes, circumstances, opinion or taste; inherent; absolute; **(3)** real; existing in fact or by the presence of something and not by its absence; **(4)** beyond all doubt or qualification; undeniable; sure; uncontestable; **(5)** confident; fully assured; firmly convinced; decided; **(6)** resolute; in agreement; affirmative; certain; **(7)** moving in an increasing direction of progress and growth; **(8)** making a definite contribution; constructive; **(9)** explicitly laid down; direct; precise; specific

Quotes:

One positive statement of good is more powerful than 1,000 negative thoughts; and two positive statements of good are more powerful than 10,000 negative thoughts.
> —CATHERINE PONDER, *The Dynamic Laws of Prosperity*

Positive thoughts can be a powerful influence for good.
> —PEACE PILGRIM, *Steps Toward Inner Peace*

When you're rooted in the positive, your destination is the brightest star.
> —STEVIE WONDER, "MASTER BLASTER"

Consideration: A study reported in the *Journal of Personality and Social Psychology* ties pessimism to poor health. In 1946, Harvard graduates were asked a series of questions designed to reflect their natural outlook when confronted with bad situations. Their health was studied for the next thirty-five years.

By matching results from the earlier questions with health status, researchers found that those who explain bad events in a relatively positive light tended to have substantially less illness than those who were less positive.

POTENTIAL

Word Forms: potent, potentially, potentiality

Definitions: (1) something that can, but has not yet, come into being; possible; unrealized, undeveloped; **(2)** a latent excellence or ability

Derivation: Latin, "powerful"

Quotes:

What lies behind us and what lies in front of us pales in significance when compared with what lies within us.
> —RALPH WALDO EMERSON

Whatever there is that ought to be, can be.
> —JAMES RAUSE

Reflection: Potentials are actuals waiting to be made real and every actuality opens up new options of unforeseen potentials.

Observations:
- One's greatest limitations are those imposed upon oneself.
- Blame is usually, and only sometimes correctly, placed on someone else for a failure to realize a potential.

Symbols: the *egg;* the *night*

POWERFUL

Word Forms: power, powerfully, powerfulness, empowered, powerhouse

Definitions: (1) great physical ability; strong; forcible; mighty; intense; **(2)** great moral force; able to persuade or convince the mind; **(3)** possessing great energy; producing great effects

Too Far: The positive qualities of desire and power taken too far end in greed. Every action can be and is justified by pointing to positive qualities.

Motto:
> *Cedant arma togae* (Latin): Let arms yield to the toga [Let military power give way to civil power].
> —WYOMING STATE MOTTO

Consideration: If a person who is immature, insecure, and fear-ridden is given power, the power will have to live within the person's emotional limits and will be subject to the constraints of the undeveloped personality. The results will be predictably negative. Decisions are made that reflect the desires of the decision maker.

Observations:
- Power can be impersonal—like the power of the ocean—or it can be personal. If personal, it can be negative or positive.
- Power is very seductive.
- The powerful are often intent on retaining their own power. And to that end, all else becomes subordinate.

Comments:
- We are still in the age of "might is right," and will be for hundreds of years. The question is how, in the face of power, to do what you know is right. Sometimes it takes great courage.
- People in power will allow the governed to expand only to the level of the consciousness that they themselves possess. Conversely, if the peoples' consciousness outgrows the consciousness of those in power, then there's a revolution or rupture of some sort. This turmoil results in one of two possibilities: a crackdown that holds the old way in place for a time or the birth of a new system to bring things back into balance.
- The temptation to enhance those qualities that serve only your personal needs is great, and the personal rewards for doing so is seductive. If you choose your needs unfairly over the needs of others, the results are unfair.

Colors: golden orange, orange

Symbols: the *crocodile;* a *hammer;* a *crown; gold;* the *Emperor* (tarot); the *whip* (Egyptian); the power to act—a *diamond key*

PRACTICAL

Word Forms: practice, practicable, practicality, practically, practicalness

Definitions: (1) exhibited in or obtained through practice or active use; (2) that which can be used in practice; that which can be applied to use <*practical* knowledge>; (3) designed for use; utilitarian; sensible; (4) concerned with the application of knowledge to useful ends or with voluntary action and ethical decisions; (5) dealing efficiently with everyday activities; (6) matter-of-fact

Too Far: mundane, mediocre

Saying: Function follows form.

Quotes:
The kingdom of heaven runs on righteousness; but the kingdom of earth runs on oil.
                                                        —SOURCE UNKNOWN

If you are motivated to do or say a mean thing, you can always think of a good thing. You deliberately turn around and use the *same energy* to do or say a good thing instead. It works!
                           —PEACE PILGRIM, *Steps Toward Inner Peace*

Tip: Reassess your situation and yourself periodically because things and you do change.

PRAGMATIC

Word Forms: pragmatist, pragmatical, pragmatism, pragmatically

Definition: concerned with practical considerations or consequences; related to matters of fact

Kindred Quality: idealistic

Comment: Some pragmatists would say that anything beyond the material or economic facts of life is not worth concerning oneself over. By this they show their range of reality. You cannot expect them to value qualities that do not apply to their view. But what is more pragmatic than to survive—not just today but forever?

PRAISEWORTHY

Word Forms: praise, praiseworthily, praiseworthiness

Definition: worthy of admiration because of good qualities or good deeds; commendable; laudable

PRAYERFUL

Word Forms: pray, prayer, prayerfully, prayerfulness

Definitions: (1) devout; **(2)** earnest; sincere; **(3)** talking to God; worshipful; meditative

Compatible Quality: intuition

Parental Quality: faith

Consequential Quality: insight

Saying: *Laborare est orare* (Latin): "To work is to pray."

Quotes:
> You can't pray a lie.
>
>   —MARK TWAIN, *The Adventures of Huckleberry Finn*

> God answers . . . prayer by giving [you] an increased revelation of truth, an enhanced appreciation of beauty, and an augmented concept of goodness.
>
>   Words are irrelevant to prayer; they are merely the intellectual channel in which the river of spiritual supplication may chance to flow. The word value of a prayer is purely autosuggestive in private devotions and sociosuggestive in group devotions. God answers the soul's attitude, not the words.
>
>   —*The Urantia Book*

Prayers: Make up your own prayers. Modify these. Remember that prayers are not the words. Your sincere heart is doing the praying. Your open mind is receiving the light. Your prayer is personal.

> Dear God, since You are everything and everyone, thank You for the gift of life. Just as the bird sits on her nest, so do you patiently and knowingly nurture our growth.

> Divine intelligence, what positive, constructive, creative thought, word, attitude or action is my next step to improve my present work? What is the next step into the abundance, satisfaction and freedom that is mine by divine right?
>
>   —CATHERINE PONDER, *The Dynamic Laws of Prosperity*

Our Mother, who art beneath us, You support us, nurture us, bring us the gift of life. Hear the prayers of your children and forgive us our trespasses. Intervene on our behalf for those other lives, great and small, which suffer when we err. Oh, Mother, we pray. Help us to face danger and be wise.

—DAVID BRIN, *Earth*

Daily Prayers

I am thankful for this new day. My mind and heart are open to all experiences because they teach me what I need to know. Those persons, places, and things that I can benefit and that can benefit me are drawn to me and I to them. I am a blessing to all whom I meet today. I am valuable and deserve to be happy.

I forgive all who need to be forgiven and everyone who needs to forgive me does so now. I can deal with whatever may happen to me today. There is nothing to fear, the Knower within me guides me perfectly in all decisions.

I am healthy and whole and respect my body. My positive, affirmative thoughts shield me from all negativity and doubt. I let go of worn out things and worn out conditions and replace them with fresh, vibrant, and abundant ideas. I am alive, alert, and aware. I walk in the paths of fairness, right action, and gratitude all of the time whether I think about it or not.

I align myself consciously and deliberately with the Supreme. I am a child of the universe and am filled with the faith that God is in charge of my life. I will that my will be The Will.

Good morning One? Thank You for this day! Thank You for me! Thank You for my friends. Thank You for the world. May all my thoughts, words and actions of today be in service to the highest good.

—ABORIGINAL, *Mutant Message*

Inspiration: Number eleven of the Alcoholics Anonymous twelve-step program:

We sought through prayer and meditation to improve our conscious contact with God (as we understand the concept), praying only for knowledge of God's will for us and the power to carry that out.

Observations:
- In the art of asking or thanking, you attempt to clarify your understanding of your intended concepts.
- In order for a prayer to be effective, you must possess and have honestly aspired to the qualities of industriousness, stamina, surrender, decisiveness, dedication, wisdom, and faith.

Comment: The sincere motive of your prayer is the payload; your faith is the propellant that sends it swiftly and surely to an eager Divine Source. Since God is always open to give and has an unlimited supply of goodness, truth, mercy, or any positive quality you need, you will get what you need. Your attitude and insight are what gets changed, expanded, and clarified.

Types of Prayers:
- Thankful, grateful, appreciative
- Wishful, needful, helpful, petitionary
- Affirming, knowing, willful
- Aligning, faithful
- Forgiving
- Contemplative
- Denial

Note: Denial should be meshed with an affirming prayer, such as, "I will not accept this negative situation. I know divine order will prevail and I accept that. The evil here does not touch me but I will learn from it."

Experience: When I used to hitchhike, I would not fret and worry about the next ride that I would get. I would instead build up a prayer that I intended to give to the person who would pick me up and bring me on down the road. I would do this by being conscious of all that was happening to me and around me. I would add special inner prayers to that. As each driver approached I would mentally let them know that a wealth of good energy would be theirs if they chose to pick me up.

I did not often get rides from female drivers, but one time I did while I was using this technique. She was amazed that she had stopped for me. I told her why and we had a very nice conversation about the important things of life.

Symbols: the *eagle;* the *bow and arrow*

Legend: A Japanese legend holds that the crane lives for a thousand years, and your prayer or wish will come true if you fold a thousand paper cranes.

Mythology: *Sandalphon*, in Jewish mythology, one of three angels who receive prayers from the faithful and weave them into crowns

PRECIOUS

Word Forms: preciously, preciousness

Definitions: (1) great in price; costly; **(2)** great in significance or worth; very valuable; **(3)** much esteemed; beloved; dear

PRECISE

Word Forms: precision, precisely, preciseness

Definitions: (1) strictly defined; accurately stated; definite; **(2)** speaking or acting explicitly or distinctly; punctilious; **(3)** with no variation; minutely exact; scrupulous

Observation: One meter is 39.37 U.S. inches or 1/299,792,458 (.0000000033) the distance light travels in a vacuum in one second. Light travels 670,616,629.4 miles per hour, 186,282.397 miles per second. Light travels 5,878,499,812,498.56 miles in one year.

Symbols: a *needle; sewing;* any fine *needlework;* the *hummingbird*

PRECOCIOUS

Word Forms: precocity, precociously, precociousness

Definition: exhibiting mature qualities at an unusually early age

Comment: Although precocious is usually attributed to a young person, if you demonstrate a quality now that is not ordinarily acquired until later, you may be considered precocious.

PREPARED

Word Forms: prepare, preparation, preparedly, preparedness

Definitions: (1) ready, fit, or qualified; in proper condition or order; (2) to have what you need because of forethought

Compatible Quality: realistic—accepting fact as fact

Motto:
Semper Paratus (Latin): "Always prepared"
—U.S. COAST GUARD

Quote:
Did you ever observe to whom the accidents happen? Chance favors the prepared mind.
—LOUIS PASTEUR

Reflection: If you permeate your consciousness with positive projections, positive thoughts, positive ideas about yourself and your future situation then you have a better chance of manifesting those happy times and the qualities that go with them.

Tip: It pays to have both a plan A and a plan B.

Comments:
- You cannot affect someone else's reality except by affecting *your* inner world. With a positive attitude you encourage other people as an example of positive living.
- One has to look at the future and imagine different options, needs, and responsibilities. Some of those possibilities are frightening. Still, allow yourself to view them objectively. You need to see them in order to steer clear of them. But since you are not actually experiencing them you need not feel them. Save the need to react to danger for real time.

PRESCIENT

Word Forms: prescience, presciently

Definition: having knowledge of events before they take place

Legend: a *sibyl,* the intuiting power of higher truths and prophesy

PRESENCE OF MIND

Definition: able to think clearly and act quickly and intelligently, especially in an emergency; cool, alert, and ready

Compatible Qualities: risible, creative

Suggestion: Recognize, in the present, what effect your actions are having upon the situation and act accordingly.

Comment: Presence of mind is a quality of "practical smarts"; it includes flexibility, intelligence, and alertness. The quick and ready retrieval of information from the mind is an essential aspect of presence of mind. But it is also the ability to put things together in new ways to fit the situation. It also implies a sense of timing and an appreciation of the subtlety of what others perceive.

PRESENT

Word Forms: presence, presently, presentness

Definition: being, existing, or occurring at this time; now; current

Proverb:
Look to this day for tomorrow is but a vision and yesterday a dream.
—SANSKRIT

Quotes:

Be here now.

—Baba Ram Das

The past and the future are the gift wrapping for the present.

—Jerry Downs

I shall tell you a great secret, my friend. Do not wait for the last judgment, it takes place every day.

—Albert Camus

[Dorothy:] "If you can't find what you are looking for right where you are then you can't find it anywhere."

—L. Frank Baum, *The Wonderful Wizard of Oz*

Consider that this day will never dawn again.

—Dante

What you do in the present creates the future. So keep your thoughts on the positive side, think about the best that could happen, think about the good things you want to happen.

—Peace Pilgrim, *Steps Toward Inner Peace*

PRESENTABLE

Word Forms: presentability, presentably, presentableness

Definitions: (1) fit to be exhibited, offered, or displayed; fit to be introduced into society; fit to be shown or seen; **(2)** attractively attired; neat; clean

PRESERVING

Word Forms: preserve, preserved, preservable, preservation, preservative

Definitions: (1) keeps from harm, damage, danger, or evil; protective;

(2) to keep alive or in existence; saving; (3) make lasting <*preserving* liberties as free citizens>

Synonyms: guard, secure, defend, maintain

Theological: *Vishnu*, the Preserver, second deity of the Hindu trinity

PRESTIGIOUS

Word Forms: prestige, prestigiously, prestigiousness

Definition: having an honored reputation; respected; esteemed

PRETTY

Word Forms: prettier, prettiest, prettily, prettiness

Definitions: (1) pleasingly attractive; handsome; implied daintiness, delicacy, or gracefulness rather than striking beauty, elegance, grandeur, or stateliness; (2) fine; good; nice; agreeable

PRINCELY

Word Forms: prince, princelier, princeliest, princeliness

Definitions: (1) characteristic of a prince; imperial, regal; (2) liberal; generous; royal; grand; noble; (3) magnificent; rich; befitting a prince; lavish

Synonyms: munificent, superb

PRINCIPLED

Word Form: principle

Definition: an accepted or professed rule of action or conduct; a guiding sense of the requirements and obligations of right behavior

PRISTINE

Word Form: pristinely

Definitions: (1) a pure and natural state; original; (2) characteristic of an earlier period or condition; (3) unblemished or untouched; uncorrupted; unspoiled

Derivation: Latin, "former," "superior"

PRIVILEGED

Word Forms: privilege, privileging

Definition: having advantage, favor, or benefit of one over another

PROBITY

Definition: adherence to the highest principles and ideals; tried virtue or integrity; upright; sincere; veracious; honest

Synonym: trustiness

PRODUCTIVE

Word Forms: produce, productivity, production, productively, productiveness

Definitions: (1) able to manifest something; generative; creative; (2) abundant; fertile; fruitful; (3) bringing into being; causing to exist; efficient <an age *productive* of great men>

PROFESSIONAL

Word Forms: profession, professionalize, professionally

Definitions: (1) having the character, spirit, or methods found in those who have had advanced training; proficient; **(2)** competent and courteous in service

Kindred Qualities: *Professional* often means efficient, and *efficient* can be moved to the point of impersonal. Add the quality of personal and enhance the quality of professional.

PROFICIENT

Word Forms: proficiency, proficiently

Definition: fully competent in an art, science, or other subject

Derivation: Latin, "to go forward," "to accomplish"

Synonyms: *Proficient, adept, skilled, skillful,* and *expert* mean having great knowledge and experience in a trade or profession. *Proficient* implies a thorough competence derived from training and practice. *Adept* implies special aptitude as well as proficiency. *Skilled* stresses mastery of technique. *Skillful* implies individual dexterity in execution or performance. *Expert* implies extraordinary proficiency and often connotes knowledge as well as technical skill.

PROFITABLE

Word Forms: profit, profitability, profitably, profitableness

Definition: yielding or bringing returns; gainful; lucrative; useful; advantageous; beneficial

Affirmation:
I've never been poor, only broke. Being poor is a frame of mind. Being broke is a temporary situation.

—MIKE TODD

PROFOUND

Word Forms: profoundly, profoundness

Definitions: (1) marked by intellectual depth; not superficial; (2) seriously or intensely felt; (3) thoroughgoing <*profound* judgments>

Synonyms: penetrating, mysterious, humble

Quote:
The first function, one might say, of every mythology has always been a mystical, metaphysical function: that of awaking in the mind and spirit of the individual a sense of awe before the mystery of being itself. This is the mystery dimension and the first function of mythology is to communicate that [mystery], so that in the field of mythological forms and of the rites by which you participate in those forms you are made aware, experientially, of the ultimate, absolute mystery of the universe which cannot be caught in words. It absolutely transcends all conceptualizations and it breaks past all fields of meaning. The world, the universe, life, *being* itself is absolutely without meaning. It is antecedent to meaning. Meanings are the mental interpretations, and these vary. . . .

Now, not only the universe itself, but also the imagery of myth is intrinsically without meaning. It is a "being" statement. And the experience of the "getting turned on" or the "ripple or buzz" comes when all of your meaning interpretations smash, break up; and what has been called the . . . fascinating, tremendous mystery of this whole thing comes zooming through.

Now, It is a tremendous mystery and it is an appalling, monstrous mystery; to think of the nature of life itself: it lives on life.

—JOSEPH CAMPBELL, *The Hero with a Thousand Faces,*
Volume II: The Cosmogonic Cycle

PROGRESSIVE

Word Forms: progress, progressing, progressively, progressiveness

Definitions: (1) moving forward or onward; (2) making use of or interested in new ideas, findings, or opportunities; (3) marked by growth, reform, or continuing improvement

Observation: To live in a complex society, progress is necessary.

Tip: If you concentrate on the openings instead of the obstacles, you will get there.

Comment: The smallest of positive decisions to do the right thing multiplied by the intention to do so creates a proliferation of positive action. This leads to the possibility of more accurate assessment of what is the best action to take under the current or new circumstances.

Symbol: spiritual evolution—*wings*

PROLIFIC

Word Forms: proliferate, prolificacy, prolificity, prolification, prolifically, prolificness

Definitions: (1) abundant inventiveness or productivity; (2) fruitful; abounding

Synonym: fertile

Consideration: Consider the trillions of seeds produced by just one tree. The oldest living tree, Methuselah, a bristlecone pine in California, is approximately 4,600 years old. In 1974, it produced 48 *live* seedlings. 48 × 4,600 = 220,800 offspring!

PROMINENT

Word Forms: prominence, prominently

Definition: eminent; distinguished above others; widely and favorably known; leading; important

PROMISING

Word Forms: promise, promised, promisingly

Definition: having reasonable grounds for hope; likely to succeed or yield favorable results; just expectations of a good outcome

Synonyms: auspicious, assuring, engaging

PROMPT

Word Forms: prompter, promptitude, promptly, promptness

Definitions: (1) ready and quick to act as occasion demands; alert; immediately or instantly at hand; expeditious; (2) done at the appointed time; exact; apt; (3) incite; to move or excite to action or exertion; active; (4) to arouse or inspire by suggestion

Saying: *Bis dat qui cito dat* (Latin): "He gives twice who gives promptly."

PROPER

Word Forms: properly, properness

Definitions: (1) appropriate to the purpose or circumstance; suitable; (2) conforming to established standards of behavior or manners; correct or decorous; chaste; modest; **(3)** fitting; right; seemly; just; fair; **(4)** normal or regular; **(5)** fine; good; excellent; becoming in appearance; handsome

PROPITIOUS

Word Forms: propitiously, propitiousness

Definitions: (1) favorably disposed; benevolent; **(2)** a good omen; auspicious; **(3)** having been blessed; advantageous

Synonyms: benign, helpful, gracious

PROSPEROUS

Word Forms: prosper, prospered, prospering, prosperity, prosperously, prosperousness

Definitions: (1) success in an enterprise or activity; achievement, usually economic well-being; **(2)** strong and flourishing; thriving; **(3)** enjoying vigorous and healthy growth
    See also: *Successful*

Synonyms: auspicious, favorable

Kindred Qualities: giving, humble, sincere

Compatible Qualities: faith, determined, persistent, focused

Familial Qualities: profitable, rich, fertile, productive

Parental Qualities: creative, talented

Consequential Qualities: relaxed, free, courageous

Quotes:
    The God of heaven, He will prosper us.
                                            —NEHEMIAH 2:20

Turn the great energy of your thinking upon "plenty" ideas and you will have plenty regardless of what men about you are saying or doing.

—CHARLES FILLMORE

You do not have to force success and prosperity. Instead, you can develop that exalted, expectant, prosperous state of mind that is a magnet for all good things

Train your mind never to be disappointed. If certain things do not come at certain expected times in the way you wished, do not consider it a failure. Since you have not received that thing, you can instead stand firm in the faith that something much better is on the way and will appear at the right time.

—CATHERINE PONDER, *The Dynamic Laws of Prosperity*

Affirmations:
- I deserve prosperity.
- I have whatever I need to fulfill my needs.

Tips:
- All wealth is created by mind.
- The more willing I am to prosper other people, the more willing other people are to prosper me.

    Balance prosperity with the qualities of sharing and giving and the recognition that your prosperity is based on the prosperity of others.

Comments:
- Prosperity is naturally associated with desire. Connect your desires with a higher purpose. Focus on the greater good. Fit your need or want into a grand scheme. Sincerity is the quality that glues your desire to that higher reality. As you "hunger for righteousness" realize that you sometimes have to look past immediate gratification to your higher and ultimate goals.
- You cannot expect to receive if your motivation is based on fear, desperation, or stress. Only in a peaceful, relaxed state can you focus your thoughts and feelings with a purity and clarity that return clean results.

Suggestions:
- Be specific.

- Take the obvious action steps.
- Open a place in your physical, emotional, mental, and spiritual self to be filled with your desire.
- Use meditation, a state of calm and openness.
- Use prayer—focused, purposeful, and sincere.

Exercises:
- Write down your desires.
- Picture your desires as completed results.
- Declare that no one or no thing can withhold your good from you.

Symbols: *rhinoceros horn* (Chinese); *maize* (Chinese)

Mythology: *Kuvera,* the Hindu god of wealth

PROTECTIVE

Word Forms: protect, protection, protectively, protectiveness

Definition: covers or shields from danger or injury; defends; guards; preserves in safety; sheltering

Symbols: an *arrow* (American Indian); self-defense—the *buckle;* the *shield;* the *wolf*

PROUD

Word Forms: pride, proudly, proudness

Definitions: (1) feeling pleasure or satisfaction over something regarded as honorable or creditable; **(2)** having or showing self-respect or self-esteem; **(3)** feeling great joy; elated; exultant; highly pleased; **(4)** stately, majestic, or magnificent; **(5)** full of vigor and spirit

Too Far: pride, the sin of

Color: green

PROVIDENT

Word Forms: providence, providential, providentially, providently

Definitions: (1) foreseeing wants and making provision to supply them; having and showing foresight; **(2)** economical; frugal; thrifty; prudent; **(3)** a manifestation of divine care and direction

Derivation: Latin, "to provide"

Symbols: Jupiter's three *thunderbolts*—Chance, Destiny, and Providence

PROVOCATIVE

Word Forms: provoke, provocation, provocatively, provocativeness

Definition: exciting; stimulating; tending to awaken or incite appetite or passion

Synonyms: arouse, stir up, move, induce

Kindred Qualities: discretion, appropriate

Comment: This is a quality with some negative connotations, but even if your actions provoke an unwanted response, if your motives are pure, you have been honorable.

PRUDENT

Word Forms: prudence, prudently, prudential

Definitions: (1) wise or judicious in practical affairs; **(2)** discreet or circumspect; cautious but sensible; **(3)** careful in providing for the future; provident

Derivation: Latin, "to discern," "to distinguish," "to separate," "to set apart"

Synonyms: considerate, sagacious, thoughtful, frugal, economical

Symbol: a *dolphin* entwined around an anchor—arrested speed

PSYCHIC

Word Forms: psyche, psychical, psychically

Definitions: (1) pertaining to the mind; psychogenic; **(2)** lying outside the sphere of the physical sciences: moral or spiritual in origin or force; not material; **(3)** sensitive to nonphysical or supernatural forces and influences; marked by extraordinary perception, understanding, or insight

People Who Exemplify This Quality: The aborigines of Australia are said to have psychic powers. They say that it is possible only when a person is totally honest.

Comment: There are degrees to everything. You may not have a clear vision of the future, or people and events in other places and times, but you can see trends. You do have hunches. You can trust and develop your intuition.

Exercise: Along with affirmations, a practical way to develop your telepathic abilities is by thinking of a situation, person, or condition about which you have some question. Write down the name or question. Sit quietly every day for a while and listen for ideas to come into your mind, which will reveal an answer.
>   —CATHERINE PONDER, *The Dynamic Laws of Prosperity*
>   (paraphrase)

PUBLIC-SPIRITED

Word Forms: public-spiritedly, public-spiritedness

Definition: exercising a disposition to advance the interest of the community; inclined to make private sacrifices for the public good

Suggestion: Give blood. For just the small price of time and a little pain, you can be of service to someone in a whole lot of pain.

PULCHRITUDINOUS

Word Form: pulchritude

Definitions: (1) physical beauty; handsomeness; grace; comeliness; that quality or form that pleases the eye; **(2)** moral beauty; those qualities of mind and soul that good people love

PUNCTILIOUS

Word Forms: punctilio, punctiliously, punctiliousness

Definitions: (1) careful in the observance of the nicer points of behavior or ceremony; **(2)** very exact; scrupulous

PUNCTUAL

Word Forms: punctuality, punctually, punctualness

Definition: carefully observant of the appointed time; on time; prompt

Synonyms: timely, precise, exact

PURE

Word Forms: purer, purest, purify, purism, purist, purity, purification, purifies, purified, puristic, purely, pureness

Definitions: (1) absolute; utter; sheer *<pure* joy>; **(2)** free from defects; perfect; faultless; unblemished; **(3)** untainted with evil or guilt; innocent; blameless; **(4)** physically chaste; virginal; spotless; **(5)** ceremonially or ritually clean; undefiled

Synonyms: clear, simple, genuine, real, immaculate, unadulterated, uncorrupted, unsullied, unspoiled, guileless, guiltless

Color: white

Symbols: the *lily; sea foam;* the three stars in the belt of Orion, which represent Purity, Righteousness, and Choice; purification—*Temperance* (tarot); the *desert; fire; rain*

PURPOSEFUL

Word Forms: purpose, purposefully, purposefulness

Definitions: (1) having a meaningful goal or an important aim; **(2)** determined; resolute

Observation: No matter how good a person's intentions, things can go wrong. No matter how bad a person's intentions, things can go right. But if your intentions are pure, the outcome will more often than not be better than if your intentions are poor.

Advice:
• Don't hurt anybody or anything on purpose.
• Whatever you do, do it on purpose.

QUAINT

Word Forms: quainter, quaintest, quaintly, quaintness

Definitions: (1) possessing an old-fashioned charm; picturesque; **(2)** peculiar or unusual in an interesting or amusing way; **(3)** skillfully or cleverly made

QUALIFIED

Word Forms: qualify, qualifiable, qualification, qualifiedly

Definitions: (1) having the qualities, accomplishments, or training that fit one for some function, office, or role; competent; **(2)** to meet the conditions required by law or custom for exercising a right or holding an office; eligible

Synonym: capable

Quote:
Sometimes it is more important to discover what one cannot do, than what one can do.

—LIN YUTANG

QUALITY

Word Forms: quality, qualities, qualitative

Definitions: (1) that which makes something such as it is; nature; **(2)** a distinguishing element or essential characteristic; **(3)** an inherent feature or peculiar attribute; property; **(4)** excellence; to aim for quality rather than quantity; **(5)** a moral or personality trait; ideal; value

Qualityism

1. The theory that people are a combination of positive qualities, that a person's existence is defined by the possession of positive qualities.
2. The adherence to the principle that by choosing to embody a quality, one can enhance that quality in their being.

Synonyms: stature, caliber, character, peculiarity, distinguishing feature, grace, principle, standard
See also: "Being" and "Meaning of Life" Quotes, Appendix 6

Quotes:

Quality is never an accident; it is always the result of high intention, sincere effort, intelligent direction and skillful execution; it represents the wise choice of many alternatives.

—JOHN RUSKIN

Observations:

- Quality is measured and known by the mind but is felt in the soul.
- Positive qualities are the fruits of the spirit.

QUICK

Word Forms: quicker, quickest, quicken, quick-minded, quickly, quickness

Definitions: (1) done, proceeding, or occurring with rapidity; brisk; **(2)** moving or able to move with speed; actively agile; **(3)** keenly responsive; lively; acute; nimble; **(4)** prompt or swift in doing, perceiving, or understanding; **(5)** sensitive; discerning; acutely perceptive; alert

QUICK-WITTED

Word Forms: quick, quick-wittedly, quick-wittedness

Definitions: (1) having a nimble, alert mind; quick in perception and understanding; keen; clever; sharp-witted; **(2)** being able to readily access memory and put ideas together in new ways

QUIET

Word Forms: quieter, quieten, quietude, quiescent, quietly, quietness

Definitions: (1) still; calm; at rest; **(2)** not noisy; hushed; **(3)** free from disturbance or tumult; tranquil; peaceful; **(4)** not ostentatious or pretentious; **(5)** not forward; unobtrusive; **(6)** gentle; mild; placid; smooth

Synonyms: pacific, unruffled, contented, satisfied, meek

Quote:
> Learn to be silent. Let your quiet mind listen and absorb.
> —PYTHAGORAS (582–500 B.C.)

Advice:
- Control your tongue. Keep your negative thoughts to yourself. Or better yet, refuse your negativity the ground to get rooted.
- Do not dissipate the energy of your ideas by talking indiscriminately about them. Share and solidify your ideas with trusted friends.

RADIANT

Word Forms: radiance, radiantly

Definitions: (1) emitting light; shining; bright; **(2)** expressing love, confidence, happiness, and joy; beaming <*radiant* smile>

RAPPORT

Definition: relation marked by harmony, conformity, accord, or affinity; the ability to get along well with others

RASCALLY

Word Forms: rascal, rascality

Definition: a mischievous person; a rogue; a scamp; especially as used jokingly and affectionately

Compatible Quality: good-natured

RATIONAL

Word Forms: rationality, rationalize, rationally, rationalness

Definitions: (1) endowed with understanding or reason; sensible; (2) sane; lucid

Kindred Quality: heart

RAVISHING

Word Forms: ravish, ravishingly

Definition: extremely beautiful or attractive; causing great joy; charming; enchanting; entrancing; captivating; delightful

READY

Word Forms: readier, readiest, readied, readying, readily, readiness

Definitions: (1) prepared or equipped to act immediately; (2) prepared in mind; unhesitant; willing; (3) clever and skillful mentally or physically; dexterous; (4) done or made without delay; prompt; (5) convenient or handy for use; immediately available

Synonyms: apt, facile, expeditious, expert

REALISTIC

Word Forms: real, reality, realism, realist, realistically

Definition: tending to face facts; concerned with or based on what is actual or practical rather than visionary

Quote:
It is the belief of mankind which shapes the world, and all of reality.
—MARION ZIMMER BRADLEY, *The Mists of Avalon*

Reflection: There is an objective reality. The more that one identifies with objective reality, the more real one is. Objective reality is described in terms of positive qualities. If one includes all of the positive qualities, then one is describing the current human understanding of objective reality: that which *is*. The more "is" you are, the more whole you are and the less concern you will have for your survival, spiritual or otherwise.

Consideration: The theory of relativity says that physical things are all moving in relation to each other and if any one thing is to be measured, a fixed point is needed. Once that one point is fixed, all other points are measured in relation to it.

This is also true of things mental and spiritual. When someone's theories can be measured and calculated and "proven," then that person's ideas become a relative beacon. The fixed point, then, is the established theory. As other observers study the ideas of this fixed point, its accuracy and objectivity are brought into relative focus. This is done by experimentation, experience, and finally agreement or belief.

We feel a satisfaction in establishing our "fixed" position. There is even greater satisfaction in confirming the accuracy of our position. If our experience verifies our belief then we stay with the belief that in turn dictates our experience. If the belief is confirmed by the agreement of our fellows, we again feel confident in staying with it. But sometimes others agree with the positive aspects of a negative belief and then the negative is also perpetuated.

As we acquire more of the stuff of the universe, positive qualities, we establish our relative position in the universe. We establish the fact that we do actually exist in the universe. This is confirmed by who we are. We have substance.

Other beings are able to navigate, if you will, based on the confirming juxtaposition of positive role models. That is why heroes and mentors are admired and are respected and emulated. We also know who not to be, by moving away from those malevolent beings who exemplify negative qualities.

Visualization: Each person experiences a personal reality. Each person has a composite of self, experiences, and beliefs that he or she calls reality. Each individual knows this reality is different from other people's experience of reality. Yet it is obvious that these realities do overlap. So, if you imagine each individual reality as a bubble and if you put a larger bubble around all of those different smaller bubbles of reality, you would get a relative objective bubble of reality, which may or may not match "true" objective reality. But if we carry this analogy out far enough, we might be able to assume that there is some kind of ultimate bubble: Ultimate Reality.

As you identify with the "correct" objective reality, you become better, you learn and grow. You will use your experience, faith and intuition to align with it. Your reality is always unfolding as you experience it. Alignment with objective reality is the ticket to expanding personal reality and therefore sanity.

Comments:
- You are in the condition you are in. It is important to understand why, but not to dwell on it. One must also simply accept reality as what is, but always with the confidence that one can change the negative aspects and sustain the positive.
- If you choose reality, you, by that choice, become reality. Then you are assuring your continuance in reality. You are inseparable from it.
- Although myth, metaphor, ritual, and rubrics often point toward reality, to view reality through these things veils the eyes. As each of the veils falls, is removed by choice or is ripped away by the cruelty of life, reality still exists and the individual learns to relate to raw reality. The more that the separators between you and reality are understood, the more they can be de-mystified and the more directly is your experience realized in its true nature.

Suggestion: Occasionally take a step back and take a look at the system, the methods, the way in which you operate—your modus operandi—not just what you do but the belief system upon which it is built.

Symbol: Absolute Reality—the *tree* (inexhaustible life, life without death)

REALIZED

Word Forms: realize, realizing, realizable, realization, realizer

Definitions: (1) real; achieved; complete; (2) to understand fully; to apprehend

REASONABLE

Word Forms: reason, reasoning, reasonability, reasonably, reasonableness

Definitions: (1) good sound judgment or thought; good sense; (2) moderate; fair; (3) logical; (4) just; rational

Familial Quality: common sense

Quotes:

> Do not put faith in traditions, even though they have been accepted for long generations and in many countries. Do not believe a thing because many repeat it. Do not accept a thing on the authority of one or another of the Sages of old, nor on the ground that a statement is found in the books. Never believe anything because probability is in its favor. Do not believe in that which you yourselves have imagined, thinking that a god has inspired it. Believe nothing merely on the authority of your teachers or of the priests. After examination, believe that which you have tested for yourselves and found reasonable, which is in conformity with your well-being and that of others.

—THE BUDDHA

Reflection: The following is quoted from *A Brief History of Time* by Stephen Hawking.

> A theory is a model of the universe, or a restricted part of it, and a set of rules that relate quantities in the model to observations that we make.

A theory is a good theory if it satisfies two requirements: It must accurately describe a large class of observations on the basis of a model that contains only a few arbitrary elements, and it must make definite predictions about the results of future observations.

Note: Mr. Hawking's answer to this final question is that natural selection gives a survival advantage to reason and logic. Therefore, it may be reasonable to assume that we would come to the "right" conclusions.

Symbols: the *left hand;* absolute or divine reason—the *temple*

RECEPTIVE

Word Forms: reception, receptivity, receptively, receptiveness

Definitions: (**1**) takes in or admits; (**2**) able or quick to receive knowledge, ideas, or persons; (**3**) willing or inclined to receive suggestions or offers

Symbol: the *cauldron*

RECHARGED

Word Forms: recharge, rechargeable, recharger, recharging, rechargeability

Definitions: (**1**) refreshed or restored; to regain energy or spirit; (**2**) inspired or invigorated; renewed; revitalized
　　See also: *Restful*

Suggestions:
Recharging Options

Sleep, humor, meditation, play, dance, exercise, entertainment, reading, imagination, vacation, commune with nature, commune with a friend, nourishment, love, be productive, be creative, sit in a rocking chair and watch the afternoon go by.

RECTITUDE

Definitions: (1) rightness of principle or practice; an upright character; conduct according to moral principles; righteousness; (2) correct method or judgment

Derivation: Latin, "straight"

Synonyms: honesty, justice, integrity

Symbol: the *lance*

RECUPERATIVE

Word Forms: recuperate, recuperated, recuperating, recuperation, recuperatory

Definition: promoting recovery; restorative; having the power to regain health or strength
See also: *Recharged*

RED-BLOODED

Word Form: red-bloodedness

Definition: vigorous; high-spirited; strong-willed

REFINED

Word Forms: refine, refining, refinement, refinable, refinedness

Definitions: (1) having cultivation or elegance; free from vulgarity or coarseness—said of manners, speech, or character; (2) possessing more than ordinary subtlety, exactness, or precision

REFLECTIVE

Word Forms: reflect, reflectively, reflectivity, reflection, self-reflective

Definitions: (1) having cognizance of the operations of the mind; capable of exercising thought or judgment <*reflective* reasoning>; **(2)** meditative; thoughtful

Comment: The universe is a personal reflection of Itself.

Symbol: the *mirror*

Mythology: *Narcissus,* a Greek youth who fell in love with his own reflection

REFRESHING

Word Forms: refresh, refreshed, refresher, refreshingly, refreshment

Definitions: (1) having the power to restore freshness, vitality, or energy; **(2)** pleasingly new or different

Symbol: *water,* cool and clean

REGAL

Word Forms: regality, regally, regalness

Definitions: (1) relating to or suitable for royalty; **(2)** exhibiting notable excellence or magnificence; splendid

REGENERATIVE

Word Forms: generate, regenerate, regeneration, regeneracy, regenerator, regeneratively

Definitions: (1) having new life; restored; **(2)** to change radically and for the better; moral reform; **(3)** to revive or produce anew; bring into existence again

Colors: black, violet, red-orange

Symbols: an *eight-petaled rose; antlers;* the *East; eight;* the *Phoenix; sprouted grain; mistletoe;* a *snake* (shedding skin); *sunrise;* rebirth or resurrection—*baptism*

REJOICING

Word Forms: joy, rejoice, rejoicer, rejoicingly

Definitions: (1) the act of expressing joy and gladness; **(2)** the experience of joy; an occasion for expressing joy

REJUVENATIVE

Word Forms: juvenescence, rejuvenate, rejuvenated, rejuvenating, rejuvenation, rejuvenator, rejuvenescence

Definition: to make young or youthful again; to bring back youthful strength, appearance, or vigor

Admonition: Go to the mountains or the ocean or the desert. From there you will bring back some insight, enthusiasm, and inspiration to create something that's honest for yourself in the world.

Color: pink

RELAXED

Word Forms: relax, relaxation

Definitions: (1) free from or relieved of tension or anxiety; **(2)** possessing an easy manner; informal
     See also: *Rejuvenative*

Too Far: lax, lazy

Saying: *En pantoufles* (French): "In slippers" [at ease, informally]

Exercise:
The Quick Crisis Escape

There are situations in which you find yourself overloaded. You are tense, uncomfortable, and wishing that you could just be someplace else or at least in a more relaxed state, but you can't. It could be a test, or an important game, or a half dozen people have to have their report done now. Neither your fight or flight mechanisms are appropriate. The only thing left is to flow. You don't have time for your usual, tried and true relaxation method, but you've just got to cool out.

Here's what you do. First, you don't get anything for free. There is some preparation necessary. You know that eventually you will find yourself in this predicament again. So you condition yourself to be momentarily and quickly transported to a special inner place of peace and strength. While you are there, you trigger an intensely positive and relaxing experience focused into a few very powerful seconds. It is best to use something that has been a real historical event in a very special place. When you do have the time, enhance the experience and keep it fresh with regular practice. As you re-experience this wonderfully refreshing place, you are creating an "energy gem." A feeling that can be released with full clarity and force on a designated clue. This gem is packed with sharp, familiar information that includes all six of the senses. The more complete your inner experience, the more intense and refreshing will be the release.

It is important that the external environment of your special place be very satisfactory but also it must include a rich internal landscape. Feel your true and most valuable qualities. And, depending upon the situation, incorporate a prime quality that would be just right to infuse into the environment at hand. You know your wants and desires. You know when you are comfortable and happy. Use these criteria as friends. Bring them with you into even the most difficult situations.

Connect the release to a common physical and socially acceptable action, such as rubbing your eyes or the back of your neck, stretching, or a deep breath. It is best if you can close your eyes for just a few seconds to close down all external information and release the internal experience into your being. This is no luxurious soak; it is a sudden wave. Your body, mind, and spirit will be fooled into staying where you have just been. The people around you need not know that you just took a delightful and powerful little trip.

Observation:
Things That Help in Relaxation

1. Hot water
2. Flotation
3. Massage
4. Cuddles
5. Laughing
6. Being in a safe situation
7. Being with somebody you like and are comfortable with
8. A diversion—something that is different
9. A diversion—something that is familiar

Colors: blue, turquoise, violet

RELIABLE

Word Forms: rely, reliance, reliant, reliability, reliably, reliableness, self-reliant

Definition: consistently dependable in character, judgment, performance, or result; worthy of confidence; one who can be counted on

Affirmation: I am reliable.

RELIGIOUS

Word Forms: religion, religiosity, religiously, religiousness

Definitions: (1) pious; devout; godly, moral; (2) scrupulously faithful; careful; conscientiously exact

Quotes:
Faith in the survival of supreme values is the core of religion.
—*The Urantia Book*

A mature religion has a universal, inclusive point of view. A mature religion encourages individual freedom, creative expression and stimulates growth.
—MEREDITH J. SPRUNGER, *Spiritual Psychology*

REMARKABLE

Word Forms: remarkably, remarkableness

Definitions: (1) worthy of particular notice; **(2)** extraordinary; unusual; arousing admiration or wonder

Synonyms: rare, striking

RENOWNED

Word Form: renown

Definition: famous; celebrated for great or heroic achievement; revered or admired for distinguished qualities; eminent; remarkable

REPUTABLE

Word Forms: repute, reputability, reputation, reputably, reputableness

Definition: being favorably known or spoken of; held in esteem; well thought of; respectable; honorable

Synonym: creditable

Color: green

RESILIENT

Word Forms: resile, resilience, resiliently

Definition: easily recovering from or adjusting to misfortune or change; quickly recovering strength, spirits, or good humor; buoyant
  See also: *Recharged*

Quote:
  I love the man that can smile in trouble, that can gather strength from distress, and grow brave by reflection.
                                                    —THOMAS PAINE

Comment: A technique to recover after a tragedy is to imagine the *you* in the future that is happy and whole. You must go through your sorrow, pain, and heartache but will emerge on the other side with a new attitude—one that can now handle even this difficulty. Bless those previous selves that have given you the resilience to carry on from here.

RESOLUTE

Word Forms: resolve, resolved, resolution, resolutely, resoluteness

Definition: having or showing a fixed, firm purpose; determined; bold; steady; persevering; steadfast

Synonyms: decided, constant, unshaken, unwavering, unflinching

Saying: *Ne cede malis* (Latin): "Yield not to misfortunes."

Quotes:
  If the going is tough and the pressure is on; if reserves of strength have been drained and the summit is still not in sight; then the quality to seek in a person is neither great strength nor quickness of

hand, but rather a resolute mind firmly set on its purpose that refuses to let its body slacken or rest.

—SIR EDMUND HILLARY

Charter of the United Nations:

We, the peoples of the United Nations

Determined to save succeeding generations from the scourge of war, which twice in our lifetime has brought untold sorrow to mankind, and

To reaffirm faith in fundamental human rights, in the dignity and worth of the human person, in the equal rights of men and women and of nations large and small, and

To establish conditions under which justice and respect for the obligations arising from treaties and other sources of international law can be maintained, and

To promote social progress and better standards of life in larger freedom, and for these ends

To practice tolerance and live together in peace with one another as good neighbors, and

To unite our strength to maintain international peace and security, and

To ensure, by the acceptance of principles and the institution of methods, that armed force shall not be used, save in the common interest, and

To employ international machinery for the promotion of the economic and social advancement of all people, have resolved to combine our efforts to accomplish these aims.

Affirmation: I resolve everything in love.

Advice: Even if the task is big, don't let that stop you from beginning it—just a part of it. Rosa Parks did a very simple thing by refusing to give up her seat on the bus. The task of ending discrimination and freeing the hearts and minds of the oppressed and oppressor was and is a daunting one, but courage and simple honesty are what it takes to begin.

If the larger task does intimidate you, focus on it long enough only to prioritize the smaller pieces. Then take the job at the top of the list and begin it.

RESOURCEFUL

Word Forms: resource, resourcefully, resourcefulness

Definition: able to deal skillfully and promptly with new situations or old difficulties; clever in finding resources; ingenious at discovering new uses for the materials at hand; inventive

Derivation: Old French, "to rise again"

RESPECTABLE

Word Forms: respect, respectful, respectability, respectably, respectableness

Definition: worthy of admiration, honor, or esteem because of a decency or correctness in station, character, or behavior; proper; honest

Quote:
The only hope of preserving what is best lies in the practice of an immense charity, a wide tolerance, a sincere respect for opinions that are not ours.
—P. G. HAMERTON

RESPONSIBLE

Word Forms: response, responsive, responsibly, responsibleness

Definitions: (1) expected or obligated to account for something to someone; (2) answerable to the cause, agent, or source of something <Who is *responsible* for this state of affairs?>; (3) accountable for actions, obligations, or duties <a *responsible* position>; (4) able to distinguish between right and wrong and to think and act rationally, and hence liable for one's behavior; (5) trustworthy; dependable; reliable; (6) able to pay debts; meet business or personal obligations

Kindred Qualities: humble, grateful, sunny

RESPONSIVE

Word Forms: respond, response, responsively, responsiveness

Definition: reacting readily and sympathetically; receptive; sensitive

Synonym: amenable

Comment: We human beings respond to and appreciate the encouragement of other people.

RESTFUL

Word Forms: rest, resting, restfully, restfulness

Definitions: (1) giving or conducive to relaxation; (2) being at rest; tranquil; peaceful; quiet
  See also: *Relaxed*

Compatible Quality: worshipful

Symbol: a *bed*

Mythologies: *Hypnos,* the Greek god of sleep; *Somnus*, the Roman god of sleep, the brother of death, and the son of night

RESTORATIVE

Word Forms: restore, restorable, restoration, restoratively

Definition: having the power to renew strength and vigor; capable of restoring health, consciousness, or life
  See also: *Resilient*

Derivation: Latin, "to renew," "to rebuild"

Symbol: the *rainbow*

REVERED

Word Forms: revere, revering, reverence

Definition: regarded with deep respect, love, awe, or affection; to venerate; to honor; to hold in esteem; admired

Derivation: Latin, "to fear"

REVERENT

Word Forms: reverence, reverently, reverential

Definition: feeling or expressing profound, adoring respect or veneration; worshipful

RHYTHMIC

Word Forms: rhythm, rhythmical, rhythmically, rhythmicity, rhythmize

Definitions: **(1)** the repetition of beat, sound, accent, or motion; usually occurring in a regular or harmonious pattern; **(2)** having a sense of the pattern and flow of things

Comment: We are surrounded by rhythm—the rhythm of our breathing, the rhythm of the seasons, the rhythm of the tides, the rhythm of the day, the sun, the rain, even the snow, the rhythm of our walking, the rhythm of our language, the rhythm of a bird tapping the bark—the rhythm of life.

Symbols: the *drum; ants;* the *centipede*

Mythology: *Terpsichore*, the Greek Muse of dancing and choral song

RICH

Word Forms: rich, richer, richest, riches, richly, richness

Definitions: (1) having abundant possessions, especially material wealth; **(2)** having high value or quality; **(3)** plentiful; ample; **(4)** elaborate; luxurious; sumptuous
See also: *Prosperous*

Synonyms: affluent, copious, fruitful, precious, luscious

Kindred Quality: gratitude

Quote:
If you are in debt, it is because someone believed in you and had enough faith in you to trust you financially. If others are in debt to you, it is because you extended your trust to them.
—CATHERINE PONDER, *The Dynamic Laws of Prosperity*

Symbols: riches of the mind and spirit—all forms of *treasure*

Legend: *Dives*, the Latin word for a rich man, thus any rich man—used in the parable of Lazarus (Luke 16:19–31)

RIGHT

Word Forms: righter, rightest, righted, righting, rightful, righteous, right-thinking, rightly, rightness, right on

Definitions: (1) in accordance with justice, law, or morality; upright; virtuous; righteous; **(2)** in accordance with fact, reason, or a set standard; conforming to truth; **(3)** correct in thought, statement, or action; **(4)** fitting; appropriate; suitable; most convenient or favorable; preferable; **(5)** normal—said of the mind; sane—said of a person; **(6)** having sound health or good spirits; **(7)** in satisfactory condition; in good order; **(8)** real; genuine

Derivation: Sanskrit. The maintenance of Cosmic order was the purpose of all the gods. The gods were conceived as "guardians of *rta*"—willing the right and making sure it was carried out.

Quotes:

This elaborate cartoon on plate tectonics was assembled, and it was beautiful, except for one detail: the earth was rotating the wrong way. When I pointed that out, nobody . . . could really see it being that important. What was the big deal? I came to realize that "right" means something different to an artist than to a physicist. To a physicist a fact is either right or wrong. To an artist "right" is more of an aesthetic question.

—SCIENCE ADVISOR TO A TV PROGRAM, 1980

Always do right. This will gratify some people and astonish the rest.

—MARK TWAIN TO THE YOUNG PEOPLES SOCIETY

Principles:
The Bill of Rights of the United States of America

    I. Right to establish and free exercise of religion
       Right to freedom of speech
       Right to freedom of the press
       Right of peaceable assembly
       Right to petition for redress of grievances
   II. Right to security (to keep and bear arms)
  III. Right to say who is to stay in your house
  IV. Right to be secure (search and seizure)
   V. Right not to be held for a crime unless indicted
       Right not to be tried for the same offense twice
       Right not to be a witness against yourself
       Right to due process of law
       Right to just compensation for private property
  VI. Right to a speedy and public trial by an impartial jury
       Right to be informed of accusations
       Right to confront witnesses for and against
       Right to have assistance of counsel for defense
 VII. Right to trial by jury
VIII. Right to be free from excessive bail, fines or cruel or unusual punishment
  IX. Constitutional rights do not "deny or disparage" other rights.

X. Powers not delegated to or prohibited by the government are reserved to the States or to the people.

Comment: I once knew a man who said that the *easy* way was the right way but he was wrong—the *best* way is the right way.

RIGHTEOUS

Word Forms: right, righteously, righteousness

Definitions: (1) upright; virtuous; acting in a just, honorable manner; **(2)** morally right or justifiable, scrupulous; **(3)** good; excellent; satisfying; pleasant; authentic

Symbol: the *tiger*

Mythology: *Varuna*, a Hindu god of righteousness and a guardian of all that is worthy and good, god of the cosmos

RISIBLE

Word Forms: risibility, risorial, risibly, risibleness

Definitions: (1) able or inclined to laugh; **(2)** causing laughter; laughable; sunny; amusing; ludicrous

Saying: Laughter is the music of grace.

Quotes:
A smile costs nothing but its value is priceless. It enriches the one who gives it, yet does not impoverish them. It happens in a flash but the memories may last for days. No one is so rich that they can get along without it. A smile generates happiness in the home and good-will in the business . . . If you meet an acquaintance or a friend who is too busy to give you a smile—leave one of yours. No one needs a smile so much as the person who has none to give.

—Anonymous

At the height of laughter, the universe is flung into a kaleidoscope of new possibilities.

—JEAN HOUSTON

If you're going to be able to look back on something and laugh about it, you might as well laugh about it now.

—MARIE OSMOND

RISK TAKER

Word Form: risk taking

Definition: (1) one willing to expose themselves to danger—this peril may range from minor change to major transformation; **(2)** to venture; to take a chance

Observation: The first circle is your comfort zone. Risk taking is lived in the second circle. And it is really risky if you get out to the third. (See *Changeable.*)

ROBUST

Word Forms: robustly, robustness

Definition: having or exhibiting sound health or great strength; vigorous; hearty; strongly built; sturdy; muscular

Derivation: Latin, "oak," "strength"

Synonyms: lusty, hale

ROLLICKING

Word Forms: rollick, rollicksome

Definition: carefree and frolicsome; boisterous; gay and lively

ROMANTIC

Word Forms: romance, romantically, romanticize

Definitions: (1) responsive to an imaginative or emotional appeal of what is heroic, adventurous, mysterious, or idealized; **(2)** loving and affectionate; **(3)** conducive to or suitable for lovemaking

Derivation: Originally, romance meant a long narrative in verse or prose, written in one of the Romance dialects about the adventures of knights and other chivalric heroes.

ROSEATE

Word Forms: rose, roseately

Definitions: (1) tinged with a rosy color; **(2)** bright and promising; cheerful and optimistic

Symbols: the *rose; rose-colored glasses*

ROUSING

Word Forms: rouse, rousingly

Definition: exciting; stirring; very active or vigorous; brisk; lively

Derivation: Middle English, "to shake the feathers"

ROYAL

Word Forms: royalty, royally, royalize

Definitions: (1) suitable for or characteristic of a king or queen; august;

princely, regal; majestic; stately; noble; **(2)** superior in quality; magnificent; splendid; **(3)** to give or receive every courtesy; extremely thoughtful; hospitable

Synonyms: monarchical, imperial, superb, magnanimous

How to Live This Quality Today: Give your guests the royal treatment.

Colors: purple, blue

Symbols: *fleur-de-lis;* the *lily*

RUGGED

Word Forms: ruggedly, ruggedness

Definitions: (1) strongly built; having a sturdy constitution; **(2)** capable of enduring hardship; austere; stern

SAFE

Word Forms: safer, safest, safety, safely, safeness, safekeeping, safeguard

Definitions: (1) free from damage, danger, or injury; secure; **(2)** having escaped injury or damage unharmed; **(3)** giving protection; **(4)** trustworthy; reliable; sure; **(5)** taking no risks; prudent; cautious

Kindred Qualities: courageous, inventive, free, adventurous

Too Far: timid

Saying: *Medio tutissimus ibis* (Latin): "You will go most safely by the middle course."

Symbol: a *fireplace*

SAGACIOUS

Word Forms: sagacity, sagaciously, sagaciousness

Definition: keenly perceptive or discerning; shrewd; farsighted in judgment; wise

Synonyms: acuity, intelligent, judicious

SAINTLY

Word Forms: saint, sainted, saintlike, saintliness

Definition: characterizes a person of great virtue, benevolence, piety, charity, patience, or any combination of the best qualities; holy

SALUBRIOUS

Word Forms: salubrity, salubriously, salubriousness

Definition: favorable to health or well-being; healthful

SALUTARY

Word Forms: salutarily, salutariness

Definitions: **(1)** favorable to or promoting health; wholesome; healthful; **(2)** encouraging or contributing to some beneficial purpose

Synonyms: salubrious, useful, advantageous, profitable

SANE

Word Forms: saner, sanest, sanity, sanely, saneness

Definitions: (1) mentally sound, especially able to anticipate and appraise the effect of one's actions; rational; **(2)** free from hurt or disease; healthy; **(3)** having or showing good reason or judgment; sensible
 See also: *Realistic*

Compatible Quality: prepared

Quotes:

Ask, "If there were only one person in the world, is there any way he could be insane?" Insanity always exists in relation to others.

—ROBERT PIRSIG, *Lila*

In the case of permanent insanity the exits to the theater have been blocked, usually because of the knowledge that the show outside is so much worse. The insane person is running a private unapproved film which he happens to *like* better than the current cultural one. If you want him to run the film everyone else is seeing, the solution would be to find ways to prove to him that it would be *valuable* to do so . . . Otherwise why should he get "better"? He already *is* better. It's the patterns that constitute "betterness" that are at issue. From an internal point of view insanity isn't the problem. Insanity is the solution.

—ROBERT PIRSIG, *Lila*

In order to be sane and adjusted as a human being, an individual must realize that he cannot know all there is to know. It is not enough to understand this limitation intellectually; the understanding must be an orderly and conditioned process, "unconscious" as well as "conscious." Such a conditioning is essential to the balanced pursuit of knowledge of the nature of matter and life.

—A. E. VAN VOGT, *The Players of Null A*

Reflection: Accepting reality is fine as long as everyone holds the same criteria for "reality." The problem comes when you are presented with a false impression of reality. Slavery was explained as necessary and accepted as "good" by a certain segment of the population. War is accepted as the only solution by a large enough group of people that it takes place. But that puts a person who sees a higher reality into a difficult position. *Truth* requires that you act as if you believe this higher reality. But *practicality* dictates that you live with the facts of the prevailing reality. Embracing *both* is sanity.

SANGUINE

Word Forms: sanguinity, sanguinely, sanguineness

Definitions: (1) cheerful; optimistic; hopeful; confident; (2) red; ruddy <*sanguine* complexion>; (3) ardent; warm

Derivation: Latin, "blood"
   In medieval physiology being sanguine meant having a warm, passionate, cheerful temperament and a healthy, ruddy complexion—one in whom the blood is the predominant humor.

Synonyms: animated, lively

SANITARY

Word Forms: sanitation, sanitize, sanitarily, sanitariness

Definition: in healthy condition, especially clean and taking precaution against disease; free from dirt, bacteria, or pollution

Symbol: *soap*
   Good hand-washing is the single most effective action against the spread of disease.

—ANITA DOWNS, RN

SAPID

Word Forms: sapidity, sapidness

Definitions: (**1**) savory; having a pleasing taste; (**2**) agreeable to the mind; interesting; engaging

Mythology: *Cawther*, the lake of paradise, in the Koran, with sweet and cool waters; anyone who drinks of it will never thirst again.

SAPIENT

Word Forms: sapience, sapiential, sapiently

Definition: possessing a capacity for great wisdom or sound judgment; discerning; knowing, sagacious

SASSY

Word Forms: sass, sassier, sassiest

Definitions: (**1**) saucy; fresh; (**2**) vigorous; lively; (**3**) distinctively smart and boldly stylish; jaunty

SATISFIED

Word Forms: satisfy, satisfactory, satisfiable

Definitions: (**1**) with fully gratified wants, needs, or desires; satiated; supplied to the full extent with what is wished for; content; (**2**) free from doubt, suspense, or uncertainty; fully assured; the mind is set at ease; convinced; (**3**) doubts or objections adequately or convincingly answered; solved

Familial Quality: grateful

Too Far: smug

SAVED

Word Forms: save, saving, savable, saver

Definitions: (1) rescued from danger or from possible harm or loss; **(2)** kept safe, intact, or unhurt; safeguarded; secured; **(3)** kept from being lost; **(4)** in religion, said of a person whose soul has been delivered from sin and punishment; redeemed from spiritual death

Synonyms: spared, preserved, protected

Symbol: salvation—the *dolphin*

SAVOIR-FAIRE

Definition: knowledge of just what to do in any situation; a polished sureness in social behavior; tact

Derivation: French, "to know how to do"

SAVORY

Word Forms: savor, savorily, savoriness

Definitions: (1) pleasing to the taste or smell; appetizing; agreeable; **(2)** morally pleasing; respectable

Synonyms: flavorous, piquant, pungent, rich, spicy, palatable

SAVVY

Word Forms: savvier, savviest, savvied, savvying, savvily, savviness

Definition: practical understanding; shrewdness or intelligence; common sense

Derivation: Spanish, "to know"

SCHOLARLY

Word Forms: school, scholar, scholastic

Definitions: (1) characteristic of a learned person; academic; (2) displaying knowledge, accuracy, and analytical ability; (3) studious; devoted to learning; (4) orderly and thorough in methods of study

SCRUMPTIOUS

Word Forms: scrumptiously, scrumptiousness

Definition: delightful; excellent; first-rate; splendid; extremely pleasing, especially to the taste; delectable, yummy

SCRUPULOUS

Word Forms: scruple, scrupulosity, scrupulously, scrupulousness

Definitions: (1) having moral integrity; acting in strict regard for what is considered right or proper; conscientiously honest; (2) punctiliously exact; careful with details; precise, accurate, and correct
    See also: *Upright*

SEARCHING

Word Forms: search, searchable, searchingly

Definitions: (1) looking into or over; exploring; examining; inquiring; seeking; investigating; (2) keen; sharp; piercing; penetrating

Synonyms: probe, examine, hunt, pursue, thorough

Quote:
Searching goes on forever.

—JUDY KAIN

Symbol: *searchlights; a lighthouse*

SEASONED

Word Forms: season, seasoning, seasoner

Definitions: (1) given a relish, zest, or interest; (2) improved quality; matured; (3) fit or competent by experience; (4) used to; accustomed; acclimatized; (5) made less harsh or severe; tempered; softened <He *seasoned* his remarks with discretion.>

SECURE

Word Forms: securer, securest, securement, security, securely, secureness

Definitions: (1) free from fear, care, doubt, or anxiety; not worried, troubled, or apprehensive; having ease of mind; (2) sure; assured; certain; (3) trustworthy; dependable; to be relied upon

Synonyms: safe, guarded, impregnable, protected, confident, undisturbed

Familial Quality: abundance

Too Far: miserly

Considerations:

- A person in solitary confinement is extremely secure, but he has very little freedom.
- All securities come down to one thing: survival. In order to survive physically, you need to maintain the things of the body: health, environment, sustenance.

   On the emotional level you need to be able to forgive and forget so that you can proceed with your life without the bonds of hate and revenge. You need also to be stress hardy to handle or deflect anxiety. To survive emotionally you need to nurture and be nurtured.

   The mind needs to be exercised and involved in creativity and problem solving. Include in that complex mental matrix the openness to accept and adapt to other points of view.

   Spiritually survival is assured only by creating a self—your soul—that will be able to fuse with the fabric of eternity. And the threads of that fabric are the positive qualities.

- Nobody is going to give up their current sense of security without some belief that they will establish a new level of security by doing so.

   The exception is the sacrifice to security that is given over to courage, loyalty, and love. The soldier will risk his security to save a friend. The parent will endure hardship and stress to support his or her child. The artist is compelled to create because of the love of beauty and the need to communicate. But even in these there is the secure knowledge of a greater good.

Quotes:

Security is mostly a superstition. It does not exist in nature, nor do the children of men as a whole experience it. Avoiding danger is no safer in the long run than outright exposure. Life is either a daring adventure or nothing.

—HELEN KELLER

The following are quoted from *The Gaia Peace Atlas,* Dr. Frank Barnaby, General Editor:

Environmental Security

True environmental security will depend on an ecologically wise economy, sustainable livelihood for all, and a re-integration of human and natural systems.

Economic Security

Ultimately, economic security will depend on conversion to a steady-state economy, and on re-creation of real wealth at local, national and regional levels.

Human and Civil Security

Human security rests on economic, environmental and spiritual security, and on the eradication of structural violence within society.

Inner Security

Personal and social well-being depends on spiritual security, and on concern for the foundations of peace: consensus, ecological wisdom, economic justice and defence of the rules of law.

Note: The above include many detailed goals to achieve, including population stabilization; pollution management; diversion of military spending to development and environment; access to rewarding work and to ideas; equality of opportunity for sexes, races, religions, and ages; responsiveness to change, diversity, and growth; and love for others.

Comment: Insecurity makes you choose to turn your will over to someone or something other than yourself: a boss, an organization, a set of ideas, or even to your concept of God.

Insecurity is based on fear.

Symbol: inside a *wall*

SEDATE

Word Forms: sedately, sedateness

Definitions: (1) composed; calm; quiet; serene; undisturbed; tranquil; (2) contemplative; sober; serious; dignified

SEDULOUS

Word Forms: sedulity, sedulously, sedulousness

Definition: assiduous; diligent in application or pursuit; constant, steady, and persevering; steadily industrious; indefatigable

SEEKING

Word Forms: seek, seeker, sought

Definitions: (1) to search for; to look for; to try to find; (2) to explore; (3) to ask or inquire for; to try to learn or discover; (4) to try to get or acquire; to aim at; pursue

Quotes:
> Seek the greater thing, and the lesser will be found therein; ask for the heavenly, and the earthly shall be included. The shadow is certain to follow the substance.
> —JESUS, *The Urantia Book*

> Seek and you shall find; knock and the door shall be opened to you.
> —JESUS, Matthew 7:7–8

Advice: Most everyone has emotional buttons that, if pushed, make them crazy. What is the underlying reason? Until you find out what it is that is really the cause, those who are willing to manipulate you will have the means to do so. The immediate solution is to remove yourself, graciously, from their presence so that they cannot continue to annoy you. The long-range solution is to remove the buttons.

Color: indigo

Symbol: the *journey*

SEEMLY

Word Forms: seem, seemlier, seemliest, seemliness

Definitions: (1) suitable; proper; fitting or becoming, especially with reference to conventional standards of conduct or good taste; decent; decorous; (2) having a pleasing appearance; fair; handsome

Synonyms: appropriate, congruous

SELFLESS

Word Forms: selflessly, selflessness

Definition: without regard for one's own interests; unselfish

Kindred Quality: service minded

Comment: If you are unselfish, you are also self-forgetful. If you are doing some service with love for someone else, your mind and heart are focused on the good that you hope the other to receive. The very thought of getting something in return lessens the value.

SELF-ACCEPTING

Word Forms: accepting, self-acceptance

Definition: regarding oneself as valid; affirming, understanding or believing in oneself

Compatible Quality: self-forgiving

Too Far: selfish

Advice: Love yourself as you are. You are often enough aware of your faults and problems. They need not be dwelt upon. Instead give yourself credit for your list of positive qualities and accomplishments. Move forward with a positive intention.

SELF-CONTAINED

Word Forms: self-containment, self-containedly, self-containedness

Definitions: (1) having within oneself all that is necessary; functioning independently; self-sufficient; self-possessed; **(2)** formal and reserved in manner

SELF-ESTEEM

Definition: a confidence and satisfaction in oneself; self-acceptance

Synonym: self-respect

Kindred Quality: humility

Too Far: arrogant, egotistical

Quotes:
When you're playing with your kids, love just happens.
> —LOUISE HART, *The Winning Family: Increasing Self-esteem in Your Children and Yourself*

Self-esteem is the most important building block for emotional health and happiness.
> —LOUISE HART, *The Winning Family: Increasing Self-esteem in Your Children and Yourself*

People who feel good about themselves tend to take good care of themselves and treat others with respect.
> —LOUISE HART, *The Winning Family: Increasing Self-esteem in Your Children and Yourself*

Self-esteem is crucial for healthy families.
　　—LOUISE HART, *The Winning Family: Increasing Self-esteem in Your Children and Yourself*

Observations:
- One of the causes of anger is a lack of self-esteem.
- One of the causes of guilt is a lack of self-esteem.
- One of the causes of insecurity is a lack of self-esteem.

One of the strange things about insecurity is the way it manifests in different people. Some turn in on themselves and feel themselves as worthless and others puff up their ego and become bullies. Still others get caught by the jealousy monster or the depression demon. The antidotes are positive qualities on different ends of the spectrum—accomplishment, loyalty, trust, humility, and thoughtfulness.

Then each kind will find a self they can esteem.

Tips:
- True self-esteem comes from doing something worthwhile.
- If you find something that you don't like about yourself, don't fall into the trap of viewing your entire self through this fault. The rest of you is still wonderful and growing.

Advice: It is more important to ask oneself, "What is right with me?" than, "What is wrong with me?"

Comment: One of the characteristics of self-esteem is the ability to be misunderstood and not be so overwhelmed that you enter into a self-pity mode. Correct the misunderstanding whenever you see the opportunity to do so. All problems are correctable eventually.

Reflection: Notice the questions that you ask yourself. Notice the motives that move you. I have a friend who told me what his inner questions are: Will I be accepted? Will people like me? How do I make people like me? There is a range of what one can do in answer to these questions. Should you be nice to others because you believe that they will like you or be kind to others because it is the right thing to do no matter what the others think about you?

Are you giving to get because you feel inadequate? Or have you transcended that need and are giving for the joy of giving? If you have a healthy sense of self-esteem you will be more likely to act without ulterior motives.

We compensate for what we think is our lack, trying to fill the hole that is in our soul. Since we are potential infinite beings, there will always be a yearning for perfection. But this can be experienced as a lack or accepted as a fact. Once you get to acceptance then you can use the fact as you would any other fact—as a building block.

Reduce the number and kind of internal mechanisms that allow you to believe that you are unworthy and undeserving. Sometimes we even have an active destructive force within that tears down the good that is in the process of growing.

SELF-GOVERNING

Word Forms: self-governed, self-government, self-governance

Definitions: (1) characterizes a state, community, or region that is governed by its own people; democratic; **(2)** having control or rule over oneself; autonomous

Quote:
That state is best which governs least.
—THOMAS JEFFERSON

SELF-MADE

Definitions: (1) having succeeded in life essentially unaided; **(2)** made by one's own efforts

SELF-POSSESSED

Word Form: self-possession

Definition: in control of one's emotions or reactions especially when under pressure and stress; having presence of mind; composed in mind or manner; calm; poised

Symbol: the *cloak*

SELF-RESPECT

Word Forms: self-respecting, self-respectful

Definition: a proper respect for oneself or for one's own character and reputation

Kindred Qualities: humility, willfulness
 Lack of or loss of self-respect results in inaction due to the diminution of will.

Advice: Idleness diminishes self-respect. Therefore, stay busy with something constructive that you love to do or have a duty to do. Then turn the duty into an act of love.

SELF-SUFFICIENT

Word Forms: self-sufficiency, self-sufficing, self-sufficiently

Definitions: (1) able to maintain oneself without outside aid; capable of providing for one's own needs; **(2)** having confidence in one's own resources or powers

How to Live This Quality Today: Wash the dishes.

SENSIBLE

Word Forms: sense, sensibility, sensibly, sensibleness

Definitions: (1) possessing or containing good or common sense, judgment, or reason; intelligent; reasonable; wise; **(2)** capable of being perceived by the senses; capable of exciting physical sensation; **(3)** having appreciation or understanding; cognizant; aware; emotionally or intellectually conscious

Quote:
 A match may start a fire, but once the fire is burning, putting out the match won't stop it. The problem is no longer the match. It's the fire.
 —MICHAEL CRICHTON, *The Terminal Man*

Suggestion: Note your reaction to the things you see or read. These reactions are an indication of your sensibilities to certain qualities. On television or in a movie or a play the writers will generate an unrealistic situation to produce a tension that represents a misunderstanding or a lack of communication so that the situation can be portrayed dramatically. You recognize and identify a more appropriate way. You will find yourself saying, "If they'd only talk to each other" or "If they had only been honest, then this would never have happened."

SENSITIVE

Word Forms: sensor, sensitivity, sensitize, sensitively, sensitiveness, supersensitive

Definitions: (1) responsive to the feelings of others; **(2)** tender or compassionate toward the feelings of others; **(3)** endowed with sensation; perceptive through the senses

Too Far: temperamental, critical

SENSUOUS

Word Forms: sense, sensual, sensuousity, sensuously, sensuousness

Definitions: (1) derived from, based on, affecting, appealing to, or perceived by the senses; **(2)** easily affected through the senses; enjoying the pleasures of sensation; **(3)** keenly appreciative of and aroused by beauty, refinement, or luxury

Too Far: licentious

Colors: violet, pink

SENTIMENTAL

Word Forms: sentiment, sentimentalism, sentimentality, sentimentally

Definitions: **(1)** showing tender emotion; having delicate feeling toward music, poetry, or drama; sensitive; **(2)** moved more by emotion than reason; acting from feeling rather than from practical and utilitarian motives

Kindred Qualities: reasonable, rugged

Symbol: *teardrops*

SERENDIPITOUS

Word Forms: serendipity, serendipitously

Definitions: **(1)** possessing an aptitude for making desirable discoveries by accident; **(2)** having good fortune; lucky

Derivation: *Serendipity,* also known as *accidental sagacity,* was so named by Horace Walpole for a faculty possessed by the heroes of a fairy tale called *The Three Princes of Serendip.*

SERENE

Word Forms: serenity, serenely, sereneness

Definition: marked by peaceful repose or quietude; tranquil; placid; undisturbed

Comment: If you are caught up in the hustle and hassle of an active life you will long for serenity and relaxation. The next vacation or retirement seems so far away. But you can always take an inner trip to your center where all peace exists.

Symbol: a *calm sea*

SERIOUS

Word Forms: seriously, seriousness

Definitions: (1) showing, having, or caused by earnestness or deep thought; grave, sober, or solemn; sincere; (2) meaning what one says or does; not joking or trifling; (3) concerned or dealing with important matters; problem solving with a focused intensity; weighty; (4) requiring careful consideration or thought; involving difficulty, effort, or considered action

Kindred Qualities: playful, lighthearted, flexible

Saying: *Au grand serieux* (French): "in all seriousness"

SERVICE MINDED

Definition: demonstrating helpful, beneficial, or friendly action or conduct; giving assistance or advantage to another or the community; thoughtful

People Who Exemplify This Quality: Martin Luther King

Proverb:

> *When I do not know who I am I serve you.*
> *When I know who I am I am you.*
>
> —INDIAN

Quotes:

Do it (what needs to be done) for yourself as if *you* were a dear friend.

—JERRY DOWNS

I don't know what your destiny will be, but one thing I know: the only ones among you who will be really happy are those who will have sought and found out how to serve.

—ALBERT SCHWEITZER

Comment: *Near versus Far*: Direct person-to-person service is what many think of as service. Even though this individual support gives you an emotional connection to the person served, it is no less important and valid to serve a wide variety of people even if you don't know them. Take entertainers for instance. They distribute their talent for your enjoyment and you get the benefit. If someone makes a tool it is up to the one who uses it to *do* something with it.

Question: How do you balance confidence and humility? Service.

Symbol: the *buffalo*

SEXY

Word Forms: sex, sexier, sexiest, sexual, sexuality, sex appeal, sexily, sexiness

Definitions: (1) suggestive or stimulating; erotic; passionate; sensual; **(2)** sensually interesting or thrilling; radiating sexuality; **(3)** excitingly appealing; glamorous

Too Far: lustful, promiscuous

Color: red

Symbol: the unification of the sexes—*hermaphrodite*

SHARING

Word Forms: share, shared, sharer, shareable

Definitions: (1) dividing and distributing in portions; apportioning; **(2)** partaking, using, experiencing, occupying, or enjoying with others; **(3)** having in common; **(4)** granting or giving a part of

Quote:
If you think a complimentary thought about someone, don't just think it. Dare to compliment people and pass on compliments to them from others.
—CATHERINE PONDER, *The Dynamic Laws of Prosperity*

SHARP

Word Forms: sharper, sharpest, sharped, sharping, sharpen, sharply, sharpness, sharp-eared, sharp-eyed, sharp-sighted, sharp-witted

Definitions: (1) clearly defined; distinct, unobstructed; **(2)** quick, acute, or penetrating in perception or intellect; clever; shrewd; **(3)** showing a keen awareness; attentive; vigilant; alert; **(4)** extremely sensitive; **(5)** full of activity or energy; brisk; active; vigorous; **(6)** attractively dressed or groomed; good-looking; handsome; beautiful

SHELTERING

Word Forms: shelter, sheltered, shelteringly

Definition: protecting from danger, violence, injury, annoyance, or attack; defending; securing or rendering safe; harboring

Derivation: Middle English, "bodyguard"

Symbol: a *roof;* a *house*

SHINING

Word Forms: shine, shined, shone, shiner, shines

Definitions: (1) radiant; gleaming; sparkling, glistening; **(2)** bright and often splendid in appearance; resplendent; **(3)** possessing a distinguished quality; illustrious; brilliant; remarkable; eminent

SHIPSHAPE

Definition: in good order; tidy; trim

SHREWD

Word Forms: shrewder, shrewdest, shrewdly, shrewdness

Definition: cunning; artful; astute or keen-witted in practical concerns; insightful; clever; perceptive

Synonyms: *Shrewd, sagacious, perspicacious,* and *astute* mean acute perception and sound judgment. *Shrewd* stresses practical, pragmatic cleverness and judgment. *Sagacious* suggests wisdom, penetrating thought, and farsightedness. *Perspicacious* implies unusual power to see through and understand what is puzzling or hidden. *Astute* suggests shrewdness, perspicacity, and diplomatic skill.

SIGNIFICANT

Word Forms: significance, significancy, significative, significantly

Definitions: (1) important; momentous; **(2)** a person of value; **(3)** the realization of one's worth; self-esteem

SILLY

Word Forms: sillies, sillier, silliest, silliness

Definition: harmless folly; simple whimsicalness; happy innocence

Familial Quality: giggly

SIMPLE

Word Forms: simpler, simplest, simplicity, simplify, simplistic, simply, simpleness

Definitions: (1) easy to understand or deal with; **(2)** elegant; not ornate or luxurious; unadorned; not elaborate or complicated; plain; unembellished; **(3)** modest; unaffected; unassuming; **(4)** sincere; free of deceit or guile; innocent; **(5)** unpretentious

Music: "'Tis a Gift to Be Simple," a Quaker traditional

Quote:

Everything should be made as simple as possible but not simpler.

—ALBERT EINSTEIN

Comment: The most complex thing can be boiled down to a simple formula or precept, for instance: $E=mc^2$ or "All You Need Is Love." As you are creating or investigating a system, its complexity can be overwhelming. But as you begin to grasp it, it begins to collapse back into its simple, unified reality. It takes time and teamwork and tenacity to arrive at simplicity.

Symbol: *one*

SINCERE

Word Forms: sincerer, sincerest, sincerity, sincerely, sincereness

Definitions: (1) without deceit, pretense, or hypocrisy; truthful; faithful; straightforward; honest; simple; innocent; **(2)** being the same in actual character as in outward appearance; genuine; real

Saying: *Ex animo* (Latin): "From the heart"

Consideration: There are some crucial qualities, a class of qualities that you really can't do without. One of them is sincerity. If you're sincere in your attempt to do the right thing, however you define that, you are succeeding in a very important aspect.

Advice: If you are motivated by and have a genuine sincerity in what you do, you should never feel guilty. If you choose correctly, it will reinforce the positive. If you choose incorrectly, you will learn that there is a better way. And if it is some of both, you will get to experience both and learn about the middle ground.

Comment: The primary quality that saves a person from being an out and out fool is sincerity.

Color: blue

SISTERLY

Word Forms: sister, sisterhood, sisterlike, sisterliness

Definition: affectionate, as the intimate kindness of a sister; characterizing congenial or loyal relationship with or among women

Familial Quality: brotherly

SKILLFUL

Word Forms: skill, skilled, skillfully, skillfulness

Definitions: (1) well-versed in an art; able to perform dexterously a manual operation in the arts or professions; adroit; (2) having a competent aptitude in management; (3) knowing; revealing intelligence; expert; ingenuity

Comment: As robots eliminate unskilled jobs, even cheap manual labor will not be as cheap as a robot, as long as there is energy to run the robots.

Mythologies: *Harpocrates*, the god of science among the Greeks and Romans; *Hermes*, the Greek god serving as messenger to the other gods; the god of science, eloquence, and cunning; the protector of boundaries and the god of commerce; he invented the lyre; *Mercury*, the Roman god of commerce, manual skill, eloquence, cleverness, and travel

SLEEK

Word Forms: sleeken, sleeking, sleekened, sleekly, sleekness

Definitions: (1) smooth, polished in manners, speech, or appearance; suave; (2) a well-groomed or healthy look; dapper; elegant; (3) slender, graceful lines; stylish

SMART

Word Forms: smarter, smartest, smarten, smartly, smartness

Definitions: (1) brisk, lively, or witty, as an insightful remark; **(2)** possessing quick intelligence; mentally alert; shrewd; brilliant; **(3)** astute; clever; capable; practiced know-how; **(4)** neat; clean; fresh; in contemporary style; flair; **(5)** sophisticated; elegant; fashionable

SMOOTH

Word Forms: smoother, smoothest, smoothed, smoothing, smoothie, smoothly, smoothness, smooth-spoken

Definitions: (1) even; not rough; calm; serene; tranquil; **(2)** equable; amiable; professional; **(3)** gentle; tender, especially to touch; **(4)** to make the way easy; to soothe emotional upset; **(5)** a sweet and soothing sound in music or voice; **(6)** pleasant; enjoyable; **(7)** charming; comfortable in the social graces

SNAZZY

Word Forms: snazzier, snazziest, snazziness

Definition: attractive in a flashy way; fancy

SNUGLY

Word Forms: snug, snugger, snuggest, snugging, snuggling, snuggled, snugness

Definition: comfortably close and safe, especially of a loved one; cozy; characterizes one who cuddles with affection

SOARING

Word Forms: soar, soaringly

Definitions: (1) high in thought or imagination; sublime; (2) aspiring to great heights; (3) a feeling of unfettered freedom

Symbols: an *albatross;* a *sailplane*

SOBER

Word Forms: soberer, soberest, sobriety, sobering, soberly, soberness, sobersided, sober-minded

Definitions: (1) temperate; practicing the reasonable and moderate use of substance or emotion; showing self-control; not extreme in any way; (2) regularly displaying calm reason; cool; (3) having a serious, earnest, or thoughtful nature; solemn; (4) quiet; not flashy; (5) honest; not exaggerated <the *sober* truth>; (6) sane or rational

Kindred Qualities: spontaneous, enthusiastic

SOCIABLE

Word Forms: social, socially, sociably, sociableness

Definition: inclined to friendly communication; open to conversing; neighborly; agreeable to a free exchange of ideas

Kindred Quality: Attentive. The best communicator is the person who is the best listener. One who is genuinely interested in the views and lives of others.

Compatible Quality: gracious

Familial Quality: companionable

Too Far: garrulous, nosey

SOFT

Word Forms: softer, softest, soften, softened, softening, softener, softy, softly, softness, softhearted, soft-spoken

Definitions: (1) not hard, rough, rigid, rude, or harsh; smooth; pleasant to the touch and feelings; gentle; comfortable; **(2)** easy to work with; malleable; pliable; flexible

Synonyms: delicate, tender, mild, mellow, engaging, kind, sympathetic, sentimental, civil, courteous, quiet, lenient, compassionate

Kindred Quality: hardy

Too Far: timid

Symbols: *fur;* a *baby's bottom*

SOFTHEARTED

Word Forms: softheartedly, softheartedness

Definition: having tenderness of heart, kindly affection; compassionate; meek; sympathetic or responsive; having a generous and giving spirit

SOLEMN

Word Forms: solemnity, solemnize, solemnify, solemnly, solemnness

Definition: serious, especially with religious reverence; sacred; devout; pious; deeply earnest; marked by veneration to God

Synonyms: profound, awe-inspiring

Compatible Qualities: liturgical, worshipful, prayerful

SOLID

Word Forms: solidify, solidity, solidly, solidness

Definitions: (1) firm; sound; real; genuine; (2) showing complete unity; in accord; (3) exhibiting substantial quality or comfort; (4) possessing moral strength; valid; true; just, said of principles and reasonings

Synonyms: stout, stable, prudent, complete, thoroughgoing

Kindred Qualities: flowing, flexible

Compatible Quality: reliable

Symbol: *granite*

SOOTHING

Word Forms: soothe, soothed, soothingly, soothingness

Definitions: (1) restores to a quiet, calm, or normal state; (2) mitigates, softens, or relieves, as pain or grief; (3) gratifying; pleasing

Synonyms: appeasing, assuaging, allaying, pacifying, composed

Colors: blue, violet

SOPHISTICATED

Word Forms: sophisticate, sophisticating, sophistication

Definition: urbane; worldly-wise; cultured; clever; knowledgeable and perceptive of modern matters or complex ideas

Derivation: Sophists, a class of men who taught rhetoric, philosophy, and politics in ancient Greece. By their use of vain subtleties and false axioms, they drew upon themselves general distrust and contempt.

Kindred Qualities: simple, natural, honest

SOULFUL

Word Forms: soul, soulfully, soulfulness, noble-souled

Definitions: (1) full of or expressive of emotion or deep feeling <All were moved by the artist's *soulful* rendition of the opera.>; **(2)** possessing positive qualities; the embodiment of a quality <Brevity is the *soul* of wit.>; **(3)** having spiritual or emotional warmth, power, or understanding

Quotes:
> The soul is the self-reflective, truth-discerning and spirit-perceiving part of man which forever elevates the human being above the level of the animal world.
> —JESUS, *The Urantia Book*

> What shall it profit you if you gain the whole world and lose your own soul?
> —JESUS, Matthew 16:26

> If the head and the body are to be well, you must begin by curing the soul.
> —PLATO

If the soul could have known God without the world, the world would never have been created.

—MEISTER ECKHART

If you would have the message of the gods to direct your life, look for that which repeats. . . . It comes again and again until you have made it part of your soul and your enduring spirit.

—MARION ZIMMER BRADLEY, *The Mists of Avalon*

Observation: Human beings, in a structural sense, are made up of five components: body, mind, spirit, personality, and soul.
Integrate your qualities into each of these aspects.

Advice: If a person is considered the embodiment of a quality or attribute, i.e., "the *soul* of generosity," emulate him or her.

Comment: Remember that your belongings are just stuff, that material possessions belong to Mother Earth. That which you are really made of is your spiritual qualities, your soul.

Symbols: the *foot;* the *gazelle; six;* a *well;* a *garden;* the *tunic; birds;* the *hawk* (Egyptian); a *butterfly* (attraction to light)

Mythology: *Psyche* is the Latin writer Appuleius' personification of the soul. Psyche was so lovely that Venus asked Cupid to destroy her, but he fell in love with her instead.

SOUND

Word Forms: sounder, soundest, soundly, soundness

Definitions: (1) whole; unimpaired; unhurt; unmutilated; not weak, diseased, or damaged; healthy; (2) firm; safe; stable; secure, especially financially; (3) founded on truth; strong; valid; reliable; sensible; (4) morally solid; honest; honorable; upright; virtuous; trustworthy; (5) thorough; complete

Saying: *Mens sana in corpore sano* (Latin): "A sound mind in a sound body"

SPECIAL

Word Forms: specially, specialist, specialty, specialize, especial

Definitions: **(1)** extraordinary; uncommon; exceptional; distinctive; unique; **(2)** particularly valued <a *special* friend>; **(3)** appropriate; proper
See also: *Important*

Synonyms: distinguished, individualistic

SPELLBINDING

Word Forms: spellbind, spellbound, spellbinder, spellbindingly

Definitions: **(1)** grippingly charming; fascinating; enchanting; **(2)** characterizes a speaker of compelling eloquence; captivating; **(3)** marks an act of extraordinary interest; riveting

SPICY

Word Forms: spice, spicing, spiced, spicer, spicily, spiciness

Definitions: **(1)** fragrant or aromatic to the smell and pungent to the taste, also applied to manners, personality, or mind; **(2)** marks something or someone who enriches, in a positive way, the quality of a thing or person; characterizes that which gives zest or interest to; piquant; **(3)** lively, spirited

Saying:
Variety is the spice of life.

—WILLIAM COWPER

Symbol: *peppers*

SPIRITED

Word Forms: spirit, spiritedly, spiritedness, inspired

Definition: having or showing mettle, courage, vigor, animation, energy

Too Far: tempestuous

SPIRITUAL

Word Forms: spiritualize, spirituality, spiritually, spiritualness

Definitions: (1) pertaining to the spirit or soul as distinguished from the body; (2) from or concerned with the higher part of the mind; (3) pertaining to or consisting of essence; incorporeal; (4) showing much refinement of thought and feeling; (5) pertaining to religion or the church; sacred, devotional or ecclesiastical; not lay or temporal; the moral aspect; (6) supernatural; suprapersonal

Reflection: On the spiritual level all potentials are actuals.

Colors: indigo, blue

Symbols: *birds; wings;* the *lamp;* the *eagle; fire*

SPLENDID

Word Forms: splendor, splendiferous, splendent, resplendent, splendidly, splendidness

Definitions: (1) magnificent; imposing; sumptuous; grand; (2) inspiring to the imagination; glorious; illustrious; heroic; brilliant; famous; celebrated; distinguished; (3) excellent; exceptionally good; very fine

Color: violet

SPONTANEOUS

Word Forms: spontaneity, spontaneously, spontaneousness

Definitions: (1) done or resulting from one's own desire; not premeditated; (2) acting upon a sudden impulse; (3) not apparently contrived or manipulated; natural; (4) playful; creative

Too Far: capricious

Saying: *Carpe diem* (Latin): "Seize the day."

Comments: Each quality has a default level. But you can change that level by being open to it when it comes up in your life. Consciously supporting it enhances it.

Automatic versus Spontaneous

Your automatic reactions are put into play immediately without thought. They could be very complex responses or as simple as flight or fight. Your reactions have been created genetically over many generations or you have built them up habitually. They are part of your basic structure.

A spontaneous response could, at the least, be the same as an automatic response. But it also could be much more flexible. If you add a wider range of possible options, you extend your responsiveness.

SPORTING

Word Forms: sport, sportive, sportful, sportability, sporty, sporter, sportingly, sportiness, sportswoman, sportsman, sportsmanlike

Definitions: (1) playful; merry; gamesome; characterizes one who indulges in a happy diversion, usually with others; frolicsome; marks an enjoyable recreation; (2) fair; plays according to the rules and courteously; accepts failure gracefully and victory graciously; (3) possessing the ability to accept defeat or jestful teasing with a good sense of humor

SPRIGHTLY

Word Forms: sprite, sprightful, sprightliness

Definitions: (1) possessing a spirit that gives cheerfulness or courage; **(2)** lively; brisk; nimble; vivacious; animated; vigorous; gay; spry; airy; buoyant

SPRINGY

Word Forms: spring, springing, springily, springiness

Definitions: (1) having an elastic quality; resilient; flexible; **(2)** showing a lively and happy gait <with a *springy* step>

SPRY

Word Forms: spryer, spryest, spryly, spryness

Definition: full of life; nimble; agile; energetic; active

SPUNKY

Word Forms: spunk, spunkier, spunkiest, spunkily, spunkiness

Definition: mettlesome; spirited; courageous; plucky; lively

STABLE

Word Forms: stability, stabilize, stabler, stablest, stably, stableness

Definitions: not easily moved or thrown off balance; not likely to break down, fall apart, or give way; steady; fixed; **(2)** firm in character, purpose, or resolution; steadfast; **(3)** resisting change; permanent; enduring; **(4)** capable of returning to equilibrium or original position after having been displaced; flexible

Kindred Qualities: changeable, lively, adventuresome

Too Far: stagnant

Quote:
Heaven is under our feet as well as over our heads.
—HENRY DAVID THOREAU

Symbol: *four*

STALWART

Word Forms: stalwartly, stalwartness

Definitions: **(1)** brave; bold; daring; valiant in character or deed; **(2)** strong; sturdy; robust in body, mind, or spirit; **(3)** resolute; firm; **(4)** one who is staunchly supportive; steadfast

Fiction: *Philip Faulconbridge*, in Shakespeare's *King John*, a daring soldier, true as steel to his friends

STAMINA

Definition: resistance to fatigue, illness, stress, or difficulty; endurance; staying power

Derivation: Latin, referring to the life-threads spun by the Fates

STATELY

Word Forms: statelier, stateliest, stateliness

Definition: lofty, dignified, elegant, or majestic in mien or manner

Synonyms: magnificent, imposing, elevated, lordly, proud, grand

STATUESQUE

Word Forms: statuesquely, statuesqueness

Definitions: (1) well-proportioned beauty; **(2)** stately; graceful; showing poise or dignity

STAUNCH

Word Forms: stanch, staunchly, staunchness

Definition: firm in principle; steady or steadfast; constant and zealous

Familial Qualities: faithful, loyal

STEADFAST

Word Forms: steady, steadfastly, steadfastness

Definitions: (1) fixed fast; established; **(2)** firmly fixed in faith or devotion to duty; constant; unchanging; resolute; not fickle or wavering; loyal

Too Far: stubborn

STEADY

Word Forms: steadier, steadiest, steadied, steadying, steadily, steadiness, steady-going

Definition: firm, constant, or resolute in action, mind, purpose, pursuit, or principle; calm; controlled; stable

Compatible Quality: dependable

STELLAR

Definitions: (1) like a star; brilliant; **(2)** outstanding

Saying: *Per aspera ad astra* (Latin): "Through difficulties to the stars"

Symbol: *stars*

STERLING

Definition: genuine; pure; of excellent quality, value, or standard

STICK-TO-ITIVE

Word Form: stick-to-itiveness

Definitions: (1) to be constant, firm, persevering, or determined; tenacious; **(2)** resolutely supportive; faithful, loyal

Observation:
Antidotes to Disappointment

- Stick-to-itiveness
- Faith in what you're doing

- Learning from information given
- Adjusting your plan to circumstances
- A sense of humor

Inspiration:
Terry Fox ran 3,339 miles across Canada raising $25 million for cancer research even though he had one artificial leg, replacing the one he lost to cancer. His story is detailed in Ann Donegan Johnson's *The Value of Facing a Challenge—The Story of Terry Fox.*

STIMULATING

Word Forms: stimulate, stimulant, stimulation, stimulator, stimulus

Definition: characterizes one who excites others to activity or growth, arouses to greater activity

Compatible Quality: Inspiration. You are inspired to begin or continue with enthusiasm if you are stimulated by some force, outside or inside, that is powerfully valuable to you.

Colors: magenta, yellow

STIRRING

Definition: active; stimulating; exciting; rousing; thrilling

Compatible Quality: inspiring

STOUT

Word Forms: stouter, stoutest, stouten, stoutly, stoutness, stouthearted

Definitions: (**1**) strong; lusty; sturdy; robust; able-bodied; (**2**) bold; intrepid; valiant; brave; courageous; (**3**) resolute; fortitude; dauntless; (**4**) powerful; forceful

Synonyms: brawny, vigorous, substantial, solid, staunch, enduring

Kindred Qualities: gentle, generous

STRAIGHTFORWARD

Word Forms: straightforwardly, straightforwardness

Definition: possessing undeviating rectitude; upright; honest; open; frank; candid

Quote:
You can run faster if you don't run into walls.
—JERRY DOWNS

Symbol: a *straight line*

STRESS HARDY

Word Form: stress hardiness

Definition: able to maintain stability when faced with the state of bodily or mental tension resulting from factors that tend to alter an existent equilibrium; emotional flexibility

Kindred Qualities: relaxation, clarity, understanding

Quote:
The mind can go either direction under stress—toward positive or toward negative: on or off. Think of it as a spectrum whose extremes are unconsciousness at the negative end and hyperconsciousness at the positive end. The way the mind will lean under stress is strongly influenced by training.
—FRANK HERBERT, *Dune*

Consideration: If your reactions are limited to your defensive mechanisms that are an established pattern, then you are almost required to follow those patterns in a wide range of situations. But if you have an abundance of options to choose from, you can respond more appropriately to individual situations. Expand your repertoire.

In order for these multiple options to be of any use, you have to have the presence of mind to choose an alternative in that split second before your automatic response triggers.

Observation:
Stress Inducers

Pet peeves, deadlines, getting in over your head, another person's pressure, another person's cruelty, blame, worry, guilt, regret, resentment, and fear

Stress Reducers

Healthy diet, stretching, exercise, meditation, deep breathing, massage, sensitive touch, musical appreciation, entertainment, stimulating conversation, laughter, creativity, goal accomplishment, playfulness, positive attitude, romance, sex, acceptance of people or situations, removing yourself from the presence of stress, rewarding yourself for progress, varying your routine, balance between work and relaxation, friendliness, an association with a loyal pet, REM sleep, love

Tips:
- Negative stress can be flipped to positive stress when you realize the growth value inherent in the turmoil.
- The more control you have the more power you feel.
- If you have a noble reason for doing what you're doing, you will be highly motivated. It makes the stress a little bit more acceptable. Committed people will do what they like to do and do something about the stress that they experience.
- Stress-hardy people like a challenge and view difficulty as opportunity.

Advice:

1. Know your life goals. Decide to concentrate on what is worth *being*, rather than what is worth *having*.
2. Stop measuring your life in quantities and begin to think in terms of qualities.
3. Cut back on the "I've got to do everything" idea—delegate.
4. Spend some quiet time to read; stare into space.
5. Cultivate a deep friendship.
   —JANE BRODY, *Type "A" Behavior: Don't Rush Your Life Away*

Note: Jane Brody also advises that we cure "hurry sickness" and conquer hostility.

Comments:

- There are real-life examples of positive qualities under very stressful extremes. Studies done on prisoners of war show that the survivors are the people who are the most flexible—people who can assess the situation, eat whatever is available, and do whatever is necessary. But the question is where to draw the line. If the only decision is to survive at all costs, then it would be okay to betray your comrades. The situation dictates the extremes but the individual dictates the boundaries. The combination of the individual and the situation governs whether a normally positive quality is negative or a normally negative quality is positive.
- If you are escaping your stress with drugs or alcohol, you are doing so to relax and forget. But you should know that you are taking a shortcut that doesn't work. The next time you reach for the temporary solution, do something that will move you onto a healthier path.
- Exercise helps create stress hardiness—all kinds of exercise: physical, emotional (friendship), psychological (reading), and spiritual (meditation).
- Another way to become stress hardy is to be forgiving. A lot of times that which stresses you out is the fact that somebody else is being a jerk. The greater ability you have to forgive them, the less stress you will feel. If the person is behaving wrongly toward you on purpose, you may need to get out of the situation or even confront him or her directly or legally.
- There is hard stress and soft stress. What is soft stress to one would be hard stress to another. But you know what you are capable of without too much trouble and you know what really gets to you.

Usually what you think will be hard stress is not too bad once you get into it. The projection is most often worse than the real thing. Soft stress is necessary to developing your quality of stress hardiness. Hard stresses that you survive will eventually be good for you too.

• It is important to know your threshold of stress. You are not going to be able to avoid the difficulties and stresses of life and it's important not to try to avoid them because there is plenty of growth that is experienced through them. But stress should be managed so that you do not get too overwhelmed.

Stress, to a greater or lesser degree, is exhilarating and positive. If something is difficult but you are coping, even if you are out on your edge, then you are discovering your threshold of stress. As you grow, this threshold changes—expands.

If you are faced with stress beyond your ability, you have to discover some way of dealing with it. You will find that you do have some methods. Note what they are and use them to your advantage—even if you dislike them. Until you learn something differently, these methods are all you've got. Try to keep your eyes open and your options varied.

• In order to measure your individual level of stress hardiness, you need to be in a situation that gives you an indication of your personal edge.

The situation can be accumulative, a build-up of stress. Then something relatively minor could push you over the edge to tell you that that is the edge of your stress hardiness. On the other hand, if you're well rested, have a good self-image, are chemically balanced, healthy, and mature, then you may be able to handle even a major blow smoothly.

Look at a current concern and compare it to a previous one. Earlier you would have folded under this situation, but now it's less of a big deal. It used to be heavy but now you take it in stride.

Symbol: *water* off a duck's back

STRETCHING

Word Forms: stretch, stretched, stretchy, stretchiness

Definitions: (1) expanding; extending; reaching; (2) opening the mind beyond its previous boundaries; (3) elongating something that has the ability to return to its original shape; (4) going beyond an original ability, usually with effort; (5) extending over a distance <*stretching* your thoughts even to the heavens>; (6) exercising the imagination

Quote:
Man's mind stretched to a new idea never goes back to its original dimension.
—OLIVER WENDELL HOLMES

STRIKING

Word Forms: strikingly, strikingness

Definition: impressive; prominent; remarkable; notable; conspicuously attractive

STRIVING

Word Forms: strive, strived, striven, striver, strivingly

Definitions: (1) making great efforts to do one's best; trying very hard; (2) making strenuous efforts toward a goal; (3) struggling vigorously, as in opposition or resistance <*striving* for justice>

Quote:
Living [is] struggling to do something impossible—to succeed, or die, knowing you had tried!
—ANNE MCCAFFREY, *Dragonflight*

Advice: Usually when people use the words *I, me,* or *mine,* they are speaking from their lower selves, their human identities. But at those times when a person is aligned with his or her higher self, that individual can speak with the voice and identity of the higher self and can dictate to the lower self what is needed or desired.

It is ideal to be aligned with one's higher self; therefore, practice that alignment, meditate, talk to your higher self, give over your will to your higher self. "It is my will that Your will be done." Heed the leadings, intuitions, hunches, knowledge, and understanding that is always trying to be impressed on your higher mind. You will filter and change it to align with your current sense of reality, but as you heed those fragments of pure, clear, accurate thought, your current reality will be transformed.

STRONG

Word Forms: stronger, strongest, strength, strongly, strong-minded

Definitions:
(1) physically powerful; having great muscular brawn; robust; stout; in healthy and sound condition; hale; hearty; (2) morally powerful; having command of character or will; (3) intellectually powerful; able to think dynamically and clearly; (4) having special competency or ability in a specified subject or field; (5) easily defended; able to endure; (6) having many resources; controlling wealth, numbers, supplies; (7) having a potent effect; conspicuously productive; (8) affecting the senses distinctly; intense in taste or flavor; (9) intense in degree or quality; not mild; specifically—ardent, passionate, warm; forceful, persuasive, cogent; felt deeply; pronounced, decided; zealous, vigorously active; forthright and unambiguous; clear, distinct; marked; (10) substantial; solid; nourishing

Kindred Qualities: In the physical realm you can't just keep your body hard, you have to keep it supple as well. Same on the emotional, mental, and spiritual levels. You can't just exemplify those qualities that give you strength. You also need to allow yourself the flexibility necessary to encompass the "softer" side of reality, becoming flexible, compassionate, gentle, friendly, helpful, et cetera.

Quote:
What does not destroy me, makes me strong.
                                   —FRIEDRICH WILHELM NIETZSCHE

Color: red

Symbols: *horns;* a coiled *snake; thighs* (Egyptian); the *tiger*

Fiction: *Kwasind,* in Henry Wadsworth Longfellow's *Hiawatha,* is the strongest man who ever lived.

STUDIOUS

Word Forms: study, studied, student, studiously, studiousness

Definitions: (1) fond of or often engaged in instruction; devoted to the acquisition of knowledge; **(2)** characterized by careful attention; diligent; earnest; **(3)** marked by or suggesting purposefulness; **(4)** deliberately or consciously planned

Derivation: Latin, "eager," "zealous"

Quote:
A pupil from whom nothing is ever demanded which he cannot do, never does all he can.
                                   —JOHN STUART MILL

STUNNING

Word Form: stunningly

Definition: possessing striking beauty or excellence

STURDY

Word Forms: sturdier, sturdiest, sturdily, sturdiness

Definitions: (1) strongly built; robust; hardy; vigorous; (2) firm; courageous; indomitable; resolute; not yielding

Consideration: Even if a person is as sturdy as an oak, you can tell by their smile if they have a gentle spirit.

STYLISH

Word Forms: style, stylishly, stylishness

Definitions: (1) characterized by or conforming to the current style or fashion; smart or chic; (2) a unique combination of elements; individualistic

Synonyms: elegant, fashionable, charming

SUAVE

Word Forms: suaver, suavest, suavity, suavely, suaveness

Definition: smoothly gracious or polite; polished; urbane; sophisticated

Derivation: Latin, "sweet," referring to sweetness to the mind versus sweetness to the tongue.

Synonyms: *Suave, urbane, diplomatic,* and *politic* mean pleasantly tactful and well-mannered. *Suave* suggests a specific ability to deal with others easily, without friction. *Urbane* implies high cultivation and poise coming from wide social experience. *Diplomatic* stresses an ability to deal with ticklish situations tactfully. *Politic* implies shrewd as well as tactful and suave handling of people.

SUBLIME

Word Forms: subliming, sublimity, sublimely, sublimeness

Definitions: (1) lofty or exalted in excellence, nature, thought, or style; (2) high honor or dignity; noble; (3) inspiring awe due to outstanding spiritual, intellectual, or moral worth

Compatible Quality: pure

Comment: In chemistry, to sublime a substance is to convert it directly from a solid to a vapor. The purpose is to purify it. Acquiring qualities transforms you from a mere collection of physical molecules into the sublime state of a spiritual being.

SUBTLE

Word Forms: subtlety, subtly, subtleness

Definitions: (1) refined; fine; (2) delicately skillful or clever; artful; cunning; crafty; (3) keen; acute; penetrating; discriminating

Questions: How can I love this person? What form of love does this person need? What do I have that I can offer? How exact and subtle can I be? How do I give the appropriate gift even to the person who is an energy sucker and a power hoarder? First, I must be willing to see the person's value and be generous enough to respect the individual need.

SUCCESSFUL

Word Forms: success, succeed, successfully, successfulness

Definitions: (1) coming about, taking place, or turning out to be as was hoped for; (2) achieving or having achieved a favorable result, specifically, having gained wealth, fame, or quality

People Who Exemplify This Quality: A successful person teaches another person how to succeed in the same way that the original person has succeeded. The student(s), in turn, promises to keep the cycle alive by teaching someone else. The commitment is not fulfilled until the student has reached the predetermined goals and knows how to do it again. The student repays the debt by becoming the teacher.

Quotes:

Success consists of a progressive realization of your own, worthwhile, predetermined goals.

—PAUL J. MEYER

Success is the progressive realization of a worthy ideal.

—EARL NIGHTINGALE

He has achieved success who has lived well, laughed often and loved much; who has gained the respect of intelligent men and the love of little children; who has filled his niche and accomplished his task; who has left the world better than he found it, whether by an improved poppy, a perfect poem, or a rescued soul; who has never lacked appreciation of earth's beauty or failed to express it; who has always looked for the best in others and given the best he had; whose life was an inspiration; whose memory is a benediction.

—A. J. STANLEY

Affirmation: I am succeeding and am helping others to succeed also.

Reflection: There are a lot of people, all of them successful, who say that anybody can make it. Well, it is possible that some of those individuals had some natural qualities that made it easier for them to be successful. They also had some talents that they developed. But even the most naturally gifted person had to reach beyond him- or herself. There is no success without an effort.

Nonetheless, it is important to know your limitations, most of which you can overcome. The time it takes to overcome a particular limitation with the skills you now possess may be longer than you want to take to reach your goal. So, change the goal, *or* acquire a new way of shortcutting the route to the other side of your limitation.

Unfortunately, we tend to get frozen if the perception of our limitations is more powerful than our vision of our desired objectives. The only thing to do is to move. Action thaws.

Considerations:

• Life does include failures, and thank goodness! For without affliction and difficulty, we would not experience the appreciation of accomplishments. But also, since failure and uncertainties do exist, we would not be realistic if we ignored or played down this fact.

You can be crushed by your defeat, thus reducing your self-esteem and hope for recovery. Or, although feeling and experiencing the devastation of the moment, you can be separate from its weight. Let the real you, the one with qualities of resilience, sympathy, courage, and hope, come forth. Watch and feel the experience so that you can learn from the occurrence and use the new knowledge to deal with the even greater successes and failures of future choices.

• Industrialists who treat people as part of the numbers are narrowing their focus down to dollars and cents. If they realized that the people are of primary importance, the quality of the product would be superior. All needs are met if one focuses on, believes in, and nurtures one's highest concepts and most cherished values. Successes are rooted in what is considered best, then success is not just superficial and material, leaving one to wonder, "Why did all this effort not satisfy me?"

Tip:
The Key Qualities to Success

1. Desire, motivation, and a clear idea of what you want
2. Decisiveness
3. Determination (try, try, try again), stick-to-itiveness
4. Patience, an expectation of results after effort
5. Balance of force with fairness

Advice: Do what you love to do. You then have a better chance to succeed because the activity will generate its own energy. The qualities you need are adaptability, courage, independence, cooperation, self-esteem, and practicality.

Admonition: Affirmations and visualizations are powerful focusing mechanisms that do bring to you a physical future that you desire. But be prepared to live the qualities that are inherent in your manifestation.

Questions:
- One can be adept at making money, but how many "successful" people are unhappy, even desperate? Are they striving for financial success because they believe they will find security, meaning, and purpose in their lives through power and comfort?
- How many parents have children and still do not experience the joy that the miracle of new life should bring?
- Ask yourself what it is people need then provide it in a way that you will enjoy.
- Ask yourself if your response in a recent situation was exemplary of the qualities that you have been striving for. Are you getting things done with more efficiency? Are you happy and proud of yourself? Have you been of service to others?

Exercises:
Facing Problems

(from Earl Nightingale's *A Course in Winning*)

1. Write down problems simply—two sentences.
   - Last sentence is a question, i.e., I need more money. How can I get it? or . . . I am in conflict with so-and-so. What can I do to get along better?
   - Do this page after page with all your problems.
2. Think about one problem at a time.
3. List all possible solutions—even if it's "impossible" or inappropriate.

Note: This is a good way of getting the internal worry and fear out in the open. This externalizing gives you the ability to face your "enemy."

Success Formula (from Catherine Ponder's **The Dynamic Laws of Prosperity***)*

1. Persist and persevere—give your best in you even though you may be mentally living beyond it. Keep your spirits high.
2. When fear or doubt arise, put your best foot forward and do something definite to effect a successful feeling.

Color: red

Symbols: *three* or *seven*

SUCCINCT

Word Forms: succinctly, succinctness

Definition: concise, particularly in speech

SUITABLE

Word Forms: suitability, suitably, suitableness

Definition: appropriate; acceptable; fitting; proper; becoming

SUNNY

Word Forms: sunnier, sunniest, sunnily, sunniness

Definition: bright; possessing a warm and cheerful disposition; optimistic

Music: "Walk on the Sunny Side of the Street"

Saying: The sun shines on the wicked and the just alike.

Symbol: *sunshine*

SUPERB

Word Forms: superbly, superbness

Definitions: (1) grand; magnificent; stately; noble; august; (2) rich; elegant; luxurious; (3) splendid; of the highest quality; extremely fine; excellent; very competent

SUPPLE

Word Forms: suppler, supplest, suppled, suppling, supplely, suppleness

Definitions: (**1**) soft and pliant; flexible; compliant; (**2**) limber; lithe; (**3**) an ability of the mind to be resilient and adaptable, especially to something new

SUPPORTIVE

Word Forms: support, supportable, supporter, supportiveness

Definitions: (**1**) upholds by aid, encouragement, or countenance; characterizes one who keeps another from fainting, falling, failing, or declining; encourages the spirits of a person, especially if in need; (**2**) assisting; furthering; forwarding; seconding; helpful

Advice: Instead of getting mad at yourself or someone else for mistakes, get over the disappointment as quickly as possible and then put as much support into the situation as you can.

Symbols: the *crutch;* the *staff;* the *throne*

SURE

Word Forms: surer, surest, surely, sureness, assured, ensured

Definitions: (**1**) unfailing; always effective <a *sure* method>; (**2**) reliable or dependable; trustworthy; (**3**) without doubt, question, or dispute; absolutely true; (**4**) showing no hesitancy; positive; confident; certain; (**5**) never missing; unerring; steady

Saying: *A coup sur* (French): "with sure stroke"; surely

SUREFOOTED

Word Forms: surefootedly, surefootedness

Definition: proceeding carefully; not likely to fail or fall

Symbol: the *ram*

SURE-HANDED

Word Forms: sure-handedly, sure-handedness

Definition: displaying dexterous use of the hands with confidence and proficiency

SURVIVING

Word Forms: survive, survival, survived, survivor

Definitions: (1) remaining alive or in existence; (2) continuing to function or manage in spite of some adverse circumstance or hardship; holding up; enduring

Quotes:
In so far as [the] evolving . . . soul becomes permeated by truth, beauty and goodness as the value-realization of God-consciousness, such a resultant being becomes indestructible. If there is no survival of eternal values in the evolving soul . . . , then mortal existence is without meaning, and life itself is a tragic illusion.
—*The Urantia Book*

Existence on a mountain is simple. Seldom in life does it come any simpler: survival, plus the striving toward a summit. The goal is solidly, three-dimensionally there—you can see it, touch it, stand on it—the way to reach it is well defined, the energy of all is directed towards its achievement. It is this simplicity that strips the veneer off civilization and makes that which is meaningful easier to come by—the pleasure of deep companionship, moments of uninhibited humor, the tasting of hardship, sorrow, beauty, joy.

—THOMAS F. HORNBEIN, *Everest, The West Ridge*

Consideration: Become positive qualities and you will survive. The first question is, What does it [your chosen quality] mean? Give it definition and scope and range so you can wrap your mind around it. Then ask, How do I make it become me? What's interesting is that the technique of making it become you is the same for making sure that you've got it, which is, to use it, to share it with somebody. You can't give it away unless you've got it.

Comment: The first impulse of a being is to survive. That is usually thought of as physical survival. This is important, of course, for a while. But we have an abundance of evidence that physical survival does end. This is why we turn to the hope and faith that there is a form of survival beyond the physical. Unless you were with Jesus when he lived and died and saw him on Easter Sunday, you do not have personal proof of life after death. So your only hope is Hope and Faith.

SUSTAINING

Word Forms: sustain, sustained, sustainer, sustainable, sustainment, sustenance, self-sustaining

Definitions: (1) upholding, supportive, maintaining, or enduring; **(2)** providing for; encouraging; confirming; **(3)** keeping up one's spirits, especially in the face of difficulty and hard times

Symbol: *Strength* (tarot)

SVELTE

Word Forms: sveltely, svelteness

Definition: slender and graceful, lithe; possessing clean lines, sleek

SWEET

Word Forms: sweeter, sweetest, sweets, sweeten, sweetened, sweetening, sweetly, sweetness, sweetheart, sweetie, sweetie pie, sweet-tempered, sweet talk

Definitions: (1) something or someone pleasing or gratifying to the mind <*sweet* words of affection>; **(2)** mild, gentle, meek, or kind; soft or delicate; pure and clean; **(3)** obliging civility; courteous; gracious; amiable manners or behavior; an affable disposition; good-humored; reasonable; **(4)** pleasant to the sense of taste; harmonious to the ear; attractive to look at; aromatic to the sense of smell; comfortable, soft, or cozy to the tactile sense; **(5)** describes a beloved friend, child, or lover
   See also: *Suave*

Saying: Sweetness and light (a harmonious association of beauty and intelligence)

Symbols: *honey; sugar; nectar*

SWEETHEART

Definitions: (1) a loved one; a darling; **(2)** a generous, friendly person; anyone that arouses loyal affection

SWIFT

Word Forms: swifter, swiftest, swiftly, swiftness, swift-footed

Definitions: (1) quick; ready to move; celeritous; prompt; speedy; **(2)** able to shift from idea to idea rapidly; quick-witted; **(3)** does what must be done without delay; efficient

Quote:
Let everyone be swift to hear; slow to speak; slow to wrath.

—JAMES 1:19

Symbols: *lightning* (American Indian); the *horse*

Fiction: *Camilla*, from Virgil's *Aeneid*, was the queen of the Volscians. She was so swift that she could run over standing grain without causing it to bend.

SYMMETRICAL

Word Forms: symmetry, symmetrically, symmetricalness

Definitions: (1) possessing beauty of form arising from balanced proportions; (2) showing similarity of form or arrangement on either side of a dividing line or plane; having correspondence of opposite parts in size, shape, and position

Quotes:
There is no excellent beauty that hath not some strangeness in the proportion.

—FRANCIS BACON

When we try to pick out anything by itself, we find it hitched to everything else in the universe.

—JOHN MUIR

Consideration: Those who study such things have calculated that the perfect proportion, the Golden Section, is the square root of 5 plus 1 divided by 2. This ratio is 1 to 1.618. A is to B as B is to A and B. This is the ratio of most of nature's most beautiful things: the physical human body, DNA, the spiral nautilus, et cetera.

Comment: Symmetry is beautiful in physical manifestation. Symmetry in the soul of a being is not only seen but is also felt.

Symbol: *Gemini* (zodiac)

SYMPATHETIC

Word Forms: sympathy, sympathize, sympathetically

Definitions: (1) demonstrating affinity between persons or of one person for another; (2) marks an action or response arising from compassion; (3) in agreement; in harmony; in accord; (4) possessing a mutual liking or understanding arising from sameness of feeling; empathetic; (5) having the ability to enter into another person's mental state or feelings; especially showing pity or empathy for another's trouble or suffering
    See also: *Nonjudgmental*

Comment: Although you can sympathize with and for another, it is not a good idea to try to sympathize for yourself. It too easily turns into self-pity and contemplation of all the reasons you have for feeling sorry for yourself. When you are in need of sympathy is just the time when you must focus on the talents you have, the things you like, the people you admire, the accomplishments you have made, and the good you can do.

Colors: red, green

SYNERGISTIC

Word Forms: synergy, synergist, synergetic, synergic, synergism, synectic, synergistically

Definitions: (1) cooperative; working together in harmony; (2) characterizes separate agents, persons, or qualities that when acting in unison have a greater total effect than the sum of their individual values; (3) describes a balanced or symmetrical collaboration, teamwork

Synonyms: A *synectic* exercise is the bringing together of a select group of diverse personalities and areas of expertise for creative thinking about a specific problem with the free use of metaphor and analogy. *Brainstorming* is the spontaneous contribution of ideas, no matter how obscure, from any group in the hope of solving a specific problem or to generate a general stimulation of creative thinking.

Symbols: cosmic synergy—the *hurricane* (American Indian); *Sagittarius* (zodiac)

SYSTEMATIC

Word Forms: system, systematical, systematics, systematize, systematizer, systemic, systematization, systematically, systematicness

Definitions: (1) methodical; precisely organized; having a logical plan; thorough; **(2)** having the need to order things, thoughts, ideas, or systems into an integrated whole

Advice: It is easy for a systematic person to get caught in the rut of efficiency by pursuing a task in a linear manner. If you add the qualities of flexibility and objectivity, you will be able to focus on detail as well as manage an overview.

TACTFUL

Word Forms: tact, tactfully, tactfulness

Definitions: (1) possessing a keen sense of what to say or do to avoid giving offense; having skill in dealing with difficult or delicate situations; diplomatic; **(2)** possessing a shrewd sense of what is appropriate, tasteful, or aesthetically pleasing; discriminating

Familial Quality: finesse

Comment: To be tactful is *not* to be compromising. One must perceive the consciousness of one's audience to understand what and how to say precisely what is needed.

TALENTED

Word Form: talent

Definitions: (1) possessing a faculty, natural gift, or endowment, from the parable of talents, Matthew 25; **(2)** exhibiting eminent abilities in art; having superior genius in science; **(3)** skilled; showing great capacity

Compatible Quality: creative

Derivation: Greek, referring to a balance or scale, also a weighed amount of precious metal

Quote:
> If you've got a talent, sometimes you've got to take that talent to where it is appreciated.
>> —JOHN RAITT to his daughter, Bonnie, when she asked why he wasn't home so much

TAME

Word Forms: tamed, taming, tamer, tamest, tamable, tamely, tameness

Definitions: (1) mild; gentle; **(2)** civilized; obedient; behaved; tractable; **(3)** humble

Kindred Qualities: courageous, spontaneous

Symbol: a *tame animal*

TASTEFUL

Word Forms: taste, tasting, taster, tasty, tastefully, tastefulness

Definitions: (1) possessing the faculty of discerning with appreciation beauty, art, order, proper behavior, style, nature, or character; **(2)** having the ability to act in a fitting or politic manner; tactful; **(3)** elegant; decorous; refined

Synonyms: sapid, flavorful, appetizing, piquant

TECHNICAL

Word Forms: technician, technology, technicality, technically

Definitions: (1) having to do with the practical, industrial, or mechanical arts or the applied sciences, recently computer skills; **(2)** showing technique <a *technical* skill>

Kindred Quality: intuitive

Observation: The following table, "Man versus Machine," is from *Human Engineering Guide for Equipment Designers* by Wesley E. Woodson and Donald W. Conover.

MAN EXCELS IN	MACHINES EXCEL IN
Detection of certain forms of very low energy levels	Monitoring people and machines
Sensitivity to an extremely wide variety of stimuli	Performing routine, repetitive, or very precise operations
Perceiving patterns and making generalizations about them	Responding very quickly to control signals
Detecting signals in high noise levels	Exerting great force, smoothly and precisely
Storing large amounts of information for long periods—recalling relevant facts at appropriate moments	Storing and recalling large amounts of information in short time periods
Ability to exercise judgment where events cannot be completely defined	Perform complex and rapid computation with high accuracy
Improvising and adopting flexible procedures and alternate solutions	Sensitive to infrared, radio waves, et cetera, beyond the human range

MAN EXCELS IN	MACHINES EXCEL IN
Ability to react to unexpected low-probability events	Able to do many different things at one time
Inductive reasoning	Deductive processes
Ability to profit from experience and alter a course of action	Insensitivity to extraneous factors
Ability to perform fine manipulation, especially where misalignment appears unexpectedly	Ability to repeat operations very rapidly, continuously and precisely the same way over a long period
Ability to continue to perform even when overloaded	Operating in environments which are hostile or beyond human tolerance
Original problem solving	

TEMPERATE

Word Forms: temperance, temperative, tempered, good-tempered, temperately, temperateness

Definitions: (1) moderate indulgence in or use of substance, speech, or action; self-restrained; self-controlled; (2) patient; calm; cool; in control of passion and feelings; (3) in proper proportion; balanced

Familial Qualities: symmetrical, synergistic

Symbol: *fourteen;* a *beach*

Fiction: *Sir Guyon*, a knight in Spenser's *Faërie Queen*, the personification of temperance and self-restraint

TENACIOUS

Word Forms: tenacity, tenaciously, tenaciousness

Definitions: (1) holding fast to ideas, habits, or possessions; (2) having a highly retentive memory

Synonyms: determined, persistent, persevering, tough, courageous

Quote:
Let me tell you the secret that has led me to my goal. My strength lies solely in my tenacity.
—LOUIS PASTEUR

Symbol: *bamboo* symbolizes tenacity and endurance.

TENDER

Word Forms: tenderer, tenderest, tenderly, tenderness

Definitions: (1) youthful and delicate; having the fragility of a baby; (2) expressive of affection, love, consideration, or friendship; gentle; (3) sensitive to impressions, emotions, or moral influences; (4) sensitive to others' feelings; sympathetic; compassionate

Synonyms: yielding, soft, careful, mild, meek, merciful

Colors: indigo, green

TENDERHEARTED

Word Forms: tenderheartedly, tenderheartedness

Definition: softhearted; sympathetic; easily moved to love or pity; compassionate; affectionate

TERRIFIC

Word Form: terrifically

Definition: unusually good; great; excellent; extraordinary; wonderful; magnificent; awesome

THANKFUL

Word Forms: thank, thanks, thankfully, thankfulness, thanksgiving

Definition: impressed with a sense of kindness received and ready to acknowledge it; grateful; appreciative

Exercise: Write out a list of what you are thankful for.

I am thankful for the following [things]. For the plenty of Mother Earth, I am grateful.

I am thankful for the following [beings]. The love I feel for and from them is healing. I thank them for their support and friendliness.

I am thankful for the following [experiences]. I know that it is through experiences that I grow. I am thankful for the happy and peaceful times in my life. I am also grateful for the difficulties and disappointments because I know that some of my greatest blessings have come from encompassing them.

I am thankful for my [qualities]. I realize that I have some of them as gifts. I have others because of my choices. I will continue to strive to enhance my positive qualities.

I am thankful for my self, my ideas, my heart, and my life. I will cheerfully and faithfully continue to grow.

THERAPEUTIC

Word Forms: therapy, therapist, therapeutical, therapeutically

Definitions: (1) concerned with healing the body, mind, or spirit; **(2)** calming; relaxing

THINKING

Word Forms: think, thought, thinker

Definitions: (1) the power of reasoning and conceiving ideas; imaginative; **(2)** the ability of a person to form ideas and mental images; **(3)** given to pondering an idea or suggestion; cogitating; **(4)** focusing on something in order to arrive at a conclusion using logic, judgment, and inference
See also: *Thoughtful*

Synonyms: fancying, realizing, envisioning, reflecting, speculating, deliberating

Saying:
Cogito, ergo sum (Latin): "I think, therefore I am."
—RENÉ DESCARTES

Quotes:
Then only are we thinking when the subject on which we are thinking cannot be thought out.
—GOETHE

If you realized how powerful your thoughts are, you would never think a negative thought.
—PEACE PILGRIM, *Steps Toward Inner Peace*

Observation:

TYPES OF THINKING

STRATEGIC	PERSONALITY RELATED	DISCIPLINARY	OVERALL QUALITY	MISCELLANEOUS
Additive	Aggressive	Anthropological	Brilliant	Aesthetic
Analytic	Extroverted	Financial	Clear	Constructive

STRATEGIC	PERSONALITY RELATED	DISCIPLINARY	OVERALL QUALITY	MISCELLANEOUS
Applied	Introverted	Historical	Deep	Creative
Backward	Kinky	Humanistic	Keen	Efficient
Broad	Optimistic	Legal	Mercurial	Expressive
Converging		Market-oriented	Methodical	Innovative
Critical		Mathematical	Quick	Insightful
Decisive		Medical	Right	Instinctive
Deductive		Product-oriented	Powerful	Literal
Diverging		Scientific	Productive	Practical
Eliminative		Sociological		Precise
Focused		Technological		Random
Forward		Verbal		Visual
Imaginative				Wishful
Incisive				
Inductive				
Intuitive				
Judgmental				
Narrow				
Objective				
Qualitative				
Quantitative				
Rational				
Speculative				
Subjective				
Theoretical				

Advice: A teacher must know the level of each student and challenge each with those things that are just outside his or her current level of understanding. But it is the responsibility of the students to commit themselves to strive for understanding. If the challenge motivates them, they will give it some thought.

Comments:
- To get from one idea to its completion you need more ideas.
- Complexity results from keeping ideas in your head. Create systems that help you express your thoughts. Holding ideas takes energy—write them down.

- Thinking people have more choice to apply their knowledge to a new situation that is unrelated to the original situation.

Color: sky blue

Symbols: thought—the *hat;* the *helmet;* the *pansy*

THOROUGH

Word Forms: thoroughgoing, thoroughly, thoroughness

Definitions: (1) very exact, accurate, attentive, or painstaking, especially in regard to details; complete; **(2)** having full command of an art or talent **(3)** executed without negligence or omissions <a *thorough* search>

Synonyms: perfect, absolute

Compatible Qualities: focused, zealous

THOUGHTFUL

Word Forms: thought, thoughtfully, thoughtfulness

Definitions: (1) showing respect for others; considerate; courteous; **(2)** possessing the power of reasoning and conceiving ideas; imaginative; **(3)** characterized by or manifesting careful thought; **(4)** occupied with or given to thought; contemplative; meditative; reflective; cognitive; **(5)** heedful; mindful; careful; attentive
See also: *Thinking*

Kindred Qualities: creative, curious, persistent, flexible, alert, open

Reflection: Others deserve your special attention because they are lovable and valuable. If you realize their worth, you will wish to be good to them—thoughtful, considerate, and courteous.

Comments:

- In order to be thoughtful you have to know (or gamble on knowing) what the other person desires, needs, or wants. There are subtle signs, but there is one way that is pretty sure: Ask.
- Positive thoughts expand. Negative thoughts contract.

THRIFTY

Word Forms: thrift, thriftily, thriftiness

Definitions: (1) practicing prudent economy; frugal; sparing; using good management of money and other resources; **(2)** thriving; successful; prosperous; fortunate

Synonym: careful

Quote:
You cannot bring about prosperity by discouraging thrift. You cannot strengthen the weak by weakening the strong. You cannot help the wage earner by pulling down the wage payer. You cannot further the brotherhood of man by encouraging class hatred. You cannot keep out of trouble by spending more than you earn. You cannot build character and courage by taking away man's initiative and independence. You cannot help men permanently by doing what they could and should do for themselves.

—Abraham Lincoln

THRILLING

Word Forms: thrill, thrilled, thrillingly, thrillingness

Definition: causing a pleasant tingling sensation, a feeling of sudden emotional excitement

THRIVING

Word Forms: thrive, thrived, throve, thriven

Definitions: (1) prosperous; experiencing increase or success, especially because of good management; **(2)** flourishing; growing

Quote:
In order that people may be happy in their work, three things are needed: they must be for it, they must not do too much of it, and they must have a sense of success in it.
—JOHN RUSKIN

TIDY

Word Forms: tidied, tidying, tidily, tidiness

Definitions: (1) in good order; neat; organized; systematic; methodical; precise; **(2)** appropriate, especially in dress and manner for a particular occasion; **(3)** characterizes an acceptable and fair solution to a problem

TIMELY

Word Forms: time, timelier, timeliest, timeless, timing, timer, timeliness, time frame, timesaving, time-honored, time-tested

Definitions: (1) happening, done, or said at a suitable time; opportune; **(2)** arriving at the appointed moment; well-timed; **(3)** appropriate or adapted to the times or the occasion; **(4)** possessing the ability to select the best time for doing or saying something in order to achieve a desired effect

Kindred Quality: prepared

Quotes:

For everything there is an appointed time, even a time for every affair under heaven.

—ECCLESIASTES 3:1

Dost thou love life? Then do not squander time, for that is the stuff life is made of.

—BENJAMIN FRANKLIN

God . . . does not recognize earth-time. To the universe, four days is no different than four billion light years.

—ROBERT JAMES WALLER, *The Bridges of Madison County*

Nobody sees a flower—really—it is so small it takes time—and to see takes time, like to have a friend takes time.

—GEORGIA O'KEEFFE

My hour has not yet come.

—JESUS

Note: Do not be forced into something that you are not ready for. Be wise in your judgment of when the best time is to act.

Affirmation: I have enough time to do everything I enjoy.

Reflection: There is an ideal pace at which you should proceed. You don't want to be going too fast or too slow. Our pace is restricted by our own lack of courage, our emotional blocks, our comfortable patterns, and our restrictive belief systems. Even so, you can only proceed from where you are.

You can accelerate your pace, but it needs to be done globally, moving forward emotionally, mentally, physically, and spiritually. Keep it all in balance. If you ignore some aspect, you will find yourself out of balance and will have to go back to it anyway. If you are going to accelerate your pace, you need to accelerate evenly.

Consideration: Take the time to do it right. Prepare as best you can so that you will be able to do your project correctly, to the best of your ability.

When there is a deadline on a job, outside pressures are creating stress and you feel badly because you have to cut some corners. Recognize the balance between efficiency and effectiveness.

If you possess a high level of attention to detail you will have to curb it. Instead of taking it to the fourth decimal, all you can do is take it to the first decimal. Ask yourself if it is good enough. Good enough doesn't mean shabby, it means high-quality work under the circumstances.

Also you have to assess the nature of the job. If you're building cabinets then you have to have a high level of perfection. If you're throwing together a shipping pallet, then you don't have to have as accurate a measurement. Same thing with any job. You have to know where the boundaries are. But within that relativity there is still the consciousness of doing it right. You know the old saying: "Take the time to do it right or you'll find there is always time to do it over."

Comments:
- One of the main reasons to do your best while you're "here," in time and space, is because you can't go back. You can't reverse time and do what you wanted to do previously. You've missed an opportunity.
- Since you have all eternity:
  1. You can give yourself a break.
  2. You can find an infinite number of ways to motivate yourself to do your best.
  3. You can take the time to find your right livelihood.
- If you are able to see exactly how to fit the luggage into the car trunk, you have a good space sense. Translate your space talent into a time talent by fitting your schedule into the day.

Question: Are you always late or put things off? What does it take to have good timing? Pay attention to organization, prioritization, focus, vision, and the ability to graciously break off from the current appointment to get to the next one on time.

A good way to motivate yourself to be on time is to have concern for the people who are waiting for you. Turn on that consideration switch.

Symbols: time—a *spindle;* a *river;* a *clock;* the *wheel*

TIRELESS

Word Forms: tirelessly, tirelessness, untiring

Definition: energetic, dynamic, untiring; indefatigable

TOLERANT

Word Forms: tolerate, tolerable, tolerance, toleration, tolerantly, tolerably, tolerableness

Definitions: (1) enduring pain or hardship; fortitude; stamina; **(2)** having sympathy or indulgence for beliefs or practices differing from or conflicting with one's own; **(3)** engaging in the act of allowing something; having forbearance; **(4)** relative capacity of an organism to grow or thrive when subjected to unfavorable environmental factors

Compatible Qualities: open-minded, perspicacious

Consequential Quality: friendship

Reflection: One of the ways that we make people less than lovable is to create or believe propaganda that dehumanizes them, i.e., calling them by vicious names. These names become negative categories that support a prejudice, that allow one to dismiss or to hate.

Drop the stereotypes. Allow yourself to accept the individual. Accept the fact that each person is striving just as you are. If they prove themselves to embrace evil, then be cautious if you have to deal with them. It is poison to you if you hate them. Hate the sin but love the sinner.

TOUCHING

Word Forms: touch, touched, touchable, touchingly

Definition: arousing emotions of tenderness or compassion; pathos; marked by sensitivity

TOUGH

Word Forms: tougher, toughest, toughen, toughened, toughening, toughy, toughly, toughness, tough-minded, tough it out

Definitions: (1) strong but pliant; yielding to force without tearing or breaking; flexible; resilient; **(2)** strong; robust; hardy; durable; vigorous; **(3)** capable of enduring hardship; sturdy; resistant; **(4)** resolute; firm; tenacious

Kindred Qualities: gentle, reasonable

Symbol: the *sword*

TRACTABLE

Word Forms: tractability, tractably, tractableness

Definitions: (1) compliant; allowing oneself to be managed; docile; **(2)** malleable; easily taught

Comments:
- It is a great joy for managers to have on their team people who are professional—people who are willing to take initiative on their own as well as cooperate within the team.
- It is a pleasure to have a student who is striving to learn. Those who learn easily because of a natural aptitude are easy. But those (gifted or not) who apply themselves are the most satisfying.

TRADITIONAL

Word Forms: tradition, traditionalist, traditionalize, traditionally

Definition: valuing the truth handed down from age to age or ancestor to posterity, originally orally but also now written

Familial Quality: conservative

Observation: There is a traditional conflict between those who hold to the established ways of the past and those who seek a more modern approach. This conflict need not be as divisive if those involved focus on the truth and value of each strategy.

TRAILBLAZING

Word Forms: trailblaze, trailblazer

Definition: pioneering in any field; pathfinding; making or finding a new way; trailbreaking

TRANQUIL

Word Forms: tranquility, tranquilize, tranquilizer, tranquilly, tranquilness

Definitions: (1) free from emotional disturbance or agitation; calm; serene; placid; (2) quiet; even; steady

Too Far: lax

Quote:
It is neither wealth nor splendor, but tranquility and occupation, which gives happiness.
—THOMAS JEFFERSON

Color: green

TREASURED

Word Forms: treasure, treasuring

Definition: greatly valued or highly prized; cherished; appreciated

Compatible Quality: abundant

Admonition: Remember that your fond memories are treasured possessions.

Symbol: supreme spirituality through purity of the soul—the *Golden Fleece*

TRIM

Word Forms: trimmer, trimmed, trimming, trimly, trimness

Definitions: (1) being in good order; firm; snug; neat; tidy; (2) being in good physical shape; (3) well-proportioned; smartly designed; (4) a modification of your viewpoint or opinion to satisfy another; compromise

TRIUMPHANT

Word Forms: triumph, triumphal, triumphantly

Definitions: (1) notably successful; victorious; (2) rejoicing for victory; exulting in success; elated

Quote:
The most important thing in life is not the triumph but the struggle.
—Baron Pierre de Coubertin, Father of the
Modern Olympic Games

Comment: Triumphant is a quality of the present and past. It is important to appreciate what has been accomplished. Contemplate the fact of having been triumphant and you can project that into the future. What is the next goal that you expect to be triumphant in? Visualize it clearly and experience the victory even before it happens.

Color: red

Symbols: inner victories over negatives—a *laurel wreath;* the *Chariot* (tarot)

TRUE

Word Forms: truer, truest, trued, truing, truly, trueness, truehearted, true love, truism, true hearted

Definitions: (1) conforming to fact; real; **(2)** genuine; pure; legitimate; **(3)** faithful; loyal to a friend, idea, or ideal; steadfast; **(4)** honest; sincere; upright; **(5)** reliable; certain; **(6)** exact; precise; accurate; conforming to a standard; **(7)** reflecting the essential character, true meaning; **(8)** in proper order; **(9)** logically necessary

Quote:

> *This above all: to thine own self be true*
> *And it must follow, as the night the day,*
> *Thou canst not then be false to any man.*
> —WILLIAM SHAKESPEARE, *King Henry IV*

TRUE-BLUE

Definition: a person of inflexible honesty and fidelity; loyal; faithful

TRUSTING

Word Forms: trust, trustable, trustworthy, trusty, trustingly, trustingness, entrust

Definitions: (1) placing confidence in; relying on; believing in the honesty, integrity, or justice of; **(2)** without fear of consequences; allowing exposure; open-hearted; confiding **(3)** certain; sure; expectant; hopeful **(4)** suppositional

Compatible Quality: trustworthy

Too Far: Gullible. Be wise to the signs that you are being played for a sap. If the person you trust is a real good liar, don't beat yourself up. You were true to your ideals. Give yourself credit and learn from the experience.

Saying: In God we trust.

Quote:

As soon as you trust yourself, you will know how to live.

—GOETHE

Consideration: A blind person takes for granted the fact that he or she occasionally needs to trust someone else; they need to put their faith in someone else as a guide from time to time. Visualize a bicycle built for two; the person in front is sighted, the person in back is blind. They enjoy being together and they each play their part.

Each person is sometimes a leader and sometimes a follower. We are all somewhat blind and somewhat sighted.

Observation: If you trust someone, you will find in their actions reasons to trust them. You do not know their motives but you will create in your mind and heart reasons enough to give them not just the benefit of the doubt but a blindness to doubt.

If you do not trust someone or if you have a suspicious nature, then even the most innocent actions will be clothed in a negative scrutiny. This is even done with the self.

Comment: Trust is linked with expectations. If someone says, "I'm going to pick you up at three," and doesn't show up until four, that person has set up and broken an expectation. There was no reason for you to believe that that person wouldn't pick you up at three. But the next time he or she makes a promise you're going to be wary.

TRUSTWORTHY

Word Forms: trustful, trustworthily, trustworthiness

Definition: reliable, worthy of confidence; dependable

Comment: There are some things that are so continuously trustworthy that we end up forgetting that they exist. One that comes to mind is gravity. But we invent a lot of others: God, beliefs, Mommy and Daddy, our job, et cetera.

Qualities that are constant are growth, choice, change, and love.

TRUTH

Word Forms: true, truths, truthful, truthfulness

Definitions: (1) honesty; integrity; veracity; **(2)** the ideal of fundamental reality apart from and transcending perceived experience; **(3)** sincerity in action, character, and utterance; **(4)** the quality of being in accordance with or conforming to experience, facts, or reality; actual existence

Sayings:

The truth will set you free.

Magna est veritas et praevalebit (Latin): "Truth is mighty and will prevail."

Vincit omnia veritas (Latin): "Truth conquers all things."

Quotes:

Nonviolence and truth are inseparable and presuppose one another. There is no God higher than truth.
—MOHANDAS KARAMCHAND GANDHI

Unless there is truth, and unless people tell the truth, there is always danger in everything outside of the individual.
—T. H. WHITE, *The Once and Future King*

Reflection: Thinking breeds facts but feeling leads to truth.

Consideration: Individuals respond to truth in their guts by the use of their "knowing centers." Even if the information or person is partially truthful, there is still an unerring response to that portion which is truthful.

Consider a good liar. He or she projects the positive qualities of sincerity and clarity and has a convincing communicative style. But the listener needs to be perceptive in judgment, so as to correctly segregate the true from the false.

This works not only externally but also internally. Listen to your "self talk" with your intuitive truth center. This is useful if you are exploring a subject of which you have a vague understanding or belief.

It is nice to share with a friend. If you say something that is inappropriate, the other person reacts with his or her truth center, and if you are sensitive and paying attention, you will both know that something needs to be adjusted. But you still have to choose whether your friend's reaction is because of objective or subjective truth.

This internal truth guide works just as well on all levels of fact, meaning, and value.

Comments:

- In Eastern philosophy, the three aspects of the Higher Nature are called Satchitananda: *sat* means "truth," *chit* means "conscious," and *ananda* means "bliss."

- Truth can be lived. You can become it. Error, evil, sin, negativity, and iniquity cannot become a permanent part of you, because, if you cling to them, you are choosing that which is unreal. If you choose to *be* unreal, you are choosing *not to be*. Truth always has an advantage over evil in that truth can be continually lived in experience. Error eventually leads to a dead end. Sooner or later error will prove its lack of value.

  Yet error has the purpose of showing us the edge that we will be able to stay away from when we encounter it again—if we're smart. Error nudges us back toward goodness and reality.

Colors: green, blue

Symbols: spiritual truths or knowledge—*gems* or *treasures;* a *hand mirror; nine;* the *torch*

Fiction: *Una,* a lovely damsel in Spenser's *Faërie Queen,* is the personification of truth.

Mythology: *Ma,* in Egyptian mythology, is the goddess of truth and justice.

UNDERSTANDING

Word Forms: understand, understood, understandingly

Definitions: (1) comprehension; knowledge; discernment; (2) the power or ability to think and learn; intelligence; judgment; sense; (3) friendly or harmonious relationship; an agreement of opinion or feeling; an adjustment of differences; (4) fully aware not only of the meaning or nature of something but also of its implications

Consequential Quality: tolerance

Sayings:
Damnant quod non intelligunt (Latin): "They condemn what they do not understand."

Tout comprendre c'est pardonner (French): "To understand all is to forgive all."

The saying "walk a mile in his moccasins" means to see things from another's perspective. Even though you will then be better able to see things how they see them, the common misunderstanding is that you will then agree with their point of view. As always, you will retain your own unique understanding. You cannot "become" the other person no matter how accurately you understand them. Knowing is not agreeing.

Quotes:
The hardest thing to understand is why we can understand anything at all.

—ALBERT EINSTEIN

It is good to give when asked, but it is better to give unasked, through understanding.

—KAHLIL GIBRAN, *The Prophet*

Love is the only way to grasp another human being in the innermost core of his personality.

—VIKTOR FRANKL

Consideration: Sometimes you have to suspend your position to understand someone else's. It is important to do both: know what your understanding is and allow for the other's understanding. If you can do both you will be able to incorporate some of the other's ideas, feelings, and sensibilities into your own. It is only fair to get a good idea of the other side, if for no other reason than to know where to draw the line.

Comment: When someone does or says something from left field, it is *your* left field that you are referring to. It may be their pitcher's mound.

Colors: yellow, indigo

Symbol: a *silver key*

UNIQUE

Word Forms: uniquely, uniqueness

Definitions: (1) existing as the only one or as the sole example; solitary in type or characteristics; **(2)** having no like or equal; unparalleled; incomparable; **(3)** singular; unusual; extraordinary

Quotes:
When strangers meet, great allowance should be made for differences of custom and training.
—FRANK HERBERT, *Heretics of Dune*

If we live truly, we shall see truly—insist on yourself; never imitate—nothing is at last sacred but the integrity of your own mind, nothing can bring you peace but yourself, nothing can bring you peace but the triumph of principles.
—RALPH WALDO EMERSON

Comment: Everybody needs something different.

UNSTOPPABLE

Word Form: unstoppably

Definition: determined; resolute; indefatigable

UPBEAT

Definitions: (1) happy; optimistic; cheerful; **(2)** marked by an increase in activity; prosperous

UPLIFTING

Word Forms: uplift, uplifted

Definitions: (1) bringing to a higher moral, cultural, intellectual, or spiritual level; **(2)** a bettering of condition; **(3)** an emotional or spiritual exaltation

UPRIGHT

Word Forms: uprighteously, uprightly, uprightness

Definitions: (1) standing erect; carrying oneself with pride; **(2)** adhering to moral rectitude

Synonyms: Pure, principled, fair, equitable, upstanding. *Upright, honest, just, conscientious, scrupulous,* and *honorable* mean having or showing a strict regard for what is morally right. *Upright* implies a strict adherence to moral principles. *Honest* stresses adherence to such virtues as truthfulness, candor, and fairness. *Just* stresses conscious choice and regular practice of what is right or equitable. *Conscientious* and *scrupulous* imply an active moral sense governing all one's actions and painstaking efforts to follow one's conscience. *Honorable* suggests a firm holding to codes of right behavior and the guidance of a high sense of honor and duty.

Symbol: the *Ch'i-lin* (Chinese)—similar to the Unicorn, with two horns

UPSTANDING

Word Form: upstandingness

Definition: having integrity; upright; honorable; straightforward

Symbol: a tall *tree*

UP-AND-COMING

Definition: enterprising; alert to opportunity; promising; industriously successful

UP-TO-DATE

Definition: modern; knowing what is in vogue in attitude or style

URBANE

Word Forms: urbanity, urbanely, urbaneness

Definition: having polite manners; courteous; civil; suave; elegant or refined; sophisticated; polished

USEFUL

Word Forms: usefully, usefulness

Definition: having the power to produce good or profit; beneficial; helpful; giving service

UTILITARIAN

Word Forms: utility, utilitarianism

Definition: possessing the quality or property of being useful; *utilitarianism:* an ethical doctrine that seeks the greatest happiness for the greatest number of people

Saying: *Abusus non tollit usum* (Latin): "Abuse does not take away use" [Abuse is not an argument against proper use].

VALOROUS

Word Forms: valor, valorously, valiant, valiancy, valiance, valiantly

Definition: possessing a strength of mind or spirit that enables a person to encounter difficulty with courage; bold or determined if facing danger

Derivation: Old French, "to be of worth"

Synonyms: brave, stout, intrepid, knightly, fearless, heroic

Symbols: the *lion;* the *wolf*

Mythology: *Hector*, in Homer's *Iliad*, was the most valiant of the Trojans and the noblest hero.

VALUABLE

Word Forms: value, valuably, valuableness

Definitions: (1) having qualities worthy of esteem; being highly thought of; considered a treasure; **(2)** having considerable worth monetarily, emotionally, personally, spiritually

Quote:

We do not believe in ourselves until someone reveals that deep inside us something is valuable, worth listening to, worthy of our trust, sacred to our touch. Once we believe in ourselves we can risk curiosity, wonder, spontaneous delight or any experience that reveals the human spirit.

—E. E. CUMMINGS

Consideration: Cloistered nuns and monks spend their whole lives in silence, praying. They pray for the pope, starving children, and the good of the planet. Their belief is that they are having a positive effect. And yet, by all accounts, things are getting worse. So are they wasting their time? No, because they are being positive. And the positive energy has a dual effect. First, on a personal level it is making them more real because they are becoming closer to the qualities that make up the universe. Those positive choices are of value in and of themselves. And second, the prayer energy is being used for something. It is positive energy; therefore, it must have a positive effect.

Comment: Einstein said that you can only chase down the facts by what is observable. On the level of science there is no question that that is the way it works. On the level of being, which is the level of experience, you can actually get inside what you are observing via feelings and recognition of values. You can be on both sides.

Question: How do you experience experience? By being existent on a higher level of reality. By embodying the higher values of positive qualities.

VENERABLE

Word Forms: venerability, venerate, veneration, venerative, venerator, venerably, venerableness

Definition: worthy of reverence, honor, or respect mingled with a degree of awe; worthy of respect because of distinction or goodness

Symbol: an *older person*

VENTILIOUS

(This is a word form that I made up.)

Word Forms: vent, ventilate, ventilation, venter

Definitions: (1) characterizes something that circulates fresh air into a space, thus driving out stale air and freshening the space; **(2)** having the ability to bring a fresh point of view into a situation, the ability to breathe new life into, as a ballplayer who makes a great play and inspires his or her teammates to excel; **(3)** marks the act of bringing something out into the open, as a grievance or a problem; **(4)** describes the person who, when angry, frustrated, or immature, has the ability to vent his or her negative energy, usually in the form of some physical or social activity, or by vocalizing with a friend or professional counsellor

Derivation: From the Latin *Ventus*, meaning "the wind"

Familial Quality: stress hardy

Quote:
Where there is no ventilation, fresh air is declared unwholesome.
—GEORGE BERNARD SHAW

Gendlerism: The following is written in the style of Janet Ruth Gendler's *The Book of Qualities*.

Ventilious entertains at children's parties with ventriloquism, juggling, and clowning around. He creates wind sculptures and kites. And he works as a volunteer for the Better Air Campaign.

Ventilious is a much sought after arbitrator. His fresh point of view and sense of humor make him perfect for the job. If you feel cluttered and confused, he will be glad to introduce you to Clarity.

He's hoping to have someday combined just the right essences in a bouquet, the fragrance of which will clear the head and open the mind.

Comments:
- Venting, if directed toward the positive, helps to neutralize the negative energy and focus the mind on possible solutions. This action is taken so that one does not act out one's negativity to the detriment of oneself or others.
- Frustration is the result of feeling trapped. You may feel trapped by circumstances outside of your control, or you could be trapped because you have not developed the ability to deal with a situation in a creative and appropriate manner. If you hold in your frustration you are susceptible to anger. Anger has only negative consequences. If you are successful in holding it in, it will manifest as some physical or mental disease, often depression. If you vent it with hatred, someone will be hurt.

    When you are feeling angry, use this high energy state as a fire that purifies thought and focuses decisiveness, which will initiate action that is directed and positive.

    When you need to be ventilious, don't hold back. Throw yourself into the activity with your whole heart. If you have to sneeze, sneeze all the way. Holding back just makes the pressure release somewhere else.

Symbol: the *wind*

VENTURESOME

Word Forms: venture, venturer, venturous, venturesomely, venturesomeness

Definition: prone to taking risks in spite of possible danger or loss; adventurous; daring

Synonyms: bold, intrepid, courageous, brave

Compatible Quality: lucky

VERACIOUS

Word Forms: veracity, veraciously, veraciousness, veridical

Definitions: (**1**) able to perceive the truth; inclined to speak the truth; honest; (**2**) accurate; precise

Comment: Not to be confused with "voracity," which refers to an excessive appetite; gluttonous or greedy.

Synonym: veridical

VERSATILE

Word Forms: versatility, versatilely, versatileness

Definitions: (**1**) competent in many things; turning with ease from one thing to another; many-sided; (**2**) having or capable of many uses or applications

Quote:
In the long run, fancier lasts longer since versatility is a virtue.
—WILLIAM H. CALVIN, *The River That Runs Uphill*

VERSED

Definition: skilled; experienced; familiar because of attentive study

VERVE

Definition: vigor, energy, or enthusiasm in the expression of ideas either verbal or physical, as in dance; vivacious; spirited

VIBRANT

Word Forms: vibrancy, vibrantly

Definition: vigorous; characterized by energetic activity; vital

VICTORIOUS

Word Forms: victor, victory, victoriously

Definitions: (1) exalted in having gained the advantage or superiority over negative passions, appetites, or temptations; (2) successful in the accomplishment of a positive goal; fulfilled

Synonyms: triumphant, successful

Symbol: the *palm tree*

Historical Figure: *El Cid*, a famous Spaniard, Rodrigo Díaz de Bivar, was always victorious in battle (1040?–1099).

VIGILANT

Word Forms: vigil, vigilance, vigilantly

Definitions: (1) ever awake and alert; (2) keenly watchful to detect danger or trouble; wary; (3) on the lookout for opportunities to do good

Observation: Birds are always vigilant even while busily feeding or drinking.

Symbol: the *cock;* the *rooster* on top of a weather vane

VIGOROUS

Word Forms: invigorating, vigor, vigorously, vigorousness

Definitions: (1) living or growing with full vital strength; robust; (2) forceful; powerful; strong; energetic; (3) acting with abundant energy and force

Color: red

Symbol: the *hippopotamus* (Egyptian)

VIM

Definition: robust energy; enthusiasm; lively spirit; vital

VIRGINAL

Word Forms: virgin, virginity, virginhood

Definitions: (1) pure; chaste; clean; modest; innocent; **(2)** pristine; fresh; new

Symbols: the *belt; six; a private room*

Fiction: *Brandamante*, the "Virgin Knight" in Ariosto's *Orlando Furioso*, wore white armor and carried an irresistible spear. (See *Chaste.*)

VIRILE

Word Forms: virility, virilely

Definitions: (1) having or exhibiting masculine strength; manly; **(2)** characterized by a vigorous spirit; forceful

Comment: One word that I wish I could have used in these listings is *virago*. I did not include it because it has taken on a common meaning that is negative. I have referred to six dictionaries in working on these writings, and four of the six gave only the negative meaning.

Virago originally referred to a woman of great stature, strength, and courage but degenerated into a description of a woman who is loud and overbearing.

Color: red

Symbol: the *lion*

VIRTUOUS

Word Forms: virtue, virtuously, virtuousness

Definitions: **(1)** possessing moral and ethical conformity; upright; righteous; **(2)** having good or great qualities; **(3)** chaste; pure; virginal
　　See also the Seven Virtues: *Faith, Hope, Charity, Prudence, Justice, Fortitude,* and *Temperance*

Quotes:
　　Virtue goes beyond mere self-interest.

—DAVID BRIN, *Earth*

　　Evil must be left behind in this world, but virtue follows the soul to heaven.

—HINDU

VISION

Word Forms: visional, visioned, visioning, envision, visionary, visual

Definitions: **(1)** the ability to anticipate and make provision for future events; foresight; **(2)** insight; a vivid imaginative conception or anticipation; **(3)** a scene, person, or artistic presentation of extraordinary beauty

Quotes:
　　Visions born of fear give birth to failing. Visions born of hope give birth to success.

—TERRY BROOKS, *Magic Kingdom for Sale—Sold*

　　I understand how scarlet can differ from crimson because I know that the smell of an orange is not the smell of a grapefruit. I can also conceive that colors have shades and guess what shades are. In

smell and taste there are varieties not broad enough to be fundamental; so I call them shades. . . . The force of association drives me
to say that white is exalted and pure, green is exuberant, red suggests love or shame or strength. Without the color or its equivalent,
life to me would be dark, barren, a vast blackness.

Thus through an inner law of completeness my thoughts are not
permitted to remain colorless. It strains my mind to separate color
and sound from objects. Since my education began I have always
had things described to me with their colors and sounds, by one
with keen senses and a fine feeling for the significant. Therefore, I
habitually think of things as colored and resonant. Habit accounts
for part. The soul sense accounts for another part. The brain with its
five-sensed construction asserts its right and accounts for the rest.
Inclusive of all, the unity of the world demands that color be kept in
it whether I have cognizance of it or not. Rather than be shut out, I
take part in it by discussing it, happy in the happiness of those near
to me who gaze at the lovely hues of the sunset or the rainbow.

—HELEN KELLER

Affirmation: After you have decided to accomplish something, visualize
it in its completion with as much detail as possible. Then see yourself,
your friends, and your family enjoying your new thing, quality, or experience. Affirm to yourself, "I appreciate the completion of this goal and am
thankful for the qualities I have acquired in gaining it. They are now part
of me for use in future endeavors."

Visualization: Practice the visualization of becoming the new you.
Continue the practice of the young with their imagination of what they
will be when they grow up.

Certainly you have a long-range vision of this wonderful person you
are going to become, but there is also the short-range recognition of your
"tomorrow self." Practice what you need to become by seeing that person
who is going to be doing the shopping tomorrow or going to change the
hose on the lawn twenty minutes from now or is going to go on vacation
next July Fourth. When each one of these things comes up, that person is
there. You have become that new you.

Each one of these events could be tied to a particular quality that you
want to exhibit between now and then as well as during the event.

When that time and person arrive, bless the previous person you were
and let him or her go.

Tip: Don't give advice unless you are asked for it or are family.

Advice: Sometimes people say, "Why don't you just . . ." and then they give you some description based on their own vision and ability. They consider their advice to be easy to follow, and it is easy for them because they have either done it or have a natural talent for it. What they are not aware of is that you do not have that same vision and do not have that same easy concept of how to proceed.

If you are going to recommend something to somebody, also take the added responsibility of finding out whether or not that person has that vision and can see what it takes to get from A to Z as easily as you do. If not, then be kind and see if you can explain it.

Admonition: People's horizons are bounded by their vision.

Color: violet

Symbols: the *eagle;* the *lynx*

Fiction: *Uriel*, an archangel in Milton's *Paradise Lost*, is the most sharp-sighted of all the angels.

Legend: *Lynceus*, a Greek Argonaut, was famed for his keen vision.

VITAL

Word Forms: vitalize, vitality, vitally, revitalize

Definitions: (1) necessary to the existence, continuance, or well-being of something; indispensable; essential; critically important; **(2)** energetic, lively, or forceful

Colors: red, orange

Symbol: *blood*

VIVACIOUS

Word Forms: vivacity, vivaciously, vivaciousness

Definition: lively, active, or sprightly in temper or conduct; spirited

Derivation: Latin, "long-lived"

VOLITIONAL

Word Forms: volition, volitionally

Definition: willful; forming a purpose or an opinion; decisive

VOLUPTUOUS

Word Forms: voluptuously, voluptuousness

Definition: luxurious; fond of pleasure; sensual

WARM

Word Forms: warmer, warmest, warmed, warming, warmth, warmly, warmness

Definitions: (1) affectionate; loving; warmhearted; kindly; (2) strongly attached; intimate; (3) cordial or hearty; (4) animated; vigorous; (5) exciting enthusiasm, cheerfulness, or vitality in someone; (6) to inspire with kindly feeling; affect with lively pleasure

Colors: red, orange-brown

Symbol: the *hearth*

WARMHEARTED

Word Forms: warm, warmheartedness

Definitions: (**1**) possessing ready affection, cordiality, kindness, generosity, or sympathy; (**2**) loving; ardent

Familial Quality: familial

Color: red-orange

WATCHFUL

Word Forms: watchfully, watchfulness

Definitions: (**1**) vigilant; carefully observant; attentive, especially with parental care; cautious; diligent; awake; aware; (**2**) guarding against danger or alert to opportunity; (**3**) mentally informed; (**4**) self-observant; self-restrained; acting with discretion

Symbol: *eyes*

Mythology: *Argus*, a Greek mythological giant who had a hundred eyes and was ever watchful, but he was killed by Hermes, and then Hera set his eyes into the tail of the peacock

WELL

Word Forms: wellness, well-advised, well-being, well-born, well-bred, well-fixed, well-groomed, well-heeled, well-informed, well-intentioned, well-known, well-off, well-rounded, well-thought-of, well-to-do, well-turned, well-wisher

Definitions: (**1**) healthy; sound in body and mind; (**2**) just; right; having reasonable propriety; (**3**) skillful; expertly accomplished; thorough; complete; done with close attention <*well* done>; (**4**) abundant; prosperous; fortunate;

in an advantageous situation; comfortable; **(5)** with a high degree of pleasure or approval; **(6)** the proper or satisfactory treatment of a person, thing, or situation; in a kindly or friendly manner; **(7)** to accept in good grace; **(8)** to behave in a moral manner; commendable; with merit; **(9)** a reservoir of feelings and emotions; **(10)** elegantly <She carried herself *well.*>

WELL-DISPOSED

Definitions: (1) feeling favorable, kind, or sympathetic; **(2)** friendly; having a pleasant character

WELL-MEANING

Word Form: well-meant

Definition: having good intentions in mind when acting; sincere

WELL-READ

Definition: one who loves literature; well-educated; well-informed

Derivation: The word *encyclopedia* comes from the Greek meaning "well-rounded."

Symbol: a *library*

Mythology: *Nebo*, the god of science and literature in Babylonian mythology, also the god of prophesy

WELL-SPOKEN

Definitions: (1) spoken with grace, kindness, or propriety; articulate; **(2)** civil; courteous; **(3)** having the ability to speak with ease; quick-minded

Comment: It can often be a greater kindness not to speak.

WHIMSICAL

Word Forms: whim, whimsy, whimsicality, whimsically, whimsicalness

Definition: spontaneously fanciful; acting with playful humor; demonstrating eccentric creativity

Compatible Qualities: rascally, changeable

WHOLE

Word Forms: wholly, wholeness

Definitions: (1) in sound health; not diseased or injured; **(2)** intact; not broken, damaged, or defective; **(3)** containing all of its elements or parts; entire; complete

Quote:
> An act is not, as young men think, like a rock that one picks up and throws, and it hits or misses, and that's the end of it. When that rock is lifted, the earth is lighter; the hand that bears it heavier. When it is thrown, the circuits of the stars respond, and where it strikes or falls the universe is changed. On every act the balance of the whole depends. . . . Having intelligence, we must not act in ignorance. Having choice, we must not act without responsibility.
> —URSULA K. LE GUIN, *The Farthest Shore*

Suggestion:
Actively function in all aspects of life.
- Appreciation
- Art, creation
- Education, teaching and learning
- Emotional
- Job, career

- Mental
- Nature
- Physical
- Playful
- Relaxation
- Relationships
- Spiritual

Symbols: the *globe;* the *peacock;* the *wheel;* the *ring;* the *bracelet;* unity and diversity, many seeds contained in one sphere—the *pomegranate*

Mythologies:
Woman, in the picture language of mythology, represents the totality of what can be known.
                —JOSEPH CAMPBELL, *The Hero with a Thousand Faces*

Yggdrasil, in Scandinavian mythology, is a huge ash tree whose roots and branches hold together the universe.

WHOLEHEARTED

Word Forms: wholeheartedly, wholeheartedness

Definition: showing devoted commitment, earnest enthusiasm, sincere and energetic focus, directed determination

WHOLESOME

Word Forms: whole, wholesomely, wholesomeness

Definitions: (1) promoting or conducive to good health, mental vitality, or well-being; vigorous; sound; (2) tending to improve the mind or morals

Compatible Quality: homey

Symbol: *bread*

WILLFUL

Word Forms: will, willfully, willfulness

Definition: deliberate, voluntary, or intentional

Parental Quality: consciousness

Symbols: *music;* the *sun*

WILLING

Word Forms: will, willingly, willingness

Definitions: (1) inclined or favorably disposed to act; ready; prompt to respond; (2) done, given, borne, or used with cheerful readiness; (3) having the power to choose; volitional

Sayings:
De bonne grace (French): "With good grace"; willingly

Energy flows on intention.

Inspirational:
> I will allow my will to be God's Will.
> I will align my will with God's will.
> I will that my will be Thy will.
> God is willing His Will to be my will.
> God is willing. I am willing.

Advice: Be willing to hear what another is saying. Are you secure enough to be open to change your behavior to conform to another's insights?

WINSOME

Word Forms: winsomely, winsomeness

Definitions: (1) innocently charming; engagingly sweet; attractive; **(2)** cheerful; merry; gay

Derivation: Anglo Saxon, "pleasant," "delightful"

WISE

Word Forms: wiser, wisest, wisdom, wisely, wiseness, worldly-wise

Definitions: (1) having or showing good judgment; having the power to discern and judge correctly; discriminating between what is true and what is false, between what is proper and what is improper; sagacious; prudent; discreet; **(2)** learned; knowing; erudite; enlightened; **(3)** calculating; crafty; cunning; subtle

Kindred Quality: appreciation

Compatible Quality: common sense

Familial Qualities: prepared, foresighted, farsighted

Sayings:
God grant me the serenity to accept the things I cannot change, courage to change the things I can and wisdom to know the difference.

Verbum sat sapienti est (Latin): "A word to the wise is sufficient."

The heart is wiser than the intellect.

Quotes:
[Merlin:] "The essence of wisdom is to know when to be doing and when it is useless even to try."
                    —MARY STEWART, *The Last Enchantment*

The beginning of wisdom is the definition of terms.
                    —SOCRATES

Comments:

- When one is able to see a broader view, to encompass a greater quantity of reality or a purer essence of reality, one possesses a fundamental aspect of wisdom. People who have a greater wisdom have a responsibility to share that larger view, and share it in such a way that those caught in the constrictive web of their own realities will be able to expand those realities.
- Wisdom is the result of balancing "opposing" positive qualities. It is also seeing the positive in a muddled and complex situation. It is the ability to contrast opposites and choose the highest possible good.

Tip: Even a little bit of wisdom helps. Say you are driving and you notice that the person in front of you is going to turn. You get over in the other lane and your progress is not impeded—small wisdom. You look even farther ahead and you take one freeway instead of another. Again you are rewarded with a smoother trip. The larger your ability to choose wisely, the greater your ability to live as you intend.

Advice: If you can't reach the heights of wisdom then be satisfied with the dregs of wisdom.

Color: yellow

Symbols: an *owl;* a *golden key;* the *dragon;* the *serpent;* an *elephant; honey;* a *ring of flames; fruit* from the Tree of Knowledge of Good and Evil; wisdom—*the Hermit* (tarot); *deep water; burnt wood;* the snake (American Indian)

Legend: *Epimenides*, a sage and prophet of ancient Greece, slept in a cave for fifty-seven years and woke possessing exceptional wisdom.

Mythologies: *Athena* or *Pallas*, the Greek goddess of wisdom and skills; *Minerva*, the Roman goddess of wisdom and liberal arts; *Neith*, the Egyptian goddess of wisdom; *Thoth*, the Egyptian god of wisdom, magic, learning, and the arts, also the measurer of time and the inventor of numbers

WITTY

Word Forms: wit, wittier, wittiest, witticism, wittily, wittiness, sharp-witted, keen-witted

Definitions: (1) amusingly or ingeniously clever in conception and execution; (2) showing humor; cleverly amusing; smartly facetious; (3) quick to see and express illuminating or amusing relationships or insights

Saying: *Sal atticum* (Latin): "attic salt" [wit]

Quote:
Wit is the salt of conversation, not the food.
                                                        —WILLIAM HAZLITT

WIZARDLY

Word Forms: wizard, wizardry

Definitions: (1) possessing amazing skill or accomplishment; very clever; (2) enchanting; charming; magical; (3) sagacious; wise; (4) praiseworthy

WONDER

Word Forms: wonderment, wondrous, wondered, wondering

Definitions: (1) a cause of astonishment or admiration; marvel; (2) the quality of exciting amazed admiration; (3) rapt attention or astonishment at something awesomely mysterious or new to one's experience

Synonyms: appreciation, curious, reverence, surprise

Quote:
Uncertainty and mystery are energies of life. Don't let them scare you unduly, for they keep boredom at bay and spark creativity.
                                                        —R. I. FITZHENRY

Tip: Deal with what happens as an answer and not as a question.

Symbol: a wide-eyed *child*

WONDERFUL

Word Forms: wonderfully, wonderfulness

Definitions: (1) excellent; grand; marvelous; astonishing; amazing; (2) unusually good; admirable; exciting; extraordinary

Proverb:
When one stops wondering at the wonderful it stops being wonderful.

—CHINESE

Quote:
If you want to find something wonderful, you have to be prepared to wonder.

—JERRY DOWNS

Tip: Don't be so interested in the ultimate spectacle that you walk unknowingly right by the simply wonderful.

WORSHIPFUL

Word Forms: worship, worshiped, worshiping, worshiper, worshipingly, worshipfully, worshipfulness

Definitions: (1) expressing adoration, veneration, and homage to a Divine person; showing devotion; (2) giving respect or honor due to a lofty character; (3) feeling intense love and admiration for a loved one

Familial Quality: liturgical

Saying: Worship leads to service. Service leads to worship.

Reflection: Remember having been, almost literally, grabbed by something of extreme interest or beauty? Remember being struck with the beauty of a flower, a butterfly, a bird? Nature can hold our fascination for moments or for a lifetime. Remember those long philosophical discussions that were so interesting that you stayed up all night? Remember that hug from a child that was so innocent and giving that you were surrounded with love? This state of appreciation and self-forgetfulness may be triggered by exquisite beauty, sublime truth, or heartwarming goodness.

During these times, you are totally absorbed. You give yourself over to your appreciation. It may be an involuntary act but you like it so much that you would not describe it as a loss of will.

Observation: During worship the ego disappears; there is a sublime self-forgetfulness. Observe that in this state of self-forgetfulness that there are a few things that are notably absent. You no longer are experiencing fear, doubt, or worry, and your prideful ego is left far behind—you are not even aware that they are gone. Love is the reason. Love evaporates the negative. Sustained love obliterates the negative.

There are a certain set of qualities that put you in this remarkable space. They are worship, play, humor, service, thoughtfulness, and love. If these positive qualities put you in a place that excludes fear, worry, doubt, and ego pride, then they are the *master keys* to conquering these negative feelings and immature habits.

Comments:
- Worship would make no sense at all without a personal Ultimate Being. We talk about worshiping a thing, but that is just desire to possess. True worship is pure unselfish love.
- Worship illuminates destiny. That is not its goal but it works because you are not only sending love but are open to receiving love.
- You may be propelled into worship by your personal experience of truth, beauty, or goodness, but you can generate this state of bliss by your own simple willingness. Take the time to focus your attention with all your heart on the wonderful.

WORTHY

Word Forms: worth, worthier, worthiest, worthily, worthiness, self-worth, worthful

Definition: demonstrating commendable excellence or great merit; possessing value or distinguished character; deserving praise; noble; estimable; virtuous

Consideration: If the parents have a strong sense of self-worth, the child can then also feel safe in having that same healthy sense of self-worth. If life is not safe, then something else will have to take its place so that the child will still have an ego identity. If the ego is built on a negative pseudo-structure, these deficiencies will eventually have to be replaced with more constructive and natural qualities.

This is one reason why people hold on to the negative even when they know that they should not, because they feel that their identities are fused with it. The fact is that you cannot disconnect from your self. It takes courage and faith to let go of something and go toward another, but if you have a bridge to your new self you will more easily let yourself do so. The bridge is made of the positive qualities that will replace the old structure.

Accept the building materials of the positive qualities to shore up your deficiencies. Tell yourself that it is necessary and that you are worthy of them, then you will start to crave them. If you seek, the way will be made clear.

WRY

Word Forms: wryly, wryness

Definition: amusing in a twisted way; exhibiting clever and ironic humor

YUMMY

Word Forms: yum, yummier, yummiest, yum-yum

Definitions: (1) delicious; delectable; tasty or tasteful; very pleasing to the senses; (2) a general quality of approval or appreciation

Symbols: the *tongue;* the *tummy*

ZANY

Word Forms: zanier, zaniest, zanily, zaniness

Definition: befitting a clown; characterizes one who makes fun in a comical way

ZEALOUS

Word Forms: zeal, zealot, zealously, zealousness

Definition: ardent in the pursuit of an object; enthusiastic; full of, characterized by, showing, or sowing fervor or enthusiasm

Too Far: fanatic

Saying: *Abeunt studia in mores* (Latin): "Practices zealously pursued pass into habits."

Comment: It is hard to be zealous in tedium, but in order for one to proceed with a tedious task, one must transcend the boredom with a higher purpose—a zealous concentration on the accomplishment of the task or the idea that one is doing some good for someone.

Color: red

ZESTFUL

Word Forms: zest, zesty, zestfully, zestfulness

Definitions: (1) piquant; adding a pleasant taste to; (2) stimulating or exciting; having gusto

Derivation: Persian, "to peel" [the woody skin of the walnut kernel, the peel of an orange or lemon]

APPENDICES

APPENDIX 1: ALPHABETICAL LIST OF POSITIVE QUALITIES

APPENDIX 2: RANDOM/RANDOM PICK LIST

APPENDIX 3: ADDITIONAL POSITIVE QUALITIES

APPENDIX 4: SYMBOLS

APPENDIX 5: MYTHOLOGICAL, LEGENDARY, HISTORICAL, FICTIONAL, AND THEOLOGICAL CHARACTERS

APPENDIX 6: "BEING" AND "MEANING OF LIFE" QUOTES

APPENDIX 7: EXERCISES AND PROJECTS

APPENDIX 8: BIBLIOGRAPHY

APPENDIX 9: END NOTES

APPENDIX 1

ALPHABETICAL LIST OF POSITIVE QUALITIES

Abiding
Able
Aboveboard
Abundant
Accepting
Accessible
Accommodating
Accomplished
Accountable
Accurate
Active
Actualized
Acumen
Adaptable
Adept
Adjusted
Admirable
Adorable
Adroit
Advancing
Adventuresome
Aesthetic
Affable
Affectionate
Affirming

Agile
Agreeable
Alacritous
Alert
Alive
Alluring
Altruistic
Amazing
Ambitious
Ameliorative
Amenable
Amiable
Amicable
Amorous
Amusing
Angelic
Animated
Aplomb
Appealing
Appeasing
Appetizing
Appreciative
Appropriate
Approving
Ardent

Arresting
Articulate
Artistic
Ascending
Aspiring
Assertive
Assiduous
Assured
Astonishing
Astounding
Astute
Attentive
Attractive
Auspicious
Authentic
Authoritative
Autonomous
Available
Awake
Aware

Backbone
Balanced
Beauty
Behaved

Believable
Beneficent
Beneficial
Benevolent
Benign
Blessed
Blissful
Blooming
Bold
Bonhomie
Bountiful
Brave
Breathtaking
Bright
Brilliant
Broad-minded
Brotherly
Bubbly
Buoyant

Cagey
Calm
Candid
Canny
Capable
Capital
Captivating
Carefree
Careful
Caring
Casual
Cautious
Celebrated
Celeritous
Centered
Cerebral
Certain
Changeable
Character
Charismatic
Charitable
Charming
Chaste

Cheerful
Cherished
Chic
Childlike
Chipper
Chivalrous
Choice
Chummy
Chutzpah
Civil
Civilized
Clairvoyant
Classy
Clean
Clean-cut
Clear
Clement
Clever
Climbing
Cogent
Cognizant
Coherent
Colorful
Comely
Comfortable
Comforting
Comical
Commanding
Commendable
Commiserative
Committed
Common Sense
Communicative
Companionable
Compassionate
Compatible
Compelling
Competent
Complacent
Complete
Compliant
Composed
Comprehensive

Compromising
Concentrative
Concerned
Conciliatory
Concise
Confident
Conforming
Congenial
Congruous
Conscience
Conscientious
Conscious
Conservative
Considerate
Consistent
Consonant
Constructive
Contemplative
Contemporary
Content
Contributive
Controlled
Conviction
Convincing
Convivial
Cool
Cooperative
Coordinated
Cordial
Correct
Courageous
Courteous
Courtly
Cozy
Creative
Credible
Cuddly
Cultured
Cunning
Curious
Cute

Daffy

Dainty
Dapper
Daring
Darling
Dashing
Dazzling
Debonair
Decent
Decisive
Decorous
Dedicated
Deep
Definite
Deft
Delectable
Deliberate
Delicate
Delicious
Delightful
Democratic
Demure
Dependable
Deserving
Desire
Determined
Developing
Devoted
Devout
Dexterous
Dignified
Diligent
Diplomatic
Direct
Directed
Discerning
Disciplined
Discreet
Discriminating
Disporting
Distinctive
Distinguished
Diverse
Divine

Docile
Down-to-earth
Dreaming
Drive
Dulcet
Durable
Dutiful
Dynamic

Eager
Earnest
Easygoing
Ebullient
Eclectic
Economical
Ecstatic
Educated
Effective
Effervescent
Efficient
Elastic
Elated
Electrifying
Elegant
Emerging
Eminent
Empathetic
Enamoring
Enchanting
Encouraging
Endearing
Endeavoring
Enduring
Energetic
Engaging
Enjoying
Enlightened
Enterprising
Entertaining
Enthusiastic
Enticing
Entrancing
Entrepreneurial

Equanimous
Equitable
Erudite
Essential
Esteemed
Ethical
Etiquette
Euphoric
Evenhanded
Even-tempered
Evolving
Exact
Excellent
Exceptional
Exciting
Exemplary
Exhaustive
Exotic
Expanding
Expeditious
Experienced
Expert
Explorative
Expressive
Exquisite
Extemporaneous
Extraordinary
Extroverted
Exuberant

Fabulous
Fair
Faith
Faithful
Familial
Famous
Fancy
Fantastic
Farsighted
Fascinating
Fashionable
Favored
Fearless

Feisty
Felicitous
Fertile
Fervent
Festive
Fetching
Fidelity
Fine
Finesse
Firm
Fit
Fitting
Flair
Flamboyant
Flexible
Flourishing
Flowing
Focused
Folksy
Forbearing
Forceful
Foresighted
Forethoughtful
Forgiving
Formal
Forthright
Fortified
Fortitude
Fortunate
Forward
Foursquare
Foxy
Fragrant
Frank
Fraternal
Free
Freethinking
Fresh
Friendly
Frisky
Frolicsome
Frugal
Fruitful

Fulfilled
Fun
Funny

Gallant
Gamesome
Gay
Generous
Genial
Genius
Genteel
Gentle
Gentlemanly
Genuine
Gifted
Giving
Glad
Glamorous
Gleeful
Glowing
Goal Oriented
Godly
Good Self-image
Good Will
Goodhearted
Goodness
Good-humored
Good-natured
Goofy
Gorgeous
Graced
Graceful
Gracious
Grand
Grateful
Great
Gregarious
Grounded
Growing
Guiding
Gumption
Gusto
Gutsy

Handsome
Handy
Happy
Happy-go-lucky
Hardy
Harmonious
Healing
Healthy
Heart
Hearty
Helpful
Heroic
High-minded
High-spirited
Holy
Homey
Honest
Honorable
Hopeful
Hospitable
Huggable
Humane
Humanitarian
Humble
Humorous
Hustle
Hygienic
Hypnotic

Idealistic
Illustrative
Illustrious
Imaginative
Imitable
Immaculate
Immune
Impartial
Impeccable
Imperial
Important
Impressive
Improving
Improvisational

Incisive
Indefatigable
Independent
Individualistic
Indomitable
Industrious
Influential
Informative
Ingenious
Ingenuous
Initiative
Inner-directed
Innocent
Innovative
Inquisitive
Insightful
Inspiring
Instinctive
Instructive
Instrumental
Integrated
Integrity
Intelligent
Interesting
Intimate
Intrepid
Intriguing
Introspective
Intuitive
Inventive
Investigative
Irresistible

Jaunty
Jocular
Joie de Vivre
Jolly
Jovial
Joyful
Jubilant
Judicious
Just

Keen
Kind
Knightly
Knowledgeable

Ladylike
Laid-back
Laudable
Law-abiding
Leadership
Learned
Legitimate
Leisurely
Lenient
Levelheaded
Levity
Liberal
Liberty
Light
Lighthearted
Likable
Limber
Lionhearted
Lithesome
Liturgical
Lively
Lofty
Logical
Long-suffering
Loose
Lovable
Love
Lovely
Loyal
Lucid
Lucky
Luminous
Luscious
Lustrous
Luxurious
Lyrical

Magical
Magnanimous
Magnetic
Magnificent
Majestic
Malleable
Maneuverable
Mannerly
Marvelous
Masterful
Maternal
Matter-of-fact
Maturing
Meditative
Meek
Mellow
Melodious
Memorable
Merciful
Meritorious
Merry
Mesmerizing
Metamorphic
Metaphysical
Methodical
Meticulous
Mettlesome
Mighty
Mild
Mindful
Ministerial
Mirthful
Moderate
Modern
Modest
Moral
Motivated
Moxie
Multidimensional
Multidisciplined
Multifaceted
Munificent
Musical

Natural
Neat
Necessary
Neighborly
Nervy
New
Nice
Nimble
No Worries
Noble
Nonchalant
Nonjudgmental
Normal
Noteworthy
Nourishing
Nurturing

Obedient
Objective
Obliging
Observant
Okay
Open
Openhanded
Open-hearted
Open-minded
Opportunistic
Optimistic
Orderly
Organized
Oriented
Original
Outgoing
Outstanding

Pacifistic
Painstaking
Panache
Paragon
Parental
Participative
Particular
Passionate

Pastoral
Paternal
Patient
Peaceful
Penitent
Peppy
Perceptive
Perfect
Perfectible
Perky
Permissive
Persevering
Persistent
Personable
Perspicacious
Perspicuous
Persuasive
Pert
Philanthropic
Philosophical
Photogenic
Physical
Pioneering
Pious
Piquant
Pity
Pizazz
Placid
Playful
Pleasant
Pliable
Plucky
Poetic
Poised
Polished
Polite
Popular
Positive
Potential
Powerful
Practical
Pragmatic
Praiseworthy

Prayerful
Precious
Precise
Precocious
Prepared
Prescient
Presence of Mind
Present
Presentable
Preserving
Prestigious
Pretty
Princely
Principled
Pristine
Privileged
Probity
Productive
Professional
Proficient
Profitable
Profound
Progressive
Prolific
Prominent
Promising
Prompt
Proper
Propitious
Prosperous
Protective
Proud
Provident
Provocative
Prudent
Psychic
Public-spirited
Pulchritudinous
Punctilious
Punctual
Pure
Purposeful

Quaint
Qualified
Quality
Quick
Quick-witted
Quiet

Radiant
Rapport
Rascally
Rational
Ravishing
Ready
Realistic
Realized
Reasonable
Receptive
Recharged
Rectitude
Recuperative
Red-blooded
Refined
Reflective
Refreshing
Regal
Regenerative
Rejoicing
Rejuvenative
Relaxed
Reliable
Religious
Remarkable
Renowned
Reputable
Resilient
Resolute
Resourceful
Respectable
Responsible
Responsive
Restful
Restorative
Revered

Reverent
Rhythmic
Rich
Right
Righteous
Risible
Risk Taker
Robust
Rollicking
Romantic
Roseate
Rousing
Royal
Rugged

Safe
Sagacious
Saintly
Salubrious
Salutary
Sane
Sanguine
Sanitary
Sapid
Sapient
Sassy
Satisfied
Saved
Savoir-faire
Savory
Savvy
Scholarly
Scrumptious
Scrupulous
Searching
Seasoned
Secure
Sedate
Sedulous
Seeking
Seemly
Selfless
Self-accepting

Self-contained
Self-esteem
Self-governing
Self-made
Self-possessed
Self-respect
Self-sufficient
Sensible
Sensitive
Sensuous
Sentimental
Serendipitous
Serene
Serious
Service Minded
Sexy
Sharing
Sharp
Sheltering
Shining
Shipshape
Shrewd
Significant
Silly
Simple
Sincere
Sisterly
Skillful
Sleek
Smart
Smooth
Snazzy
Snugly
Soaring
Sober
Sociable
Soft
Softhearted
Solemn
Solid
Soothing
Sophisticated
Soulful

Sound
Special
Spellbinding
Spicy
Spirited
Spiritual
Splendid
Spontaneous
Sporting
Sprightly
Springy
Spry
Spunky
Stable
Stalwart
Stamina
Stately
Statuesque
Staunch
Steadfast
Steady
Stellar
Sterling
Stick-to-itive
Stimulating
Stirring
Stout
Straightforward
Stress Hardy
Stretching
Striking
Striving
Strong
Studious
Stunning
Sturdy
Stylish
Suave
Sublime
Subtle
Successful
Succinct
Suitable

Sunny
Superb
Supple
Supportive
Sure
Surefooted
Sure-handed
Surviving
Sustaining
Svelte
Sweet
Sweetheart
Swift
Symmetrical
Sympathetic
Synergistic
Systematic

Tactful
Talented
Tame
Tasteful
Technical
Temperate
Tenacious
Tender
Tenderhearted
Terrific
Thankful
Therapeutic
Thorough
Thoughtful
Thrifty
Thrilling
Thriving
Tidy
Timely
Tireless
Tolerant
Touching
Tough
Tractable
Traditional

Trailblazing
Tranquil
Treasured
Trim
Triumphant
True
True-blue
Trusting
Trustworthy
Truth

Understanding
Unique
Unstoppable
Upbeat
Uplifting
Upright
Upstanding
Up-and-coming
Up-to-date
Urbane
Useful
Utilitarian

Valorous
Valuable
Venerable
Ventilious
Venturesome
Veracious
Versatile
Versed
Verve
Vibrant
Victorious
Vigilant
Vigorous
Vim
Virginal
Virile
Virtuous
Vision
Vital

Vivacious

Volitional

Voluptuous

Warm

Warmhearted

Watchful

Well

Well-disposed

Well-meaning

Well-read

Well-spoken

Whimsical

Whole

Wholehearted

Wholesome

Willful

Willing

Winsome

Wise

Witty

Wizardly

Wonder

Wonderful

Worshipful

Worthy

Wry

Yummy

Zany

Zealous

Zestful

Appendix 2

Random/Random Pick List

To use this Random/Random list, pick one or two numbers at random. If you pick two numbers, decide on the two qualities of the four available to work on.

The two columns include the 988 qualities listed in a totally random order. Therefore, the combinations are completely accidental. This gives you the option of focusing on the range of positive qualities no matter how (seemingly) dissimilar or aligned.

First decide how often you want to choose qualities to focus on—daily, weekly, monthly, annually (New Year's, birthday)—then pick a set of qualities.

There are a few ways to do this.

1. Without looking at the list, pick a number at random from 1 to 988. If you don't like what you've picked, just pick again—you might as well suit yourself. Check off that number so that you know you've used it. This does not mean you cannot focus on those qualities again. It's your choice.

2. Pick a quality that you want to work on. Find it in the first column and see what it is paired with. Find it in the second column and see what it is paired with.

3. Read through the list and see what jumps out at you and accept that combination.

|__1 Saintly . . . . Essential
|__2 Assertive . . . . Willing
|__3 Trailblazing . . . . Wise

|__4 Tranquil . . . . Savvy
|__5 Subtle . . . . Laid-back
|__6 Wry . . . . Simple
|__7 Lovable . . . . Wonder
|__8 Alert . . . . Prominent
|__9 Long-suffering . . . . Available
|__10 Supportive . . . . Ethical
|__11 Steadfast . . . . Important
|__12 Gentle . . . . Loose
|__13 Imaginative . . . . Trustworthy
|__14 Aplomb . . . . Salutary
|__15 Versatile . . . . Levity
|__16 Feisty Civil
|__17 Open-minded . . . . Sedate
|__18 Assured . . . . Systematic
|__19 Fancy . . . . Extroverted
|__20 Determined . . . . Personable
|__21 Perspicacious . . . . Entrancing
|__22 Wholehearted . . . . Focused
|__23 Frisky . . . . Pure
|__24 Commanding . . . . Assertive
|__25 Abundant . . . . Emerging
|__26 Effective . . . . Self-sufficient
|__27 Constructive . . . . Eclectic
|__28 Virile . . . . Chutzpah
|__29 Believable . . . . Satisfied
|__30 Self-governing . . . . Up-and-coming
|__31 Affectionate . . . . Canny
|__32 Timely . . . . Provocative
|__33 Maternal . . . . Witty
|__34 Simple . . . . Impartial
|__35 Courteous . . . . Fabulous
|__36 Sane . . . . Obedient
|__37 Succinct . . . . Genuine
|__38 Felicitous . . . . Genius
|__39 Searching . . . . Vim
|__40 Committed . . . . Genteel
|__41 Outstanding . . . . Swift
|__42 Enticing . . . . Gleeful
|__43 Refined . . . . Remarkable

|__44 Prosperous . . . . Sincere
|__45 Shipshape . . . . Prestigious
|__46 Sustaining . . . . Prepared
|__47 Aware . . . . Assured
|__48 Eclectic . . . . Sure
|__49 Balanced . . . . Soaring
|__50 Natural . . . . Pious
|__51 Endearing . . . . Wholesome
|__52 Symmetrical . . . . Inquisitive
|__53 Munificent . . . . Down-to-earth
|__54 Lovely . . . . Original
|__55 Forceful . . . . Etiquette
|__56 Rejuvenative . . . . Disporting
|__57 Love . . . . Goodness
|__58 Sophisticated . . . . Amiable
|__59 Peppy . . . . Popular
|__60 Well-meaning . . . . Fashionable
|__61 Masterful . . . . Philosophical
|__62 Sapid . . . . Concise
|__63 Relaxed . . . . Modest
|__64 Delectable . . . . Rectitude
|__65 Amusing . . . . Ladylike
|__66 Pastoral . . . . Choice
|__67 Concentrative . . . . Progressive
|__68 Genteel . . . . Potential
|__69 Royal . . . . Trailblazing
|__70 Adept . . . . Pizazz
|__71 Delicate . . . . Painstaking
|__72 Nourishing . . . . Democratic
|__73 Supple . . . . Gutsy
|__74 Stellar . . . . Conscientious
|__75 Orderly . . . . Frolicsome
|__76 Sporting . . . . Appetizing
|__77 Enlightened . . . . Reliable
|__78 Festive . . . . Sophisticated
|__79 Prepared . . . . Thorough
|__80 Fortitude . . . . Surefooted
|__81 Thrilling . . . . Fortunate
|__82 Dulcet . . . . Sanguine
|__83 Upright . . . . Passionate

|__84 Treasured . . . . Forward
|__85 Receptive . . . . Whimsical
|__86 Authoritative . . . . Pretty
|__87 Sturdy . . . . Pioneering
|__88 Sagacious . . . . Charming
|__89 Accountable . . . . Regenerative
|__90 Ecstatic . . . . Fragrant
|__91 Scrupulous . . . . Dulcet
|__92 Liberal . . . . Distinctive
|__93 Fraternal . . . . Adept
|__94 Religious . . . . Attentive
|__95 Comely . . . . Sound
|__96 Flowing . . . . Solemn
|__97 Unstoppable . . . . Sprightly
|__98 Profound . . . . Knowledgeable
|__99 Thorough . . . . Diligent
|__100 Mighty . . . . Refined
|__101 Dazzling . . . . Hospitable
|__102 Rousing . . . . Confident
|__103 Skillful . . . . Felicitous
|__104 Composed . . . . Caring
|__105 Merciful . . . . Decisive
|__106 Solid . . . . Advancing
|__107 Fabulous . . . . Concerned
|__108 Rectitude . . . . Enthusiastic
|__109 Prolific . . . . Impeccable
|__110 Jovial . . . . Sleek
|__111 Refreshing . . . . Blessed
|__112 Good Self-image . . . . Affirming
|__113 Enterprising . . . . Improvisational
|__114 Celeritous . . . . Superb
|__115 Elated . . . . Persistent
|__116 Multidisciplined . . . . Celeritous
|__117 Magnificent . . . . Receptive
|__118 Able . . . . Magnanimous
|__119 Devoted . . . . Engaging
|__120 Self-sufficient . . . . Surefooted
|__121 Pulchritudinous . . . . Verve
|__122 Esteemed . . . . Alive
|__123 Bountiful . . . . Staunch

|__124 Effervescent . . . . Risk Taker
|__125 Tidy . . . . Thankful
|__126 Even-tempered . . . . High-minded
|__127 Cognizant . . . . Responsible
|__128 Proper . . . . Bonhomie
|__129 Erudite . . . . Persevering
|__130 Handsome . . . . Smooth
|__131 Remarkable . . . . Careful
|__132 Propitious . . . . Common Sense
|__133 Urbane . . . . Open-minded
|__134 Down-to-earth . . . . Sweet
|__135 Open-hearted . . . . Delightful
|__136 Snazzy . . . . Deft
|__137 Progressive . . . . Alert
|__138 Autonomous . . . . Laudable
|__139 Funny . . . . Hustle
|__140 Entertaining . . . . Quality
|__141 Luscious . . . . Aspiring
|__142 Ventilious . . . . Consistent
|__143 Potential . . . . Self-respect
|__144 Sympathetic . . . . Actualized
|__145 Service Minded . . . . Objective
|__146 Fit . . . . Exemplary
|__147 Gifted . . . . Healing
|__148 Understanding . . . . Believable
|__149 Melodious . . . . Companionable
|__150 Plucky . . . . Pert
|__151 Neat . . . . Humane
|__152 Winsome . . . . Glad
|__153 Complete . . . . Stimulating
|__154 Forethoughtful . . . . Immune
|__155 Obedient . . . . Sentimental
|__156 Statuesque . . . . Smart
|__157 Daring . . . . Enduring
|__158 Goofy . . . . Amazing
|__159 Chipper . . . . Incisive
|__160 Imperial . . . . Forthright
|__161 Hustle . . . . Cool
|__162 Enthusiastic . . . . Aboveboard
|__163 Colorful . . . . Homey

|__164 Perfectible . . . . Sexy
|__165 Seeking . . . . Meritorious
|__166 Venerable . . . . Elated
|__167 Just . . . . Convivial
|__168 Thankful . . . . Changeable
|__169 Controlled . . . . Realized
|__170 Admirable . . . . Heroic
|__171 Aboveboard . . . . Authoritative
|__172 Gracious . . . . Moxie
|__173 Smooth . . . . Precious
|__174 Complacent . . . . Fortitude
|__175 Favored . . . . Opportunistic
|__176 Comprehensive . . . . Grounded
|__177 Praiseworthy . . . . Scholarly
|__178 Etiquette . . . . Appropriate
|__179 Passionate . . . . Gamesome
|__180 Comforting . . . . Delectable
|__181 Goodness . . . . Elegant
|__182 Energetic . . . . Tidy
|__183 Coherent . . . . Committed
|__184 Deserving . . . . Forethoughtful
|__185 Carefree . . . . Synergistic
|__186 Judicious . . . . Empathetic
|__187 Delicious . . . . Vision
|__188 Alacritous . . . . Intimate
|__189 Sensitive . . . . Unique
|__190 Humble . . . . Meticulous
|__191 Trusting . . . . Forbearing
|__192 Levity . . . . Genial
|__193 Careful . . . . Frugal
|__194 Warmhearted . . . . Pity
|__195 Saved . . . . Grand
|__196 Resilient . . . . Deserving
|__197 Precious . . . . Respectable
|__198 Entrancing . . . . Conscious
|__199 Graced . . . . Striking
|__200 Virtuous . . . . Paragon
|__201 Public-spirited . . . . Fertile
|__202 Sheltering . . . . Robust
|__203 Civil . . . . Giving

|__204 Ascending . . . . Curious
|__205 Cool . . . . Farsighted
|__206 Reliable . . . . Significant
|__207 Alive. . . . . Excellent
|__208 Diplomatic . . . . No Worries
|__209 Motivated . . . . Fortified
|__210 Hygienic . . . . Spontaneous
|__211 Maneuverable . . . . Up-to-date
|__212 Conscience . . . . Behaved
|__213 Radiant . . . . Liturgical
|__214 Upstanding . . . . Promising
|__215 Wizardly . . . . Credible
|__216 Attractive . . . . Clear
|__217 Knightly . . . . Perky
|__218 Illustrative . . . . Famous
|__219 Hopeful . . . . Provident
|__220 Huggable . . . . Snugly
|__221 Stamina . . . . Nice
|__222 Consistent . . . . Psychic
|__223 Springy . . . . Cheerful
|__224 Musical . . . . Proficient
|__225 Enchanting . . . . Royal
|__226 Electrifying . . . . Certain
|__227 Ministerial . . . . Cute
|__228 Unique . . . . Ingenuous
|__229 Meek . . . . Ardent
|__230 Magical . . . . Uplifting
|__231 Chic . . . . Punctual
|__232 Savoir-faire . . . . Vivacious
|__233 Sleek . . . . Zany
|__234 Ebullient . . . . Propitious
|__235 Godly . . . . Enticing
|__236 Courageous . . . . Well-spoken
|__237 Salubrious . . . . Touching
|__238 Clairvoyant . . . . Upbeat
|__239 Lenient . . . . Temperate
|__240 Upbeat . . . . Sassy
|__241 Rich . . . . Compliant
|__242 Graceful . . . . Chummy
|__243 Sure . . . . Meek

|__244 Systematic . . . . Reputable
|__245 Fidelity . . . . Qualified
|__246 Self-possessed . . . . Persevering
|__247 Credible . . . . Compelling
|__248 Conviction . . . . Faithful
|__249 Brave . . . . Benign
|__250 Laudable . . . . Philanthropic
|__251 Intimate . . . . Tame
|__252 Shrewd . . . . Authentic
|__253 Canny . . . . Steady
|__254 Responsible . . . . Assiduous
|__255 Perky . . . . Precise
|__256 Charitable . . . . Plucky
|__257 Extemporaneous . . . . Mesmerizing
|__258 Cerebral . . . . Great
|__259 Openhanded . . . . Amenable
|__260 Organized . . . . Comprehensive
|__261 Knowledgeable . . . . Recharged
|__262 Truth . . . . Freethinking
|__263 Innocent . . . . Surviving
|__264 Insightful . . . . Perfect
|__265 Tactful . . . . Adjusted
|__266 Realistic . . . . Peaceful
|__267 Civilized . . . . Considerate
|__268 Secure . . . . Guiding
|__269 Giving . . . . Ecstatic
|__270 Sociable . . . . Beneficent
|__271 Appetizing . . . . Romantic
|__272 Straightforward . . . . Accomplished
|__273 Willful . . . . Initiative
|__274 Tough . . . . Adventuresome
|__275 No Worries . . . . Profound
|__276 Romantic . . . . True
|__277 Auspicious . . . . Brave
|__278 Eminent . . . . Light
|__279 Sassy . . . . Fine
|__280 Matter-of-fact . . . . Stirring
|__281 Fortified . . . . Fancy
|__282 Prestigious . . . . Liberty
|__283 Familial . . . . Watchful

|__284 Touching . . . . Inspiring
|__285 Service Minded . . . . Devoted
|__286 Rascally . . . . Creative
|__287 Informative . . . . Earnest
|__288 Fantastic . . . . Lighthearted
|__289 Strong . . . . Outgoing
|__290 Mettlesome . . . . Eminent
|__291 Cooperative . . . . Clean-cut
|__292 Productive . . . . Mannerly
|__293 Pious . . . . Indefatigable
|__294 Liberty . . . . Productive
|__295 Darling . . . . Gentle
|__296 Genius . . . . Lofty
|__297 Cherished . . . . Softhearted
|__298 Exhaustive . . . . Courageous
|__299 Frugal . . . . Upright
|__300 Stable . . . . Alluring
|__301 Forgiving . . . . Ambitious
|__302 Forward . . . . Just
|__303 Earnest . . . . Independent
|__304 Glamorous . . . . Comfortable
|__305 Exuberant . . . . Contributive
|__306 Tolerant . . . . Fulfilled
|__307 Significant . . . . Soft
|__308 Punctual . . . . Sure-handed
|__309 Solemn . . . . Dainty
|__310 New . . . . Majestic
|__311 Ready . . . . Soulful
|__312 High-minded . . . . Acumen
|__313 Prayerful . . . . Participative
|__314 Nice . . . . Flourishing
|__315 Memorable . . . . Special
|__316 Integrated . . . . Glamorous
|__317 Tenderhearted . . . . Bold
|__318 Approving . . . . Pacifistic
|__319 Advancing . . . . Exciting
|__320 Cute . . . . Easygoing
|__321 Zealous . . . . Helpful
|__322 Sunny . . . . Commanding
|__323 Self-contained . . . . Public-spirited

|__324 Persistent . . . . Imperial
|__325 Deliberate . . . . Drive
|__326 Essential . . . . Open-hearted
|__327 Aesthetic . . . . Suitable
|__328 Choice . . . . Rhythmic
|__329 Jolly . . . . Adorable
|__330 Pert . . . . Clever
|__331 Sterling . . . . Altruistic
|__332 Good Will . . . . Keen
|__333 Neighborly . . . . Serious
|__334 Mesmerizing . . . . Intelligent
|__335 Expanding . . . . Shipshape
|__336 Noble . . . . Stout
|__337 Correct . . . . Spry
|__338 Healthy . . . . Proud
|__339 Triumphant . . . . Improving
|__340 Contributive . . . . Integrated
|__341 Popular . . . . Awake
|__342 Ethical . . . . Aware
|__343 Whole . . . . Legitimate
|__344 Equitable . . . . Fraternal
|__345 Distinctive . . . . Handy
|__346 Introspective . . . . Self-esteem
|__347 Mild . . . . Tireless
|__348 Endeavoring . . . . Dexterous
|__349 Softhearted . . . . Princely
|__350 Affable . . . . Sporting
|__351 Free . . . . Maternal
|__352 Jaunty . . . . Responsive
|__353 Well-read . . . . Astonishing
|__354 Gumption . . . . Congruous
|__355 Considerate . . . . Affable
|__356 Gregarious . . . . Dependable
|__357 Inventive . . . . Merry
|__358 Bright. . . . . Evolving
|__359 Maturing . . . . Tasteful
|__360 Modern . . . . Stalwart
|__361 Therapeutic . . . . Exceptional
|__362 Caring . . . . Integrity
|__363 Astonishing . . . . Gay

|__364 Hearty .... Likable
|__365 Parental .... Breathtaking
|__366 Respectable .... Cuddly
|__367 Responsive .... Whole
|__368 Goal Oriented .... Prudent
|__369 Folksy .... Powerful
|__370 Pacifistic .... Energetic
|__371 Improving .... Balanced
|__372 Clement .... Capable
|__373 Persuasive .... Astute
|__374 Tenacious .... Prompt
|__375 Gay .... Vibrant
|__376 Tame .... Sheltering
|__377 Beneficent .... Courtly
|__378 Entrepreneurial .... Rejuvenative
|__379 Glowing .... Conviction
|__380 Breathtaking .... Lively
|__381 Perspicuous .... Dignified
|__382 Foursquare .... Enamoring
|__383 Benign .... Able
|__384 Regal .... Preserving
|__385 Extemporaneous .... Instrumental
|__386 Perfect .... Controlled
|__387 Deep .... Forgiving
|__388 Immune .... Spicy
|__389 Spontaneous .... Delicate
|__390 Precocious .... Favored
|__391 Hypnotic .... Prayerful
|__392 Surviving .... Penitent
|__393 Agile .... Lucky
|__394 Placid .... Honorable
|__395 Bubbly .... Imaginative
|__396 Wonder .... Sturdy
|__397 Joie de Vivre .... Coordinated
|__398 Merry .... Sensuous
|__399 Photogenic .... Fetching
|__400 High-spirited .... Adaptable
|__401 Stick-to-itive .... Jocular
|__402 Sensible .... Aesthetic
|__403 Contemporary .... Decent

|__404 Artistic . . . . Reverent
|__405 Synergistic . . . . Venturesome
|__406 Swift . . . . Magical
|__407 Satisfied . . . . Nervy
|__408 Exciting . . . . Patient
|__409 Zany . . . . Perspicacious
|__410 Legitimate . . . . Delicious
|__411 Reverent . . . . Blissful
|__412 Prominent . . . . Skillful
|__413 Traditional . . . . Renowned
|__414 Content . . . . Endearing
|__415 Compliant . . . . Triumphant
|__416 Dainty . . . . Modern
|__417 Presence of Mind . . . . Ministerial
|__418 Cuddly . . . . Ravishing
|__419 Ameliorative . . . . Vigilant
|__420 Risk Taker . . . . Spiritual
|__421 Reasonable . . . . High-spirited
|__422 Preserving . . . . Restful
|__423 Democratic . . . . Discreet
|__424 Innovative . . . . Equitable
|__425 Fascinating . . . . Prosperous
|__426 Suitable . . . . Good-natured
|__427 Serene . . . . Courteous
|__428 Clean . . . . Indomitable
|__429 Svelte . . . . Goal Oriented
|__430 Astounding . . . . Idealistic
|__431 Idealistic . . . . Law-abiding
|__432 Charming . . . . Warmhearted
|__433 Climbing . . . . Resourceful
|__434 Ingenious . . . . Natural
|__435 Backbone . . . . Gracious
|__436 Valorous . . . . Ameliorative
|__437 Profitable . . . . Therapeutic
|__438 Nonjudgmental . . . . Carefree
|__439 Wholesome . . . . Meditative
|__440 Sanguine . . . . Glowing
|__441 Precise . . . . Nurturing
|__442 Fragrant . . . . Irresistible
|__443 Commendable . . . . Poetic

|__444 Up-to-date . . . . Sharp
|__445 Sublime . . . . Cordial
|__446 Worshipful . . . . Cooperative
|__447 Bold . . . . Sterling
|__448 Venturesome . . . . Rousing
|__449 Fortunate . . . . Sympathetic
|__450 Striking . . . . Artistic
|__451 True-blue . . . . Composed
|__452 Spunky . . . . Flair
|__453 Practical . . . . Seeking
|__454 Philosophical . . . . Casual
|__455 Growing . . . . Formal
|__456 Agreeable . . . . Elastic
|__457 Conscious . . . . Vital
|__458 Broad-minded . . . . Wholehearted
|__459 Sapient . . . . Chivalrous
|__460 Valuable . . . . Daring
|__461 Appealing . . . . Serene
|__462 Polished . . . . Climbing
|__463 Chaste . . . . Happy
|__464 Paternal . . . . Neat
|__465 Studious . . . . Motivated
|__466 Decent . . . . Fidelity
|__467 Emerging . . . . Definite
|__468 Exact . . . . Bubbly
|__469 Flamboyant . . . . Joie de Vivre
|__470 Direct . . . . Generous
|__471 Privileged . . . . Right
|__472 Sweetheart . . . . Versatile
|__473 Outgoing . . . . Amicable
|__474 Pity . . . . Accurate
|__475 Kind . . . . Desire
|__476 Observant . . . . Distinguished
|__477 Fair . . . . Hardy
|__478 Pioneering . . . . Faith
|__479 Regenerative . . . . Moral
|__480 Right . . . . Honest
|__481 Princely . . . . Veracious
|__482 Okay . . . . Clement
|__483 Honest . . . . Enchanting

|__484 Robust . . . . Appealing
|__485 Engaging . . . . Flamboyant
|__486 Adjusted . . . . Feisty
|__487 Initiative . . . . Nonjudgmental
|__488 Impeccable . . . . Harmonious
|__489 Pure . . . . Orderly
|__490 Chummy . . . . Agreeable
|__491 Economical . . . . Docile
|__492 Interesting . . . . Comforting
|__493 Reflective . . . . Luxurious
|__494 Disporting . . . . Tender
|__495 Amicable . . . . Diverse
|__496 Victorious . . . . Profitable
|__497 Courtly . . . . Religious
|__498 Recharged . . . . Extraordinary
|__499 Conservative . . . . Deliberate
|__500 Multidisciplined . . . . Concerned
|__501 Discriminating . . . . Oriented
|__502 Tractable . . . . Sensible
|__503 Oriented . . . . Succinct
|__504 Integrity . . . . Noteworthy
|__505 Conscientious . . . . Admirable
|__506 Splendid . . . . Judicious
|__507 Divine . . . . Volitional
|__508 Moxie . . . . Sunny
|__509 Luxurious . . . . Cherished
|__510 Indomitable . . . . Successful
|__511 Liturgical . . . . Compatible
|__512 Educated . . . . Magnetic
|__513 Important . . . . Calm
|__514 Individualistic . . . . Normal
|__515 Equanimous . . . . Nimble
|__516 Adroit . . . . Determined
|__517 Distinguished . . . . Hygienic
|__518 Behaved . . . . Splendid
|__519 Spellbinding . . . . Effervescent
|__520 Active . . . . Soothing
|__521 Vivacious . . . . Appeasing
|__522 Lucky . . . . Masterful
|__523 Demure . . . . Astounding

|__524 Sweet .... Gorgeous
|__525 Grounded .... Illustrative
|__526 Acumen .... Recuperative
|__527 Astute .... Humorous
|__528 Resolute .... Trusting
|__529 Handy .... Outstanding
|__530 Wise .... Enjoying
|__531 Focused .... Well-read
|__532 Blissful .... Appreciative
|__533 Spicy .... Persuasive
|__534 Present .... Evenhanded
|__535 Helpful .... Goofy
|__536 Permissive .... Statuesque
|__537 Independent .... Shrewd
|__538 Brotherly .... Rich
|__539 Good-natured .... Grateful
|__540 Recuperative .... Praiseworthy
|__541 Loose .... Truth
|__542 Character .... Candid
|__543 Empathetic .... Terrific
|__544 Savvy .... Understanding
|__545 Whimsical .... Ebullient
|__546 Participative .... Self-made
|__547 Generous .... Knightly
|__548 Philanthropic .... Purposeful
|__549 Extraordinary .... Spirited
|__550 Amorous .... Lovable
|__551 Stylish .... Humble
|__552 Comfortable .... Alacritous
|__553 Provocative .... Sober
|__554 Likable .... Reflective
|__555 Exemplary .... Okay
|__556 Enamoring .... Charitable
|__557 Zestful .... Festive
|__558 Marvelous .... Lionhearted
|__559 Influential .... Presence of Mind
|__560 Lively .... Silly
|__561 Enjoying .... Discriminating
|__562 Uplifting .... Polite
|__563 Mellow .... Colorful

|__564 Capital . . . . Competent
|__565 Rejoicing . . . . Entrepreneurial
|__566 Grand . . . . Complacent
|__567 Promising . . . . Introspective
|__568 Purposeful . . . . Obliging
|__569 Intelligent . . . . Self-accepting
|__570 Assiduous . . . . Svelte
|__571 Gleeful . . . . Limber
|__572 Tender . . . . Metamorphic
|__573 Rugged . . . . Good Will
|__574 Opportunistic . . . . Bountiful
|__575 Decorous . . . . Influential
|__576 Hardy . . . . Expanding
|__577 Sprightly . . . . Animated
|__578 Humorous . . . . Stellar
|__579 Steady . . . . Fervent
|__580 Devout . . . . Utilitarian
|__581 Fearless . . . . Roseate
|__582 Accepting . . . . Presentable
|__583 Trim . . . . Venerable
|__584 Mirthful . . . . Seasoned
|__585 Noteworthy . . . . Precocious
|__586 Stirring . . . . Aplomb
|__587 Spry . . . . Instinctive
|__588 Red-blooded . . . . Moderate
|__589 Appropriate . . . . Valorous
|__590 Tireless . . . . Cognizant
|__591 Angelic . . . . Willful
|__592 Lionhearted . . . . Positive
|__593 Sharp . . . . Exact
|__594 Rhythmic . . . . Present
|__595 Self-esteem . . . . Entertaining
|__596 Sedulous . . . . Impressive
|__597 Leadership . . . . Permissive
|__598 Stress Hardy . . . . Dashing
|__599 Well . . . . Clairvoyant
|__600 Faithful . . . . Blooming
|__601 Aspiring . . . . Liberal
|__602 Contemplative . . . . Contemporary
|__603 Dedicated . . . . Supportive

|__604 Accurate . . . . Objective
|__605 Fervent . . . . Stress Hardy
|__606 Immaculate . . . . Upstanding
|__607 Certain . . . . Observant
|__608 Bonhomie . . . . Brilliant
|__609 Brilliant . . . . Rascally
|__610 Grateful . . . . Instructive
|__611 Buoyant . . . . Instrumental
|__612 Special . . . . Useful
|__613 Dependable . . . . Rejoicing
|__614 Vibrant . . . . Cerebral
|__615 Directed . . . . Informative
|__616 Freethinking . . . . Efficient
|__617 Compatible . . . . Hopeful
|__618 Beauty . . . . Captivating
|__619 Actualized . . . . Practical
|__620 Inquisitive . . . . Commiserative
|__621 Probity . . . . Sublime
|__622 Intriguing . . . . Healthy
|__623 Vigorous . . . . Mirthful
|__624 Roseate . . . . Parental
|__625 Heroic . . . . Capital
|__626 Sanitary . . . . Constructive
|__627 Eager . . . . Arresting
|__628 Euphoric . . . . Vigorous
|__629 Thoughtful . . . . Economical
|__630 Seemly . . . . Quiet
|__631 Righteous . . . . Cautious
|__632 Fruitful . . . . Secure
|__633 Scholarly . . . . Cagey
|__634 Inspiring . . . . Charismatic
|__635 Light . . . . Noble
|__636 Trustworthy . . . . Trim
|__637 Suave . . . . Physical
|__638 Incisive . . . . Righteous
|__639 Classy . . . . Lyrical
|__640 Frank . . . . Neighborly
|__641 Striving . . . . Conservative
|__642 Comical . . . . Comely
|__643 Lithesome . . . . Familial

|__644 Cogent . . . . Expressive
|__645 Warm . . . . Regal
|__646 Rational . . . . Zestful
|__647 Arresting . . . . Expert
|__648 Quick-witted . . . . Stylish
|__649 Nurturing . . . . Auspicious
|__650 Convincing . . . . Rapport
|__651 Instinctive . . . . Sharing
|__652 Nervy . . . . Deep
|__653 Particular . . . . New
|__654 Amenable . . . . Compromising
|__655 Spiritual . . . . Virtuous
|__656 Altruistic . . . . Pleasant
|__657 Rollicking . . . . Multifaceted
|__658 Harmonious . . . . Quick
|__659 Expert . . . . Centered
|__660 Compassionate . . . . Forceful
|__661 Professional . . . . Wizardly
|__662 Pulchritudinous . . . . Foxy
|__663 Magnanimous . . . . Suave
|__664 Adventuresome . . . . Photogenic
|__665 Creative . . . . Spellbinding
|__666 Obliging . . . . Fitting
|__667 Presentable . . . . Durable
|__668 Multifaceted . . . . Salubrious
|__669 Pristine . . . . Tough
|__670 Stimulating . . . . Jolly
|__671 Stunning . . . . : Nourishing
|__672 Punctilious . . . . Wry
|__673 Utilitarian . . . . Tactful
|__674 Fresh . . . . Zealous
|__675 Watchful . . . . Electrifying
|__676 Competent . . . . Conscience
|__677 Perceptive . . . . Backbone
|__678 Dapper . . . . Broad-minded
|__679 Loyal . . . . Particular
|__680 Elastic . . . . Heart
|__681 Concise . . . . Quaint
|__682 Vigilant . . . . Traditional
|__683 Restful . . . . Worthy

|__684 Fine . . . . Equanimous
|__685 Congenial . . . . Joyful
|__686 Quality . . . . Amorous
|__687 Terrific . . . . Thrifty
|__688 Self-respect . . . . Mellow
|__689 Sure-handed . . . . Good Self-image
|__690 Exceptional . . . . Malleable
|__691 Learned . . . . Multidimensional
|__692 Intrepid . . . . Sane
|__693 Qualified . . . . Conforming
|__694 Clear . . . . Expeditious
|__695 Prompt . . . . Safe
|__696 Patient . . . . Sensitive
|__697 Investigative . . . . Direct
|__698 Talented . . . . Rugged
|__699 Sedate . . . . Technical
|__700 Willing . . . . Funny
|__701 Lustrous . . . . Sapient
|__702 Experienced . . . . Coherent
|__703 Ingenuous . . . . Investigative
|__704 Exquisite . . . . Eager
|__705 Clever . . . . Chaste
|__706 Blessed . . . . Warm
|__707 Fetching . . . . Refreshing
|__708 Lighthearted . . . . Euphoric
|__709 Happy-go-lucky . . . . Kind
|__710 Inner-directed. . . . . True
|__711 Spirited . . . . Frisky
|__712 Psychic . . . . Abiding
|__713 Pragmatic . . . . Panache
|__714 Reputable . . . . Yummy
|__715 Attentive . . . . Spunky
|__716 Soaring . . . . Tenacious
|__717 Clean-cut . . . . Serendipitous
|__718 Cultured . . . . Scrupulous
|__719 Original . . . . Intriguing
|__720 Hospitable . . . . Wonderful
|__721 Confident . . . . Punctilious
|__722 Celebrated . . . . Privileged
|__723 Prudent . . . . Principled

|__724 Accommodating . . . . Approving

|__725 Worthy . . . . Gregarious

|__726 Flexible . . . . Conciliatory

|__727 Painstaking . . . . Saved

|__728 Accessible . . . . Solid

|__729 Successful . . . . Seemly

|__730 Evolving . . . . Intrepid

|__731 Nimble . . . . Disciplined

|__732 Yummy . . . . Cogent

|__733 Staunch . . . . Correct

|__734 Risible . . . . Maturing

|__735 Inner-directed . . . . Celebrated

|__736 Captivating . . . . Compassionate

|__737 Matter-of-fact . . . . Ravishing

|__738 Discreet . . . . Openhanded

|__739 Revered . . . . Debonair

|__740 Homey . . . . Valuable

|__741 Levelheaded . . . . Complete

|__742 Impressive . . . . Quick-witted

|__743 Communicative . . . . Cultured

|__744 Developing . . . . Bright

|__745 Capable . . . . Educated

|__746 Paragon . . . . Fun

|__747 Deft . . . . Intuitive

|__748 Fulfilled . . . . Savoir-faire

|__749 Voluptuous . . . . Revered

|__750 Faith . . . . Ascending

|__751 Calm . . . . Unstoppable

|__752 Available . . . . Handsome

|__753 Dignified . . . . Interesting

|__754 Principled . . . . Sisterly

|__755 Technical . . . . Optimistic

|__756 Seasoned . . . . Love

|__757 Gutsy . . . . Sociable

|__758 Panache . . . . Voluptuous

|__759 Open . . . . Restorative

|__760 Witty . . . . Maneuverable

|__761 Expressive . . . . Stamina

|__762 Forthright . . . . Sanitary

|__763 Physical . . . . Foursquare

|__764 Meticulous . . . . Imitable
|__765 Penitent . . . . Tolerant
|__766 Polite . . . . Poised
|__767 Stalwart . . . . Mettlesome
|__768 Proud . . . . Exhaustive
|__769 Genuine . . . . Relaxed
|__770 Casual . . . . Directed
|__771 Necessary . . . . Attractive
|__772 Luminous . . . . Clean
|__773 Efficient . . . . Inventive
|__774 Fashionable . . . . Talented
|__775 Fitting . . . . Innovative
|__776 Ardent . . . . Graceful
|__777 Sound . . . . Autonomous
|__778 Drive . . . . Paternal
|__779 Serious . . . . Logical
|__780 Conciliatory . . . . Musical
|__781 Positive . . . . Firm
|__782 Indefatigable . . . . Good-humored
|__783 Playful . . . . Sweetheart
|__784 Genial . . . . Benevolent
|__785 Charismatic . . . . Cozy
|__786 Congruous . . . . Exuberant
|__787 Durable . . . . Mighty
|__788 Lofty . . . . Contemplative
|__789 Definite . . . . Stunning
|__790 Consonant . . . . Fascinating
|__791 Abiding . . . . Enterprising
|__792 Shining . . . . Darling
|__793 Ladylike . . . . Prescient
|__794 Foxy . . . . Dapper
|__795 Changeable . . . . Thriving
|__796 Sisterly . . . . Supple
|__797 Guiding . . . . Snazzy
|__798 Sober . . . . Fantastic
|__799 Centered . . . . Insightful
|__800 Quaint . . . . Consonant
|__801 Ambitious . . . . Risible
|__802 Veracious . . . . Resilient
|__803 Impartial . . . . Shining

|__804 Awake .... Dutiful
|__805 Appreciative .... Innocent
|__806 Scrumptious .... Lovely
|__807 Leisurely .... Long-suffering
|__808 Sexy .... Brotherly
|__809 Magnetic .... Self-contained
|__810 Superb .... Probity
|__811 Decisive .... Dazzling
|__812 Frolicsome .... Divine
|__813 Useful .... Learned
|__814 Holy .... Gentlemanly
|__815 Formal .... Content
|__816 Conforming .... Classy
|__817 Coordinated .... Urbane
|__818 Lyrical .... Dynamic
|__819 Dashing .... Flowing
|__820 Humanitarian .... Huggable
|__821 Happy-go-lucky .... Industrious
|__822 Stretching .... Chic
|__823 Tasteful .... Pastoral
|__824 Animated .... Demure
|__825 Stick-to-itive .... Compromising
|__826 Cunning .... Frank
|__827 Self-made .... Character
|__828 Pleasant .... Active
|__829 Extroverted .... Loyal
|__830 Happy .... Developing
|__831 Individualistic .... Amiable
|__832 Fertile .... Accessible
|__833 Serendipitous .... Folksy
|__834 Dutiful .... Tractable
|__835 Authentic .... Well
|__836 Mindful .... Gifted
|__837 Exotic .... Gusto
|__838 Cagey .... Magnificent
|__839 Normal .... Exotic
|__840 Healing .... Metaphysical
|__841 Gentlemanly .... Foresighted
|__842 Keen .... Peppy
|__843 Famous .... Buoyant

|__844 Foresighted . . . . Lithesome
|__845 Sentimental . . . . Articulate
|__846 Firm . . . . Luscious
|__847 Straightforward . . . . Mannerly
|__848 Optimistic . . . . Luminous
|__849 Alluring . . . . Playful
|__850 Discerning . . . . Growing
|__851 Evenhanded . . . . Mild
|__852 Diligent . . . . Jaunty
|__853 Law-abiding . . . . Pristine
|__854 Savory . . . . Selfless
|__855 Metaphysical . . . . Ventilious
|__856 Forbearing . . . . Hypnotic
|__857 Multidimensional . . . . Victorious
|__858 Dynamic . . . . Cunning
|__859 Gusto . . . . Open
|__860 Common Sense . . . . Munificent
|__861 Appeasing . . . . Ingenious
|__862 Adorable . . . . Adroit
|__863 Blooming . . . . Industrious
|__864 Lucid . . . . Well-meaning
|__865 Imitable . . . . Sapid
|__866 Poised . . . . Beneficial
|__867 Explorative. . . . . Winsome
|__868 Heart . . . . Civilized
|__869 Moral . . . . Symmetrical
|__870 Expeditious . . . . Even-tempered
|__871 Methodical . . . . Holy
|__872 Volitional . . . . Melodious
|__873 Intuitive . . . . Merciful
|__874 Proficient . . . . Nonchalant
|__875 Soulful . . . . Leadership
|__876 Flair . . . . Fresh
|__877 Commiserative . . . . Searching
|__878 Prescient . . . . Decorous
|__879 Affirming . . . . Explorative
|__880 Well-spoken . . . . True-blue
|__881 Renowned . . . . Professional
|__882 Metamorphic . . . . Encouraging
|__883 Gamesome . . . . Accepting

|__884 Articulate . . . . Sustaining
|__885 Personable . . . . Endeavoring
|__886 Pliable . . . . Enlightened
|__887 Chutzpah . . . . Chipper
|__888 Selfless . . . . Amusing
|__889 Daffy . . . . Dreaming
|__890 Silly . . . . Scrumptious
|__891 Debonair . . . . Organized
|__892 Dreaming . . . . Stable
|__893 Thriving . . . . Commendable
|__894 Moderate . . . . Perfectible
|__895 Vision . . . . Savory
|__896 Benevolent . . . . Worshipful
|__897 Realized . . . . Convincing
|__898 Soothing . . . . Godly
|__899 Glad . . . . Illustrious
|__900 Desire . . . . Reasonable
|__901 Joyful . . . . Childlike
|__902 Instructive . . . . Proper
|__903 Compelling . . . . Memorable
|__904 Soft . . . . Comical
|__905 Quick . . . . Perspicuous
|__906 Modest . . . . Agile
|__907 Easygoing . . . . Abundant
|__908 Piquant . . . . Thoughtful
|__909 Cordial . . . . Fair
|__910 Farsighted . . . . Striving
|__911 Cautious . . . . Diplomatic
|__912 Companionable . . . . Congenial
|__913 Meritorious . . . . Communicative
|__914 Delightful . . . . Accountable
|__915 Irresistible . . . . Piquant
|__916 Provident . . . . Accommodating
|__917 Disciplined . . . . Exquisite
|__918 Chivalrous . . . . Springy
|__919 Powerful . . . . Rollicking
|__920 Peaceful . . . . Pragmatic
|__921 Verve . . . . Humanitarian
|__922 Poetic . . . . Methodical
|__923 Childlike . . . . Sedulous

|__924 Amazing . . . . Studious
|__925 Sensuous . . . . Self-governing
|__926 Improvisational . . . . Hearty
|__927 Accomplished . . . . Treasured
|__928 Logical . . . . Steadfast
|__929 Vim . . . . Dedicated
|__930 Sincere . . . . Necessary
|__931 Rapport . . . . Sagacious
|__932 Encouraging . . . . Virginal
|__933 Self-possessed . . . . Leisurely
|__934 Illustrious . . . . Tranquil
|__935 Elegant . . . . Saintly
|__936 Self-accepting . . . . Radiant
|__937 Temperate . . . . Prolific
|__938 Curious . . . . Realistic
|__939 Meditative . . . . Timely
|__940 Laid-back . . . . Experienced
|__941 Stout . . . . Versed
|__942 Pizazz . . . . Stretching
|__943 Honorable . . . . Free
|__944 Safe . . . . Gallant
|__945 Diverse . . . . Placid
|__946 Salutary . . . . Mindful
|__947 Sharing . . . . Strong
|__948 Flourishing . . . . Marvelous
|__949 Restorative . . . . Tenderhearted
|__950 Thrifty . . . . Discerning
|__951 Candid . . . . Erudite
|__952 Friendly . . . . Resolute
|__953 Snugly . . . . Perceptive
|__954 Cheerful . . . . Ready
|__955 Virginal . . . . Friendly
|__956 Malleable . . . . Fit
|__957 Beneficial . . . . Lustrous
|__958 Good-humored . . . . Angelic
|__959 Vital . . . . Polished
|__960 Cozy . . . . Affectionate
|__961 Nonchalant . . . . Thrilling
|__962 Humane . . . . Daffy
|__963 Quiet . . . . Lenient

|__964 Enduring .... Esteemed
|__965 Docile .... Red-blooded
|__966 Adaptable .... Virile
|__967 Majestic .... Flexible
|__968 Pretty .... Beauty
|__969 Limber .... Jubilant
|__970 Up-and-coming .... Jovial
|__971 Protective .... Well-disposed
|__972 Finesse .... Goodhearted
|__973 Resourceful .... Fruitful
|__974 Excellent .... Immaculate
|__975 Gallant .... Subtle
|__976 Dexterous .... Concentrative
|__977 Smart .... Protective
|__978 Convivial .... Lucid
|__979 Versed .... Rational
|__980 Well-disposed .... Effective
|__981 Wonderful .... Fearless
|__982 Gorgeous .... Pliable
|__983 Jocular .... Stately
|__984 Stately .... Gumption
|__985 Great .... Graced
|__986 Fun .... Devout
|__987 Goodhearted .... Levelheaded
|__988 Jubilant .... Finesse

Appendix 3

Additional Positive Qualities

These qualities are generally positive but were not included on the primary list because of the following reasons:

- Too Godlike—see the Divine List
- Expressed better in one word—see the Positive Phrase List
- Too close—i.e., Assure and Reassure
- Concept included in a quality on the list
- Too nebulous
- Too obscure
- Too colloquial
- Too situational
- Too specific to a particular group
- Too extreme
- More passive than active
- Not positive enough
- Negated negative—i.e., Nonoffensive
- More an attitude than a quality
- More a quality of a thing than a person
- Sometimes considered negative
- The most recent meaning is not positive—e.g., *Virago*

THE DIVINE LIST

This is a list of qualities attributed to a Divine Being. A finite being can conceptualize owning these qualities, but the actualization of them is beyond the everyday experience of a mortal human. Albeit, people are sometimes characterized with these qualities.

1. Absolute	23. Flawless	45. Mysterious	67. Sanctified
2. Ageless	24. Foremost	46. Omneity	68. Self-generated
3. Almighty	25. Glorious	47. Omnicorporeal	69. Self-perpetuated
4. Amaranthine	26. Hallowed	48. Omnifarious	70. Spotless
5. August	27. Immortal	49. Omnific	71. Stupendous
6. Awesome	28. Immutable	50. Omnipercipient	72. Supernal
7. Beatific	29. Imperishable	51. Omnipotent	73. Supernatural
8. Beloved	30. Incomparable	52. Omnipresent	74. Supreme
9. Blameless	31. Incorruptible	53. Omniscient	75. Timeless
10. Boundless	32. Incredible	54. Omnispective	76. Transcendent
11. Ceaseless	33. Indispensable	55. Paramount	77. Ubiquitous
12. Changeless	34. Inexhaustible	56. Peerless	78. Ultimate
13. Cosmic	35. Infallible	57. Perpetual	79. Unchangeable
14. Effulgent	36. Infinite	58. Preeminent	80. Unequaled
15. Endless	37. Invaluable	59. Premier	81. Unified
16. Eternal	38. Invincible	60. Priceless	82. Unimpeachable
17. Ethereal	39. Inviolate	61. Prime	83. Universal
18. Everlasting	40. Invulnerable	62. Quintessential	84. Unlimited
19. Exalted	41. Irrepressible	63. Replete	85. Unmatched
20. Existential	42. Irreproachable	64. Resplendent	86. Unrivaled
21. Faultless	43. Matchless	65. Sacred	87. Unsurpassed
22. First	44. Miraculous	66. Sacrosanct	88. Zenithal

THE POSITIVE PHRASE LIST

1. A brown study
2. A can-do attitude
3. A cut above
4. A defender of righteousness
5. A good listener
6. A green thumb
7. A laugh that opens hearts
8. A longing for the highest ideals
9. A mover and shaker
10. A problem solver
11. A rosy outlook
12. A smile that lights up the room
13. A straight arrow
14. A straight shooter
15. A straight talker
16. A team player
17. Able to accept disappointment
18. Able to ask for what is needed

19. Able to be here now
20. Able to defuse an argument
21. Able to get to the heart of the matter
22. Able to give credit where due
23. Able to give relief
24. Able to handle conflict
25. Able to hold up under close scrutiny
26. Able to hold your tongue
27. Able to keep an even keel
28. Able to laugh at yourself
29. Able to leap tall buildings in a single bound
30. Able to like what you don't want to do
31. Able to overcome inertia
32. Able to put forth the maximum effort
33. Able to recognize inner intentions
34. Able to recognize inner motivations
35. Able to save face
36. Able to see a global view
37. Able to size up a situation
38. Able to take things in stride
39. Able to view difficulty as an opportunity
40. An interesting conversationalist
41. Being idea-minded
42. Capable of giving solace
43. Capable of mutual respect
44. Clearly see the overview
45. Esprit de corps
46. Following the straight and narrow
47. Free of illusion
48. Full of ideas
49. Full of life
50. Get-up-and-go
51. Good at give-and-take
52. Having high aspirations
53. Having high morale
54. Heart of gold
55. Held in the highest regard
56. In contact with higher self
57. In fine fettle
58. Joyfully discontent
59. Knowing one's limitations
60. Knowing what to do next
61. Knowing when to let go
62. Loving kindness
63. On a roll
64. Par excellence
65. Peace of mind
66. Service oriented
67. Thought provoking
68. Understanding the basics
69. Up-front

OTHER POSITIVE QUALITIES

1. Abetting
2. Able-bodied
3. Abounding
4. Absolving
5. Abstaining
6. Accordant
7. Achieved
8. Acknowledged
9. Acme
10. Acquiescent
11. Acquitting
12. Acuity
13. Address
14. Adequate
15. Advisable
16. Affecting
17. Affiance
18. Affinity
19. Afflatus
20. Affluent
21. Agape
22. Aggressive
23. Aglow
24. Aiding
25. Aligned
26. Allegiance
27. Allowing
28. An Ally
29. Amatory
30. Ample
31. Analytical
32. Answerable
33. Anxious
34. Apostolic
35. Apotheosis
36. Apposite

37. Apprehension
38. Approachable
39. Approbatory
40. Apt
41. Ardor
42. Aristocratic
43. Artifice
44. Asseverative
45. Assimilative
46. At Onement
47. Atonement
48. Audacious
49. Averring
50. Avid
51. Avouching
52. Avuncular
53. Awarded
54. Balmy
55. Basic
56. Bearing
57. Becoming
58. Befitting
59. Belonging
60. Benison
61. Best
62. Better
63. Bewitching
64. Beyond
65. Big-hearted
66. Blessing
67. Blithe
68. Blossoming
69. Bonding
70. Bonny
71. Bouncy
72. Brash
73. Bravado
74. Brawny
75. A Buddy
76. Camaraderie
77. Capacious
78. Capricious
79. Caressing
80. Caritas
81. Catholic

82. Celestial
83. Challenging
84. Chary
85. Chimerical
86. Christlike
87. Circumspect
88. Clairaudient
89. Clear-minded
90. Close
91. Cocky
92. Cohesive
93. Collected
94. Comity
95. Competitive
96. Complaisant
97. Complimentary
98. Concerting
99. Conclusive
100. Concrete
101. Confidant
102. Congratulatory
103. Connected
104. Consecrated
105. Conserving
106. Constant
107. Continuous
108. Contrite
109. Convenient
110. Conventional
111. Copasetic
112. Coping
113. Copious
114. Corrigible
115. Corroborative
116. Couth
117. Crackerjack
118. Craftsmanship
119. Crafty
120. Creditable
121. Crisp
122. Critical
123. Crucial
124. Cultivated
125. Curing
126 A Cut-up

127. Dancing
128. Dandy
129. Dash
130. Dauntless
131. Dear
132. Dear Heart
133. Defensible
134. Deferential
135. Definitive
136. A Demigod
137. Demonstrative
138. Derring-do
139. Destined
140. Detached
141. Didactic
142. Different
143. Ditzy
144. Dogged
145. Dominant
146. Doubtless
147. Doughty
148. A Dove
149. Doxological
150. Droll
151. Earning
152. Eccentric
153. Ecumenical
154. Effortful
155. Effortless
156. Egalitarian
157. Elaborate
158. Elan
159. Eloquent
160. Eleemosynary
161. Emotional
162. Empowered
163. Endorsed
164. Endowed
165. Enraptured
166. Enriching
167. Ensured
168. Enthralling
169. Entreating
170. Entrusted
171. Enviable

172. Equable
173. Equipoise
174. Esoteric
175. Especial
176. Established
177. Eustress
178. Even
179. An Example
180. Excelling
181. Exculpating
182. Excusable
183. Exonerating
184. Experimental
185. Exultant
186. Fair-minded
187. Fair play
188. Familiar
189. Far-reaching
190. Fast
191. Fastidious
192. Fealty
193. Fecund
194. Fervid
195. Fighter
196. First-class
197. First-rate
198. Flabbergasted
199. Flashy
200. Flattered
201. Fleet
202. Flirtatious
203. Flowering
204. Fluent
205. Flush
206. Follow-through
207. Fond
208. Foolproof
209. Forewarned
210. Forging
211. Formidable
212. Fostering
213. Free will
214. Freehanded
215. Full
216. Functional

217. Funky
218. Furtive
219. Futuristic
220. Gaining
221. Gambol
222. A Gem
223. Giggly
224. Gladsome
225. Gleaming
226. Glib
227. Glistening
228. Glittery
229. Global
230. Glorifying
231. God-seeking
232. A Go-getter
233. Golden mean
234. Good judgment
235. Good looking
236. Good taste
237. Good-tempered
238. Grandeur
239. Gratified
240. Greathearted
241. Groovy
242. Guileless
243. Guilt-free
244. Gung ho
245. Habitual
246. Halcyon
247. Hale
248. Hardworking
249. Harmless
250. Heartsease
251. Heartsome
252. Heavenly
253. Hedonistic
254. Heedful
255. High
256. Hilarious
257. A Honey
258. Hot
259. Humdinger
260. Hunky-dory
261. Husky

262. Idyllic
263. Illuminated
264. Impassioned
265. Imperative
266. Imperturbable
267. Impervious
268. Impetus
269. Imposing
270. Impregnable
271. Impromptu
272. Impulsive
273. Inconspicuous
274. Incontrovertible
275. Incorruptible
276. Increasing
277. Indispensable
278. Indisputable
279. Indubitable
280. Indulgent
281. Informed
282. Inoffensive
283. Insouciant
284. Inspirited
285. Insuperable
286. Insured
287. Intense
288. An Intermediary
289. Intrinsic
290. Introverted
291. Inured
292. Invigorating
293. Inviting
294. Involved
295. Irreplaceable
296. Irresistible
297. A Jewel
298. Jocose
299. Juicy
300. Justifiable
301. Keen-witted
302. Kempt
303. Kissable
304. Kooky
305. Lambent
306. Lasting

307. Latitude
308. Laughing
309. Lavish
310. Legendary
311. Legerity
312. Lickerish
313. Limpid
314. Listening
315. Literal
316. Literate
317. Longing
318. Long-lived
319. Loony
320. Loopy
321. Lordly
322. Lush
323. Lusty
324. Manageable
325. Manful
326. Meaningful
327. Mediator
328. Mellifluous
329. Mental
330. Mercurial
331. Meteoric
332. Mischievous
333. Model
334. Momentous
335. Momentum
336. Monarchical
337. Monumental
338. A Moonbeam
339. Morale
340. Multicultural
341. Multileveled
342. Museful
343. Mutual
344. Mystical
345. Mystifying
346. Naive
347. Natty
348. Neat-handed
349. Negotiative
350. Nestling
351. Nifty
352. Noble-souled
353. No doubt
354. Nonabrasive
355. Nonculpable
356. Nondisruptive
357. Nondogmatic
358. Nonobstructive
359. Nonoffensive
360. Nonrigid
361. Nonviolent
362. Non-attached
363. Noticeable
364. Novel
365. Obligatory
366. Offbeat
367. Ongoing
368. Ontological
369. Oomph
370. Open-eyed
371. Open-faced
372. Optimal
373. Oratorical
374. Orgasmic
375. Orgiastic
376. Outrageous
377. Pacifying
378. A Paladin
379. Palatable
380. Palmy
381. Pampered
382. Pardonable
383. Passing
384. Pathos
385. Patriotic
386. A Peach
387. A Pearl
388. Peculiar
389. Pellucid
390. Penetrating
391. Performing
392. Periscopical
393. Pertinacious
394. Pertinent
395. Pervious
396. Phenomenal
397. Picturesque
398. A Pillar
399. Pithy
400. Placable
401. Plainspoken
402. Planetary
403. Platonic
404. Plausible
405. Pleading
406. Pleasurable
407. Plentiful
408. Pliant
409. Plush
410. Poignant
411. Pointed
412. Pollyanna
413. Ponderous
414. Posh
415. Potent
416. Practiced
417. Precautionary
418. Predominant
419. Preferred
420. Prepossessing
421. Prevailing
422. Prim
423. Prodigious
424. Promethean
425. Promoting
426. Prophetic
427. Proportionate
428. A Protagonist
429. Prototypical
430. Prowess
431. Puissant
432. Pull
433. Pure-hearted
434. Quick-minded
435. Quirky
436. Quizzical
437. Racy
438. Rambunctious
439. Rank
440. Rapid
441. Rapt

442. Rapturous
443. Rare
444. Rate
445. Ratiocinative
446. Rattling
447. Reassuring
448. Reborn
449. Recognizable
450. Recommended
451. Reconcilable
452. Redeemed
453. Redoubtable
454. Reformed
455. Regarded
456. Regular
457. Reinforcing
458. Renascent
459. Renewed
460. Repentant
461. Rescued
462. Reserved
463. Resistant
464. Resonant
465. Restraint
466. Retentive
467. Revamped
468. Revised
469. Revitalized
470. Revived
471. Rewarding
472. Rhapsodic
473. Right-on
474. Ripe
475. Rising
476. Riveting
477. Rounded
478. Ruthful
479. Salty
480. Sanctity
481. Sang-froid
482. Satisfactory
483. Satyagraha
484. Saucy
485. Savoir vivre
486. Scientific

487. Seductive
488. Selective
489. Self-acting
490. Self-actualized
491. Self-assertive
492. Self-assured
493. Self-centered
494. Self-composed
495. Self-confident
496. Self-contained
497. Self-controlled
498. Self-correcting
499. Self-defensive
500. Self-determined
501. Self-disciplined
502. Self-educated
503. Self-effacing
504. Self-expressive
505. Self-forgetful
506. Self-guided
507. Self-reflective
508. Self-regulating
509. Self-reliant
510. Self-restrained
511. Self-ruling
512. Self-sacrificing
513. Self-starter
514. Self-subsisting
515. Self-sufficing
516. Self-sustaining
517. Self-taught
518. Self-worth
519. Settled
520. Sharp-sighted
521. Shimmery
522. Sholom
523. Showy
524. Shy
525. Sidereal
526. Simpatico
527. Singing
528. Single-hearted
529. Single-minded
530. Singular
531. Sky-high

532. Slick
533. Sly
534. Smiling
535. Solicitous
536. Somebody
537. Sovereign
538. Spacious
539. Sparing
540. Sparkly
541. Spectacular
542. Speculative
543. Speedy
544. Spick-and-span
545. Spiffy
546. Spotless
547. A Star
548. Stealthy
549. Steely
550. Stewardship
551. Still
552. Stoic
553. Stouthearted
554. Straight
555. Streamlined
556. Studly
557. Stupefying
558. Submissive
559. Substantial
560. Sufficient
561. Sultry
562. Sumptuous
563. Super
564. Supercharged
565. Superfine
566. Superhuman
567. Superior
568. Supernormal
569. Supersensible
570. Superstar
571. Supraliminal
572. Supranational
573. Suprarational
574. Surpassing
575. Swank
576. Swell

577. Swinging
578. Synthesis
579. Tantalizing
580. A Teacher
581. Telepathic
582. Telling
583. Theistic
584. Theosophical
585. Thunderstruck
586. Tight
587. Tip-top
588. Titanic
589. Toasty
590. Together
591. Tops
592. Towering
593. Transcendental
594. Transformed
595. Trenchant
596. Tricky
597. Trooper
598. Trow
599. True-hearted
600. True-to-self
601. Unadulterated
602. Unaffected
603. Unafraid
604. Unambiguous
605. Unashamed
606. Unassuming
607. Unblemished
608. Uncomplaining
609. Uncomplicated
610. Unconcerned
611. Unconquerable
612. Uncontaminated
613. Uncorrupted
614. Undaunted
615. Undefiled
616. Undeniable

617. Unemotional
618. Unencumbered
619. Unerring
620. Unfailing
621. Unfaltering
622. Unflappable
623. Unflinching
624. Unforgettable
625. Unhurried
626. Uniform
627. Unimpaired
628. Uninhibited
629. United
630. Unmistakable
631. Unobjectionable
632. Unobstructed
633. Unobtrusive
634. Unorthodox
635. Unperturbed
636. Unpolluted
637. Unpredictable
638. Unprejudiced
639. Unpretentious
640. Unquestionable
641. Unreserved
642. Unruffled
643. Unselfish
644. Unshakable
645. Unsoiled
646. Unspotted
647. Unsullied
648. Unswerving
649. Untroubled
650. Unwavering
651. Valid
652. Vehement
653. Veridical
654. Viable
655. Vindicating
656. Virago

657. Virtuosity
658. Visionary
659. Vivid
660. Vocal
661. Voluntary
662. Waggish
663. Wanted
664. Warrior
665. Wealthy
666. Welcome
667. Well-advised
668. Well-balanced
669. Well-being
670. Well-beloved
671. Well-born
672. Well-bred
673. Well-favored
674. Well-fixed
675. Well-groomed
676. Well-grounded
677. Well-heeled
678. Well-informed
679. Well-intentioned
680. Well-known
681. Well-mannered
682. Well-off
683. Well-ordered
684. Well-rounded
685. Well-thought-of
686. Well-to-do
687. Well-turned
688. A Well-wisher
689. Winning
690. Wishful
691. With-it
692. Worldly
693. Worthful
694. Yielding
695. Youthful
696. Zippy

SYMBOLS

Graphic images are the picture language of the mind. A graphic symbol is a quick imprint of a concept. Use symbols to activate your visualization of your desired qualities.

QUALITY	SYMBOL(S)
Abiding	The elephant (long-lived)
Abundant	Vegetation; a big mountain (American Indian)
Accurate	A bull's-eye
Active	Children playing; Mars; the sail; the spur
Actualized	A golden rose
Adventuresome	A ship
Affectionate	A hug; a kiss
Affirming	Shaking the head up and down yes; the column
Agility	The stag; the rabbit
Alert	An arrowhead (American Indian)
Alive	Air—the breath of life; bread; fire (like the living, both must consume life to stay alive); the fountain; the vine
Articulate	An orator
Assertive	The flag raised above on a pole
Authoritative	The fist; the hand
Balanced	Libra (zodiac); the scales of justice; the wheel of fortune (tarot); two; yin and yang
Beauty	The eagle; the flower

Blooming	A flower in bloom
Bold	A youth
Buoyant	A boat
Carefree	A bird (American Indian)
Centered	One; the tree as the world axis
Changeable	Crossing of the fingers (hoping to change an expected outcome); death; eleven; the bridge (transition from one stage to another)
Charity	The girding of the loins
Chaste	The swan; the unicorn
Choice	Crossroads
Clairvoyant	The third eye
Clear	A clear blue sky
Clever	The fox
Colorful	The rainbow
Comical	A clown
Commanding	Clubs (the suit in cards); the scepter
Commiserative	A nurse
Communicative	Music; the infinity symbol; the mouth (Egyptian); water
Companionable	The Round Table of King Arthur fame
Compassionate	The elephant
Conscious	An island front; Jupiter (superconscious); right; Saturn; the mirror; window(s)
Consonant	Ouroboros—a dragon or serpent biting its own tail
Contemplative	A mandala; a mountaintop
Controlled	The chariot (self-control)
Cool	An ice cube; an icicle
Cooperative	Fish (team work)
Courage	The sword
Creative	A volcano; Aries (zodiac); weaving; a storm; Fabric (warp = passive, yin; woof = active, yang); the letter R; dance; the Minstrel (tarot); the mouth (speech); the spider (web spinning); the spiral
Cuddly	A teddy bear
Curious	The brown bear
Daring	A tightrope walker
Deep	The abyss
Delicate	The almond tree (sweet blossoms that can be destroyed by frost); the wing of a butterfly
Desire	A siren; fruit; the apple; the hunter
Developing	Hair, abundant and beautiful (spiritual development)

Dexterous	A juggler
Dignity	Sunshade (Chinese)
Diligent	Wings
Disciplined	The yoke
Diverse	Nature
Divine	The meteorite (any object that falls from heaven is sacred)
Down-to-earth	Four; the cube; the square
Dreaming	A stormy sea
Dutiful	The ox
Dynamic	The ocean
Easygoing	A hammock
Ecstatic	Jumping
Educated	The cap and gown
Electrifying	A bolt of lightning
Emerging	A cocoon
Endeavoring	The search for the Holy Grail
Enduring	A long-distance runner; Saturn (endurance)
Energetic	Fire; hair; the snake; the sun
Enlightened	The crown
Equitable	Wyoming is the Equality State
Evolving	A ladder; steps; the fossil; the sword; the ziggurat or minaret; the zigzag
Fabulous	The dragon
Faith	The feather; the shield
Faithful	The dog
Familial	The chain; the Ruby Slippers ("There's no place like home.")
Farsighted	The telescope
Feisty	The badger
Fertile	Grapes; seeds; the frog; the cat
Festive	Streamers
Fidelity	Turtledoves
Firm	The leg; the column
Flowing	River water
Forbearing	The ox
Fragrant	Perfume; flowers
Fraternity	The garland (fellowship)
Friendly	Shaking hands; crossed arrows (American Indian)
Fulfilled	A single rose
Funny	Laughter
Generosity	A mountain (Chinese)
Genius	A single pearl, usually hidden (Chinese)

Gentle	Unicorn (Chinese)
Giving	Infinity (∞)
Graceful	A ballet dancer; the swan; the hummingbird
Growth	A field of grain; any growing vegetation; the stag; the tree
Happy	A leaf (Chinese); the bat (Chinese); Water maidens; the thunderbird (American Indian); the sun (American Indian)
Harmonious	Justice (tarot); the lyre; three; the whale
Healing	The month of June; the Staff of Aesculapius
Health	Five
Heart	Gold (the heart of the earth); the heart (the center of the body and therefore eternity); the lotus; the sun (the heart of the universe)
Heroic	Hercules (heroic striving); the sun
Holy	The halo
Honorable	The turtle
Hope	Seed; the anchor; the helmet
Humility	Shoes
Imaginative	Flight; wings; Gemini (zodiac); the moon
Individualistic	Leo (zodiac)
Industrious	Bees
Informative	Ravens (Odin had two ravens who told him what was happening in the world)
Innocent	A sleeping baby; sheep
Inquisitive	A question mark (?)
Inspiring	The torch
Instinctive	The house; the steed
Integrated	A sheaf or bundle; interlocking fingers of two hands; the necklace
Integrity	A rock or stone; the Lover (tarot)
Intelligent	A lamp; the heart (the seat of intelligence); the sun; Virgo (zodiac); wings
Intrepid	The boar
Intuitive	The planet Mercury; the sound of the flute; the sun; water; window(s)
Inventive	A light bulb
Joie de Vivre	A full head of hair
Joyful	A ship plowing through the sea; the butterfly (Chinese)
Judicious	Jupiter
Justice	Fourteen; Lady Justice; the crane; the sword
Kind	The dolphin; the elephant (Hindu)

Knightly	The sword
Knowledge	A rolled papyrus scroll; the Tree of Knowledge
Law-abiding	The Archpriestess (tarot)—law
Liberty	Footwear (since slaves walked barefoot)
Light	Dew; diamond(s); gold; the lamp
Lofty	Winged sandals
Long-suffering	The ox
Love	Five; the heart; the hearth; the pyramid; Venus; the elephant
Loyal	The dog
Lucky	A lidded urn (supreme intelligence, which triumphs over life and death); a shell (Chinese); horseshoes; gold
Luminous	Aquarius (zodiac) (illumination)
Magical	A net; abnormal objects or persons; the right hand; the wand; the whistle
Maternal	The oven; forest; a goose; a gorge; ocean; water
Meek	Lamb
Melodious	The flute
Metamorphic	The butterfly; the frog
Moral	The caduceus (a wand entwined with two serpents and wings, representing moral equilibrium)
New	Thirteen
Nonjudgmental	Nothingness; the void (not the absence of life but the absence of conflict)
Nurturing	Earth; mother
Openhanded	The removal of the right glove
Orderly	Seven (moral or perfect); ten (universal); three (spiritual); twelve (cosmic)
Oriented	A pyramid (four cardinal directions and a central apex); sunrise; the East; the North Star
Passionate	A storm; blood
Pastoral	The farmer; the shepherd
Paternal	The sun; the umbrella
Patient	The tortoise
Peace	The dove; the olive tree; the crane (Japanese)
Perfect	Ten; the circle
Persuasive	The Empress (tarot)
Philosophical	The Archpriest (tarot)
Pioneering	A covered wagon; a space capsule
Pious	The stork (filial piety)
Playful	Swings; the seal
Poetic	Words

Potential	The egg; the night
Power	A crown; gold; the Emperor (tarot); the whip (Egyptian)
Powerful	A diamond key (the power to act); the crocodile; the hammer
Prayerful	The bow and arrow; the eagle; origami crane
Precise	A needle; sewing; any fine needlework; the hummingbird
Prescient	A sibyl (legend)
Progressive	Wings (spiritual evolution)
Prosperity	Maize (Chinese); rhinoceros horn (Chinese)
Protective	The buckle (self-defense); the shield; the wolf; an arrow (American Indian)
Provident	Jupiter's three thunderbolts (Chance, Destiny, and Providence)
Prudent	A dolphin entwined around an anchor (arrested speed)
Pure	Sea foam; stars in Orion's belt (Purity, Righteousness, and Choice); the lily
Purification	Temperance (tarot); the desert; fire; rain
Reality	The tree (inexhaustible life—Absolute reality)
Reasonable	The left hand; the temple (Absolute or Divine reason)
Receptive	The cauldron
Rectitude	The lance
Reflective	Narcissus; the mirror
Refreshing	Water, cool and clean
Regenerative	An eight-petaled rose; antlers; baptism (rebirth, resurrection); eight; mistletoe; sprouted grain; sunrise; the East; the Phoenix; the snake (shedding skin)
Relaxed	A hammock
Restful	A bed
Restorative	The rainbow
Rhythmic	Ants; the centipede; the drum
Rich	All forms of treasure (riches of the mind and of the spirit)
Righteous	The tiger
Roseate	Rose-colored glasses; the rose
Royal	Fleur-de-lis; the lily
Safe	A fireplace
Sanitary	Soap
Saved	The dolphin (salvation)

Searching	Searchlights; a lighthouse
Secure	Inside a wall
Seeking	The journey
Self-possessed	The cloak
Sentimental	Teardrops
Serene	A calm sea
Service minded	The buffalo
Sexy	Hermaphrodite (the unification of the sexes)
Sheltering	A house; a roof
Simple	One
Soaring	An albatross; a sail plane
Soft	Fur; a baby's bottom
Solid	Granite
Soul	A well; birds; six; the butterfly (because of its attraction to light); the foot; the garden; the gazelle; the hawk (Egyptian); the tunic
Spicy	Peppers
Spiritual	Bird(s); fire; the eagle; the lamp; wings
Stable	Four
Stellar	Star(s)
Straightforward	A straight line
Stress Hardy	Water off a duck's back
Strong	A coiled snake; horn(s); thighs (Egyptian); the tiger
Successful	Seven; three
Sunny	Sunshine
Supportive	The crutch; the staff; the throne
Surefooted	The ram
Sustaining	Strength (tarot)
Sweet	Honey; nectar; sugar
Swift	The horse; lightning (American Indian)
Symmetrical	Gemini (zodiac)
Synergistic	Sagittarius (zodiac); the hurricane (American Indian)—cosmic synergy
Tame	Any tame animal
Temperate	A beach; fourteen
Thinking	The hat; the helmet; the pansy
Time	A clock; a river; a spindle; the wheel
Tough	The sword
Treasured	The Golden Fleece (supreme spirituality through purity of the soul)
Triumphant	A laurel wreath (inner victories over negatives); the Chariot (tarot)

Truth	A hand mirror; gems or treasures (spiritual truths or knowledge); nine; the torch
Understanding	A silver key
Unity	Pomegranate (diversity—many seeds contained in sphere)
Upright	The Ch'i-lin (Chinese)—similar to the Unicorn, with two horns
Upstanding	A tall tree
Valorous	The lion; the wolf
Venerable	An older person
Ventilious	The wind
Victorious	The palm tree
Vigilant	The cock; the rooster atop a weather vane
Vigorous	The hippopotamus (Egyptian)
Virginal	A private room; six; a belt
Virile	The lion
Vision	The eagle; the lynx
Vital	Blood
Warm	The hearth
Watchful	Eye(s)
Well-read	A library
Whole	The bracelet; the globe; the peacock; the ring; the wheel
Wholesome	Bread
Willful	Music; the sun
Wisdom	Burnt wood; deep water; the Hermit (tarot); the snake (American Indian)
Wise	An elephant; a golden key; a ring of flames; an old man; an owl; honey; the dragon; the fruit of the Tree of Knowledge of Good and Evil; the serpent
Wonder	A wide-eyed child
Yummy	The tongue; the tummy

MYTHOLOGICAL, LEGENDARY, HISTORICAL, FICTIONAL, AND THEOLOGICAL CHARACTERS

For more information about these characters in relation to the qualities, look under the specific quality heading in the body of the book.

QUALITY	CHARACTER(S)
Abundant	Amalthea; the land of Cockaigne
Agile	Tarzan
Alive	Merodach
Beauty	Frigga; Helen of Troy; Venus; Blouwedd
Blessed	Pandora
Brave	Henry Fleming; Sir Lancelot
Bright	Aglaia
Chaste	Bona Dea; Britomart; Sir Galahad
Chivalrous	Don Quixote
Choice	Janus
Civilized	Isis
Comical	Aristophanes; Thalia
Committed	Juno
Compassionate	Androcles
Content	Roger Bontemps
Courteous	Sir Calidore; Sir Gawain
Creative	Bel; Osiris; Ormuzd; Brahma; Shiva
Curious	Curious George
Dignified	Hermione
Dreaming	Sleeping Beauty

Dutiful	Javert
Faithful	Abdiel
Fertile	Baal
Flowing	Alpheus
Forethoughtful	Prometheus
Fortunate	Fortuna
Friendly	Damon and Pythias; Nisus and Euryalus
Fruitful	Vertumnus
Giving	Kris Kringle; Santa Claus; St. Nicholas
Glad	Pollyanna
Guiding	Mentor; Nestor
Healing	Aesculapius; Hippocrates
Heroic	Hercules
Hospitable	Baucis and Philemon
Jolly	King Cole
Joy	Euphrosyne
Just	Astraea
Knightly	King Arthur
Light	Balder
Love	Anteros; Aphrodite; Ashtoreth; Astarte; Beauty and the Beast; Cupid; Eros; Freya; Kama
Magical	Merlin
Merry	Momus
Musical	Apollo; Euterpe; Orpheus; St. Cecilia
Obedient	Griselda
Observant	Sherlock Holmes
Panache	Cyrano de Bergerac
Pastoral	Beulah; Ceres; Cybele; Demeter; Rhea
Patience	Enid
Poetic	Calliope; Bragi; Erato; Chaucer; Homer
Prayerful	Sandalphon
Preserving	Vishnu
Prosperous	Kuvera
Reflective	Narcissus
Restful	Hypnos; Somnus
Rhythmic	Terpsichore
Rich	Dives
Righteous	Varuna
Sapid	Cawther
Skillful	Harpocrates; Hermes; Mercury
Soulful	Psyche
Stalwart	Philip Faulconbridge
Strong	Kwasind

Swift	Camilla
Temperate	Sir Guyon
Truth	Ma; Una
Valiant	Hector
Victorious	El Cid
Virginal	Brandamante
Vision	Lynceus; Uriel
Watchful	Argus
Well-read	Nebo
Whole	Yggdrasil; woman
Wise	Athena; Pallas; Epimenides; Minerva; Neith; Thoth

"BEING" AND "MEANING OF LIFE" QUOTES

The concept of focusing on your desire in order to attain it is an ancient and primal element of human understanding. People have always realized that learning comes from experience. Here are assembled quotes highlighting this concept. Also included are quotes on the meaning of life.

THE LAW OF KARMA

A person's actions determine a person's fate.

BIBLE QUOTES

As a man thinks within himself, so he is.

—SOLOMON, PROVERBS 23:7

You shall decree a thing and it shall be established to you and light shall shine on your way.

—JOB 22:28

Where your treasure is, there also will your heart be.

—JESUS, MATTHEW 6:21

Ask and it shall be given; seek and you shall find; knock and the door shall be opened.

—JESUS, MATTHEW 7:7

All things are possible to they who have faith.

—JESUS, MARK 9:23

Whatsoever you sow, so also shall you reap.

—PAUL, GALATIANS 6:7

ANCIENT HISTORICAL QUOTES

All that we are is the result of what we have thought. The mind is everything. What we think, we become.

—BUDDHA

The way to gain a good reputation is to endeavor to be what you desire.

—SOCRATES

We are what we repeatedly do.

—ARISTOTLE

Character is guided by the nature of things most often envisaged, for the soul takes on the color of its ideas.

—MARCUS AURELIUS ANTONINUS

A man's life is what his thoughts make of it.

—MARCUS AURELIUS ANTONINUS

HISTORICAL QUOTES

What is now proved was once only imagined.

—WILLIAM BLAKE

Life has a value only when it has something valuable as its object.

—HEGEL

A man is what he thinks about all day long.

—RALPH WALDO EMERSON

The reward of a thing well done, is to have done it.

—RALPH WALDO EMERSON

I know of no more encouraging fact than the unquestionable ability of man to elevate life by conscious endeavor.

—HENRY DAVID THOREAU

Human beings, by changing the inner attitudes of their minds, can change the outer aspects of their lives.

—WILLIAM JAMES

If you only care enough for a result, you will most certainly attain it.

—WILLIAM JAMES

The greatest use of life is to spend it for something that will outlast it.

—WILLIAM JAMES

Lives based on having are less free than lives based either on doing or being.

—WILLIAM JAMES

He who attains his ideal, by that very fact transcends it.

—FRIEDRICH WILHELM NIETZSCHE

To be what we are and to become what we are capable of becoming is the only end of life.

—ROBERT LOUIS STEVENSON

Picture yourself vividly as a winner and that alone will contribute immeasurably to your success.

—HARRY EMERSON FOSDICK

CONTEMPORARY QUOTES

Great occasions do not make heroes or cowards; they simply unveil them to the eyes. Silently and imperceptibly, as we wake or sleep, we grow strong or weak; and at last some crisis shows what we have become.

—BROOKE FOSS WESTCOTT

You could be better than you are
You could be riding on a star.

—JIMMY VAN HEUSEN

What lasts from an educational experience is not the enhancement of memory but the enhancement of being. . . . It is beliefs about the nature of man, what he may become and what is his destiny, with the morality that flowed from these, that enhance a man's being.

—BASIL FLETCHER

What you are becoming day by day is of infinitely more importance than what you are today.

—*The Urantia Book*

The past is already incorporated in me.

—DR. GEORGE SHEEHAN

> *'To be is to do'—Socrates*
> *'To do is to be'—Jean-Paul Sartre*
> *'Do-be-do-be-do'—Frank Sinatra*
>
> —KURT VONNEGUT
>
> *Who wills, can.*
> *Who tries, does.*
> *Who loves, lives.*
>
> —ANNE MCCAFFREY, *Dragon Flight*

If you can imagine it, you can achieve it; if you can dream it, you can become it.

—WILLIAM ARTHUR WARD

You are what you pay attention to.

—WILLIAM H. CALVIN, *The River That Runs Uphill*

The behavior of animals is determined mostly by evolution, while humans have options for self-improvement in line with their civilized ideals.

—SARAH BLAFFER HRDY, ETHOLOGIST

Natural selection won't matter soon, not anywhere near as much as conscious selection. We will civilize and alter ourselves to suit our ideas of what we can be.

—GREG BEAR

If you think in positive terms, you will achieve positive results.
—NORMAN VINCENT PEALE

Believe and succeed.
—NORMAN VINCENT PEALE

We become what we think about.
—EARL NIGHTINGALE

Life is a self fulfilling prophecy, and you usually get what you expect.
—DENIS WAITLEY

It's not having information that is going to make you happy and successful; it's using that information that's going to make the dramatic difference in your life.
—ZIG ZIGLER

We become what we do.
—FRANK HERBERT, *Dune*

There is a direct connection between what occurs in your consciousness and what occurs in your external life.
—ROBERT FRITZ, *The Path of Least Resistance*

As you create, you naturally evoke that which is highest in you.
—ROBERT FRITZ, *The Path of Least Resistance*

Whatever you think about, give your attention to, or are interested in, begins to reveal its secrets to you.
—CATHERINE PONDER, *The Dynamic Laws of Prosperity*

Whatever the mind is taught to expect, *that* it will build, produce, and bring forth for you.
—CATHERINE PONDER, *The Dynamic Laws of Prosperity*

You, indeed, become what you want to be by affirming that you already are!
—CATHERINE PONDER, *The Dynamic Laws of Prosperity*

What most you admire, that shall you become.
—RICHARD BACH, *One*

Transformation is *being* the answer. Be *now* . . . even if "you" think you can't!
—JACQUELYN SMALL, Transformers

Transforming is effortless because there is nothing to be done, there is only someone to *be*.
—JACQUELYN SMALL, Transformers

It's what you do that makes your soul.
—BARBARA KINGSOLVER, Animal Dreams

As the twig is bent, so grows the tree.
—BARBARA KINGSOLVER, Animal Dreams

Be all that you can be.
—FRANK BURNS, U.S. ARMY SLOGAN

Whatever you are fascinated with, you want to create more of.
—AVINASH, TEACHER

Working hard and methodically to attain a skill can actually provide you with that skill.
—BILL LITTLEFIELD

When you bless it you can own it. Our eye is how God sees the world. Our hand is how God holds the world. Our job is simply to be.
—JERRY DOWNS AND JOE BURULL

Don't let what you're being get in the way of what you might become.
—HARRY PALMER (ON A SWAN POSTER)

Being on the tightrope is living. Everything else is waiting.
—KARL WALLENDA, TIGHTROPE WALKER

You know, "nothing ventured, nothing won" is true in every hour. It is the fiber of every experience that signs itself into memory.
—J. N. FIGGIS

What we dwell upon we help bring into manifestation.
                    —PEACE PILGRIM, *Steps Toward Inner Peace*

Causes and effects are a result of thought.
   —ROBERT M. PIRSIG, *Zen and the Art of Motorcycle Maintenance*

The social pathology, existential vacuum and meaninglessness experienced by contemporary society is the result of intrinsic values starvation, Being-value deficiency. Transpersonal values command adoration, celebration, and reverence. They are worth living and dying for. Contemplating and becoming one of these values gives the greatest sense of worth and joy that human beings can experience.
                    —MEREDITH SPRUNGER, *Spiritual Psychology*

Every time we say, "Let there be!" in any form, something happens.
                    —STELLA TERRILL MANN

We can have more than we've got because we can become more than we are.
                    —JIM ROHN

Undoubtedly, we become what we envisage.
                    —CLAUDE M. BRISTOL

Your life will be filled with what you fill it. If you want to live with anger—be angry, but if you want to live with peace, happiness, goodness, love . . . then fill it with these—at least to the best of your ability. Why have a life filled with hate or any other kind of ugliness when you have the power to fill it with beauty?
                    —JUDY KAIN

JIM DOWNS'S QUOTES

By considering yourself and others as possessing specific qualities, you are helping to make it so.

By following the good, you learn to be good. Everything you do, which is good, contributes positively to your future self.

Don't expect immediate results. Those qualities which you possess most securely are the result of many layers of experience.

If you sincerely seek to understand any one quality, you will find all others. As you acquire your favorites, you will be discovering the rest along the way.

"MEANING OF LIFE" QUOTES

The goal of life is living in harmony with nature.

—ZENO, 335–263 B.C.

The grand essentials to happiness in this life are something to do, someone to love and something to hope for.

—ADDISON

All the way to heaven is heaven.

—ST. CATHERINE OF SIENNA

As far as we can discern, the sole purpose of human existence is to kindle a light in the darkness of mere being. It may even be assumed that just as the unconscious affects us, increase in our consciousness likewise affects the unconscious.

—CARL G. JUNG

This is the true joy in life, the being used for a purpose recognized by yourself as a mighty one.

—GEORGE BERNARD SHAW

The only true security that can be found in this world is in the process of giving love.

—PUNDITJI

Survival of self, of species, and of environment, these are what drive humans. You can observe how the order of importance changes in a lifetime. What are the things of immediate concern at a given age? Weather? The state of digestion? Does she (or he) really care? All of those various hungers that flesh can sense and hope to satisfy. What else could possible matter?

—FRANK HERBERT, *Heretics of Dune*

The mystery of life isn't a problem to solve but a reality to experience.
—FRANK HERBERT, *Dune*

A purpose of life, no matter who is controlling it, is to love whomever is around to be loved.
—KURT VONNEGUT, *The Sirens of Titan*

The ultimate purpose of life, which is to keep alive, is impossible, but this is the ultimate purpose of life anyway.
—ROBERT M. PIRSIG, *Zen and the Art of Motorcycle Maintenance*

The secret of life is enjoying the passage of time.
—JAMES TAYLOR

People say that what we are all seeking is a meaning for life. I don't think that's what we're really seeking or thinking. I think what we're seeking is an experience of being alive. That the life experiences that we have on the purely physical plane will have resonances within . . . our own innermost being and reality, so that we actually feel the rapture of being alive. That's what it's all finally about and that's what these clues help us to find within ourselves.

Myths are clues to the spiritual potentialities of the human life.

We're having experiences all the time which . . . render some sense of this, a little intuition of where your joy is: grab it. No one can tell you what it's going to be. You've got to learn to recognize your own depths.
—JOSEPH CAMPBELL, "INTERVIEW WITH BILL MOYERS"

Buddhist Eight-fold Path:
• Right belief or view
• Right intention
• Right speech
• Right action
• Right livelihood
• Right endeavoring or effort
• Right mindfulness
• Right concentration or collectedness
If realized, one will be detached from illusion.
—BHIKKHU PHRA KHANTIPALO, *Calm and Insight*

The Principles of Kwanzaa
• Unity
• Self-determination
• Teamwork and responsibility
• Cooperative economics
• Purposeful
• Creativity
• Faith

DESIDERATA

Go placidly amid the noise and haste, and remember what peace there may be in silence. As far as possible without surrender be on good terms with all persons. Speak your truth quietly and clearly; and listen to others, even the dull and ignorant; they too have their story. Avoid loud and aggressive persons. They are vexations of the spirit. If you compare yourself with others, you become vain and bitter; for always there will be greater or lesser persons than yourself. Enjoy your achievements as well as your plans. Keep interested in your own career, however humble; it is a real possession in the changing fortunes of time. Exercise caution in your business affairs; for the world is full of trickery. But let this not blind you to what virtue there is; many persons strive for high ideals; and everywhere life is full of heroism. Be yourself. Especially do not feign affection. Neither be cynical about love; for in the face of all aridity and disenchantment it is perennial as the grass. Take kindly the counsel of the years, gracefully surrendering the things of youth. Nurture strength of spirit to shield you in sudden misfortune. But do not distress yourself with imaginings. Many fears are born of fatigue and loneliness. Beyond a wholesome discipline, be gentle with yourself. You are a child of the universe, no less than the trees and the stars; you have a right to be here. And whether or not it is clear to you, no doubt the universe is unfolding as it should. Therefore be at peace with God, whatever you conceive Him to be, and whatever your labors and aspirations, in the noisy confusion of life keep peace with your soul. With all its sham, drudgery and broken dreams, it is still a beautiful world. Strive to be happy.
—FOUND IN OLD SAINT PAUL'S CHURCH, BALTIMORE, DATED 1692

OATHS

On my honor, I will do my best to do my duty to God and my country and to obey the Boy Scout law; to help other people at all times; to keep myself physically strong, mentally awake and morally straight.

—THE BOY SCOUTS' OATH

A scout is trustworthy, loyal, helpful, friendly, courteous, kind, obedient, cheerful, thrifty, brave, clean and reverent.

—THE BOY SCOUTS' LAW

On my honor, I will try to serve God and my country, to help people at all times and to live by the Girl Scouts' law.

—THE GIRL SCOUTS' PROMISE

I will do my best to be honest; to be fair; to help where I am needed; to be cheerful; to be friendly and considerate; to be a sister to other Girl Scouts; to respect authority; to use resources wisely; to protect and improve the world around me and to show respect for myself and others through my words and actions.

—THE GIRL SCOUTS' LAW

ELEMENTARY SOLUTIONS

Most of what I really need to know about how to live, and what to do, and how to be, I learned in kindergarten. Wisdom was not at the top of the graduate school mountain, but there in the sandbox at nursery school.

These are the things I learned. Share everything. Play fair. Don't hit people. Put things back where you found them. Clean up your own mess. Don't take things that aren't yours. Say you're sorry when you hurt somebody. Wash your hands before you eat. Flush. Warm cookies and cold milk are good for you. Live a balanced life. Learn some, and think some and draw and plan and sing and dance and play and work every day some.

Take a nap every afternoon. When you go out into the world, watch for traffic, hold hands, and stick together. Be aware of wonder. Remember the little seed in the plastic cup. The roots go down and plant goes up and nobody really knows how or why, but we are all like that.

Goldfish and hamsters and white mice and even the little seed in the plastic cup—they all die. So do we.

And then remember the book about Dick and Jane and the first word you learned: the biggest word of all, LOOK. Everything you need to know is in there somewhere. The golden rule and love and basic sanitation. Ecology and politics and sane living.

To think of what a better world it would be if we all—the whole world—had cookies and milk about 3 o'clock every afternoon and then lay down with our blankets for a nap. Or if we had a basic policy in our nation and other nations to always put things back where we found them and clean up our own messes. And it is still true, no matter how old you are, when you go out into the world, it is best to hold hands and stick together.

—ROBERT FULGHAM

EXERCISES AND PROJECTS

The following are exercises and projects that you may decide to do in order to increase your possession of a specific quality or a set of qualities.

EXERCISES

JOURNAL

Keep a daily journal on the qualities that you have chosen.

PERSONAL PROFILE

Go through the list with a pencil, very quickly, as fast as you can, read each word, and decide if you possess (even a little bit) of that quality, and check it off if you do.

Write your thoughts on what that process was like. Are you surprised by how many you marked off?

Go through the list again and ask yourself,
Do I possess this quality?
To what degree do I possess it? (rating 0 to 9)
How am I already like that?

How is this quality present in my life?
Do I want to acquire this quality?
What can I do to become this quality in my daily life?
How are other qualities associated with this quality?

IDEALS EXERCISE

Make a list of your highest ideals. Your most important ideals are personal and they may change over time.

CAREER EXERCISE

If you are thinking about a career focus or are thinking about changing life-styles, pick out those characteristics, qualities, and aspects of being that are your most valuable ideas and ideals. If becoming truth is your highest ideal, then pick a life-style, such as that of a teacher or author, where that is the predominant quality.

What profession are you in? What are the qualities that someone in that field needs? Do you have those naturally? Have you acquired them while working in the field?

PICKING QUALITIES

If you have decided to pick qualities, here are some other ideas on how to play with them.

- Above all practice your chosen qualities.
- Talk about them with a friend.
- Read about them fifteen minutes per day.
- Think about them fifteen minutes per day.
- Write about them fifteen minutes per day.
- Write the qualities on a mirror with soap.
- Think about and feel them while doing what you are doing.

Once a year pick a quality that is not random. A special quality that will be the guiding principle for your life for a year. Make it one of the "big" qualities. This may be when you make a contract with yourself.

I promise to myself (and also promise to somebody you can trust, if you want a partner) to work on becoming the quality of _____ for the next year. I will remember to think about and apply this quality when I see

_____, when I hear _____, when I smell _____, when I taste _____, and when I touch _____.

I also promise to you, my friend, to work on this quality. I give you permission to help me remember it, in a tactful, loving way. When I deviate from the quality or don't see the opportunity for exhibiting it, you may point it out to me.

Signed: _____

THE "I AM" EXERCISE

This is a meditation. Go through the list creating simple declarative sentences. Start each sentence with "I am" or "I have." Go through the list any way you wish. Accept the images, feelings, memories, and other thoughts that arise as you proceed. At first you will experience that the statements are too absolute but soon you will realize that your quest for qualities is infinite and therefore your possession of a quality is relative.

Variation: Go through a list of qualities starting each sentence with "Am I _____?" Listen to your answers.

PROJECTS

"SCOUT" PROJECTS

The Boy Scouts and Girl Scouts have programs that teach them how to do various things. These projects result in the scout getting a badge for having accomplished the task. Those who designed the scouting organizations are interested in what a person becomes in addition to the facts that he or she learns. You could set up your own badge system. Design an activity that will give you the personal experience of the quality that you are interested in. Then give yourself a badge.

WRITING PROJECTS

Write a story using every quality at least once.
Write a short story that exemplifies a particular quality.
Write a story or an interview about a person who exemplifies a specific set of qualities.

MISCELLANEOUS PROJECTS

Take an historical inventory of your activities and experiences to see what qualities you have lived.

Talk to someone who knows you quite well, and find out what he or she thinks your qualities are.

Take a class that will help you become the quality you are interested in.

As you are living your life, live positively.

APPENDIX 8

BIBLIOGRAPHY

The references to *Being* and *Meaning of Life* were used in appendix 6. All other parenthetical references refer to the alphabetical listings.

Some listings do not have a quote under the quality but are generally about the quality, e.g., *A Courage to Be,* Paul Tillich.

14,000 Things to Be Happy About, Barbara Ann Kipfer. New York: Workman, 1990. (*Happy*)

The Adventures of Huckleberry Finn, Mark Twain. New York: Clarkson N. Potter, Inc. 1981. (*Prayerful*)

Age of Mountaineering, James Ramsey Ullman. Philadelphia: J. B. Lippincott, 1954. (*Harmonious*)

The American Heritage Dictionary, Second College Edition. New York: Dell, 1983. (*Definitions*)

The Ancient Art of Color Therapy, Linda Clark. New York: Pocket, 1975. (*Colors*)

Angel® Cards, Narada Media, 4650 N. Port Washington Rd., Milwaukee, WI 53212-1063; and InnerLinks, P.O. Box 16225, Seattle, WA 98116-0225. (*Angelic*)

The Anger in All of Us and How to Deal with It, Abigail Van Buren, P.O. Box 447, Mt. Morris, IL 61054. (*Just*)

Animal Dreams, Barbara Kingsolver. New York: Harper Collins, 1990. (*Being*)

Another Roadside Attraction, Tom Robbins. New York: Bantam, 1971. (*Adventuresome, Aware*)

"Anxiety—Recognition and Intervention." *American Journal of Nursing,* (September 1965): 132–133. (*Good Self-Image*)

BARD, The Odyssey of the Irish, Morgan Llywelyn. New York: TOR, 1984. (*Empathetic*)

The Bible (*Abundant, Being, Cheerful, Light, Love, Merry, Motivated, Peaceful, Perfect, Prosperous, Seeking, Soulful, Swift, Timely*)

The Black Unicorn, Terry Brooks. New York: Del Ray, 1987. (*Independent*)

The Book of Qualities, J. Ruth Gendler. New York: Harper and Row, 1988. (*Confidence, Impeccable, Ventilious*)

The Bridges of Madison County, Robert James Wallers. New York: Warner, 1992. (*Timely*)

A Brief History of Time, Stephen Hawking. New York: Bantam, 1988. (*Reasonable*)

Brightness Reef, David Brin. New York: Bantam Books, 1995. (*Hopeful, Original*)

Calm and Insight, A Buddhist Manual for Meditators, Bhikkhu Phra Khantipalo. London: Curzon Press, 1981. (*Meaning of Life*)

Centering, in Pottery, Poetry, and the Person, Mary Caroline Richards. Middletown, CT: Wesleyan University Press, 1964. (*Centered*)

Chapterhouse: Dune, Frank Herbert. New York: Ace/G. P. Putnam, 1985. (*Disciplined, Moral*)

Charm, Margery Wilson. Philadelphia: J. B. Lippincott, 1928. (*Charm*)

City, Clifford D. Simak. New York: Ace, 1952. (*Civilized*)

The Courage to Be, Paul Tillich. Binghamton, NY: Vail-Ballou Press, 1980. (*Courageous*)

A Course in Winning, Earl Nightingale (*Being, Goal Oriented, Successful*), Denis Waitley (*Being, Changeable, Motivated*), Jimmy Calano and Jeff Salzman (*Motivated*), Norman Vincent Peale (*Being*), Zig Zigler (*Being, Goal Oriented*). Nightingale-Conant Corp., 7300 N. Lehigh Ave., Chicago, IL 60648, 1-800-525-9000.

The Dhammapada (*Fragrant*)

The Diary of Anne Frank, Anne Frank. New York: Doubleday, 1967. (*Heart, Natural*)

A Dictionary of Symbols, J. E. Cirlot. New York: Dorset, 1991. (*Creative, Symbols*)

Dragon Flight, Anne McCaffrey. New York: Ballantine/Fawcett, 1968. (*Being, Striving*)

Dune, Frank Herbert. New York: Berkley, 1965. (*Appreciative, Awake, Being, Diverse, Great, Meaning of Life, Stress Hardy*)

The Dynamic Laws of Prosperity, Catherine Ponder. Marina Del Rey, CA: DeVorss, 1985. P.O. Drawer 1278, Palm Desert, CA 92261. (*Abundant, Accomplished, Affirming, Being, Confident, Desire, Forgiving, Godly, Healthy, Independent, Mindful, Persistent, Positive, Prayerful, Prosperous, Psychic, Rich, Sharing, Successful*)

Earth, David Brin. New York: Bantam, 1990. (*Conscious, Flexible, Passionate, Prayerful, Virtuous*)

Eight Skilled Gentlemen, Barry Hughart. New York: Bantam, 1991. (*Content*)

"The End of Physics?" Frank Wilczek. *Discover* (March 1993): 34. (*Knowledgable*)

Even Cowgirls Get the Blues, Tom Robbins. Boston: Houghton Mifflin, 1976. (*Magic*)

Everest, The West Ridge, Thomas F. Hornbein. New York: Ballantine, 1966. (*Surviving*)

EYE, Death of a City, Frank Herbert. New York: Berkley, 1973. (*Love*)

The Farthest Shore, Ursula K. Le Guin. New York: Bantam, 1972. (*Whole*)

Fortkamp Publishing Company, c/o Center for Peace Studies, Georgetown University, Washington, DC 20057 (*Peaceful*)

Frames of Mind: The Theory of Multiple Intelligences, Howard Gardner. New York: Basic, 1983. (*Intelligent*)

The Gaia Peace Atlas: Survival into the Third Millennium, Dr. Frank Barnaby, general editor. New York: Dell, 1988. (*Secure*)

Gender and Stress, Rosalind C. Barnett, Lois Biener, and Grace K. Baruch, editors. New York: Free Press, 1987. (*Stress Hardy*)

Green Mars, Kim Stanley Robinson. New York: Bantam, 1995. (*Objective*)

The Guinness Book of World Records 1992, Donald McFarlan, editor. New York: Facts on File. (*Discerning, Meticulous*)

Heretics of Dune, Frank Herbert. New York: G. P. Putnam, 1984. (*Meaning of Life, Growing, Peaceful, Unique*)

The Hero with a Thousand Faces, Joseph Campbell. Princeton, NJ: Princeton University Press, 1968. (*Dreaming, Heroic, Whole*)

The Hero with a Thousand Faces, Volume II: The Cosmogonic Cycle, Joseph Campbell. Los Angeles: Audio Renaissance Tapes, 1990. (*Profound*)

Hiawatha, Henry Wordsworth Longfellow, 1855. (*Strong*)

The Hollow Hills, Mary Stewart. New York: Fawcett Crest, 1973. (*Knowledgeable*)

How Good People Make Tough Choices, Rushworth M. Kidder. New York: William Morrow, 1995. (*Obedient*)

How to Be Popular, Abigail Van Buren, P.O. Box 447, Mt. Morris, IL 61054. (*Popular*)

Human Engineering Guide for Equipment Designers, Wesley E. Woodson and Donald W. Conover. Berkeley: University of California Press, 1964. (*Technical*)

"Interview with Bill Moyers," Joseph Campbell. Big Sur, CA: Dolphin Tapes, 1990. (*Blissful, Meaning of Life*)

The Joy of Stress, Peter G. Hanson, M.D. Kansas City, MO: Andrews, McMeel and Parker, Universal Press Syndicate. (*Stress Hardy*)

The Last Enchantment, Mary Stewart. New York: Fawcett Crest, 1979. (*Peaceful, Wise*)

"Law and Manners," Lord Moulton of Bank. *Atlantic Monthly* (July 1924). (*Law-abiding*)

The Leader, A New Face for American Management, Michael MacCoby. New York: Simon and Schuster, 1981. (*Leadership*)

Learned Optimism, Dr. Martin Seligman. New York: Knopf, 1990. (*Optimistic*)

"The Lessons of Love: Have We Learned Anything Yet About Love," Beth Livermore. *Psychology Today* (March/April 1993). (*Love*)

Lest Innocent Blood Be Shed: The Story of the Village of Le Chambon and How Goodness Happened There, Philip P. Hallie. New York: Harper and Row, 1979. (*Pacifistic*)

"Letter from Birmingham City Jail, Speeches and Sermons," Dr. Martin Luther King, Jr., audiotape, Martin Luther King Jr. Center for Nonviolent Social Change, 449 Auburn Ave. NE, Atlanta, GA 30312, 1963. (*Just*)

Lila: An Inquiry into Morals, Robert M. Pirsig. New York: Bantam, 1991. (*Efficient, Growing, Moral, Perceptive, Sane*)

The Lost Princess of Oz, L. Frank Baum. New York: Del Rey, Ballantine/Fawcett, 1917. (*Individualistic*)

Magic Kingdom for Sale—Sold, Terry Brooks. New York: Del Rey, 1986. (*Vision*)

Man's Search for Himself, Rolo May. New York: Bantam Doubleday Dell, 1953. (*Decisive*)

Mark Twain's Notebook, Samuel Clemens. New York: Cooper Square, 1972. (*Cheerful, Optimistic*)

Mind as Healer, Mind as Slayer, Kenneth Pelletier. New York: Delta, 1977. (*Stress Hardy*)

The Mists of Avalon, Marion Zimmer Bradley. New York: Ballantine/Fawcett, 1982. (*Reality, Soulful*)

The Mote in God's Eye, Larry Niven and Jerry Pournelle. New York: Pocket, 1974. (*Choice*)

Mutant Message Down Under, Marlo Morgan. 1991, MM Co., P.O. Box 100, Lees Summit, MO 64063. (*Prayerful*)

The Nonsexist Word Finder: A Dictionary of Gender-free Usage, Rosalie Maggio. Boston: Beacon Press, 1988. (*Humane*)

On the Loose, Terry and Renny Russell. New York: Ballantine/Fawcett, 1967. (*Adventuresome*)

The Once and Future King, T. H. White. New York: Ace Books/G. P. Putnam, 1939. (*Learned, Truth*)

One, Richard Bach. New York: Bantam Doubleday Dell, 1988. (*Being, Changeable, Character, Choice, Imaginative*)

"Organizations Don't Run on Information," Michael Schrage. *Lotus* (September 1991). (*Companionable*)

Otherness, David Brin. New York: Bantam Spectra, 1994. (*Honest*)

The Patchwork Girl of Oz, L. Frank Baum. New York: Del Rey, Ballantine/Fawcett, 1913. (*Brave, Kind*)

The Path of Least Resistance, Robert Fritz. Norman, OK: Fawcett/Columbine, 1989. (*Being, Creative*)

"Peak Performance: Coaching Your Internal Team," Dr. George Sheehan. *Taking Care* (January 1991). (*Goal Oriented*)

The Players of Null-A, A. E. van Vogt. New York: Berkley Medallion, 1948. (*Sane*)

The Prophet, Kahlil Gibran. New York: Knopf, 1973. (*Understanding*)

Puddin'head Wilson, Mark Twain. New York: Bantam, 1894. (*Joyful*)

The Rainbow Book, The Fine Arts Museums of San Francisco, F. Lanier Graham, editor. New York: Random House, 1975. (*Colors*)

The Red Badge of Courage, Stephen Crane. New York: Tom Doherty Associates, 1895. (*Brave*)

Refiner's Fire, Mark Helprin. Orlando, FL: Harcourt Brace Jovanovich, 1977. (*Loyal*)

The River That Runs Uphill: A Journey from the Big Bang to the Big Brain, William H. Calvin. New York: Macmillan, 1986. (*Being, Effective, Farsighted, Foresighted, New, Versatile*)

The Road to Oz, L. Frank Baum. New York: Del Rey, Ballantine/Fawcett, 1909. (*Industrious*)

Sadhana, A Way to God, Anthony de Mello S.J., published by X. Diaz der Rio S.J., Gujarat Sahitya Prakash, Anand, Gujarat. 388-001, India. (*Lucky*)

Serendipity and the Three Princes, The Peregrinaggio of 1557, edited by Theodor G. Remer. Norman: University of Oklahoma Press, 1965. (*Serendipitous*)

Shakespeare, William: *As You Like It* (*Love*), *Hamlet* (*Controlled, Playful*), *King John* (*Beauty, Stalwart*), *The Merchant of Venice* (*Honest*), *Twelfth Night* (*Musical*), *King Henry IV* (*True*)

Speaker for the Dead, Orson Scott Card. New York: Tor, 1991. (*Restorative*)

Spiritual Psychology: A Primer, Meredith J. Sprunger. Wilmette, IL: Jemenson, 1988. (*Being, Religious*)

Standard Encyclopedic Dictionary, Chicago: J. G. Ferguson, 1968. (*Definitions*)

Steps Toward Inner Peace, Peace Pilgrim. Published by Friends of Peace Pilgrim, 43480 Cedar Ave., Hemet, CA 92544, 1981. (*Being, Changeable, Communicative, Forgiving, Godly, Harmonious, Law-abiding, Light, Peaceful, Positive, Practical, Present, Thoughtful*)

The Story of the Stone, Barry Hughart. New York: Bantam, 1988. (*Patient*)

The Talmud. (*Angelic, Peaceful*)

The Terminal Man, Michael Crichton. New York: Bantam, 1972. (*Sensible*)

Tik-Tok of Oz, L. Frank Baum. New York: Del Rey, Ballantine/Fawcett, 1914. (*Brave, Desire, Economical, Equitable, Just*)

Transformers, Jacquelyn Small. Marina Del Rey, CA: DeVorss, 1982. (*Being, Choice, Important, Perfect*)

"Type "A" Behavior: Don't Rush Your Life Away," Jane Brody. In *New York Times Guide to Personal Health.* New York: Times Books, 1982. (*Stress Hardy*)

"Understanding Why People Reject New Ideas, Helping Industrial Engineers Convert Resistance into Acceptance," J. Randolph New and Daniel D. Singer. *Industrial Engineering Magazine* (May 1983). (*Changeable*)

The Urantia Book, Urantia Foundation, 533 Diversey Parkway, Chicago, IL 60614, 1955. (*Active, Artistic, Being, Character, Civilized, Friendly, Godly, Great, Idealistic, Loyal, Merciful, Motivated, Poised, Prayerful, Religious, Soulful, Seeking, Surviving*)

The Value of Facing a Challenge: The Story of Terry Fox, Ann Donegan Johnson. Stamford, CT: Value Communications Inc., Oak Tree Publications, Inc., Division of Vizcom, Inc., 1983. (*Stick-to-itive*)

Walden and Other Writings, Henry David Thoreau. New York: Bantam, 1854. (*Dreaming*)

Webster's College Dictionary. New York: Random House, 1991. (*Definitions*)

Webster's New Universal Unabridged Dictionary. New York: Simon and Schuster, 1983. (*Definitions*)

Webster's Ninth New Collegiate Dictionary. Springfield, MA: Merriam-Webster, 1991. (*Definitions*)

Webster's Unabridged Dictionary: An American Dictionary of the English Language, Noah Webster. Chicago: Donohue and Henneberry, 1891. (*Definitions*)

"Whose Genome Is It, Anyway?" Jerold M. Lowenstein. *Discover* (May 1992). (*Individualistic*)

"Why Bother?" Joann C. Autin quoting Michael Rose. *Discover* (June 1992). (*Inventive*)

The Winning Family: Increasing Self-esteem in Your Child and Yourself, Louise Hart. Berkeley, CA: Celestial Arts, 1993. (*Self-esteem*)

The Witching Hour, Anne Rice. New York: Ballantine/Fawcett, 1990. (*Choice*)

The Wonderful World of Oz, L. Frank Baum. New York: Del Rey, Ballantine/Fawcett, 1900. (*Familial, Present*)

Zen and the Art of Motorcycle Maintenance: An Inquiry into Values, Robert M. Pirsig. New York: William Morrow, 1974. (*Being, Contemplative, Meaning of Life*)

Appendix 9

End Notes

Our language is constantly changing, and I want this work to reflect the full and rich diversity of our culture. The material in this book should be kept fresh and rejuvenated.

Please write to me:

If you know of new positive concepts that I have not listed,
If you have other ideas on how to acquire qualities,
If you have had experience in becoming a quality,
If you disagree with something.

My address is:

Jim Downs
The Positive Qualities Company
2888 Bluff St., #428
Boulder, CO 80301-9002
1-800-484-9668; Extension: 0984

Thank you for your qualities. Keep on expanding.

OTHER POSITIVE QUALITY PRODUCTS AVAILABLE

Ask your local bookseller or contact me at the above address.

THE POSITIVE QUALITIES CHART

The Positive Qualities Chart is a hierarchical representation of Love and all its aspects. There are 988 positive qualities displayed in nine concentric circles. I started with more than 1800. See appendix 3 for those qualities that are not on the chart. The original is twenty-two inches square in full color.

The qualities named in the inner rings are the "indispensable" qualities; but any quality is the crucial quality if it is the one that is most appropriate at the time.

Since we tend to categorize reality, I thought it would be easier to conceptualize the relationships between the qualities with a chart.

I consider Love, Truth, Beauty, and Goodness to be the most important and essential of all of the qualities, and therefore all other qualities are subattributes of these. The size of each word is dependent on the circle it is in and on the number of words behind it, that is, in the outer circles. The qualities in each circle are of more or less equal value. Open spaces occurred when I purposefully put a quality in a more external position due to my judgment of the nature of the qualities in each circle. The words in the outer two circles are somewhat interchangeable.

It was sometimes difficult to choose where to locate a quality since some could easily have been placed in more than one place, but the linear nature of the chart dictated that I decide. This was a subjective and individual exercise and I realize that anyone deciding these relationships would create a unique arrangement.

The chart includes an eleven-by-twenty-two-inch Locator Guide.

$10.00 each, plus $5.00 postage and packaging.

A Spanish version of the chart will be available soon.

BUTTONS

Love, Truth, Beauty, Goodness button:
Like the center of the chart. Love is in the center and Truth, Beauty, and Goodness around the edges of each button.

There are two sizes available. The small one is one inch in diameter, for $1.00. The large one is one and three-quarter inches in diameter, for $2.00.

Other single and various combination buttons also available by special order.